SOCIALISTS, LIBERALS
AND LABOUR

STUDIES IN POLITICAL HISTORY

Editor: Michael Hurst
Fellow of St. John's College, Oxford

CHIEF WHIP: The Political Life and Times of Aretas Akers-Douglas 1st Viscount Chilston by Eric Alexander 3rd Viscount Chilston.
GUIZOT: Aspects of French History 1787–1874 by Douglas Johnson.
MARGINAL PRYNNE: 1660–9 by William M. Lamont.
LAND AND POWER: British and Allied Policy on Germany's Frontiers 1916–19 by H. I. Nelson.
THE LANGUAGE OF POLITICS in the Age of Wilkes and Burke by James T. Boulton.
THE ENGLISH FACE OF MACHIAVELLI: A Changing Interpretation 1500–1700 by Felix Raab.
BEFORE THE SOCIALISTS: Studies in Labour and Politics 1861–81 by Royden Harrison.
THE LAWS OF WAR IN THE LATE MIDDLE AGES by M. H. Keen.
GOVERNMENT AND THE RAILWAYS IN NINETEENTH CENTURY BRITAIN by Henry Parris.
THE ENGLISH MILITIA IN THE EIGHTEENTH CENTURY: The Story of a Political Issue, 1660–1802 by J. R. Western.
SALISBURY AND THE MEDITERRANEAN, 1886–96 by C. J. Lowe.
VISCOUNT BOLINGBROKE, Tory Humanist by Jeffrey Hart.
W. H. SMITH by Viscount Chilston.
THE McMAHON LINE: A Study in the Relations between India, China and Tibet, 1904–14; in two volumes by Alastair Lamb.
THE THIRD REICH AND THE ARAB EAST by Lukasz Hirszowicz.
THE ELIZABETHAN MILITIA 1558–1638 by Lindsay Boynton.
JOSEPH CHAMBERLAIN AND LIBERAL REUNION: The Round Table Conference of 1887, by Michael Hurst.
SOCIALISTS, LIBERALS AND LABOUR: The Struggle for London 1885–1914 by Paul Thompson.
POLAND AND THE WESTERN POWERS, 1938–9 by Anna M. Cienciala.
DISRAELIAN CONSERVATISM AND SOCIAL REFORM by Paul Smith.

SOCIALISTS, LIBERALS AND LABOUR

The Struggle for London 1885–1914

by
PAUL THOMPSON

LONDON: Routledge & Kegan Paul
TORONTO: University of Toronto Press
1967

*First published 1967
in Great Britain by
Routledge & Kegan Paul Ltd
and in Canada by
University of Toronto Press*

*Printed in Great Britain
by Western Printing Services Ltd
Bristol*

© *Paul Thompson 1967*

*No part of this book may be reproduced
in any form without permission from
the publisher, except for the quotation
of brief passages in criticism*

TO
MY FATHER AND MOTHER

CONTENTS

		page
	Preface	vii
	Introduction	1
I.	London	5
II.	Religion	17
III.	Trade Unionism	39
IV.	Politics and Parties	68
V.	Liberals, Radicals and Labour	90
VI.	The Social Democratic Federation	112
VII.	The Socialist League, the Fabians and the Independent Labour Party	136
VIII.	The Liberal Revival and After	166
IX.	The Lean Years of Social Democracy	190
X.	The Fabians and the Independent Labour Party after 1900	212
XI.	Local Labour Parties	239
XII.	The Founding of the London Labour Party	265
	Epilogue	286
	Conclusion	294
	Appendices	299
	Select Bibliography	322
	Maps	335
	Index	367

MAPS
Page 336–366

1. Growth of London
2. Edge of London
3. Middle Class Districts and Poverty
4. Domestic Servants
5. Overcrowding
6. Applicants to Distress Committees 1905–8
7. Commercial Occupations
8. Tailors
9. Engineering and Metal Workers
10. Railways, Port and Heavy Industry
11. 1886: Attendance under 20 per cent of Resident Population
12. 1903: Worshippers under 20 per cent of Resident Population
13. Constituencies: Conservative and Liberal Safe Seats, 1885–1914
14. 1886: Nonconformists Exceeding Anglicans
15. 1903: Nonconformists Exceeding Anglicans
16. Constituencies: Liberal Seats 1885
17. Constituencies: Liberal and Labour Seats 1906
18. 1851: Nonconformists Exceeding Anglicans
19. 1903: Nonconformists Exceeding Anglicans and 10 per cent of Resident Population
20. Irish Colonies
21. Jewish Colony. c 1900
22. (a) Constituencies
22. (b) Constituencies
23. 1911: Electorates over 17 per cent and under 13 per cent of Resident Population
24. Boards of Guardians
25. Vestries and District Boards
26. London School Board
27. Boroughs and Urban Districts
28. Constituencies: Social Composition 1885–1900
29. Constituencies: Social Composition 1900–1914
30. Growth of Labour Seats

PREFACE

THE help of two people has been outstanding in making this book. Henry Pelling was the supervisor of my thesis and my colleague at the Queen's College, Oxford, and his advice and criticism have been continuous and invaluable. My wife shared much of the research with me, in particular the section on trade unionism, and the half million issues of local newspapers which we ought to have read; she has helped in many other ways, and her encouragement has been essential.

This book is a reduced and revised version of a thesis on 'London Working Class Politics and the Formation of the London Labour Party, 1885–1914', and I am particularly grateful in the revision for the comments of Royston Lambert. Very useful criticisms were also made by Hugh Clegg and A. F. Thompson. Chapter 5 is based on an article published in *Past and Present*, April 1964, and in this I was much helped by the comments of Trevor Aston and Eric Hobsbawm. I am grateful for other suggestions and help to Nicholas Walter, Ken Weller, Walter Kendall, Philip Bagwell and Betty Grant, and for assistance in securing access to documents to the Rt. Hon. Anthony Greenwood, M.P. It will be seen from the Select Bibliography that I have been assisted by a large number of librarians, trade unions, political parties and clubs, and I should like to thank them all for allowing me to use their collections; and also to thank those others unmentioned who helped me in similar ways. I owe a particular debt to the national Labour Party, the London Labour Party, Woolwich Labour Party, Deptford Labour Party, South Kensington Conservative Party, St. Pancras Reform Club and the Boro' of East Ham Club for access to their records; to the British Library of Political and Economic Science and the British Museum Department of Manuscripts for assistance in the use of their collections; and to Francis Johnson and Julius Jacobs for allowing me to see the manuscripts in their possession. In addition Karl Walter and Tom Braddock gave me

PREFACE

an evening to discuss their memories of the period. Among many others who generously helped in this way were Lord Morrison of Lambeth, and—most memorably—Bob Streetley and Jimmy Jacques of Bermondsey.

I am grateful to all the sources acknowledged in the notes. The Passfield Collection is quoted by kind permission of the Passfield Trustees, and Table 4 of Peter Hall and Messrs Hutchinson and Co.

PAUL THOMPSON

INTRODUCTION

IN the period between 1885 and 1914 national parties in British politics depended upon local and regional strongholds. Because a wide electoral franchise had been introduced, these strongholds could no longer be maintained by a network of personal patronage and influence. But the national leaders still required intermediaries through which to win the electorate. There was no radio and television through which they could speak directly to the people as a whole. Nor, until the very end of the period, was there a national press with a wide circulation.

The press, it is true, was changing. But in the 1880s and 1890s its most striking expansion was in local rather than national newspapers. At this time in London a flourishing weekly press sprang up in the districts, and the *Star*, started as a London evening paper in 1888, was able to achieve an unprecedented circulation exceeding 250,000. The development of a mass circulation national press followed, with the launching of the *Daily Mail* in 1896, and by 1906-7, with its onslaught upon the London Progressives, this new popular national press could be seen to be a formidable political weapon. As late as 1904 the circulation of the two London Liberal morning papers, the *Daily News* and the *Daily Chronicle*, had been as little as 30,000 each. They now changed their character, and by 1914 there were also two daily papers supporting the Labour Party. But even in 1914 it is unlikely that the majority of electors were directly influenced in their politics by the national press.

Lacking a direct approach to the electorate, the parties relied on the enthusiasm of local political activists to bring their supporters to the poll, and in the words of the Liberal organiser Herbert Gladstone, 'on the degree of this enthusiasm elections are won or lost'.[1] Local personalities, local party organisation, local government contests, churches, trade unions and clubs were all of vital importance. They made up the regional differences of the period, the regional strengths of Nonconformity and trade unionism, the regional political figures and political leaders. It was these local and regional characteristics which produced the Liberal strength in Wales and

[1] H. Gladstone, *After Thirty Years*, London 1928, p. 161.

INTRODUCTION

Scotland, the Liberal Unionist power in Birmingham, the Conservative hold on London, the growth of independent Labour in the north of England and of Marxist socialism in London and Lancashire.

These regional differences have been pointed out by general historians but they have been very little studied. It has been rarely possible in this book to make precise comparisons between London and other regions. Most local histories are either antiquarian, shunning the unromantic 19th century, or social and administrative, avoiding political controversy. Of the great cities, only Liverpool, Birmingham and Manchester have histories which bring together social and economic growth and local and national politics. Purely local studies of political-sociological development are equally rare. The contrast with the United States, where urban historians have long been sufficiently active and numerous to hold conferences and produce a newsletter, is startling.[1]

It is especially remarkable that London in this period has been ignored. It is of special interest for a number of reasons. It was the capital city, drawing to itself an unusual concentration of talent: trade unionists, churchmen and journalists as well as politicians. With over seventy constituencies its political weight far exceeded that of any other city. Because of the socialist revival and the clashes in Trafalgar Square, the dock strike and the new unionism, and the Fabians and their claims, London in the 1880s and 1890s attracted special attention as a focus of political discontent. In addition, the special characteristics of the London region, its growth into a conurbation, its commuters, its social segregation, its religious apathy, its relative lack of heavy industry and its growing number of office workers, far from making it a peculiar region of marginal importance, anticipate the pattern of development of most British cities in the 20th century.

There are a number of studies of national politics which touch on London. In particular, H. J. Hanham's *Elections and Party Management* comments on the London Liberals before 1885; A. M. McBriar's *Fabian Socialism and English Politics* analyses the influence of Fabian policies on the London Progressives; and E. P. Thompson's *William Morris* describes the Socialist League in London. C. Tsuzuki's

[1] B. D. White, *A History of the Corporation of Liverpool; 1835–1914*, Liverpool 1951; C. Gill and Asa Briggs, *The History of Birmingham*, Oxford 1952; A. S. Redford and I. S. Russell, *The History of Local Government in Manchester*, Manchester 1940; W. H. Chaloner, *The Social and Economic Development of Crewe, 1780–1923*, Manchester 1950; T. C. Barker and J. R. Harris, *A Merseyside Town in the Industrial Revolution: St. Helens, 1750–1900*, Liverpool 1954; A. H. Birch, *Small Town Politics, A Study of Political Life in Glossop*, Oxford 1959.

INTRODUCTION

H. M. Hyndman and British Socialism is less useful on local movements. H. M. Pelling's *Origins of the Labour Party* and F. Bealey and H. M. Pelling's *Labour and Politics 1900–1906* give exceptional attention to regional differences and their comments on London are helpful. There is, however, no study of the Conservatives in this period, and nothing on the Liberals after 1885, the local peculiarities of the Social Democrats, the tactics rather than programmes of the Fabians, or the local development of the independent Labour movement. Moreover on one aspect of London politics, the part played by the Fabians, much misleading literature exists, some by the original protagonists, but recently added to (in spite of the publications of Dr. McBriar) by Margaret Cole's *The Story of Fabian Socialism* and a chapter in Asa Brigg's *Victorian Cities*.[1] In the standard histories of the period by R. C. K. Ensor and E. Halévy, London is generally ignored, but a number of misleading comments are made, especially sneers at the allegedly alien character of the Social Democratic Federation (S.D.F.) and suggestions that local elections were unrelated to national policies; and these comments can be found repeated in more recent works.[2]

In addition to correcting some of these common impressions, a study of London politics can throw direct light on certain problems of national political history: in particular, the failure of the Liberal Party to prevent the development of an independent Labour Party, the small influence of Marxist socialism on the Labour Party, and the comparative prospects of Liberals and Labour at the end of the period. But because London politics have been so little studied the principal purpose here is to establish rather than to correct historical interpretation. This is an attempt to show the relationship of the social, religious and industrial characteristics of the London region and the development of working class political activity and organisation. It is only concerned with Ministers, administration and Acts of

[1] See Chapters 5 and 7.
[2] R. C. K. Ensor, *England 1870–1914*, Oxford 1936: e.g. p. 222, 'the incurable exoticism' of the S.D.F. contrasted with the 'thoroughly English lines' of the I.L.P.; p. 296 that the L.C.C. 'was fortunate in avoiding at the outset a mechanical party division as between conservatives and liberals; the special municipal parties which were created instead—the "moderates" and "progressives"—succeeded nearly till 1906 in excluding the irrelevances of national politics'; E. Halévy, *History of the English People*, trans. E. I. Watkin, 1951 edn: e.g. V, p. 221, the S.D.F.'s 'sour creed, imported from abroad, which refused to set before its adherents an ideal which made appeal to the heart'; p. 239, 'politics played very little part in municipal elections'; H. M. Pelling, *The Origins of the Labour Party, 1880–1900*, London 1954, pp. 97 and 182 describing the S.D.F. as 'dogmatic and sectarian' and a 'weedy growth'; Asa Briggs, *Victorian Cities*, London 1963, p. 348, 'neither Liberals nor Conservatives fought the (1889 L.C.C.) election on party grounds'.

INTRODUCTION

Parliament where they affect political development. In this perspective the lack of Liberal Councillors in Limehouse will demand more attention than the Limehouse speech of Lloyd George. The focus is on the infra-structure of politics.

I
LONDON

LONDON was a conurbation before the word was invented. By the end of the 19th century it was the most populous and extensive city in the world, a source of wonder and anxiety to both natives and visitors. It seemed to be as unceasing in its growth as it was unhealthy in its nature. London, 'like a swelled pudding', had 'splashed beyond its envelope'.[1] Lord Rosebery, speaking as first chairman of the London County Council in 1891, found 'no thought of pride associated in my mind with the idea of London. I am always haunted by the awfulness of London ... Sixty years ago a great Englishman, Cobbett, called it a wen. If it was a wen then, what is it now? A tumour, an elephantiasis sucking into its gorged system half the life and the blood and the bone of the rural districts.'[2] The French commentator, H. Taine, described how on arrival the visitor's 'astonishment ends by turning into bewilderment'. As his ship moved up the Thames past mile on mile of wharves and warehouses, and ships in long rows massed against the chimneys of the dockland houses, a pale sun penetrated the foggy atmosphere, reflected in 'the brackish, tawny, half-green, half-violet water', like 'a smile upon the face of a shaggy and blackened Cyclop'.[3] London seemed endless, a vast blotch of population, a heated, crowded, glaring, noisy magnet 'drinking up the best life of the country', transforming the rural English to 'a race which prowls at night along the lamp-lit streets'.[4]

At the end of the 18th century the population of London and its suburbs had been a million. By 1881 it had risen to four and a half million, and by 1911 to over seven million. At a time of rapid increase in the national population, London's share had risen from 18 per cent to 23·6 per cent.[5] Its physical growth had been equally rapid

[1] C. F. G. Masterman, 'The English City', in Lucian Oldershaw (ed.), *England a Nation*, London 1904, p. 56.
[2] Ebenezer Howard, *Garden Cities of Tomorrow*, London 1902, p. 11.
[3] H. A. Taine, *Notes on England*, trans. W. F. Rae, London 1872, pp. 6–8.
[4] *England a Nation*, op. cit., pp. 52–58.
[5] PP 1939–40 IV, p. 294.

(Map 1). In 1800 the built-up area was dense and compact. To the east it reached as far as Limehouse, to the north Camden Town and to the west Mayfair. South of the river Bermondsey and Vauxhall linked up. Chelsea and Hampstead were still fashionable villages, Deptford, Woolwich and Poplar independent dockyard towns, and Barking a fishing port. The river was the chief means of transport.

The coming of the railways, particularly the suburban network built in the 1860s and 1870s, made a much more dispersed growth possible. By 1880 the built-up area stretched from Hammersmith to Poplar on the north, and Battersea to Greenwich on the south side of the river. A ribbon stretched northwards to Tottenham, and across the county boundary in Essex West Ham was growing rapidly. The southern suburbs were more scattered, growing around railway stations. Woolwich remained an independent industrial town.

After 1880, with the extensive introduction of cheap workmen's trains, the beginning of the first electric underground railways in the 1890s, the electrification and extension of the tramway system, and the introduction of motor buses in the 1900s, dispersal became increasingly rapid. In the mid-century it had still been usual for London workmen to walk to work, often considerable distances. This new rapid transport, and the advent of the bicycle, brought about a far more general mobility. The annual number of tram, bus and railway journeys per head by Londoners in 1881 had been only 56; by 1913 it was 271. The millions of passengers carried rose from 269 in 1881 to 2,007 in 1913.[1] By 1913 over 2,000 'cheap' and workmen's trains were running daily and new working class suburbs had sprung up, especially in north and east London. By 1914 the built-up area had lost all its original compact appearance. Undeveloped stretches of country, such as the Lea valley and Dulwich fields, were left as islands cut off by the tide of building. Although less sharply defined, the continuous built-up area north of the river stretched from Ealing in the west to East Ham in the east and Wood Green in the north. Fingers stretched out to Enfield and Ilford. South of the river Wimbledon and Sydenham had linked up, and ribbons stretched out to Croydon and Woolwich. Woolwich in turn had stretched out to Erith. London, which in 1800 had covered less than twenty square miles, now occupied more than ten times that area.

The built-up area itself represented only one edge of London. Even in the 18th century it had been common for London stockbrokers to live in Brighton, and by 1914 colonies of professional and businessmen could be found far out along most of the radial railway lines. Similarly the railway works at Watford, the ordnance industry at Enfield, the paper and printing industry at Dartford, the cement

[1] *London Statistics*, 1913–14, pp. 477–8.

works at Grays and Northfleet, the dockyards at Tilbury and Chatham, although industrial settlements surrounded by countryside, were economically closely dependent on London. The boundary of the county of London fixed in 1889 had been over-run by building except on the south-east side, but other administrative boundaries, such as those of the Metropolitan Police and the Water Board, extended into the home counties.

There is thus some problem in defining the boundary of London appropriate for a political study. A rigid line would be somewhat arbitrary, and in the discussion of some of the rarer aspects of London politics examples have been taken from as far afield as Dartford, Croydon and Watford. But in general, and in the presentation of statistics, a narrower boundary has been taken, comprising the county area, and those suburbs beyond it absorbed into the built-up area or directly dependent upon it. Separate suburban residential villages and independent small industrial towns with a definite life of their own have been excluded, but industrial villages on the fringe of the built-up area have been included. The area chosen is shown in Map 2.

It was the out-county suburbs which were most rapidly developing between 1881 and 1911. The rise in population passed outwards like a tidal wave. In the built-up area of 1800 population had ceased to grow by 1860. The rest of the county area was growing most rapidly in the 1840s and 1850s, and by 1900 was approaching its maximum population. The spectacular growth of the out-county suburbs began in the 1860s and was still quickening in the 1900s, population increasing in each decade by between 400,000 and 600,000. At the same time population began to decline in the central area. This was partly because of the expanding needs of office and warehouse accommodation, partly the demolition of slums for railway building or rehousing, and partly the migration of the middle classes to more salubrious districts. The old City of London began to lose population after 1851, and the inner area which had been built-up in the 18th century started to lose population after 1871. In the 1900s this central decline was sufficient to offset the population increase at the edge of the county, so that, in striking contrast to the outer suburbs, the county of London showed a slight decrease in population.

One of the most important features of this development of London was the separation of the social classes into distinct residential districts. 18th century London had been a tangled mixture, fashionable squares and aristocratic town houses jostled up against overcrowded slum tenements, sharing the same epidemics, the same polluted water and insanitary drainage. Social segregation began as an estate policy: exclusive residential development of the Bloomsbury type brought the best financial returns. The old urban pattern was finally undermined by the combined influences of the romantic movement, which brought rustic suburbs into fashion, and the Victorian sanitary campaigns, which brought home to the middle classes the dangers of living next to slums. First the wealthy, then the professional classes and smaller businessmen, finally even the shopkeepers, began to leave the old mixed districts for either the new West End suburbs or the higher ground to the north and south (Maps 3 and 4). By the 1890s, when Charles Booth wrote his *Life and Labour of the People in London*, each district had its distinct social character. Except in the West End, the lower ground—the river valleys and former Thames marshes—were almost always working class districts. But the working class population was continually increasing, fed by immigration from rural England, and to a lesser extent by Irish and Jewish immigration. The old Jewish colony in Whitechapel was rapidly growing, adding to the population pressures in the East End. In the West End the redevelopment of Chelsea for the wealthy had a similar effect. Pushed by central overcrowding, the working class population was expanding into middle class areas wherever it could. There was thus a tendency for all but the most successful districts to decline in respectability as the middle classes retreated yet further outwards. Parts of Paddington such as Westbourne Park, although laid out with consistent grandeur, early became slums. Islington, a stronghold of respectable clerks and Nonconformity, the home of the meticulous Mr. Pooter of G. and W. Grossmith's *The Diary of a Nobody*, was becoming more a working class borough in the 1900s. Even in working class districts the same process could be observed. Silvertown, next to the West Ham docks, was built for 'artisans of a good class, stevedores, regular dockhands, ship painters, bricklayers, carpenters, etc. . . . As the outlying districts developed, the more prosperous inhabitants moved out to new houses in better neighbourhoods, and their place was taken by people of another class, chiefly casual dock labourers, costers and hangers-on.'[1]

Although similar developments could be found in most large towns in the country, the very scale of the metropolis exaggerated the distance between the classes in London. The middle class Londoner, with his 'swarms of happy, physically efficient children', his garden, 'today the lilac and syringa, to-morrow the scattered autumn leaves', knew little of working class conditions. 'Every day, swung high upon embankments or buried deep in tubes underground, he hurries through the region where the creature lives. He gazes darkly from his pleasant hill villa upon the huge and smoky area of tumbled tene-

---

[1] E. G. Howarth and M. Wilson, *West Ham*, London 1907, p. 57.

ments which stetches at his feet. He is dimly distrustful of the forces fermenting in this uncouth laboratory.'[1]

Had he cared to look more closely his distrust could scarcely have been diminished. The condition of the working classes in this period gave ample cause for discontent. There had, it is true, been some changes for the better since the mid-century. London had then been like a polluted sponge, a honeycomb of cesspools and wells, water supply taken from the rivers which were used as drains, perpetual fever haunting the slums, and thousands dying in successive epidemics of cholera. The Metropolitan Board of Works set up in 1855 had built the main London sewerage system by the mid-1860s, and by the 1880s the water supply, although insufficient, was taken from better sources, stored in reservoirs and properly filtered. This must be one reason why London, in spite of its size and its rapid growth, was a relatively healthy city. Although its mortality rates had changed little since the mid-century, they were as low as those of any large English city, and very much lower than those of the great European cities.

The achievement should not, however, be exaggerated. As yet only a quarter of London houses had constant water supply, and most working class tenements still had only a single tap for the whole block, with intermittent supply; drainage was frequently faulty and water closets shared very often by dozens of families. Moreover housing conditions had scarcely improved. Some of the old slum rookeries, warrens of old houses often built overhanging open sewers, had been cleared, but chiefly for railway and street improvement schemes. Those displaced were rarely rehoused, and increased the crowding of other districts. The model dwellings, grim barracks though they were, and often raising population to a higher density than the old slums, housed only 30,000, mostly artisan families. The 1884 Royal Commission on Housing found evidence that 'crowding has become more serious than it ever was'. Cellar dwellings though illegal were numerous.[2] The local vestries, whether or not they attempted to do so, were quite unable to enforce sanitary maintenance. The medical officer for Bethnal Green reported in 1883 that of 2,000 houses visited not one was without 'some grave sanitary defect; in a very large number the walls of the staircases, passages and rooms are black with filth, the ceilings are rotten and bulging, the walls damp and decayed, the roofs defective, and the ventilation and lighting most imperfect. . . . In almost every house I visited I found the yard, paving, and surface drainage, in a more or less defective

[1] C. F. G. Masterman, *The Condition of England*, London 1909, pp. 72–80.
[2] PP 1884–5 XXX, pp. 6–12.

condition, a quantity of black foetid mud having accumulated in places.'[1]

By 1914 there had been a marked improvement in the public health statistics (Table 1). Probably compulsory elementary education, by providing a better physical environment for school children, was a major reason. The death rates for children over five fell especially early. The school medical services and free meals gradually introduced from the 1890s helped to maintain this improvement.

Table 1

	Crude Death Rate			Infant Death Rate per 1,000 Live Births		
	1851–60	1881–90	1911–14	1851–60	1881–90	1911–14
England & Wales	22·2	19·1	13·5	154	142	110
London	23·7	20·5	14·5	155	152	108
County Boroughs			15·9		160[2]	125
More Urban Counties	24·7	20·3				

(PP. 1899 xvi, 1900 xv, and 1939–40 iv; *London Statistics* 1903–4 p. 464.)

Rising real wages must also have contributed, and the relative prosperity of London helps to explain why the improvement was more marked in London than in other urban areas. There were significantly fewer undernourished children found in London than in other town schools (Table 2).

Table 2

Percentage of Verminous and Undernourished Children in 1914

	London	County Boroughs	England and Wales
Unclean head	21·1	17·8	18·1
Unclean body	21·4	7·1	14·8
Nutrition good	27·6	13·7	21·1
Nutrition normal	62·9	72·6	67·5
Nutrition below normal	9·5	13·7	11·4

(PP. 1914–16 xviii, p. 731–2.)

London's prosperity, stimulating its continual growth, must on the other hand have aggravated the housing situation, and consequently limited the spread of improved health. By 1914 the artisan dwellings

[1] H. Jephson, *The Sanitary Evolution of London*, London 1907, p. 298.
[2] 78 principal towns, *Population Studies*, xvii, p. 254 (1964).

companies had built extensive suburban estates, particularly in north-east London, housing 100,000. Further slum clearance schemes by the L.C.C. had displaced 45,000 and new housing had been provided for a similar number, but only a very small proportion of council tenants were unskilled manual workers.[1] Consequently in the inner working class districts overcrowding was as serious as ever in 1911 (Map 5). In the county as a whole the census of 1911 revealed a slight improvement since 1891 (Table 3), but the improvement was less than the national average and London remained far more crowded than towns in general. Its 17·7 per cent of population crowded in fact showed a slight increase since 1901, and was much worse than that of any other large town except Newcastle.

Table 3
Percentage Living More Than Two Per Room

	1891	1911
U.K.	11·2	9·5
London	19·7	17·7
Large Towns (London, County Boroughs and Urban Districts over 50,000)		9·8

There can be no doubt of the effect of these conditions upon health. In the 1900s there was a rising infant death rate in those areas where overcrowding was increasing. The Select Committee on Physical Deterioration was told that the death rate of those living in one room tenements in Finsbury was twice the average for the borough. The report of the committee showed how as a whole the physical conditions and health of the working classes were far inferior to those of the middle classes. In middle class Hampstead the expectation of life was 50·8 years, in working class Southwark 36·8 years. A table of mortality by occupation showed the lowest expectancy of life to be that of unskilled labourers. In giving evidence of the health of London children a School Board medical officer said that 'physical infirmity is practically confined to the lowest and poorest strata of the population, whose children are improperly and insufficiently fed and inadequately housed'.[2] One should remember not only that nearly a tenth of London school children were undernourished in 1914, but that a 'normal' working class diet could mean little more than bread and tea; and that, despite their relative prosperity, London school children were exceptionally dirty. As late as 1914, despite continuous cleansing campaigns, a survey found that a fifth were verminous

[1] G. Gibbon and R. W. Bell, *History of the London County Council 1889–1939*, London 1939, pp. 374–5.
[2] PP 1904 XXXII, pp. 20–23.

(Table 2). Although the improvement in public health was indubitable, it still had a long way to go.

The same may be said of the economic situation of the London working classes. Certainly their overcrowded housing, for which they paid higher rents than were common in the provinces, was partly due to the economic buoyancy of London. Throughout this period London wages were higher and London hours in general shorter than those in the rest of the country.[1] In spite of the continued influx of workmen, indicated by the exceptionally rapid growth of population, the demand for labour remained high and was generally reflected by special higher London district wage rates. There is no reason for doubting that in periods of rising real wages, such as the 1880s and 1890s, Londoners took their full share.

Nevertheless, even in the best decades prosperity was no more than relative. Many of the principal London trades, such as the building industry, tailoring, gasworks and docks, suffered especially seriously from unemployment, both seasonal and cyclical. Not only were the regular seasonal fluctuations of the London building industry more violent, but the collapse of the late 19th century housing boom after 1900 was more catastrophic in Greater London, despite its continued population growth, than in any other region.[2] In depressed periods unemployment was widespread. A government survey of 29,000 London working men in 1887 revealed that over 70 per cent of the dock labourers, building craftsmen, tailors and bootmakers had been unemployed during the winter, most for more than two months.[3] The winter of 1886–7 was bad, but by no means alone. Between 1884 and 1887, 1892 and 1895, 1901 and 1905, and in 1908–9 the economy was depressed. Little relief for unemployment was provided under the Poor Law, but when Distress Committees were set up in 1905 more than a third of the families applied for relief in many boroughs, particularly those close to the docks and heavier industry (Map 6). Thus although at times there were good wages to be earned, the general picture in these years was far from real prosperity. In his survey of London, Charles Booth, defining the poor as those barely able to obtain the necessaries of life, found that 30 per cent of the whole population was living in chronic poverty.[4] In working class districts the figure was frequently over 40 per cent, and in some areas 60 per cent or 70 per cent (Map 3). Well might Charles

[1] F. W. Lawrence, *Local Variations in Wages*, London 1899, p. 7.

[2] S. B. Saul, 'House Building in England, 1890–1914', *Economic History Review*, August 1962; N. B. Dearle, *Problems of Unemployment in the London Building Trades*, London 1908.

[3] PP 1887 LXXI, pp. 313, 321.

[4] C. Booth, *Life and Labour of the People in London*, 1892–7, I, p. 33, and II, p. 21.

Masterman, a young Liberal politician writing in the 1900s, years in which even the relative rise of real wages had been halted, regard the London multitude as a threat to the peace of the country. 'One feels that the smile might turn suddenly into fierce snarl or savagery.'[1]

Yet there were reasons for moderating these fears. Firstly, revolt does not often spring from chronic poverty. A socialist propagandist, visiting North Kensington in 1906, described the 'long streets of overcrowded houses, let out in single rooms, filthy streets, dirty children', the appalling death rate. 'But not a revolt had they amongst them. . . . It is absolutely no use talking about socialism to people who die at the rate of 40 per 1,000. What they want—and need—is Drink. Yet, between the extremes there is a class of people who try to live cleanly and think clearly.'[2] If protest was to come, it was rather from the more prosperous working classes of the new districts than from the real poverty of the inner slums.

Secondly, there was less local community feeling in London than in the provinces. This factor is hard to assess, and can be easily exaggerated. There were certainly local personalities, local meeting places and especially in the suburbs local newspapers. But contemporary commentators often noticed the lack of neighbourliness and co-operation among working class Londoners.[3] The rootlessness of the London population might lead one to expect this. Although a few districts, such as Bethnal Green, were relatively stable, it was common for a third of the population in working class districts to move during each year.[4] The size of the city meant that a change of work frequently caused a change of residence. There was also movement in search of better accommodation. Many artisans were settling in the suburbs, commuting to work on overcrowded workmen's trains, so that they had less time and energy left to give to local life. The segregation of even artisans and unskilled workers into different districts meant that local communities, as well as being unstable, were socially unbalanced. The commuting artisan was not only a weakness to the suburban community: his migration was leaving the poorer districts without their natural leaders.

This impersonality and sprawling vastness, residential segregation and commuting, this rootless population, made London in 1880 more like the conurbation of the future than the city of the past. But the political effect of impersonality was increased by another characteristic inherited from the past: the small scale of London industry,

[1] *Condition of England*, op. cit., p. 121.
[2] *Clarion*, 28 September 1906.
[3] E.g. J. Grant, *The Great Metropolis*, London 1837, I, p. 324; T. H. S. Escott, *England: its People, Polity and Pursuits*, London 1885 edition, pp. 160–1.
[4] Booth, op. cit., I, pp. 26–27; III, p. 148 (Map); PP 1905 XXX, p. 560.

which hindered the development of a new sense of working class solidarity in a common occupation.

The broad occupational pattern of London has changed surprisingly little over the past century. An analysis of census occupations shows that while Greater London's share of manufacturing industry is close to the national average, its service occupations are notably important, while its primary industry is negligible (Table 4).

Table 4
Industrial Occupations: England and Wales

Percentage of Total Labour Force Employed in:	England and Wales			Greater London			Greater London as Percentage of England & Wales		
	1861	1921	1951	1861	1921	1951	1861	1921	1951
Primary industry (agriculture, fishing, mining)	24	13·9	8·6	3·0	0·9	0·5	1·9	1·2	1·2
Manufacturing industry (excluding building, gas and electricity services)	33·2	34·8	37·8	31·7	32·7	35·5	14·9	17·6	20·2
Services	39·2	49·0	53·6	61·0	65·0	63·9	24·3	24·8	25·7
Not stated	3·7	2·2	0·1	4·3	1·4	0·1	Total employed		
	100	100	100	100	100	100	15·6	18·7	21·5

(P. G. Hall, *The Industries of London Since 1861*, London 1962, p. 21)

The detailed analysis in Table 5 (for the county only) confirms this impression. There was, first of all, the substantial share of the civil services, professional and commercial classes that one would expect of the capital city, mostly working in central London but living in the suburbs, and attended by a large class of domestic servants (Map 4 and 7). These middle class occupations were expending rapidly during the period: the number of clerks, for example, rose from 90,000 in 1881 to 172,000 in 1911.

The characteristic London industries were trades serving the capital city. The printing, furniture, boot and dress trades had developed on the fringes of the city (Map 8). So had specialised trades such as goldsmiths, watchmakers, piano-makers, precision instrument makers, and during this period the new electrical industry. None of these occupations produced any heavy industry. They were small-scale

Table 5
Percentage of Persons over 10 Grouped by Occupations as Defined by the Census of 1911 (PP 1913 lxxviii)

	England & Wales	London County	London County as Percentage of England & Wales
Government, Defence, Professions and Commerce	12·9	18·7	19·3
Hotel and Domestic Service	13·6	17·6	17·1
Food and Lodging	8·9	11·1	16·6
Transport, Gas, Water and Electricity	9·8	12·9	17·6
Service Trades	32·3	41·6	16·9
Print and Paper	2·1	4·9	30·6
Dress Trades	7·6	11·7	19·5
Skin Manufacture	0·7	1·5	26·0
Furniture	1·8	3·2	23·8
Building	6·0	6·1	13·4
Electrical Trades	0·6	0·9	20·8
Precious Metals	0·7	1·5	27·9
Service Manufacture	19·7	30·1	22·5
Metal Manufacture	9·5	4·9	6·9
Chemical, Brick, Cement, Pottery and Glass Industries	2·2	1·7	10·7
Textile manufacturing	8·4	2·3	3·5
Agriculture, Fishing and Mining	14·8	0·5	0·4
Primary and Manufacturing Industry	35·0	9·5	3·6
Total	100·0 (15 million)	100·0 (2 million)	13·3

sweated trades, and several minor industries which seem typical, such as brush and basket making, artificial flowers and soap manufacture, in fact accounted for very small numbers.

Heavier industry thus developed from services such as the docks or gas works rather than directly from manufacturing (Map 10). The great national heavy industries, textiles, iron and steel and mining, were conspicuously absent. Building was no more important than in the national pattern, although the building slump and the fact that operations were principally in the out-county suburbs affected the figure. There were nearly 4,000 building firms employing 126,000 in 1911. Transport was more important, employing double this number, nearly half on the roads. Vehicle building was consequently important, and in the 1900s London became a centre of the rapidly expanding motor car industry. Similarly the port of London—the busiest in the country—ensured that, in spite of the collapse of the Thames shipbuilding industry in the mid-19th century, London remained a centre for ship-repairing. The railways also required engineering workshops, and further stimulus came from the government. Although the admiralty dockyards had been removed from Woolwich and Deptford, Woolwich remained the centre of government armament manufacture, and later in the 19th century the rifle industry was established at Enfield. Cable for the telegraph service was produced in Erith and West Ham. Altogether in the county 120,000 were employed in the metal and engineering industry, concentrated on Woolwich and Poplar and to a lesser extent Battersea, and outside the county equally large numbers could be found in Erith, West Ham and up the Lea Valley (Map 9). Although the spectacular growth of light engineering in outer north-west London which took place after 1920 had scarcely started, it is easy to see that the industry had a good foundation in London.

London is not usually considered to be an industrial city, and it is true that it lacks the heavy manufacturing industries which are prominent in the national industrial structure. But the impression created by the West End and West London can be misleading (Map 10). Parts of London are quite different. Along the north London canal between the railway terminals, by Limehouse Creek, the river Lea and the Thames banks east of the vast area of wharves and docks, factories tower up as menacingly as in any northern city. The Beckton gasworks at East Ham was the largest in the world, with seventy miles of railway line within its bounds. In West Ham alone the docks, railway shops and engineering and chemical industry employed over 20,000 men, more than in many provincial industrial towns.[1] The lower Thames-side was a minor industrial region, combining the factory life of the north with the shifting rootlessness of the conurbation. In the future, as the older central areas decayed and their trades became industrialised, and a second light industrial region developed in Middlesex, London was to seem as much an industrial as a capital city.

[1] Howarth and Wilson, op. cit., pp. 149–52.

II
RELIGION

RELIGION had no hold upon the working classes of 19th century London. Bishop Walsham How, in charge of East London, said in 1880 that East Enders thought of religion 'as belonging to a wholly different class from themselves, and to a class looked upon with no kindly regard'. Religion was associated 'with a prosperity they envy, and a luxury which they resent'.[1]

The three religious surveys of 1851, 1886 and 1903 make the facts clear. Although the first survey[2] is least reliable, the result was plain enough: with the exception of Preston, (where the Catholics were not properly counted), East and South London had the lowest church attendance in the country, and London as a whole compared very badly with other large towns.

The *British Weekly* survey of 1886 elaborated the relationship between low attendance and working class districts.[3] Although no allowance was made for those who attended twice (and the third survey showed that half the morning congregation reappeared in the evening), it showed that the fashionable City and West End churches were surrounded by a continuous working class area in which attendances were less than 20 per cent of the population (Map 11).

The third survey, organised by Richard Mudie-Smith for the *Daily News*, was definitive in its accuracy. Summing up the results, Mudie-Smith wrote, 'the poorer the district the less inclination is there to attend a place of worship'.[4] An area was shown in which 80 per cent of the population did not go to church or chapel, much more extensive than that of low attendance in 1886 (Map 12). It included the whole of inner south London, the East End and inner north London

---

[1] Church Congress report, 1880, pp. 94–95.   [2] PP 1852–3 LXXXIX.
[3] *British Weekly*, November-December 1886.
[4] R. Mudie-Smith (ed.), *The Religious Life of London*, London 1904, p. 26. This survey is supplemented and confirmed by Booth, op. cit., *Religious Influences*, London 1902, e.g. 7, p. 47.

out to the northern and eastern suburbs, and a great western ring from Battersea to Willesden where the working class were ousting the earlier middle class suburban population. Better attendances were only recorded in the West End and middle class suburbs. In most East End boroughs, St. Pancras and Tottenham, Deptford and Battersea, Willesden, Hammersmith and Fulham, less than 15 per cent attended any place of worship.

In a working class district like Walworth even the small congregations which were achieved consisted chiefly of middle class families still living in the once respectable Walworth Road and attending the great Baptist tabernacles. 'In these districts at least, Nonconformists form the aristocracy, and the Church and the Roman Catholics work with a lower social stratum.'[1] But the Church worked with little success. Even Sunday Schools, which accounted for over a third of the attendance, were 'not to any large extent slum children. . . . Even the so-called Ragged Schools do not reach the ragged children to any extent.'[2]

This weakness of religion among the working classes, a danger in any great impersonal city, had been made inevitable by a long period of neglect by the Church, which had failed to adapt to the growth and changing structure of London after 1600. By 1812 the total church accommodation for a population of one million was only 163,000, and even the vigorous church building efforts of the Victorians failed to keep up with the growth of population. Moreover, not only was there never enough room for the working classes in church, but before 1850 most churches were exclusive, the pews reserved for those who could afford pew rents, and in the poorer parts their vicar an absentee. By the time when clergy began to take up residence in the slum parishes it was already too late: the Gospel was 'as unknown as in Thibet'.[3]

The Nonconformists were even weaker in London than the Church of England and they made less notable efforts to improve their position in the 19th century. Of the older denominations, only the Baptists succeeded to a small extent with artisans in north east London, but they relied on the lower middle classes.[4] The others remained solidly middle class. There were no strong working class sects such as the Primitive Methodists or the Plymouth Brethren in London.[5] Even the Salvation Army, begun in Whitechapel where William Booth set up his missionary tent in 1865, showed an atten-

[1] *Mudie-Smith*, op. cit., pp. 197–200.   [2] Ibid., pp. 202, 326.
[3] (Rev. E. B. Pusey, 1855) K. S. Inglis, *Churches and the Working Classes in Victorian England*, London 1963, p. 8.
[4] Booth, op. cit., *Religious Influences*, 7, p. 123; Mudie-Smith, op. cit., p. 200.
[5] The sects which existed are well described in C. M. Davies, *Unorthodox London*, London 1873 and 1875.

RELIGION

dance in 1886 of only 53,000 out of 367,000 Nonconformists, and in the poorest districts such as Bethnal Green and Whitechapel it had scarcely a member. It reached a lower social class than most Nonconformists, but its headquarters were appropriately in Clapton, among artisans and clerks.[1] The attitude of the working classes to Nonconformity is well illustrated by the fate of the Walworth Jumpers, one of the very few examples of a genuine working class sect, who met under a railway arch near the Elephant and Castle. Their inspired convulsions provoked such ridicule among the local population that they were forced to charge an admission fee of 3d, and on occasions when the service failed to inspire sufficiently dramatic hoppings and twitchings the congregation demanded its money back.[2]

Some of the weakness of religion in London resulted from the impersonality of the metropolis and the lack of strong social pressures to attend church which could operate in a small community. At the same time the failure of the churches exaggerated the lack of local community feeling in London. Equally it had direct political consequences. In some parts of England the Nonconformist chapels had provided the training ground in public speaking and in organisation upon which trade unions could be based. Similarly they influenced the socialist movement and gave it a distinctly Nonconformist ring. Nonconformity also provided an important bond between the middle and working classes in the Liberal Party. In London, where Nonconformity was weak and working class sects insignificant, trade unions and co-operation were less easily organised. Secularism developed in the place of working class sectarianism, and the London socialist movement became secular and Marxist rather than Nonconformist in tone. Political clubs tended to be more influential than chapels. Without the political bond of Nonconformity a social and religious conflict, which is described in Chapter 5, developed in the London Liberal Party.

On the other hand, since the immediate impact of this religious weakness was in working class politics, it is still possible to trace the traditional religious affiliations of the Liberal and Conservative Parties.

Between 1885 and 1914 the Conservative Party held fifteen safe seats in the county of London (Map 13). In twelve of these there was

---

[1] Inglis, op. cit., pp. 195–7; Booth, op. cit., *Religious Influences*, 7, pp. 326–7: 'as regards spreading the Gospel in London, in any broad measure, the movement has altogether failed'; in the rare cases where regular congregations had been formed 'they consist of the better sort of working-class people . . . but not of "the poor" '.

[2] Davies, op. cit., pp. 89–100.

an Anglican majority in both 1886 and 1903, and Anglican worshippers exceeded 10 per cent of the population in 1903 (Maps 14 and 15). Of the three exceptions, Norwood and Dulwich were counted with Lambeth and Camberwell but in fact were probably Anglican areas. In Hammersmith Anglicans and Nonconformists were equal, but attendance was low, and Conservative success was primarily due to internal Liberal squabbles. It is also clear that except for Hammersmith these safe seats were in the wealthiest parts of London. Thus there seems no reason to suppose that the backbone of the London Conservative Party was less Anglican than its provincial counterparts: support for both Church and Party were equally on a class basis. In many districts the Anglican clergy were open in their support for the Conservatives, and church halls were used as Conservative committee rooms at general elections.[1] In local elections too the local vicar was often chairman of the vestry until 1894, and notorious as a champion of vested interests.[2] It is only when the supporters rather than the stalwarts are considered that the religious connection becomes less marked. Beyond the safe seats Conservative success is clearly linked to the class composition of constituencies, but there is no longer any relationship with Anglican church attendance.

Liberalism is harder to analyse, because it was less successful. There were only two Liberal safe seats, and one was Whitechapel, where the Jewish community accounted for Liberal success. Nor is there a clear relationship between the 1885 election result, before the middle class desertions over Home Rule, and the 1886 survey. Only just over half the constituencies were in Nonconformist areas (Maps 15 and 16). On the other hand, of the 39 seats captured in 1906, 32 were in areas shown as Nonconformist in 1903 (Maps 16 and 17), and of the 18 seats which the Liberals held three times in the period (excluding bye-elections and January 1910), 15 were recorded in 1903 with a Nonconformist majority, although Nonconformist attendance exceeded 10 per cent of the population in only two. The connection between Nonconformity and Liberal success in thus slight, especially when compared with the effect of working class strength in the electorate.[3] There is, however, one significant variation. In both 1886 and 1900 the very poorest constituencies were less resistant to the Conservatives than those in which the middle class element was slightly larger. It appears that both Nonconformity and Liberalism benefited from a backbone of artisan and lower middle class support.

It should be emphasised that the vast area of Nonconformist

[1] E.g. *Woolwich Pioneer*, 21 January 1910.
[2] E.g. (Bermondsey) F. W. Soutter, *Recollections of a Labour Pioneer*, London 1923.
[3] See Appendix A.

superiority shown by the 1903 survey gives a false picture of its strength. Because the shopkeepers were the last to migrate from a working class area to the suburbs, there was a phase in which chapel attendance exceeded that in churches. But before long both would dwindle to insignificance. The three surveys show the growing area of low attendance following the Nonconformist majority (Maps 12–14, 18–19). By 1903 areas of real Nonconformist strength were all suburban; and on the heels of the migrant chapel-goers were the irreligious. Nonconformity was thus a dwindling political asset, and in a situation in which elections could only be won on a class basis the traditional Liberal connection with Nonconformity produced such internal conflict as to be a source of weakness.

The general political effect of the churches is easier to assess than the influence of individual clergy. Nevertheless this is important. For the churches London was a mission field, and the political role of religion not unlike that in colonial mission fields. In areas where churchpeople were absent the influence of the missionaries with the heathen was often more powerful, and their identification with the political causes of the natives more likely. In a working class district the clergy because of their education and social standing were inevitably prominent, and their political influence could be greater than their religious following.

Influence was not acquired simply through a 'social conscience'. Nearly all the slum clergy played a part in social work, but from the mid 1870s social work in London was dominated by the local committees of the Charity Organisation Society. These committees attempted to revive the pure doctrine of the 1834 Poor Law, modified by experience, that no relief should be given that did not make the recipient self-supporting. They granted loans to tradesmen in difficulty or to artisans who had lost their tools, and gave emigration grants, and pensions to the respectable poor. The rest were offered resident relief at the workhouse or nothing. They opposed out-relief under any circumstances, even to those unemployed through trade fluctuations. They campaigned against free education, against state pensions, the feeding of undernourished schoolchildren, the provision of winter relief works by local authorities for the unemployed, against Salvation Army shelters and soup kitchens, and the Lord Mayor's relief funds of the 1880s, all of which they thought eroded self-help. They stood as candidates for the Poor Law Guardians and in Stepney, St. George's in the East and Whitechapel succeeded in imposing their rigorous system.[1]

[1] H. Bosanquet, *Social Work in London 1869–1912; a History of the Charity Organisation Society*, London 1914.

It is easy to understand why no Victorian institution was more disliked by the working classes than the Charity Organisation Society. Samuel Barnett's activities as a Whitechapel Guardian provoked such bitterness that his windows were stoned, and although he later adopted a more humane attitude there can be little doubt that his earlier reputation remained a serious handicap in his work as Warden of Toynbee Hall.[1] In contrast the popularity of the Salvation Army can be attributed to its work after 1890 in helping the really destitute classes, refusing to discriminate between the 'deserving' and 'undeserving'.[2]

Although no other sect won the respect of the Salvation Army, the influence of a minority of clergy rested on a similar basis, and enabled them to play a vital part in the Labour movement. The mid-19th century Christian Socialism of F. D. Maurice had lain dormant until its revival in the 1870s by Stewart Headlam, then a curate in Bethnal Green. A friend of secularists and trade unionists, a defender of music halls, and a bitter opponent of the Charity Organisation Society, Headlam called himself a socialist largely through a desire not to be identified with middle class Liberalism.[3] 'We are liberals and radicals and therefore socialists,' he wrote in 1893: 'we think that the true position of a socialist, politically, is on the extreme left of the liberal party.'[4]

Headlam never advanced beyond a belief in land nationalisation and trade unionism: he strongly opposed the I.L.P.[5] But other members of his Guild of St. Matthew, founded in 1877 and reaching some 350 members in the early 1890s, were more adventurous. In Lambeth the Rev. W. A. Morris, vicar of St. Anne's Nine Elms, ran a workmen's club from which the 1890 gas strike was organised and the first Mayday demonstration planned. He became a trustee of the Gas Workers' Union, and in 1895 a Labour member of the Lambeth vestry.[6] In Poplar the Rev. H. A. Kennedy was first treasurer of the Labour Electoral Committee formed in 1892. His successor in this post, Dr. Chandler, was probably not a member of the Guild, but equally important as an early Labour supporter.[7] It was principally Chandler's support of George Lansbury as a fellow-member of the Board of Guardians which made the Board, while still con-

[1] A. F. Young and E. T. Ashton, *British Social Work in the 19th Century*, London 1956, p. 112; c.f. G. Lansbury, *My Life*, London 1928, pp. 130–1.
[2] Inglis, op. cit., pp. 194–212.
[3] F. G. Bettany, *Stewart Headlam: a Biography*, London 1926.
[4] *Church Reformer*, December 1893.
[5] E.g. ibid., September 1892, October 1895.
[6] *Labour Annual*, 1895; Thorne, op. cit., p. 118.
[7] G. Haw, *From Workhouse to Westminster: the Life Story of Will Crooks, M.P.*, London 1907, p. 76.

trolled by the local Moderates, the most progressive in policy in London.[1]

In Woolwich the clergy were perhaps even more influential. Canon Escreet, a member of the Guild, became rector in 1892, and brought a socialist curate with him.[2] The Rev. J. W. Horsley, vicar of Holy Trinity in 1888, 'took up the sword of sanitation' in Woolwich, campaigned in local elections and became a member of the Local Board.[3] Both he and Escreet were elected as Labour Guardians in 1893. When Horsley left Woolwich for Walworth in 1894 (where he once again became a Guardian, as well as Newington Vestry chairman), he received an address from 'the wage-earning class . . . Your name, sir, has been a terror to slum-owners, rackrenters, and other exploiters.'[4] As rector Escreet became chairman of the local Charity Organisation Society committee, and probably secured the choice of another socialist, C. H. Grinling, as its secretary in 1894. Grinling,[5] a young man of independent means, had settled in Woolwich in 1889 after working as a curate in Nottingham and living as one of the first residents in Toynbee Hall. In later life he appears to have been an anarchist agnostic of the William Morris type, but in the 1890s he was probably still a Christian, and certainly an advocate of state assistance for the poor. He had already founded the Woolwich Dispensary and an Invalid Children's Aid Committee, but his obvious ability did not prevent a clash with the central Charity Organisation Society and his dismissal from the post. During the next five years he added to his social efforts work for adult education, and finally in 1900 threw himself into political work, leading the formation of the Woolwich Labour Party and publishing the *Woolwich Pioneer*. Throughout the 1890s and 1900s Escreet and Grinling, Horsley and three or four other clergy are prominent figures in any political labour agitation. Most of them were connected either with Headlam's Guild or with the more respectable Christian Social Union, founded in 1889, whose 2,300 London members in 1895 included Horsley and Chandler.

There was no similar general movement among Nonconformist ministers. Most of those who supported social reform, even if they called themselves socialists, William Lax of Poplar, Scott Lidgett of the Bermondsey Settlement, Dr. John Clifford of Paddington,

[1] E.g. *London*, 6 July, 17 August, 12 October 1893.
[2] (Rev. Wragge) *Church Reformer*, February 1894.
[3] *London*, 14 March 1896.
[4] Ibid., 22 February 1894.
[5] H. Snell, *Men, Movements and Myself*, London 1936, pp. 66–73; C. H. Grinling, *Settlement Work in Woolwich*, London 1906; C. H. Grinling to G. Wallas, 6 April 1894, Wallas Collection; K. Walter to P. Thompson, 20 April and 26 May 1960.

remained firmly attached to the Liberal Party.[1] Only after 1906, with the conversion to socialism of the Rev. R. J. Campbell of the fashionable Congregationalist City Temple, is a leading Nonconformist pastor found as an open Labour Party supporter in London, and it is symptomatic that Campbell ended his life as an Anglican.[2] J. H. Belcher, minister of St. Thomas' Square chapel in Hackney, who was elected a vestryman in 1895 and supported the Hackney Labour League and Fabian Group, was certainly a socialist, but apparently something of an oddity if his Ministers' Union, which he tried to propagate by outdoor meetings in Hackney Fields, was intended seriously. Later he moved to the provinces and became a militant I.L.Per.[3]

In contrast to their clergy, two Nonconformist settlements gave a lead in their support for the Labour movement. Only four of the twenty-six slum settlements founded between 1884 and 1900 took any part in local affairs, and of these Toynbee Hall and Bermondsey tended to be neutral or Liberal. The two Congregationalist settlements acted corporately and explicitly for Labour. Browning Hall in Walworth under Herbert Stead, brother of the journalist, ran notable campaigns for housing, work for the unemployed and old age pensions. For the pensions campaign, which was especially vigorous, the National Committee of Organised Labour was set up in 1898.[4] In West Ham, Mansfield House and the women's settlement were closely involved with local politics. They sent representatives to the joint socialist electoral committees, and one resident, a nurse, Edith Kerrison, was a Guardian, a delegate to the 1895 I.L.P. conference and organiser of the local Socialist Sunday School. Percy Alden the Warden was a Labour borough councillor and Deputy Mayor in 1898. Two other residents were on the School Board. Alden, although a Liberal rather than a socialist, made it the settlement's policy 'to support all honest and intelligent labour candidates', and disassociated himself from the Liberal tradesmen who had formerly controlled the council.[5] The policy of the settlement helped to secure the first Labour Party majority on any local council in 1898. It was acknowledging rather than leading local political feeling: but the support in West Ham of the settlement, and in Woolwich and Poplar

[1] W. E. Lax, *Lax of Poplar*, London 1927; J. Scott Lidgett, *My Guided Life*, London 1936; Sir J. Marchant, *Dr. John Clifford; Life, Letters and Reminiscences*, London 1924.

[2] R. J. Campbell, *A Spiritual Pilgrimage*, London 1916.

[3] Hackney Fabian Group minutes, 1893; Mann, op. cit., p. 121.

[4] F. H. Stead, *How Old Age Pensions Began to Be*, London 1909; Anon., *Browning Hall and Settlement, Eighteen Years in the Central City Swarm*, London 1913.

[5] Anon., *Twenty-One Years at Mansfield House, 1890–1911*, London 1911; W. Reason (ed.), *University and Social Settlements*, London 1898.

of the clergy, help to explain why these were the first areas in London to maintain successful independent Labour Parties.

There were a number of other Christian Socialist groups in London, but none had any prolonged existence or influence. We must therefore turn from this socialist minority, whose political influence was exerted amidst religious indifference, to a second kind of religious minority, whose political importance was due to a religious following among the working classes.

The first two religious minorities, the Jews and Roman Catholics, were alike in consisting largely of immigrant groups and to an unusual extent of the working classes and the very poor.

Like the Jews, the Irish, the largest Catholic group, had formed colonies in London as early as the 17th century. Their migration was at first seasonal, providing harvest labour. Later they found work on the riverside, the canals and in building.[1] The real influx of Irish into London, however, was from the 1830s to the 1870s, when four million Irish emigrated. How many settled in London is unknown, but Garwood estimated their numbers in 1853 as a tenth of the London population.[2] They crowded into slum rookeries in St. Giles, Smithfield, Camberwell and by the riverside, especially in St. George's in the East and in Southwark, their insanitary conditions made worse by the fact that many still kept cows and pigs.

Since the census returns give no indication of the cumulative growth of the Irish colony and the religious surveys do not distinguish Irish from other Catholics it is not possible to give precise estimates of Irish numbers. Certainly the religious surveys suggest that the vigorous Catholic efforts to hold the faith of immigrants had not been without effect. Attendances at West Ham were 6,500; and the figures for Stepney, Woolwich, Bermondsey, Southwark and Clapham were also impressive. In these and other riverside areas Catholics accounted for between 11 and 15 per cent of the total church attendance. More important, in such districts Charles Booth found Roman Catholic congregations alone to 'include the very poorest'.[3] Contemporary estimates suggest that in these districts the Irish numbered roughly four times the Catholic church attendance, so that they were well over 10 per cent of the population. Probably in the whole of London there were 350,000 Irish in 1900 (Map 20).[4]

[1] M. D. George, *London Life in the 18th Century*, London 1925, pp. 111–13.
[2] J. Garwood, *The Million Peopled City*, London 1853, pp. 245, 314–15; c.f. F. Engels, *The Condition of the Working Class in England in 1844*, London 1952 edition, p. 90.
[3] Booth, op. cit., *Religious Influences*, 1, p. 87.
[4] Ibid., 5, p. 17; C. Russell, *The Catholics of London and Public Life*, London, 1907.

What impression did this large number of Irish make on London politics? Impressive claims were sometimes made for the Irish vote and its influence, as in 1885, when the Nationalists said that there were 57,000 Irish voters in London.[1] But a more likely estimate by the *Pall Mall Gazette* at the same time was only 10,000.[2] As the poorest section of the working class, the most frequently disqualified by receipt of poor relief or by removal to another district, the Irish widely escaped registration as electors. Figures given by the *London Catholic Herald* in 1910 suggested that the highest numbers, in Limehouse and Poplar, were no more than 1,000.[3] It is unlikely that Irish voters were more than 10 per cent of the electorate except in St. George's in the East, Poplar and possibly Limehouse and Rotherhithe, and nowhere more than 20 per cent.

Irish influence was further weakened by poor organisation. Insufficiently assimilated to join in a large measure in metropolitan political life, they were nevertheless equally insufficiently alien to develop the political features of a well organised minority, with its own culture, press and communal institutions. The *London Catholic Herald*, although a Home Rule paper with a working class circulation, was largely made up of religious parish news, anecdotes and Shamrockiana. Apart from the L.C.C. election of 1907 it gave very little coverage to local politics, and the lists of Irish candidates which it sometimes published were extraordinarily inaccurate.[4] The various Home Rule organisations proved a very limited success in London, in spite of the presence of the Irish M.Ps in Westminster. At the height of the anti-coercion campaign of 1880 a number of branches of the Land League were formed, and its successor the National League had as many as thirty-eight London branches in 1887. But they were transitory, and in the later 1890s the National League and in the 1900s the United Irish League had less than ten London branches. Their influence after 1902 was weakened by a hostile rival organisation, the Irish National Society.[5] Although the League organiser was

[1] *Freeman's Journal*, 4 December 1885.   [2] *Pall Mall Gazette*, 20 August 1886.
[3] *London Catholic Herald*, 1 January 1910. Even so, the figures were not closely reliable. For Limehouse, the estimate was 800, but the *Daily Chronicle*, 3 January 1906, suggested 450. The figure for St. George's in the East varied from 500–600 (*London Catholic Herald*, 23 October 1909) to 600–700 (*Standard*, 14 December 1909). For Poplar the 1910 estimate was 1000, for Bow and Bromley 400. No figures were given for south London constituencies, although *South London Press*, 24 September 1909, gave 1000 for Bermondsey and Rotherhithe together. The failure of the political agents to give reliable estimates is itself significant.
[4] E.g. 8 April 1892, list of Catholic candidates including well-known Protestant clergy such as Scott Lidgett and Arthur Jephson.
[5] E. P. M. Wollaston, 'The Irish Nationalist Movement in Great Britain, 1880–1908', London M.A. thesis, 1958.

usually in London, election organisation seems to have been strikingly ineffective. In 1885, for example, some of the League branches were not even informed of the election policy of hostility to the Liberals.[1]

Consequently the distinctive Irish part in London politics was very limited. Apart from the anti-coercion agitation of the radical clubs in 1880 and the support for the Dublin strike led by the *Daily Herald* in 1913, there was little general interest in Irish issues. Irishmen prominent in London politics, such as T. P. O'Connor of the *Star*, Jim Connell and John Scurr the socialists, Pete Curran and Tom McCarthy the trade unionists, worked with the radical or labour rather than the Irish political movement. There were Catholics put up for the London School Board and occasionally elected, a few borough councillors in Deptford and West Ham, and B. F. C. Costelloe represented Stepney on the L.C.C. from 1889 until 1899; but these were exceptions. In 1907 Charles Russell could find only a dozen Catholic borough councillors, 50 of 824 Guardians, and not a single county councillor.[2]

Drawn to Conservatism by the Catholic schools question, by the priest and the publican, to socialism by their poverty, and to Liberalism by the Home Rule issue, the Irish were the most unstable element in London politics. If organised, they would have probably been of most advantage to the Liberal Party, but the registration effort of the English Liberal agent, 'however zealous, signally fails, because he is so often taken for a School Board visitor, a broker's man, or some equally obnoxious individual'.[3] The socialists encountered similar problems. Perhaps typically, Keir Hardie's defeat at West Ham in 1895 was blamed on the Irish. Their main effect was simply to add to the apathy and unreliability of the poorest riverside constituencies, Deptford, Rotherhithe, Limehouse and St. George's in the East.

Politically the contrast with the Jewish colony could not be more striking, despite the fact that among the Jews poverty and votelessness was as common as among the Irish. The traditional Jewish colony had been in the East End since the arrival of the Spanish and Portuguese Jews in the 17th century. Like successive immigrants, as they prospered they tended to move to north and west London. They were followed in the mid 19th century by German Jews, a mixture of wealthy merchants and small tailors and shopkeepers. Finally, as a

---

[1] C. D. H. Howard, 'The Parnell Manifesto of 1885 and the Schools Question', *English Historical Review*, 1947.

[2] Russell, op. cit.

[3] J. Denvir, *The Irish in Britain from the Earliest Times to the Fall and Death of Parnell*, London 1892, p. 391.

result of the persecutions of 1881–2 and 1903, large numbers of Russian and Polish Jews arrived. Unlike the earlier immigrants, these were poor artisans and tradesmen without special skills who had lived in the ghettoes of Eastern Europe, segregated, and debarred from public work, agriculture or large-scale industry. They were not easily assimilated into the existing Jewish community. They did not join the large synagogues which elected the communities organs of justice and charity, the Beth Din and the Board of Guardians. But the problems which their arrival provoked, crowding into already overcrowded Whitechapel and the already sweated furniture and tailoring trades, could not be ignored by the community.

The Jewish area in the 1870s had been between Houndsditch and Whitechapel High Street, but by 1900 had spread southwards to Cable Street, which formed a frontier with the Irish in St. George's (Map 21).[1] It was compact, with most streets over 75 per cent Jewish. Although there were also Jews in Mile End, and more prosperous Jews in Hackney and North-west London, these did not form similar communities, and all the great synagogues and community institutions continued in the East End.

The conditions of the new immigrants could have been most effectively raised by trade union organisations, and this was recognised by the support given to trade unionism by the community's leaders, notably by Samuel Montagu, but even by the conservative *Jewish Chronicle*. Some small Jewish crafts, such as mantlemaking, Hebrew printing or Jewish butchers, sustained small unions, and the Jewish boot finishers were organised by English unionists, but in tailoring, the largest trade, all attempts at organisation proved transient. The elaborate subdivision of labour in the East End wholesale trade resulted in a series of small unions whose scope was frequently in dispute. Of the thirty-two known unions in 1902, only four or five had existed in 1896. There was never any Jewish organisation to compare with the strong craft unionism of the West End tailors.[2]

Consequently the Jewish Board of Guardians, set up in 1859 with power to raise money by assessment of all Jews in London, remained the only protection of living standards. It was both efficient and enlightened, with its own investigating officers, sanitary inspectors and voluntary visitors, offering aid which was always intended to be adequate; there was no Jewish workhouse. The Guardians maintained an orphan's home, provided several hundred pensions, and in the 1900s enforced improvements on over a thousand dwellings annually.

---

[1] C. Russell and H. S. Lewis, *The Jew in London*, London 1900.

[2] S. Lerner, 'The History of the United Clothing Workers' Union', London Ph.D. thesis, 1956; L. P. Gartner, *The Jewish Immigrant in England 1870–1914*, Detroit 1960; Booth, op. cit., IV, p. 37.

RELIGION

In addition the community ran an impressive series of boys' and athletic clubs and secured the provision of Jewish education through private schools and sixteen London Board Schools run 'on Jewish lines'.[1]

It is not surprising that these conscientious leaders of the community were not successfully challenged during this period. Whitechapel returned the wealthy Samuel Montagu and his successor and nephew Montagu Samuel with unfailing regularity; it was one of the two Liberal safe seats. As aliens a high proportion of the Jews were voteless, and the Whitechapel electorate declined sharply during the period; probably only a third of the electors were Jewish. But the Jewish vote was enough to turn the balance, and it was united by anti-alien feeling to both left and right. Trade union hostility to immigrants was strong during the depressions of the 1890s and 1900s, while the Social Democrats were led by the anti-semitic Hyndman. David Hope Kyd, Conservative candidate in the 1900s, appealed directly to 'the British working man' to vote against 'Pro-Alien Radical Jews' and 'push back this intolerable invasion'.[2]

If Kyd failed in Whitechapel, the Conservative Party had a better chance of profiting from anti-alien feeling in the neighbouring East End constituencies. The explosive situation was indicated by the crusade launched in 1902 by the sinister British Brothers' League, at whose opening meeting 260 stewards, 'big, brawny stalwarts, dock labourers, chemical labourers from Bromley' and other workers watched for 'the sallow face of the Pole or the squat features of the Russian exile', so that 'when an alien angrily rose from his seat to protest, he forthwith received the attention of the stewards and was unceremoniously bundled outside into the cold, biting atmosphere'.[3] The East End Liberal M.P.s, including Sydney Buxton, bowed to local feeling, supporting anti-alien legislation and sending encouraging messages to the British Brothers' League. In fact the Aliens Act passed by the Conservatives proved an insufficient barrier, so that they were unable to claim much credit for it. Moreover, although the anti-alien agitation was obviously anti-semitic in tone, the Conservative Party rejected its racialistic implications and put up Jewish candidates for some East End constituencies. Finally, in a triangular racial situation, with Jews, Irish and English, too close an identification with one group could lose as many votes as it gained. If the Irish, for the most part neighbours to the Jewish colony, became enthusiastic Conservatives, the English vote might well be lost. These

[1] Gartner, op. cit., p. 227; V. D. Lipman, *A Century of Social Service, 1859–1959: the Jewish Board of Guardians*, London 1959.
[2] *Whitechapel Constitutional Almanac*, 1906, copy in Kyd Collection.
[3] Cutting from *East London Observer*, 18 January 1902, Kyd Collection.

complications make it dangerous to ascribe any Conservative success in the East End to the anti-alien issue. Certainly the Liberal Central Office thought its importance exaggerated.[1]

Although the Jewish community had no strong Labour movement in these years, it produced an interesting minority of socialists and anarchists. The Russian and Polish immigrants normally organised themselves in small 'Landmanschaft' associations, combining a social club, benefit society and religious congregation and study group. Children were taught to read the Bible and discuss its theological meaning in the 'cheder', the primary schools maintained in the ghettoes. Socialist or anarchist Jews were usually free-thinkers, but they did not abandon the passionate concern with doctrine or the gathering in small clubs.

The first of these groups were socialist, notably that which founded the Yiddish *Arbeiter Freind* and Berners Street Club in 1885. The hostility of Hyndman and the Social Democrats assisted the influence of anarchism, which was an attractive doctrine to the voteless alien. Apart from Lewis Lyons, whose reputation as a trade unionist was lost when he became a small master tailor, the leaders of the 1889 East End tailors strike were anarchists, and in 1890 *Arbeiter Freind* and the Berners Street Club were captured by the anarchists. Both, however, soon collapsed, and there was little socialist or anarchist activity until the 1900s.

The leader of the revival was Rudolf Rocker,[2] a German Gentile by birth, educated as a Roman Catholic, a bookbinder, who married (without legal ceremony) an agnostic Ukrainian Jewess and identified himself completely with Yiddism both politically and culturally. He started *Germinal*, a literary and political Yiddish journal, in 1900, and translated Shaw and Ibsen into Yiddish. In 1903 he was able to revive *Arbeiter Freind* and its club, which settled in Jubilee Street in 1906, becoming an international centre for political refugees. He started an anti-sweating campaign, led a bakers' strike in 1904 and 1912 a successful tailors' strike, coinciding with strikes by the English tailors and the dockers, which drew the tailoring trade together and led to the formation in 1916 of the United Clothing Workers' Union.

Rocker was also a founder of the 800 strong socialist Workers' Circle, a club and benefit society. It was internationalist and anti-Zionist, and there was a rival Zionist socialist group, Poale Zion. Also

---

[1] H. Gladstone to H. Campbell Bannerman, 26 January 1905, Campbell Bannerman Collection: '*Aliens*, your correspondents of course exaggerate considerably. The Tories can't do more than they did at Mile End and we should have won if we had had a good British candidate.' And at Mile End the issue lost for the Conservatives the important local support of Lord Rothschild: J. Sandars to Short, 18 January 1905, Balfour Collection.

[2] R. Rocker, *The London Years*, trans. J. Leftwich, London 1956.

in the 1900s Hyndman and the Social Democrats redeemed their reputation by their strong opposition to anti-alien legislation, an East London Jewish branch of the S.D.F. was formed and a Jewish Social Democrat, Joseph Finn, was able to build up a relatively strong United Ladies' Tailors and Mantle Makers' Union.

Although within the community anarchism was more important, outside it the influence of the Jewish Social Democrats was more significant. Their instinct for doctrine made them the leading theorists in the S.D.F., winning many branches to a more clearly Marxist and internationalist standpoint, providing the resistance to Hyndman's increasing jingoism, and eventually helping to prevent him from carrying the party with him during the First World War. Like converts from Scottish Calvinism or Roman Catholicism, their religious training made them more formidable than their numbers warranted.

One final religious minority remains to be considered, the religious tradition produced by and peculiar to the lower classes. In provincial England this commonly took the form of sectarianism, such as Primitive Methodism. In London it was secularism.

Secularism represented a particular stage in religious development, fulfilling the religious needs of those who could no longer believe in Christianity. Its vocabulary, activities, and intellectual concerns were decidedly religious. The *National Reformer* called its supporters 'the sect' and Charles Bradlaugh's audiences at the Finsbury Hall of Science the 'congregation'.[1] Lectures, whether positive or destructive were almost all on biblical subjects. The 'Gospel of Freethought' even acquired its own ritual, a *Secular Song and Hymnbook* and ceremonies for naming children, marriage and burial. In the last the sentiments are conventionally religious: 'his belief sustained him in health; during his illness, with the certainty of death before him at no distant period, it afforded him consolation and encouragement; and in the last solemn moments of his life, when he was gazing as it were into his own grave, it procured him the most perfect tranquillity of mind.'[2] It is not surprising that secularism appealed only to the section of the working class, the artisans, who had a significant minority of church-goers.

London secularism first came into the open in the period of the French Revolution, when a Temple of Reason was opened in Finsbury. Its doctrines were spread by 'field-preaching' in Moorfields and through benefit societies where, 'after the business of the evening was over, the disciple of Paine was sure to introduce the subject of religion; and by these means, several copies of the Age of Reason

---

[1] E.g. 14 January, 4 February 1866.
[2] C. M. Davies, *Heterodox London*, London 1874, 2, p. 181.

were circulated.'[1] Paine remained the father of the movement, but by the 1870s its character had somewhat changed. Between Chartism and the radical revival of the 1880s, secularism was largely apolitical. Although few militant secularists maintained the tradition of open-air lectures, tea parties and evening discussion meetings had become more characteristic. Of those attending 'the large majority, perhaps, were of the tradesman and artisan class'.[2]

It was with the radical revival of the 1880s, however, that secularism reached the peak of its influence. In 1885 there were 30 secular societies in London, including 25 branches of the National Secular Society, and about 70 societies in the provinces. Stimulated by the organising work of G. W. Foote, militant editor of the *Freethinker*, between 1880 and 1897 there were usually ten or twenty summer outdoor meetings weekly. The epic struggle of Bradlaugh to take his seat as an atheist M.P. made secularism once more a radical political issue. The radical clubs were found supporting secularist measures, while secularists came forward for selection as parliamentary candidates, and secular societies participated in the formation of the Metropolitan Radical Federation and in the radical committees for the 1888 School Board election.

By 1889, however, the movement was already in obvious decline. The number of branches both in London and the provinces had halved, and the annual report complained of the diversion of energy into purely political activity.[3] There was a slight recovery in the next four years, as radicalism itself revived; but by 1897 the National Secular Society was extinct.[4] The radical association had in fact brought short benefits. The secular movement depended on the annual winning of large numbers of members, most of whom lapsed after the shock of 'conversion' had worn off.[5] By 1890 far more

[1] W. H. Reid, *The Rise and Dissolution of Infidel Societies of London, including the Origin of Modern Deism and Atheism*, London 1800, pp. 18–23.
[2] Davies, op. cit., 2, p. 119.   [3] *National Reformer*, 16 June 1889.
[4] *Radical*, final issue, February 1897; *Freethinker*, 1890–7.
[5] E.g. *National Reformer*, annual reports, 31 May 1885, 1367 new members; 20 June 1886, 988 new members; 5 June 1887, 505 new members; 27 May 1888, 'slight improvement'; 16 June 1889, 492 new members, but a pessimistic report: 'members do not often secede or withdraw, but there are many hundreds of persons on the books, who joined during the exciting struggles of a few years ago, whose membership is almost nominal'. The total number of subscribers was not given, but the income of £137 of the National Secular Society from members' subscriptions sent by branches, at a rate of 4d per member, represents 7820 members. The branch incomes totalled £2896, with a minimum subscription of 4/–. Assuming that some of this income came from wealthier subscribers of other sources, the National membership of the movement would have been about 7000, over half recruited in the previous four years. At the same time the number of branches had fallen from 101, *National Reformer*, 31 May 1885, to 40, 16th June 1889.

converts were being made directly to the socialist movement than to the older creeds of secularism and radicalism. Secularism and socialism need not have conflicted; indeed much of the tone of the London socialist movement can be ascribed to the secularist tradition, and two of the most prominent secularists, Annie Besant and Edward Aveling, as well as a number of lesser figures, worked for both movements in the 1880s. But the older secularists, Bradlaugh, Watts and Foote, who retained control of the movement, insisted on a narrow radicalism—land reform, disestablishment and public economy—which by 1890 was quite out of touch with advanced political feeling. Led by anti-socialists secularism could not play its role as the religious companion of working class political thinking, and withered away.

Yet it was not left without a successor. The ethical movement grew out of secularism just as socialism grew out of radicalism. The positive religious qualities in secularism have been noticed. They were more marked among parallel organisations of middle class agnostics, such as the Liberal Social Union, the Victoria Institute of Atheism and Pantheism, or Dr. Congreve's Positivist Sunday School. From the late 1880s several secularists, including Annie Besant and Herbert Burrows, were converted to Theosophy. George Standring, former editor of the *Radical*, was attracted to Buddhism, while the great Liberal journalist W. T. Stead became a spiritualist. Beatrice Webb practised agnostic prayer and Bernard Shaw invented an agnostic form of God. All reflected the current of feeling which produced the ethical movement. An early working class example of the same tendency was the Humanitarian sect in Pentonville, 'the religion of the omnipresent God of Nature', whose members were urged to 'take an interest in the material and political welfare of all human beings'.[1]

Another forerunner of the ethical movement, the Fellowship of the New Life, was the religious counterpart of the Fabian Society, formed in 1882–3 from the same group around the American scholar Thomas Davidson. Its tone was Positivist, and its membership chiefly Fabian, with Ramsay MacDonald secretary in 1891–3 and afterwards J. F. Oakeshott. Sydney Olivier contributed to its journal, *Seedtime*, published from 1889 to 1898, which like the Fabians supported the Progressive Party but scorned the Liberals and the I.L.P.[2] Its hundred members centred on Croydon, where Oakeshott and its editor Maurice Adams lived, and eventually in 1898 it merged with the Croydon ethical movement. Its religious tone is suggested by the comment of its first secretary, Percival Chubb, that *News from Nowhere* would have been improved by 'a pruned Christianity . . . a

[1] Davies, op. cit., I, pp. 55–86.   [2] E.g. April 1892, July 1894.

moral sensitiveness which feels sin as a stain'.[1] It provided the 'level-headed enthusiasm' which was the aim of the shortlived Hampstead Fabian church of 1893 for those middle class socialists who needed a 'communion of inspiration ... a Collectivist Church'.[2] It stood between the ethical movement and the Labour Churches, sharing members with both.

The ethical movement began with the visit of Dr. Stanton Coit, a member of Felix Adler's New York circle of ethical culture, to lecture at Toynbee Hall in 1886. Although the Ethical Society's first secretary Muirhead and other early members were hostile to socialism, it quickly adopted a different standpoint. Its 1889 report claimed that the Ethical Society needed 'the interest of social and political reformers. It aims at co-operating with these by means of its lectures and publications, in the formation of a true conception of human good. ... It holds, moreover, that the improvement of the present surroundings of many is an indispensable condition of the moral welfare of all.'[3] During its most successful years in the 1900s the movement was able to include liberal collectivists, such as Massingham and J. A. Hobson, and socialists of working class origin who through different routes had reached the I.L.P. and Fabian Society, such as Harry Snell, William Sanders, and Ramsay MacDonald. Its political tone was social reformist rather than socialist, but its periodical, published from 1898 under varying titles, *Ethical World*, *Ethics* and *Democracy*, printed articles by both Liberal and Labour supporters. It also drew on a wide variety of religious support, from secularism to the primitive Christianity of the Labour Churches.

The ethical movement was strongly intellectual. Its magazine printed the advanced views on economics of J. A. Hobson, on education of Margaret McMillan, and on town planning of Ebenezer Howard.[4] When an appeal was issued in 1899 for a lecturers' training fund it was suggested that all candidates should be university graduates and that it was 'desirable that they should also have pursued a three years' course of post-graduate study'.[5] The movement supported a London School of Ethics and Philosophy and for children provided a Moral Instruction League. No wonder, with this high tone, that *Ethical World*, while urging the 'imperative duty' not to 'cut ourselves off from the working classes', feared that ethical teaching 'can appeal only to those whose mental training has been a little above the average of what obtains among our working classes today'.[6]

[1] *Seedtime*, October 1891.
[2] Ibid., April 1895; *Workman's Times*, 2 September 1893.
[3] G. Spiller, *The Ethical Movement in Great Britain*, London 1934, p. 7.
[4] E.g. 29 October 1898, 7 October 1899; Spiller, op. cit., p. 164.
[5] Spiller, op. cit., p. 173.   [6] *Ethical World*, 17 September 1898.

RELIGION

Even so the ethical movement provided a successor for secularism for the working classes. Coit again came to England in 1888 as pastor to the former Unitarian congregation at South Place, which he converted into an Ethical Society. He was unable to get on with its middle class congregation and shortly left to start a social centre in Kentish Town, and ethical Neighbourhood Guild. [South Place remained a centre of advanced thinking, with Progressive and Fabian preachers, including Sidney Webb, who 'preached on "Peace on Earth (London)"—all my London programme in rhetorical form'.[1]] Of the three other ethical societies founded by 1892, one was in middle class Kensington, but the others were in Peckham and Mile End, the last meeting in a dancing saloon. They organised classes, clubs and Sunday Schools, and George Lansbury sent his children to F. J. Gould's school in Mile End. These schools were copied by the secularists and socialists.[2] The West Ham Secular Society began a children's service in 1890 with 'secular hymns',[3] and the first Socialist Sunday School began in 1892 in Battersea, although it remained a rarity for some years.

The ethical movement followed the secularist in providing services for the naming of children, marriage and burial; and through it, the Socialist Sunday Schools of the 1900s adopted the naming service and probably some of their songs. In other ways it led the secularists: in its positive interest in non-dogmatic morality and its benevolent attitude to political reformers of different schools. During the 1890s the *Freethinker* gave increasing prominence to Ethical Society meetings, and an article by Charles Watts in 1893 declared secularists to be 'strong in our confidence in the potency of ethical culture'.[4] Foote, who succeeded Bradlaugh as President of the National Secular Society, proved an impossible leader, and after the Society collapsed in 1897 the surviving propagandists, Watts, J. M. Robertson and Joseph McCabe, rapidly became ethical lecturers. With this important addition to its forces the ethical movement was able to expand considerably during the 1900s 'especially among the working class élite'.[5] There were six societies affiliated to the Ethical Union in 1900; numbers reached a peak of twenty-six in 1905, and fell back to sixteen in 1913—its fortunes thus closely reflecting those of the Labour movement in general. The London societies were mostly in the less poor working class suburbs—Harringay, Holloway, Peckham, Plumstead, Hammersmith, Fulham, Wood Green, Forest Gate, East Ham

[1] S. Webb to B. Potter, 27 September 1891, Passfield, Collection.
[2] Spiller, op. cit., pp. 83, 96; F. J. Gould, *The Life Story of a Humanist* London 1923, pp. 76–77.
[3] *Freethinker*, 23 March 1890.   [4] Ibid., 9 July 1893.
[5] Spiller, op. cit., p. 116.

and Hackney—although the middle class societies, particularly Kensington, were the most stable.

During the 1900s the ethical movement also attempted with some success to digest the remains of the Labour Church movement. There was never a complete combination, because in spite of its provincial branches the atmosphere of the ethical movement was metropolitan and sophisticated. 'Practically the whole of the available speakers reside in London.'[1] Their vocabulary often failed to meet those rooted in provincial Nonconformity.

Labour Churches were never successful in London, although the movement's founder John Trevor was trained under Philip Wicksteed in London and the fund-raising Labour Church Brotherhood was staffed by Londoners, its Secretary and Treasurer being two Croydon Fabians.[2] But neither the Limehouse Labour Church started by Margaret McMillan and Paul Campbell in 1892–3 nor Trevor's Labour Church settlement of 1902 came to anything.[3] A Tottenham Church maintained a frail existence from 1896 until 1901 and ran a Sunday school, and a Labour Church met for a year in the I.L.P. rooms in Harrow Road, Paddington, but the only genuine Labour Churches were outside London, in Croydon and Watford.[4]

More successful and similar to the Labour Churches was the Brotherhood Church in Islington, a decayed Congregational chapel taken over by Bruce Wallace in 1892. He invited Keir Hardie to preach, started conferences and smoking concerts, and built up a congregation of 200. Although his Brotherhood Trust, intended to take over the national economy by encroaching co-operative control, produced only an insignificant store and suburban rambling and discussion groups, he made his church a socialist centre. It was the scene of the Russian Social-Democratic Party conference of 1907, and after his retirement it was burnt down by hooligans in 1917 after being chosen for the conference intended to organise soviets in London.[5] Wallace had some influence in London. Most of the Labour Churches were alternatively known as Brotherhood Churches, J. H. Belcher tried to run his chapel on similar lines, and unsuccessful imitations were attempted in Hoxton and Walthamstow.[6] In Croydon

---

[1] Ibid., p. 117.   [2] *Labour Prophet*, July 1896.
[3] Ibid., May 1892; *Workman's Times*, 18 February 1893; *Fabian News*, December 1902; *Brotherhood*, December 1902.
[4] *Labour Prophet*, January and September 1896, April 1898; *Labour Church Record*, January 1899, April 1901; *Brotherhood*, June 1897, April 1901; *Labour Leader*, 21 September 1895.
[5] *Workman's Times*, December 1892; *Labour Annual*, 1895; *Brotherhood*, passim.
[6] *Labour Leader*, 23 January 1897; *Brotherhood*, May and November 1895, October 1896, July 1899.

a Brotherhood Church, supported by some members of the Fellowship of the New Life and the Labour Church Brotherhood, together with a Tolstoyan settlement for commuters and an Ethical Guild, kept going until 1902.¹

After the collapse of the *Labour Church Record* in 1902 the movement had less contact with London, although in the 1900s it was experiencing something of a revival.² A successful Labour Church was founded in Watford, providing a meeting place and leaders for local labour and socialist activity.³ The revival did not otherwise touch London. The Labour Churches had no trained ministry, no coherent religious movement and after 1902 no common journal. The ethical movement had all these, and also had Sunday Schools and its own religious forms of service before the Labour Churches. The only possible development of the Labour Churches was in fact in an ethical direction and in 1902 their conference debated a fusion with the Ethical Union. Although no decision was reached, five Labour Churches joined the seven Ethical Societies then comprising the Ethical Union, and it was only after this that the ethical movement spread to the provinces.⁴

The role of the ethical societies in the working class movement did not survive the 1914–18 war. Nearly all the post-war societies were wholly middle class. Before this an increasing ritualism in the movement suggested its declining purpose. The Hampstead Society devised a 'declaration of belief' which took its place between music and readings, while from 1909 Coit's Bayswater church acquired stained glass, statues of Christ and Buddha, and eventually an altar, while a 'universal litany' and 'Ten Words of the Moral Life' were added to his services. When in 1914 he led the ethical movement into full support of the war with the discovery of 'God Indwelling in the British People', its moral bankruptcy was apparent.⁵ The need which produced it had disappeared. By 1914 it required less moral courage to become an agnostic. Respectable artisans often still sent their children to Sunday School, but adult disbelief did not produce social concern or troubled consciences.

¹ *Labour Prophet*, December 1897, January 1899; *Labour Annual*, 1898; *Seedtime*, April 1895; *Brotherhood*, July 1896.
² Labour Church Union conference, *Clarion*, 10 March 1905, reported four new churches; delegates 'gave encouraging reports, and those not represented are known to be experiencing a revival'.
³ *Labour Church Record*, April and October 1901; *Clarion*, 3 April 1903, 10 March 1905; *Labour Leader*, 23 March 1901, 23 June 1905; Watford I.L.P. branch minutes; and P. J. Heady to H. Bryan, 27 June 1913, I.L.P. London Divisional Council correspondence.
⁴ *Democracy*, 15 June 1901; *Ethics*, 3 May, 14 June, 5 July 1902, 15 August 1903.
⁵ Spiller, op. cit., pp. 75–83, 158.

RELIGION

Because Sunday schools did remain a social need with the more respectable working classes, providing parents with an afternoon by themselves, it was through them that the ethical and secularist tradition was passed on to socialism. The first London Socialist Sunday School of 1892 at Battersea had been followed by four others by 1901, when the magazine of the movement, the *Young Socialist*, first appeared.[1] Its editor, Alex Gossip, was a Scottish founder member of the I.L.P. and a militant trade unionist and socialist until his death in 1952 at the age of 90. He led the furniture trade unions from craft caution to aggressive industrial unionist. He was a pacifist in 1914–18, and in the 1920s a leader of the non-Communist left wing.[2] When his union work brought him to London in 1902 he pursued the Socialist Sunday School work which he had started in Glasgow, working with both S.D.F. and I.L.P., inducing branches to open schools, teaching them methods, and building up a successful joint school in Fulham. There were a dozen London Schools within two years, and in spite of the refusal of premises by the L.C.C. after 1907 they reached nineteen by the end of 1913. The average attendance was forty, but Walthamstow and West Ham, schools run by Christian socialists and Social Democrats, reached over 150 weekly. By 1913 they had largely superseded the ethical schools, from which they took their naming service and their doctrine. Gossip told the L.C.C. in 1907, 'we neither teach atheism nor orthodoxy but strive to instil in the minds of the children the highest ethical ideals'; and although the purely S.D.F. schools introduced some primitive Marxist ideas, Gossip was in general correct. It is perhaps strange to find this tough trade unionist in his children's 'Magazine of love and service' asking 'What is socialism but brotherhood put into practice in wise ways?' Yet it was in this gentle doctrine that 'our young soldiers are trained for their noble and peaceful warfare'.[3] Here the parallel developments of working class political and religious thinking are interwoven.

[1] *Young Socialist*, March 1901.
[2] S. Harrison, *Alex Gossip*, London 1962; *Reformers Year Book*, 1907; N. Robertson, 'A Study of the Development of Labour Relations in the British Furniture Trade', Oxford B.Litt. thesis, 1955.
[3] *Young Socialist*, May 1907 (c.f. Wood Green school, March 1913, and a scheme of lessons, April 1903), March and April 1901.

III
TRADE UNIONISM

LONDON was never a trade union stronghold. Writing in 1914, Ben Tillett the dockers' leader called it 'the ever great problem ... the Sphinx of Labour.'[1] Even at the height of the trade union expansion of 1889–91, in London there were only 3·52 per cent of trade unionists in the population, less than the national average of 4 per cent, while there were 6–7 per cent in South Wales and parts of Yorkshire and the Midlands, 8 per cent in Lancashire, and over 11 per cent in north east England.[2]

Two causes of this weakness are evident. Firstly, the character of London industry—the characteristic small-scale sweated trade and the rarity of large factories—weakened working class solidarity and made union organisation difficult. Secondly, the instability of the London population, the distances travelled to work and the lack of strong local community feeling, hindered the development of trade unionism outside the workshop. There was none of the social pressure to join a trade union which could be exerted in a closely-knit community of mine or textile workers. Nor were there the strong working class sects which had sometimes provided a training in speaking and organisation for future trade unionists.

Exactly the same difficulty was found in London by the Co-operative movement. At the time of the 1896 Co-operative Congress there were only two strong London societies, Woolwich with 7,600 members and Stratford (West Ham) with 5,600, and both districts had 'a compact thriving industrial population, each clustered round a large manufacturing establishment', in the first case the Arsenal and in the second the Great Eastern Railway workshops. In the rest of London the difficulty was the 'migratory life, which means a shifting of home

---

[1] Dock, Wharf and Riverside Labourers' Union triennial report, May 1914.
[2] S. and B. Webb, *The History of Trade Unionism*, 1666–1920, London 1920, pp. 423–7.

when fresh jobs have to be found ... The people of London lack corporate life, they are more fickle and thriftless.'[1]

London Co-operation, if a somewhat weakly plant, had ancient and distinguished roots in the Chartists, Owenites and Christian Socialists of the 1820s to 1850s. Similarly trade unionism in London had a long history. Craftsmen in the printing and dress trades had a continuous organisation from the 18th century, and there were unions of watermen, shipwrights, carpenters and cabinetmakers by the early 19th century. Although the formal constitution of many of these societies only dates from the repeal of the Combination Acts in 1824, it is possible that the organisation of London artisans was never stronger than in the period 1800–20. Then, but not later in the century, the engineers and cabinetmakers were powerful enough to drive away provincial immigrants. There were strong hereditary traditions, supported by the apprenticeship system, in most of these crafts; and even among riverside and building workers family tradition was still strong in the late 19th century. In some cases the same restrictions and fixed rates of pay were secured by the survival of paternalistic corporate organisations. The market and wharf porters were organised in fellowships under the control of the City dating from the 16th century, reaching their highest membership in the 1820s, while the watermen, who had been ruled by a Company under the control of the City from 1556, were fully incorporated in 1827 as a City Livery Company.

The national reputation of London trade unionism was also strong at this period. A Metropolitan Trades Committee, led by John Gast of the Shipwrights, organised resistance to the repeal of the Combination Acts in 1824, while Gast's attempt to form a national trade union in 1818 was a precedent for the efforts of the Chartist period.

Although London, as an attractive headquarters for national societies, remained a trade union centre, the development of more strongly organised trade unionism in other regions meant that by the 1880s its reputation had changed from one of strength to weakness. It kept its nucleus of craft unions, often with a strong hold on a small trade. The tailors, hatters, brushmakers, cigar makers, coopers and bookbinders' unions not only survived, but even between 1880 and 1914 produced occasional leaders of importance, such as Will Crooks of the Coopers, Ben Cooper of the Cigar Makers and Will Steadman of the Bargebuilders. Among the printers new unions were formed of pressmen, printers' warehousemen, machine rulers and vellum binders, while the London Society of Compositors became the largest of all the London craft unions. Compositors were required by their work to be intelligent and literate, and until the advent of machine-

[1] *Handbook of the 28th Co-operative Congress.*

setting in the 1890s they were not threatened by technical change in the industry. By the 1880s more than half the 12,000 London compositors belonged to the union. Led by a series of able secretaries, it was notable for the financial assistance which it gave to less strong unions, and for the agitation for trade union conditions in government and local authority contract work which it began in 1884.

In contrast to this some of the most effective organisations of the earlier period had been broken by industrial change. The Thames shipbuilding industry collapsed in the 1860s, thus ending the power of the Shipwrights. The city porters failed to extend their fellowships into the docks and railways, began to lose membership rapidly, and in spite of the efforts of 'ginger groups' were finally abolished in 1893.

More important was the relative failure of London to consolidate the extension of trade unionism among poorly organised or unorganised workers, in spite of the prominence of Londoners in several periods of expansion. Of all the national building unions formed in the 1830s, only the Stonemasons survived with a London membership. Similarly, when national unions recovered in the mid-century on the basis of more centralised organisation with higher subscription rates and better benefits, London influence again proved transient. The classic 'new model' union, the Amalgamated Society of Engineers, was formed in 1852 through the efforts of William Newton, a Lancashire factory boy who had come to London in the 1840s, and who in addition to his union work stood as an independent parliamentary candidate for Tower Hamlets in 1852. The financial support of the Engineers helped to secure victory in a major London building strike in 1859. This strike resulted in the formation of new unions among the carpenters, plasterers and painters and a new permanent co-ordinating body, the London Trades Council.

George Howell of the Manchester Bricklayers became secretary of the London Trades Council, and for a while it served as the mouthpiece of the group of national unions with London headquarters—notably the Engineers, the Ironfounders, the Carpenters and the London Bricklayers. At the end of the 1860s the formation of the Trades Union Congress provided a more appropriate alternative and the Trades Council lost its national significance. At the same time a wave of trade union expansion in the early 1870s, while establishing the power of the coal and cotton unions in the north, left little permanent mark in London. The most successful new London unions, the Machine Rulers and Vellum Binders and George Shipton's House Painters, were not important new departures. The most important national union founded, the Amalgamated Society of Railway Servants, proved a dismal failure in London. Some of the less successful unions did however represent real advances, such as the unions of cabdrivers, postmen and civil service writers.[1] There were especially significant attempts to organise semi-skilled and unskilled workers, such as builders' labourers, and one such union, the London and Counties Labour League, even survived to enjoy a second prosperity in the 1890s. Successful strikes at the docks resulted in the formation of a conservative Amalgamated Society of Watermen and Lightermen, a more aggressive Amalgamated Society of Stevedores, and a general Labour Protection League which survived in a small way among north side stevedores and south side cornporters. Most spectacular of all was a strike of gas workers, which was eventually broken by the arrest of eighteen of its leaders at the Beckton gas works.

With the deterioration of the economic situation after 1875 the weaker unions mostly collapsed and the stronger unions had to struggle to survive. In the mid 1880s London trade unionism thus seemed exceptionally weak. Only two unions, the Compositors and Engineers each with 6,000 members, were of any strength. Of the other larger unions, the Tailors, Bricklayers and Carpenters had about 2,000 and the Stonemasons, Boilermakers, Railway Servants and Boot Operatives scarcely 1,000 members. Whole aspects of London industry were virtually unorganised. The labourers and semi-skilled workers in the docks, gasworks, road transport and railways were scarcely touched. There were no unions for shop assistants and warehousemen, domestic and hotel servants, bakers, and many of the sweated trades. Although the teachers had formed associations the growing number of clerks and administrative workers were unaffected by trade unionism.

Yet in this critical situation the London Trades Council showed no sense of urgency. The Compositors, by now the only large union affiliated, were outvoted by the delegates of tiny bodies of less than 100 members, who seemed content that its main activity should be the agitation against sugar bounties which was an enthusiasm of George Shipton, its secretary from 1872 to 1896. So far from being a national body, the London Trades Council now expressed a particularism which was a persistent London weakness. Because of their higher wages, London artisans, including the Compositors, were afraid that national unions would neglect their special interests. They were content to belong to local London unions, in many cases to unions which only covered one of the several London wage districts, and to waste energy in boundary disputes with provincial unions.

It is hardly surprising that in the 1880s the radicals and the early socialists overlooked the political possibilities of London unionism.

[1] The National Union of Teachers and the Metropolitan Board Teachers, Association were also founded in 1870-2.

Neither George Howell nor Randal Cremer, the two trade unionists elected for London in 1885, owed anything to union organisation; both in fact belonged to Manchester unions with insignificant London membership.[1]

London trade unionism at the beginning of our period was, in short, restricted to a few artisan crafts, poorly organised in most of these, plagued by particularism, without any strong central voice, and politically insignificant.

The next three decades brought marked changes, even if the relative weakness of London in the national scene remained. Trade unionism was extended to the semi-skilled and unskilled workers, and by 1914 the exclusiveness of artisan organisation was weakening, while many more London trades had amalgamated into national unions. After 1889 London trade unionism was a force in politics, and for a short but crucial period it spoke through a powerful Trades Council.

Most of these changes occurred in two short bursts. Organisation is much easier when demand for labour is high, so that trade union development closely reflected the changing economic situation (Figure 1). Between 1887 and 1891 there was a strong recovery of the economy, and a notable expansion of trade unionism. This was followed by a sharp depression 1892–5 which seriously weakened the unions; a recovery of 1896–9 accompanied by a revival of trade union militancy; a deepening depression in 1901–4, a slight recovery in 1905–7 and further depression in 1907–9, marked by a prolonged weakening of the unions, scarcely affected by the slight recovery of 1905–7; and finally, at the end of the period, a sharp recovery and boom reaching its peak in 1913, which was marked by a second notable expansion of trade unionism.

The marked fluctuations of the London labour market, with its exceptional buoyancy in boom periods and the equally striking unemployment in depressions, also helps to explain why London was the scene of several great strikes in this period yet less often capable of sustained organisation. To a certain extent the movement of real wages must also have been important. No doubt the long upward trend of real wages had reduced militancy by the late 1890s, while the great expansion in the no more favourable conditions after 1909 was probably stimulated by the fall in real wages after 1900.

These economic explanations are not, however, sufficient in themselves. A final factor was the climate of opinion. A determined hostility among employers, as in 1890–7, or a national crisis, as during the Boer War, might check the unions; while militant socialist

[1] R. Postgate, *The Builder's History*, London 1923, pp. 221–2, 290–2, 336; H. Evans, *Sir Randal Cremer, his Life and Work*, London 1909, p. 26.

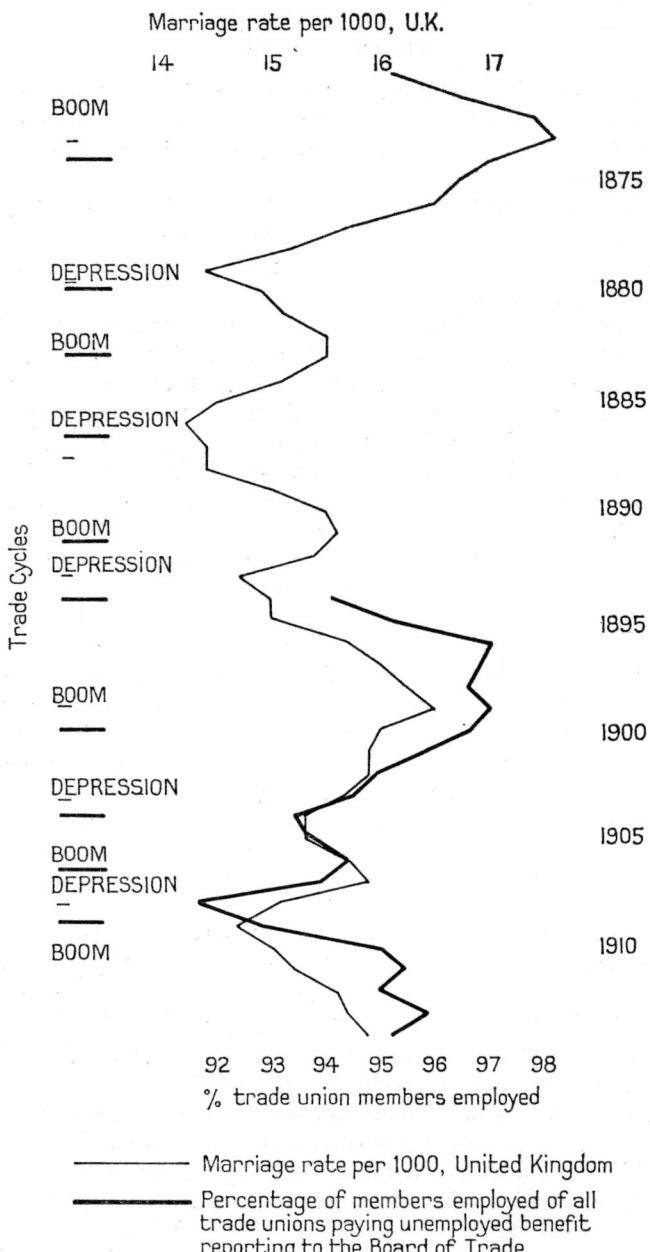

FIGURE I. ECONOMIC BOOMS AND DEPRESSIONS

London Statistics, 1914–16, p. 116. Trade cycles as reported by the Board of Trade; PP 1909 XXXVII. *Note:* unemployed statistics are available for the County of London, but both suffer from excluding outer London, and do not show significant variations from national figures.

or syndicalist doctrines, as in 1889–91 and 1910–14, could help to stimulate a great upsurge of trade union activity.

The great expansion of 1889–91 was a turning point in trade union history. As in 1871–4 there was a wave of strikes and agitation among unorganised unskilled and semi-skilled workers, notably dockers and gasworkers. This time, however, the agitation proved less transient, and a 'new unionism' was permanently established which rejected both the craft traditions and the moderate Liberal-Labour or neutral politics of the older unions.

The movement did not begin in London. Already before the summer of 1888 new labour unions were successfully recruiting unskilled labour, while a more aggressive attitude among the miners was shown by Keir Hardie's appearance at the 1887 T.U.C. and the emergence in 1888 of the Miners' Federation. Havelock Wilson's National Amalgamated Sailors and Firemen's Union and Ben Tillett's Tea Operatives and Dock Workers' Union, both founded in 1887, had failed to make much progress in London, and Tillett's union nearly collapsed after an unsuccessful strike at Tilbury in 1888.[1] The strike of matchgirls in July 1888, organised by two socialists Herbert Burrows and Annie Besant and resulting in a trade union of 800 members, at that time the largest women's trade union in England, was relatively isolated and consequently given exaggerated publicity. The real start of the 'new unionism' in London was not until the gasworkers' agitation of 1889.

As in 1872 the source of the gasworkers' movement[2] was the Beckton works. The causes of discontent were various: the technical advances of the period, the compressed air stoking machine and hotter retort houses which made the work harder, the long twelve hour day, and in particular the longer week-end shifts followed for Canning Town workers by a four mile walk home on an empty stomach. At the end of March 1889 a socialist gas stoker Will Thorne called a meeting, at which Ben Tillett and Clem Edwards of the Tea Operatives and H. W. Hobart the socialist compositor were speakers, resulting in the formation of the National Union of Gas Workers and General Labourers. 800 men joined on the first day, and the union headquarters was set up in a temperance bar. An enthusiastic missionary campaign was organised to recruit men in other London gasworks, and the union grew with astonishing rapidity. It had 3,000

---

[1] The Sailors had 950 London members in January 1889, *Labour Elector*, 2 November 1889; for the Tea Operatives, see H. L. Smith and V. Nash, *The Story of the Dockers' Strike*, London 1890, p. 31.
[2] B. Grant, *Beckton's Struggles*, London 1955; and W. Thorne, *My Life's Battles*, London 1925.

members within a fortnight. The agitation was supported by the radical *Star* and the socialist *Labour Elector*. John Burns the Battersea socialist organised a branch among the men at the Vauxhall and Nine Elm works, and at Brentford a branch was started at a meeting of 3,000 men formed by three convergent processions.[1] In August the Beckton employers, the Gas, Light, and Coke Company, decided to concede an eight hour day without a strike, and the first half-yearly report of the union claimed 'we are at present one of the strongest Labour Unions in England', with forty-three branches in London. Although no figures were published, the national membership of the union was said to be 30,000.[2]

This early prosperity was soon challenged. The employers at Beckton were unusually flexible in attitude. They had started a pension scheme for manual workers as early as 1870, and a week's paid holiday in 1886. The other large London company, the South Metropolitan Company, had also granted paid holidays and the eight hour day,[3] but soon found itself pushed into concessions which it was very reluctant to accept. Moreover, it had to deal with union branches less discreet than those close to the union headquarters at Beckton. When its chairman, George Livesey, found his men refusing to oil the retort lid hinges, he warned: 'Well, if your Union is going to act in this way it will not last twelve months'. He agreed to the union demand for double time on Sundays only under protest: 'I will take it back again as soon as I can'.[4] He had already started to prepare for a major strike, ordering beds, building huts and drafting advertisements for substitute labour. The strike was eventually fought against the introduction of a bonus scheme, offering 1 per cent additional wages for every penny by which increased productivity reduced the price of gas, but conditional on an agreement to obey all orders and do any work for a year. The scheme was denounced by the *Star* as a 'base and obvious trick' to break the union,[5] but it was attractive enough to win over some employees, and with the aid of the substitute labour he had recruited Livesey was able to defeat the union. The strike lasted from December 1889 to February 1890 and cost the union £10,000. Before this a long strike at the large india rubber factory in Silvertown, West Ham, had also ended in failure. Consequently in its second half-yearly report the union admitted that it was no longer 'very prosperous'. But it was strong enough to survive these setbacks.

[1] *Justice*, 22 June, 11 May 1889.
[2] *Star*, 17 October 1889.
[3] E. H. Phelps-Brown, *The Growth of British Industrial Relations*, London 1959, pp. 77–80.
[4] H. A. Clegg, A. Fox and A. F. Thompson, *A History of British Trade Unions since 1889*, Oxford 1964, p. 59.
[5] *Star*, 7 December 1889.

Its London region (which extended over most of southern England) had sixty branches in 1891 and 16,000 members in 1892.

From the start the Gas Workers broke the pattern of the old unionism. Without a wider unionism effective organisation was impossible in an industry in which gas labourers were in the habit of working as brickmakers, navvies or vestry labourers during slack periods, and in any dispute the employers could draw on unskilled provincial labour. In 1889 the union was already recruiting brickmakers in Tottenham, vestry employees in west London, and workers in the Woolwich Arsenal and the Silvertown india rubber factory.[1] It opened a women's branch in Silvertown. The Battersea branch, of which the Fabian de Mattos was secretary and the Social Democrat John Ward chairman, enrolled the carmen at a local yard, and in October turned their attention to the 'grievances of the employees of the London and South Western Railway'.[2] The policy of the union was to attract as wide as possible a membership through its low membership fee, twopence a week. Although there could be no other substantial benefits offered beyond strike pay, in a struggle the union could 'command £2,000 per week if all our forces are concentrated on one place'.[3] In addition, it aimed at a close co-operation with other unions, and in particular an interchangeability of union tickets rather than the closed shop 'one ticket, one job' policy. In 1889 Thorne was advocating a grand federation with the miners and coal porters. His ultimate hope was one great union or federation of unions, strong enough to raise the standards of workers of all kinds.

In practice the union did not function in this way. There were always too many workers unorganised. Despite its enthusiasm for women's branches, it had only 800 women members in 1908. In fact the strength of the union depended upon its strongly entrenched position in certain dispersed provincial trades rather than in its more mixed London membership.[4] But the general policy of the union was important, and led directly to its equally revolutionary political standpoint. The gasworkers were the first union to run a series of independent Labour candidates for local elections in London, and in this way they initiated a transformation of the political scene. In the London branches there was a strong socialist element, and Thorne himself belonged to the Social Democratic Federation. The union corresponded with socialist and union leaders in America and 'nearly

[1] *Labour Elector*, 29 June, 26 October 1889; *Justice*, 27 April 1889.
[2] *Labour Elector*, 5 October, 19 October 1889.
[3] National Union of Gas Workers and General Labourers report, 1890.
[4] E. J. Hobsbawm, 'General Labour Unions in Britain, 1889–1914', *Economic History Review*, 1949.

all continental countries',[1] and Thorne attended as its delegate at the socialist International Congress. In his reports he defended the standpoint of the union. 'It has been contended that we are too Socialistic; that the general officials of the union were hostile to the Liberal party. ... We are hostile to any party that will use gunboats and soldiers against the workers.'[2] 'To be a trade unionist and fight *for* your class during a strike, and to be a Tory or Liberal and fight *against* your class at election time is folly.'[3] 'So long as the trade of this and other countries is carried on for profit only,' unemployment was inevitable. 'This question I now leave for the consideration of each member.'[4] He was no doubt confident of the conclusion they would draw.

The dockers' movement which followed the gasworkers' agitation was a less straightforward development. The workers on the river and port were a strikingly contrasted mixture of skilled craftsmen and unskilled manual labourers. The watermen and lightermen, who had formed a strong union in 1872, were true aristocrats of labour. Recruited from 'old riverside families', apprenticed in the ceremonial atmosphere of the Watermen's Company, their ancient grandeur was recalled by annual festivals, river races and processions. In spite of the elimination of the many small masters through the growth of large fleets, and the tough work, long hours at the mercy of the weather on the sewage-ridden river, they remained politically Conservative at least until the 1900s. They were strongly aware of craft and class differences. 'The men who navigated sailing barges, for instances, were distinct from those who navigated dumb lighters, and the difference between licensed men who navigated the river and unlicensed men who attended to craft on non-tidal waters was as pronounced almost as difference in nationality. ... The wife of a lighterman felt that she was with her equals when she went out shopping with the wife of a stevedore or the wife of a shipwright, but never with the wife of a docker or an unskilled labourer.'[5]

Stevedores in the London docks, unlike other ports, were better paid trained men who loaded ships for export, and they were the best organised men within the docks themselves. They were not employed by the dock companies, but by master stevedores who supplied the necessary equipment. The backbone of the Labour Protection League was its stevedores' branches, and they also had a strong Amalgamated Society.[6]

The remaining workers were scarcely touched by trade unions, and

---
[1] National Union of Gas Workers and General Labourers report, 1891.
[2] Ibid., 1896.   [3] Ibid., 1897.   [4] Ibid., 1895.
[5] Harry Gosling, *Up and Down Stream*, London 1927, pp. 18-51, 144-5.
[6] Smith and Nash, op. cit., p. 23.

were among the most depressed class in London. The main cause was the uncertain and fluctuating demand for labour. The amount of work fluctuated daily as well as seasonally not only in the port as a whole, but between the various docks and riverside wharfs. Before the Port of London Authority was set up in 1908 there was little co-ordination between them. The dock companies developed systems[1] by which they could call on a certain amount of regular labour, assisted by any amount of temporary casual assistance. The systems differed, resulting in a complex variety of pay systems. In most of the north side docks there was a nucleus of directly employed regulars, and a list of more reliable casuals ('royals' or 'ticket men') who were chosen first; the remaining casuals were employed by sub-contractors, notorious for their sweating. The Millwall docks were exceptional, employing only 800 men in specialised corn and timber work, and the men not employed directly were taken on by small contractors with their own lists, so that there were no real casuals. At the south side Surrey docks all the men were employed by contractors, while the river wharfs were worked by casual labour taken on by the wharfingers foremen.

Geographically isolated on the Isle of Dogs, with a labour force which had been based on provincial labour brought in to break the 1872 strike, the Millwall docks had a tradition somewhat separate from the other docks. Generally both regulars and casuals were Londoners with a strong family tradition. There was a considerable number of London Irish on the north side and among the stevedores, but few were recent migrants to London. Nevertheless the pool of labour available was about 30 per cent above the average demand. Fluctuation was most spectacular at the Surrey docks, where trade varied for example in 1891 from 22,000 tons in January to 137,000 tons in August. In the same year the numbers employed by the north side docks fluctuated in a single fortnight between 5,000 and 7,000.[2] In the West Ham docks the daily numbers varied between 2,500 and 5,000.[3]

Many of these casual dockers were thus forced, day by day, to queue up at the 'cage' in the hope of securing a work ticket from a ganger. The wage was the symbol of all that was wrong with the system. 'Calls at any period of the day or night kept men for a week at a time hungry and expectant for the food and the work which never came. Night and day watches, the scraping of refuse heaps, the furtive, miserly storing of refuse rice the coolies had thrown away. . . .

---

[1] Ibid., pp. 18–22; Booth, op. cit., *Industry*, London 1902, 3, pp. 405–21; PP 1892 XXXV, 1893–4 XXXIII, XXXIX Part 1.
[2] Dock, Wharf and Riverside Labourers' Union annual report, 1891.
[3] Howarth and Wilson, op. cit., p. 229.

There can be no ennobling in an atmosphere in which we are huddled and herded together like cattle; there is nothing refining in the thought that to obtain employment we are driven into a shed, iron-barred from end to end, outside of which a foreman or contractor walks up and down with the air of a dealer in a cattle-market, picking and choosing from a crowd of men, who, in their eagerness to obtain employment, trample each other under foot, and where like beasts they fight for the chances of a day's work.'[1]

The author of this protest was Ben Tillett. Born in Bristol, he had worked as circus hand and sailor before settling in the East End. A little man with a restless spirit but not much physical stamina, an emotional and at times dramatic speaker, an instinctive political rebel, Tillett was not naturally suited to the consistent routine of trade union organisation. In 1887 he found himself unexpectedly elected secretary of the Tea Operatives and General Workers' Union, a tiny new union at the docks, and during the next two years he was working without much success to build up its strength. At the same time the Sailors and Firemen's Union was also attempting to recruit members in London. The development of both unions was suddenly transformed by the dock strike of 1889.

The strike was unplanned.[2] It started from an insignificant bonus dispute which was unexpectedly followed by a strike of the South-West India dockers as a whole. Their demands, 6d an hour, overtime pay, engagement for at least four hours, and the abolition of sub-contract, were formulated by Tillett and sent to the directors at once. He then sought to rally the rest of the docks to his aid. These hasty tactics provided an excuse for the London Trades Council secretary George Shipton, who had little sympathy with unskilled unionism, to refuse assistance.[3] But he was almost alone. The other docks, the Stevedores, the socialists Tom Mann and John Burns, the Gas Workers and the Compositors all responded. Most of the press supported the strike, and the *Star*, which gave its main leader in support from 24 August to 16 September with the exception of only one day, published long lists of subscribers. In all £48,000 was raised, of which £30,000 was sent by supporters in Australia. John Burns acted as publicity manager and fund-raiser, and devised an elaborate system of strike pay. With the aid of the Sailors and the Stevedores effective picketing was organised. Huge processions marched through the City with impressive discipline. This excellent organisation together

---

[1] Ben Tillett, *A Brief History of the Dockers' Union*, London 1910, p. 9.

[2] Ibid., Smith and Nash, op. cit.; S. and B. Webb, op. cit.; H. H. Champion, *The Great Dock Strike*, London 1890.

[3] B. Webb, *Our Partnership*, London 1948, p. 21; London Trades Council minutes, 12 September 1889.

with the pressure of public opinion enabled the dockers eventually to win most of their demands. They secured 6d an hour, 2d an hour extra for overtime, four hours minimum and the replacement of contract by 'co-operative piecework', by which the men elected a gang leader, usually a union official, to supervise the taking on of labour and the distribution of bonus.

As a result of the strike the Dock, Wharf and Riverside Labourers' Union was formed, with Tillett as its secretary and Mann as president. In important ways it resembled the Gas Workers. It spread with astonishing rapidity, claiming 60,000 members by October 1890, 24,000 in London, its London branches extending from Brentford to Gravesend.[1] It was soon recruiting not only workers in other ports, but agricultural labourers, principally because they were a source of blackleg labour. The union later came to rely for stability on its strength among the South Wales tinplate and Bristol waterside workers.[2]

Although in fact the union relied on its diversity for survival, the Dockers never shared the 'one man, one ticket' policy of the Gas Workers. They hoped to replace the casual labour system by a smaller permanent labour force. Like a craft union they sought a monopoly of the supply of labour, demanding high entrance fees and seeking to put a 'ring fence' round the docks.[3] At a meeting in November Mann announced that they were 'determined to eliminate the riff-raff: the wretched wastrels that have disgraced the Docks. The end of this week we close our books.... The other men at the Dock Gates must clear off; with us there is no room for them; no doubt there are other social movements to provide for them, but our movement is to eliminate them.'[4]

The closed shop policy proved a failure. When Tom McCarthy the Stevedores' secretary became one of the Dockers' organisers, bringing some of his former members with him, the union's hopes of raising all dock work to craft status seemed reasonable. But most of the stevedores remained with their own society, which had been greatly strengthened by the strike, while the Watermen, whose numbers had jumped to 7,000, remained typically aloof. The Dockers were not even able to monopolise the organisation of the dock labourers. On the south side only a single cornporters' branch of the old Labour Protection League had survived before the strike, but this became the nucleus of a strike committee organised by Thorne, Harry Quelch and other Social Democrats. Mann had only been able to turn to

---

[1] Dock, Wharf and Riverside Labourers' Union annual congress report, October 1890.
[2] Hobsbawm, op. cit. [3] Thorne, op. cit., p. 90.
[4] B. Webb, diary, 19 November 1889.

them after three weeks in order to formulate a set of demands applicable to their special pay system. After the strike Quelch formed a south side Labour Protection League, which recognised all other trade union tickets and recruited in Woolwich arsenal and other factories as well as the docks. In November 1889 it claimed 14,000 members and twenty-three branches. Tillett tried to break it up, but was unable to obtain much following on the south side.[1] The closed shop policy also produced a clash with the Gas Workers, to whom the Dockers lost other members.

Most serious of all was the continued conflict with the employers. The new systems of pay produced as many conflicts as the old and the union found itself involved in a number of minor and unsuccessful strikes. It also supported the Hay's Wharf strike, a bitter five months struggle to recover payment for mealtimes, which had been eliminated under the dock strike settlement. This ended in defeat in May 1890. In November 1890 the Dockers refused to vary the 1889 settlement in order to provide more incentive, as the companies wished, but when the companies refused to renew the co-operative system the union gave in without a struggle. It thus lost its crucial influence through elected gang leaders, and membership fell disastrously. Only Millwall, where the employers preferred to work through the union, remained well organised.[2]

The industrial strength of the Dockers was thus shortlived. To some extent this was also true of their political influence. Like the Gas Workers they put up independent Labour candidates. Mann was particularly important in the transformation of the London Trades Council and Tillett became a Labour alderman of the L.C.C. in 1892. But although their part in the strike made Burns, Mann and Tillett the best-known of the new unionist leaders, the long-term influence of all three was reduced by their political inconsistency. They were socialists, but of a peculiarly individualistic kind. Burns' egotism was already drawing him towards the Liberal Party. Mann proved restless and erratic during the next few years. He first turned from the Dockers to the London Trades Council, then campaigned for the reform of the Engineers, and between 1891 and 1894 worked as a member of the Royal Commission on Labour, at the same time acting as secretary of the L.C.C. Progressive Party organisation. After announcing that he was considering ordination as an Anglican priest, he became secretary of the Independent Labour Party in 1894. Three years later he returned to trade unionism to work for the

---

[1] C. Tsuzuki, *H. M. Hyndman and British Socialism*, Oxford 1961, pp. 89–91; D. Torr, *Tom Mann and his Times*, London 1956, p. 293; *Star*, 26 September, 22 November 1889; PP 1892 XXXV, pp. 83–95.

[2] Clegg, Fox and Thompson, op. cit., pp. 71-72.

International Federation of Ship, Dock and River Workers, but this required much time abroad, and after a brief return to politics as secretary of the radical National Democratic League, he set off in 1901 for nine years in Australia and South Africa.[1] Tillett kept to his post of Dockers' secretary, but he too was abroad between 1895 and 1898 on account of ill-health, and proved a somewhat erratic political rebel. He stood as an independent Labour candidate at Bradford in 1892 and soon dropped out of the L.C.C. when he realised its dependence on the Progressives. He was 'never a Lib-Lab'.[2] But his socialism was based on confused emotion, and his exhortations in the union's annual reports on 'the ethical conception of duty', and a trades unionism 'not limited to the mere sordid sphere', obscure his protests against the status of the worker as 'a mere wage slave'.[3] As a result of this lack of an effective lead from Burns, Tillett and Mann, other leading officials of the Dockers can be found playing somewhat contradictory political roles. Harry Kay, the union treasurer, after dabbling in Fabianism turned to the I.L.P. and eventually became a Social Democrat.[4] Clem Edwards, an early independent Labour man, became Labour editor of the radical *Sun* in 1893 and stood as a Liberal-Labour candidate for Tottenham in 1895.[5]

The dock strike set off a whole series of agitations, strikes, the formation of new unions and the expansion of those already existing. Although membership figures for many unions are missing at the height of the boom, Charles Booth's estimates of trade union membership in the county in 1893–4 indicate the scale of the expansion. In 1885 there had been only three unions with more than 2,000 London members: now there were twenty-six (Table 6).

In some fields, such as the old London trades, the changes in leadership caused by this activity proved more important than the expansion of organisation. The reorganisation and eighteen week strike of the Bargebuilders, for example, made Will Steadman's reputation. Most of the new unions were either transient or very small, and the most striking expansion was in older unions, the Tailors, Boot Operatives and Compositors.

The tailors' agitation was led by two socialists, James Macdonald and Lewis Lyons, who succeeded in uniting the workers in the sweated sub-divided East End wholesale industry with the highly paid

[1] T. Mann, *Memoirs*, London 1923.
[2] B. Tillett, *Memories and Reflections*, London 1931, p. 191.
[3] Dock, Wharf and Riverside Labourers' Union annual report, 1892.
[4] Fabian Society minutes, elected 5 January 1892, purged February 1896; I.L.P. annual conference report, 1896; S.D.F. annual conference report, 1900.
[5] I.L.P. London District Council minutes, 8 August 1892; *Labour Annual*, 1895.

West End bespoke trade craftsmen. As London District secretary of the Amalgamated Society, Macdonald evolved an ingenious reform policy, combining proposals for opening membership to factory workers and women with a demand for local autonomy which appealed to the special interests of the West End craftsmen. The London delegates failed to carry this programme at the union's 1891 conference and Macdonald was expelled after a dispute with the union executive in 1892, but his plan for wider membership was gradually accepted.[1]

Table 6

Trade Union Membership in the County of London in 1893–4

10,000: London Compositors
8,000: Gas Workers
7,000: Bricklayers; Engineers
6,000: Amalgamated Carpenters; Dockers
5,000: London Carmen; Coal Porters
4,000: Boot and Shoe Operatives; Metropolitan Cabdrivers; Municipal and Vestry Employees; Navvies
3,000: General Union of Carpenters; Amalgamated General Labourers; Postmen; (London) Stevedores; (London) Watermen
2,000: Bakers; Boilermen; Fawcett Association; London Painters; Plasterers; (London) Labour Protection League; London and Counties Labour League; Railway Servants; Stonemasons; Tailors
1,000: London Bookbinders; London Boot and Shoemakers; Alliance Cabinet Makers; (London) Cigar Makers; Farriers; United Builders Labourers; Plumbers; Postal Telegraph Clerks; (London) Printers' Assistants; London Printing Machine Managers; General Railway Workers; London Shipwrights; Smiths and Hammermen

[Booth, *Industry*, Vols 1–5, except for Dockers (union accounts) and Labour Protection League (Board of Trade reports); compare London district membership of e.g. Gas Workers, 12,000 (1892 annual report) or Railway Servants, 3,000 (Gupta)]

In contrast, the militants and socialists in the Boot Operatives, whose leadership in London was established by a strike of 10,000 in 1890, were attempting to reassert craft standards in a period of mechanisation and subdivision in their industry.[2] Nor was there any change in the enlightened conservatism of the Compositors, although they were active in support of other unions, including the new Printers' Assistants. A Reform League was started in 1891, princi-

[1] Clegg, Fox and Thompson, op. cit., pp. 137–8.
[2] Ibid., pp. 200, 295.

pally to attack the 'gifts', exclusive local cliques within the union which dominated the executive supplementing union benefits and finding work for their members. The Reform League won three seats on the executive in 1892 and as a result the union's secretary, Drummond, resigned and was replaced by the less outspoken Bowerman, but it won no further successes and shortly disbanded.[1]

Some of the new unions formed in other fields were to prove important. The Shop Assistants' Union, formed by two socialists, James Macpherson and John Turner, and the National Union of Clerks, both had great opportunities in London although they were initially small. Two of the new unions formed among post office workers were of political interest: the Fawcett Association for the sorters led by two Liberals, W. E. Clery and W. C. Cheesman, and the Postmen's Union, dominated by John Mahon, A. K. Donald and Thomas Binning of the socialist Labour Union, who led it into a disastrous strike in 1890. Nevertheless it was revived as the Postmen's Federation. A trade union was also formed for vestry employees, which was soon active in local elections.

In the building industry three substantial new unions were formed for builders' labourers. The largest was the socialist John Ward's Navvies, Bricklayers' Labourers and General Labourers' Union. The older craft unions expanded dramatically, and although their leaders were Liberal-Labour men they gave support, through the London Building Trades Federation formed in 1892, to 'Labour and Advanced candidates' at local elections.[2] Otherwise the building craft unions were little influenced by the new unionism.

Nor were the attitudes of the Engineers easily shaken. They had voted grants to the Dockers and Gas Workers, but did not trouble to support their strikes by withdrawing their own members. But there was considerable feeling against the part-time executive and restrictive membership of the union. As a result of the refusal of admission to electricians in London, the Electrical Trades Union was allowed to become a rival organisation. A series of strikes in west London in 1889 led to the formation by John Ward of the National Federation of Labour Union, calling on the mechanics 'to throw off all prejudices and distinctions of trades and join with the labourers for one common object'. By the end of the year it had thirteen branches, mostly in south-west London, and was also recruiting among waiters, leather dressers and railway workers.[3] At the same

[1] Ibid., p. 144.
[2] London Building Trades Federation quarterly circular, June 1896.
[3] National Federation of Labour Union manifesto, 1890; Tsuzuki, op. cit., p. 90.

time other strikers at Erith, although loyal to the union, were equally critical of its executive.[1] These events had some impact; the 1890 union conference declared support for the legal eight hour day, and in 1891, after Mann with the support of a big committee of reformers had narrowly missed election as secretary, in a poll of unequalled size, much of what he had demanded was won by the reorganisation of the union with a full-time executive and the opening of membership to electricians and machinemen.[2]

Among the transport workers the principal existing union, the Railway Servants, was also unsympathetic to the new unionism. Consequently a General Railway Workers' Union was started, with support from Burns and a strong nucleus in Battersea. It was not at first well organised, claiming 30,000 members when its real strength was never above 10,000, and by 1893, after a change of leadership, its London membership had fallen to 1,000. The socialist Labour Union formed a new Coachbuilders' Union and helped the more successful Coal Porters, formed immediately after the dock strike in 1889. The London Carmen's Trade Union, founded at the same time, was another strong union. In contrast the Cabdrivers' and Busmens' unions proved transient in spite of successful strikes. The busmen were paid partly from a 'spoils system' of takings from fares, and when a new ticket system was introduced in 1891 eliminating their profits they decided to strike for a twelve hour day. Their union president Sutherst, a middle class lawyer, appealed to the London Trades Council for help, admitting 'that there was scarcely any organisation of busmen or money in the funds'.[3] The Trades Council responded by providing a team of organisers which secured a complete stoppage through effective picketing. But although the strikers won after a week, eight were prosecuted and imprisoned and under this added strain the union collapsed. The Trades Council had to raise a defence fund and left Fred Hammill to organise a new Amalgamated Omnibus and Tram Workers' Union. Hammill was an able man who had trained as a veterinary surgeon before becoming an engineer, but as a keen Labour politician was anxious not 'to be boxed up in a union's office engaged on incidental detail work'. In any case his health broke.[4] By 1893 the union had few London members.

The London Trades Council thus played a vital part in the last great London strike of the new unionism: a part which demonstrated

[1] J. B. Jefferys, *The Story of the Engineers, 1800–1945*, London 1946, p. 109.
[2] Ibid., pp. 98, 113, 136–8.
[3] London Trades Council minutes, 5 June 1891.
[4] F. Hammill to J. Burns, 31 August 1891, Burns Collection; *Labour Annual* 1895; *Fabian News*, August 1901.

its own transformation. The Council had not at first welcomed the movement. Although it had been glad to support the matchgirls, two requests for assistance from Tillett in October 1888 and April 1889 were treated with scorn and it refused to help in the dock strike.[1] This provoked the largest affiliated union, the Compositors, who had already been angered by the failure of the Trades Council to back its local election work for trade union contracts, to disaffiliate from the Council for seven months.[2] Meanwhile the *Star* began to publish hostile reports of the Council,[3] and after criticism of his attitude to the strike Shipton offered to resign and a vote of censure on him was narrowly defeated.[4] During the next few months large numbers of new unions and branches affiliated to the Council, including the Engineers at Battersea and Woolwich, two Gas Workers' branches and thirty-two Dockers' branches. Through the *Labour Elector*, Tom Mann urged the new unionists to send more delegates. The Council had been 'reserved for the delegates of the skilled trades only. This must not be so in future. You have the fullest right to be there.'[5]

The Council was still unwilling to support socialist demands for a London labour exchange in January 1890 or to agree to Mann's request for fortnightly meetings in February, but it agreed to admit women delegates, and by April Mann was able to carry a resolution in favour of an eight hours demonstration.[6] In July the reformers secured a narrow majority through new elections to the executive, although Hammill's effort to replace Shipton as secretary failed. By April 1891 the whole executive consisted of reformers and socialists. They did not agree to Mann's scheme for a grand federation of local trades councils, but the Council was reorganised with nine committees on kindred trades, a finance committee, and a lecture bureau organised by Hammill and Tillett.[7] As the bus strike success indicated, it was at the height of its powers. It had an affiliated membership of 67,000, treble that of 1888, a third of the trade unionists in the whole London district, in spite of the formation, in the same period, of local trades councils in West Ham, East Ham, Woolwich, Tottenham and South West London.

Even if London trade unionism in 1893 still compared unfavourably with the provinces, the situation had been transformed since the

[1] London Trades Council minutes, 25 October 1888 and 18 April 1889.
[2] Ibid., 12 September 1889; London Society of Compositors annual report, 1889; *Labour Elector*, 15 March 1889.
[3] E.g. 29 July 1889.
[4] London Trades Council minutes, 3 October and 7 November 1889.
[5] *Labour Elector*, 1 February 1890.
[6] London Trades Council minutes, 30 January, 13 February, 10 April 1890.
[7] Ibid., 27 August 1891, 2 March 1893; *Trade Unionist*, 16 May 1891; G. Tate, *The London Trades Council, 1860–1950, a History*, London, 1950.

1880s. Two thirds of the adult printing workers and skilled rivermen were trade unionists. So were half the stevedores, between a third and half of the building craftsmen, a third of the metal and engineering workers and the boot makers, and nearly a third of the dock labourers, gasworkers, coal porters and general labourers.[1] These were good figures: and almost as good for labourers as for artisans. This was the London trade unionism which could give strength to the socialists and create the political force of independent Labour—and which, through the London Trades Council, could form its own Labour Party.

The next fifteen years proved an anticlimax. The London Trades Council and its party lost their momentary significance; and if trade union organisation did not disintegrate, it failed to make important advances. It was a period of slow change; and only here and there an amalgamation into a national union, or an artisan trade facing new challenges, indicates the direction of the current. The growth of an independent Labour Party at the expense of both independent socialism and Liberal-Labourism parallels this phase of trade unionism, and was equally slow and inconclusive.

Between 1893 and 1909 membership fluctuated with the economic situation, but there were no dramatic shifts (Table 7). The industry with the most important changes was building.

During these years all the building craft unions declined seriously. The three unions of builders' labourers held together, although at first the United Builders' Labourers increased their London strength at the expense of the other two. After the removal for fraud of the controversial W. Stevenson in 1904, its secretary became an Irish Londoner from Stepney, Dan Haggerty.[2] Of the other major labourers' unions, the Dockers shrank to a tiny London membership, while the National Federation of Labour disappeared. The Gas Workers, although never losing their hold on London, fluctuated very considerably between 15,000 and a nadir of less than 4,000 in 1909. Their most serious losses were among builders' labourers who grew to nearly half their local membership in 1899 and then fell away again.

Few important new unions emerged during the period. Tom Mann's Worker's Union, formed among unskilled engineers in 1898, had little following in London. After 1903, however, the Shop Assistants entered a phase of rapid growth, reaching 7,000 London members by 1909. The National Amalgamated Furnishing Trades Association, formed from the old cabinet makers' unions in 1902, and

[1] Booth, op. cit., *Industry*, 5, p. 144.
[2] C. A. Smart to J. Burns, n.d. 1892, Burns Collection; W. Parker to J. R. MacDonald, 30 December 1904, Labour Party correspondence.

Table 7
Membership of the Larger Unions in the London District
1900

- 15,000: Gas Workers
- 11,000: London Compositors
- 9,000: Bricklayers; *Amalgamated Carpenters*; Engineers
- 7,000: *Amalgamated General Labourers*
- 6,000: Railway Servants; *United Builders' Labourers*
- 4,000: Plasterers; Postmen
- 3,000: London Cab Drivers; London Carmen; *Coal Porters*; Fawcett Association; United General Order of London Labourers; (London) Stevedores; (London) Watermen
- 2,000: *Bakers*; *Boilermakers*; General Union of Carpenters; (London) Cigar Makers; (London) Labour Protection League; (London) Printers' Assistants; London Printing Machine Minders; *Shop Assistants*; Stonemasons; *Tailors*
- 1,000: London Bookbinders; *London Boot and Shoemakers*; Boot Operatives; *Alliance Cabinet Makers*; London French Polishers; Ironfounders; Dockers; *Locomotive Engineers and Firemen*; Municipal Employees; *Navvies*; London Painters; Plumbers; *Postal Telegraph Clerks*; *Railway Clerks*; *General Railway Workers*; Upholsterers

1910

- 13,000: Shop Assistants
- 12,000: London Compositors
- 9,000: Engineers
- 8,000: Railway Servants
- 6,000: Postmen
- 5,000: London Carmen; Amalgamated Carpenters; *Fawcett Association*
- 4,000: Bricklayers; Gas Workers; (London) Stevedores
- 3,000: London Cab Drivers; Postal Telegraph Clerks; *General Railway Workers*
- 2,000: *Bakers*; Boilermakers; Furnishing Trades Association (Cabinet Makers, etc.); (London) Labour Protection League; London Painters; Plasterers; *Printers' Assistants*; *Printers' Warehousemen*; London Printing Machine Minders; *Tailors*; (London) Watermen
- 1,000: London Bookbinders; *London Boot and Shoemakers*; Boot Operatives; (London) Cigar Makers; *Clerks*; Civil Service Assistant Clerks; Coal Porters; Dockers; Farriers; *United Builders' Labourers*; United General Order of London Labourers; *Amalgamated General Labourers*; *Locomotive Engineers and Firemen*; Municipal Employees, *Railway Clerks*; *Tinplate Workers*; *Upholsterers*

(Approximate estimates *italicised*: figures are taken from union reports, reports of the Board of Trade and Registrar of Friendly Societies, and affiliation figures to the Labour Party: see thesis) the Municipal Employees' Association—despite great hostility, especially from the Gas Workers, for poaching members—were also firmly established during the 1900s.

Nevertheless the ebbs and flows in trade union strength were far more evident than any changes in the main outline. The chief reason for this was that while the two periods of economic recovery, 1896–9 and 1905–7, helped the unions to weather the worst years, neither stimulated another dramatic trade union expansion. In 1905–7 this was partly because the recovery was insufficient. In 1896–9, however, there was another reason: the continuance of the strong resistance of the employers, which had first checked the new unions in 1890.

The most important movement was among the Engineers. Technical change, including the introduction of American methods of work-timing, had made the workmen more militant, while at the same time the formation of the Employers' Federation of Engineering Associations in June 1896 showed a new determination among the masters. In the union socialist influence was strongest in London, and its ascendancy seemed assured when George Barnes, who had been secretary of Mann's election committee in 1891, finally captured the post himself in 1896. In May 1897 a trade committee of engineering unions presented a demand for an eight hour day to 800 London firms, and although at first it seemed that this would be conceded, resistance was stimulated by the Employers' Federation, and led in July to a national lock-out. A bitter six-month struggle ensued. The employers enrolled ex-policemen as counter-pickets and replaced the strikers by 'drafts from the provinces' of up to 9,000 men. The Poplar employer Alfred Yarrow bought a mail steamer which he moored in the Thames to house his blackleg labour. In all this a prominent, although not very effective part was played by the National Free Labour Association, founded in 1893 by William Collison, an able ex-trade unionist with a fierce dislike of 'the tyranny and dictation of Socialistic Trade Union leaders'.[1] With the backing of industrialists such as Livesey who had formed rudimentary 'free labour' associations from 1890, Collison's organisation became an effective source of unskilled and semi-skilled substitute labour, but in a craft struggle of this kind its main effect was to heighten tension. There was widespread support for the Engineers from other unions, including gifts of £3,000 from the Compositors who were concerned at the new 'military element' among employers.[2] Nevertheless in January 1898 the Engineers were forced to accept defeat and agree to non-union labour, piecework and work-timing, and an arbitration machinery to avoid future disputes.

[1] *Free Labour*, 15 July 1897; Clegg, Fox and Thompson, op. cit., p. 171.
[2] London Society of Compositors annual reports, 1897–8.

The employers' victory cowed the Engineers for a decade. Their numbers kept up, but Barnes found his initiative crippled by his union executive, and eventually resigned in protest in 1907. The defeat of the strongest of the craft societies also crushed the optimism of the other unions. Free Labour was used to defeat dock strikes in 1899–1900 and also in disputes in the printing industry. The London Master Printers' Association had been reformed in 1890 in response to union growth, and in 1894 they attempted to break the Printers' Assistants. The Compositors were similarly threatened in 1896, when they were negotiating a pay scale for the new linotype machine setter, but although the Free Labour Association opened a printing trade bureau and enrolled 7,000 men, the new scale was agreed without a strike.[1] Eventually in 1899 the outbreak of the Boer War overshadowed industrial developments, and the London Trades Council reported that no union had applied for strike credentials, 'a sure index of the peaceful state of affairs in the industrial circles of the Metropolis'.[2]

Thus in 1909 the general scene remained little altered. Although many of the trade union secretaries had changed, no new figures had emerged in London to rival those like Thorne and Tillett whose reputations had been made in 1889. Perhaps the most significant change had been not in the individual unions but in the London Trades Council, which had relapsed from its position of authority in 1891 to an ineffective debating chamber for the smaller societies. Its affiliated membership had fallen to 52,000 in 1896, and remained in most years below 60,000. Its industrial ineffectiveness was shown by its failure to help the Engineers. Its political attitudes were largely obstructive. James Macdonald, the Social Democrat and former new unionist who succeeded Shipton as secretary in 1896, proved a poor organiser and a supporter of the narrowest London particularism. In his own union, for example, instead of throwing himself into the strike of East End wholesale tailors in 1906, he led a secession of West End craftsmen from the national society in 1905 to form the London Society of Tailors and Tailoresses, which asserted that 'never again would a provincial organisation be allowed to interfere with London trade regulations and London ambitions'.[3] Meanwhile the importance of the local Trades Councils had been growing. By 1909 they numbered over twenty, and in many cases they had gained stature through acting as constituency organisations for the Labour Party.

. . . .

[1] *Free Labour*, 15 September 1897.
[2] London Trades Council annual report, 1899.
[3] Clegg, Fox and Thompson, op. cit., pp. 440–3.

This placid phase ended in 1909. The last years of the period saw a second great upheaval on the scale of that of 1889–91, once again transforming the pattern of trade unionism, greatly extending its organisation, and giving it a new political importance.

While in 1889–91 socialism had helped to create a militant climate of opinion, this time industrial unionism and syndicalism were responsible. Of these two new doctrines, industrial unionism, although introduced earlier, had fewer supporters. They wanted a single militant trade union in each industry, and to this end waged a continuous campaign against both employers and existing trade unions. In London they were first represented by the Socialist Labour Party, a body strongly influenced by the American Daniel de Leon, and by the London Alliance of Industrial Unionists formed with its support of E. J. B. Allen in 1906.[1] In 1907 an Industrial Union of Direct Actionists groups, with the future libertarian socialist orator Guy Aldred as secretary, was formed in the same spirit with the *Voice of Labour* as its organ: 'its mission being to overthrow, not to perpetuate, it provides strike pay, and strike pay only. ... By trade strikes would the way be paved for the final principle of the Social General Strike.'[2]

These somewhat vague revolutionary ideas were given a more coherent purpose by syndicalism. The syndicalist movement was set off by the return of Tom Mann from his long period overseas, and his visit to Paris with Guy Bowman, a Walthamstow journalist, to study French trade unionism. They returned in July 1910 eager to spread the new theory of revolution through the general strike, with the future community organised nationally through democratic industrial unions and locally through Trades Councils. They were willing to work through existing organisations, and especially to promote amalgamation movements in the unions. In July 1910 they launched the *Industrial Syndicalist*, published under various titles until 1914. In November the Industrial Syndicalist League was formed at a Manchester conference, and a second conference was held in London in November 1912. In March 1912 however Mann and Bowman were imprisoned for printing a 'Don't Shoot' appeal to soldiers, and both then dropped out of the movement. The Walthamstow Trades Council, whose secretary was a young syndicalist carpenter, A. G. Tufton, also lost their initial interest at this point.[3] But

---

[1] B. Pribicevic, *The Shop Stewards' Movement and Workers' Control*, Oxford 1959, pp. 12–13; *Socialist*, April 1907.

[2] *Voice of Labour*, 15 June 1907.

[3] Tufton was a delegate to the first conference, and the Walthamstow Trades Council decided to call a London conference of hearing his report: *Industrial Syndicalist*, March 1911.

the movement continued with the publication of *Solidarity* in 1913–14 by Jack Wills, a Bermondsey bricklayer, secretary of the Industrial Democracy League, whose hope was to build on the Amalgamation Committees which had developed in the building, engineering and other industries. The amalgamation committees were in fact the clearest result of syndicalist influence; but the general effect of its propaganda for trade union solidarity, against 'our foolish and criminal sectionalism',[1] for the sympathetic strike and the general strike, and its hostility to political means of change, especially as reflected in the policies of the *Daily Herald*, was widely influential.

The printers had first brought out the *Daily Herald* as their strike organ in 1911 and later supported it rather than the moderate *Daily Citizen*,[2] but the only London success of the amalgamation movement in this industry was with the bookbinding unions. Among the East End tailors and also the rapidly expanding National Union of Clerks there were active industrial unionist groups, but most of the direct influence of syndicalism was confined to the building, engineering and transport industries. The Shop Assistants, another fast growing union, showed little interest, while the Gas Workers and other general unions were naturally unsympathetic to a doctrine which would have broken up their organisations.

Among the transport workers the most publicised conflict was again in the docks. Ben Tillett had been immediately attracted by syndicalism, and at his suggestion a conference was called in September 1910 which led to the formation of a National Transport Workers' Federation, including the Stevedores and Sailors, with Harry Gosling of the Watermen as President. The Federation at once launched into a strike in July 1911, and secured an increase in basic pay from sixpence (the 1889 rate) to eightpence, a minimum engagement of four hours, fixed 'hours of call' and the hiring of labour outside the dock gates under union supervision. Once more in control of the labour supply, the Dockers grew rapidly and were able to bring in the south side Labour Protection League, so that they reached a London membership of 7,000. But again their strength proved transient. Lord Devonport, chairman of the new Port of London Authority which was now the chief employer, decided that union dominance must be challenged, and prepared for a struggle. The Federation was caught unexpectedly by a minor dispute in April 1912, which it unwisely attempted to convert into a national strike, and defeated by Devonport's determination and organisation of blackleg labour. The unions lost their control of the hiring of labour and the Dockers had lost nearly half their members within a year.

[1] *Solidarity*, September 1913.
[2] *London Typographical Journal*, December 1911.

With the railwaymen there was more success. In the unions syndicalism was a 'doctrine fervently held by a minority of active and influential members',[1] including Charles Watkins, a Derbyshire railway servant who in the autumn of 1911 edited the *Syndicalist Railwayman* from Walthamstow. Although there was considerable support for syndicalism in the Great Eastern works at West Ham, the London Railway Servants were notably conservative and the Walthamstow branch had as secretary W. V. Osborne, whose legal pursuit of his Liberal sympathies had resulted in the decisions that union political levies were illegal. The branch can hardly have welcomed Watkin's exhortations to 'get ready for the fray . . . Law and order means the dominance of the capitalist cut-throat and his watchdogs; the dominance of the sweater and the fat-bellied idle rich . . . Let us make it clear to them that if ever again they put a weapon in our hands, be it a police staff, a rifle, or any other instrument of destruction, we shall know how to use it.'[2] Nevertheless, as a result of a series of unofficial provincial strikes, the unions were forced into a national strike in 1911, and, in the atmosphere of solidarity produced by victory, negotiations for amalgamation, which had failed on several previous occasions, were reopened. The General Railway Workers Union pressed for a comprehensive industrial union, and although the Railway Servants at first rejected the idea that 'every Tom, Jack and Harry that works upon the railway, irrespective of his position', should be able to join the union, eventually the National Union of Railwaymen was formed on very much this basis.[3] Both the Railway Clerks and the Locomotive Engineers and Firemen refused to join, but the new union grew rapidly to a London membership of some 30,000 in 1914. For the first time the London railwaymen were remarkable for the strength rather than the weakness of their organisation.

Support for industrial unionism was also strong among the building workers, led by Jack Wills and George Hicks of the Bricklayers. Haggerty the Builders' Labourers' secretary spoke for the movement, but the Bricklayers were the only craft union to support amalgamation. When the unions were forced into a major London strike in 1914 the militants attacked the 'spineless leaders' of the London Building Trades Federation for their willingness to settle before victory, and denounced its secretary George Dew as 'a past master at marking time'.[4] Supported by the *Daily Herald*, with Hicks

[1] P. Bagwell, *The Railwaymen, the History of the National Union of Railwaymen*, London 1963, p. 327.
[2] *Syndicalist Railwaymen*, October 1911.
[3] Report of conference on fusion, December 1911.
[4] *Solidarity*, September 1913, January-February 1914.

declaring the strikers had 'nothing to be robbed of but a very uncertain third-class life',[1] the dispute was not settled before the outbreak of war in August 1914. Some 60,000 men were involved.

There was an especially vigorous amalgamation movement among the London engineers, in which W. F. Watson of Chiswick and F. S. Button on Erith played leading roles, but it failed to achieve an industrial union in the industry or even to make a success of the unskilled workers' section started by the Engineers. There was, however, another upheaval in the union. In 1910 J. T. Brownlie of Woolwich published a notable attack on the autocratic full-time executive, which could only be challenged by a triennial delegate meeting whose powers were limited to rules revision. The 1913 delegate meeting dismissed and forcibly ejected the full-time executive. The ineffective secretary was replaced by Robert Young, and Brownlie was elected chairman under the new regime. There were also signs that the advance of division of labour and work-timing, which had undermined the assurance of the craftsmen, were creating a new solidarity and militancy among the London engineering workers. In Woolwich an 'all grades' movement in the Arsenal began in 1914 for the first time, showing an important 'broadening of mind' among the skilled men.[2] A strongly organised Arsenal Shop Stewards' Committee developed with Tom Rees, a Welsh Marxist who had been to Ruskin College and then to the Central Labour College, as its secretary. Rees became London district secretary of the Engineers in 1913.[3] The Woolwich Trades Council was reorganised with a strike fund, and raised £286 for the Dublin strikers, and during the 1914 builders conflict a single strike committee of all the unions was organised in Woolwich.[4] Early in July a dispute started in the Arsenal when a man was dismissed for refusing to work with blackleg building labourers. For the first time the skilled and unskilled men stood together against victimisation. The Engineers' Shop Stewards Committee became a strike committee, and within three days the strike was won.[5]

This new spirit moving among the strongholds of craft unionism produced a decisive change in the character of trade unionism. At the same time there was a startling expansion of trade union membership among those classes which had been most difficult to organise, from office clerks at one extreme to unskilled workers, especially women, at the other. The pioneering efforts of Mary MacArthur, Margaret MacDonald and Margaret Bondfield were at last rewarded by a substantial London membership in the National Federation of

[1] Ibid., April 1914.　　[2] *Woolwich Pioneer*, 6 February 1914.
[3] Ibid., 18 April 1913.
[4] Ibid., 19 June 1914, and Woolwich Trades Council minutes, 1911–14.
[5] *Woolwich Pioneer*, 10 July 1914.

Women Workers, and the number of women in other unions, especially the Dockers, Gas Workers and the Workers' Union, also grew rapidly. The Workers' Union increased from 6,000 to 60,000 in two years, but most of this membership was provincial. The Gas Workers, however, increased their London membership from under 4,000 in 1909 to 25,000 in 1914.

Table 8

London District Membership of the Larger Unions in 1914

- 30,000: Railwaymen
- 25,000: Gas Workers
- 20,000: *Shop Assistants*
- 13,000: Engineers
- 12,000: London Compositors
- 8,000: Amalgamated Carpenters; Postmen
- 7,000: *Vehicle Workers* (formerly Carmen)
- 6,000: Fawcett Association; *Licensed Vehicle Workers* (formerly Cab Drivers)
- 5,000: London Painters; (London) Stevedores
- 4,000: Bricklayers; *Clerks*; Dockers; (London) Watermen
- 3,000: Boilermakers; Furnishing Trades Association; (London) Labour Protection League; United Builders' Labourers; Municipal Employees; *Postal Telegraph Clerks*; *Printers' Assistants*; *Railway Clerks*
- 2,000: *Bakers*; Boot Operatives; Civil Service Assistant Clerks; Plasterers; London Printing Machine Minders; *Sheet Metal Workers*; *Tailors*; *Workers' Union*
- 1,000: *Bookbinders*; London Boot and Shoemakers; General Union of Carpenters; (London) Cigar Makers; *Coopers*; Electricians; *Farriers*; London French Polishers; Ironfounders; *Locomotive Engineers and Firemen*; Plumbers; (London) Scientific Instrument Makers; *Ships Stewards*; Smiths and Hammermen; Stonemasons; *Upholsterers*

(Approximate estimates *italicised*; no figures obtained for Coal Porters, Amalgamated General Labourers, United General Order of London Labourers, or Printers' Warehousemen; sources as Table 7)

This expansion has often been attributed to the National Insurance Act of 1911, under which benefits were available through trade unions registered as 'approved societies'. This may have helped some unions, but it cannot have helped generally because the act did not come into operation until July 1912, after the period of most rapid expansion, and only a quarter of trade union members registered for insurance through their unions. It is possible, however, that the Insurance Act helped the unions to hold their members, for after the peak of the boom had passed in 1913 there was no sign of the usual falling off in membership. Certainly their active involvement in government was to be a source of strength in the future; and in any case their membership figures, with the Gas Workers' 25,000, the Shop Assistants' 20,000, the Railwaymen's 30,000, the Compositors' 12,000 and the Engineers' 13,000, had never been more impressive (Table 8).

A new phase of far more extensive and powerful trade unionism had begun. Moreover, while almost a third of the significant unions in 1893–4 had been local London unions, by 1914 nearly four fifths were national unions. A national outlook, the new militancy of the artisans and the general growth of the financial and numerical strength of trade unionism, provided a foundation upon which the Labour Party in London was at last able to absorb both socialists and Liberal-Labour men.

IV

POLITICS AND PARTIES

BETWEEN 1885 and 1914 there were eight general elections. Although the franchise was still far from the adult suffrage of a fully developed democracy, the elections of this period more closely resemble those of the 20th century than elections under the restricted franchise of before 1867.

There were no important alterations in the parliamentary electoral system in these years. London was divided in 1885 into 27 parliamentary boroughs. Of these one, the City of London, was a two-member constituency, while the others were split into 57 single-member divisions. Adjacent to London were two single-member borough seats in West Ham and ten single-member county divisions in Middlesex, Essex, Kent and Surrey. (Croydon was also adjacent but is omitted from this survey) (Map 22). There was also a member elected for the University of London. Altogether, therefore, there were 72 London Members of Parliament—one tenth of the whole House of Commons.

The basic franchise qualifications were three: firstly, as a male head of household of a separate dwelling who had resided a year within the borough or county; secondly, as a male lodger over 21 who had occupied for a year the same rooms worth £10 unfurnished annually; and thirdly, as the male occupier of premises worth £10 annually who had lived six months within seven miles of the borough. For this last qualification an elector could vote in any number of boroughs, but only in one division in each borough. In addition over 2,000, rising by 1910 to 6,000, London graduates made up the electorate of the University of London; 6,000 freemen of the City of London had votes in the City and constituted a fifth of its electors; and nearly 10,000 were qualified as county ownership voters, by being owners but not occupiers of freehold property worth £2 annually or by other tenure of property worth £5 annually. These last voters were apportioned to the adjacent county divisions, since there was no parliamentary county of London.

How close did this come to adult suffrage? Women were completely excluded from the vote. As a proportion of the men over 21 the electorate rose from just under half in 1885 (594,000) to about 55 per cent (1,016,000) in 1910. This improvement, however, was principally because of the growth of population in the adjacent county divisions, which always had a much higher proportion of electors than the inner divisions. In 1892 half the county divisions had 17 per cent of their population on the register (which was the national average),[1] but only two inner constituencies, the City and Strand. By 1911 only two more had reached this figure, and the inner electorate as a whole had only increased from 13·2 per cent to 14·7 per cent of the population. In one sense even this growth aggravated an injustice of the system, the variation in constituency size. In 1892 and again in 1910 six constituencies had less than 6,000 electors, but while in 1892 only four exceeded 15,000, by 1910 there were twenty with over 15,000, including five with over 30,000.

In a number of other ways the system was far from that of a fully developed democracy. It contained a strong social bias. It was possible for a graduate with the requisite property qualifications to vote for twenty-nine borough members, seven county members and one university member, thirty-seven votes in all. A middle class family could register not only the head of household, but also the adult sons living in rooms in the house and the coachmen in the mews. A working class family of the same size living in lodgings would be very unlikely to be able to register more than the head of family. If a period of unemployment had forced him to apply for poor relief, even he would be disqualified. If he moved in search of work, and in many working class districts a third of the population moved each year, he would require another year's residence before again qualifying. Finally, while owners and occupiers were registered by the Guardians without personal application, lodgers, who constituted a high proportion of the London working class, were obliged to make annual applications for the vote. If the registration agent of one of the political parties raised an objection to the lodger's application he might be obliged to attend a revision court, which would only sit during his hours of work. As a result of these difficulties, added to the frequency of removal, it was common for half the lodgers on the register to disappear from the voters list in the following year.[2]

[1] J. A. Baines, 'Parliamentary Representation in England illustrated by the Elections of 1892 and 1895', *Journal of the Royal Statistical Society*, 1896, and S. Rosenbaum, 'The General Election of (January) 1910', ibid., 1910.

[2] E.g. *Londoner*, 22 September 1894.

This bias in the franchise is reflected clearly in the registers. Although in most divisions the non-resident ownership vote was negligible, in the City, St. George's Hanover Square, Westminster, Strand, and all the out-county suburban divisions, it accounted for some 10 per cent of the electorate.[1] These outvoters exaggerated the difference between the inner constituencies and the outer suburbs. Even so it is clear that in the suburbs the relative stability of middle class inhabitants and the smaller proportion of working class lodgers produced a much higher proportion of electors. Throughout the period 17 per cent to 23 per cent of the population in middle class suburbs and 15 per cent to 16 per cent in working class suburbs were electors. In contrast, in 1892 there were 24 constituencies in which less than 12 per cent of the population were electors. Four of these were West End constituencies, where there were large numbers of transient lodgers, hotel guests, living-in servant girls and living-in shop assistants. In the others the low figure is explained by the large working class element in the population. In constituencies like St. George's in the East, where there were large numbers of poor Irish, the figure was below 10 per cent. By 1911 there had been some improvement, and in only five constituencies was the electorate below 12 per cent of the population, but in fifteen, all but one working class, it was still below 13 per cent (Map 23).

It would appear from these figures that while probably one fifth of the middle classes were electors, only one tenth of the working class were registered in many areas. But there was probably a sharp distinction between the more comfortable working class, such as that found in the suburbs, and the poorer working class. While perhaps a sixth of the comfortable working class were electors, among the poor, especially those qualifying as lodgers, the number may have been less than a twelfth. One of the few startling inconsistencies in the register is the lodger vote. Although there is no sign of fluctuations in the proportion of the population in lodgings in this period, the number of constituencies in which lodgers were more than 15 per cent of the electorate varied from 5 in 1888 to 13 in 1889, 9 in 1899 and 21 in 1911. The total lodger vote within the county was 75,000 in 1893, 70,000 in 1903 and 108,000 in 1914. In the earlier period these fluctuations can be ascribed to the varying energy and funds spent by the political parties on registration work. It is clear enough that in a marginal constituency in the 1880s and 1890s the party which secured the registration of the largest number of its supporters would benefit far more from this work than from any purely political campaigning.

[1] The number of non-resident voters in all but three constituencies is given in PP 1888 LXXIX, p. 909; for these three constituencies, and for other years, it is possible to consult the registers in the London County Council Record Room.

Party activity in fact centred upon annual canvassing for the electoral register. The poorer Liberal Associations were forced to rely largely on voluntary work, but a wealthy Conservative Association such as South Kensington can be found employing an agent, clerk and three full-time canvassers.[1]

This work became less important after 1900, when registration became a responsibility of the London boroughs, and many, led by Battersea, made it their policy to improve the quality of the parliamentary register. The South Kensington Conservative Association by 1905 only required to 'supplement the official work of the town clerk', and in 1907 alluded 'to the excellent way in which the Registration work is performed by the Borough Council officials, reducing, of course, the need for claims and objections'.[2] It is no doubt the particular local efficiency of the borough councils in Southwark and Battersea which explain why the electorate reached unusually high figures in their constituencies, rising to 19 per cent of the population in the Battersea division in 1911. The fact that this division was almost entirely working class, and had had only 12·7 per cent of its population registered in 1892, strongly suggests the degree to which the working classes were usually penalised by the registration system.

The lodger vote was also affected after 1906 by the legal decision in Kent v. Fittall, which allowed the registration as occupiers of those householders in separate lodgings who had their own housekey, in spite of the fact that the landlord was resident on the premises. As a result in 1906–7 the lodger vote dropped by 31,000, while the other voters increased by 129,000, a net gain of 98,000 representing 'practically a new class of elector'.[3] Former lodger voters were now enabled to dispense with annual claims, continuous residence in the same lodging, and the qualification of an annual value of £10. In fifteen constituencies, all but one predominately working class, the electorate was increased by 20 per cent. Subsequently, due to 'stricter scrutiny' and the decision in Douglas v. Smith, nearly half of this gain was lost, and the lodger vote in fact increased again. There is, however, some reason for believing that the legal decisions were interpreted differently by the different revision courts. Although the electorate was unusually extensive in Battersea and Southwark, the lodger vote was not notably large. On the other hand in all the fourteen divisions in the boroughs of Hackney, Camberwell, Islington and Lambeth lodgers were more than 15 per cent of the electorate, although they included

[1] South Kensington Conservative Association executive committee minutes, 15 May and 11 December 1888, 9 July 1890, etc. The agent was paid £200 a year, the clerk £85, and the canvassers 5/– daily.
[2] South Kensington Conservative Association annual reports, 1905 and 1907.
[3] *London Statistics*, 1906–7, pp. 14–15.

middle class constituencies such as Dulwich and Norwood. These illogical variations were reflections of a franchise in which the right of the poor to the vote was still much less secure than that of the prosperous.

This bias in the electoral registers was further exaggerated at elections. The same frequent migration which made it more difficult for the working classes to register made it more likely that they would have removed before the parliamentary election took place. By the last month of validity of the register it was common for a quarter or even a third of the electorate to have left the district.[1] Middle class removals were easier to trace, and more likely to be able to vote in spite of removal. In addition the long distances which many Londoners travelled to work, and long working hours, meant that many working men, particularly those living in the suburbs, would find it difficult to reach the polls before they closed. It was noticeable that in those local elections in which polling continued until 10 p.m. by far the heaviest vote occurred in the last three hours.[2] In general elections the polling stations closed at 8 p.m. There was a distinct tendency immediately after the 1885 redistribution for the lowest polls to be in working class constituencies. Later, as safe seats came to be recognised, the poll also dropped in many middle class Conservative constituencies.[3] In some working class boroughs, such as Battersea and Woolwich, perhaps due to the excitement caused by a popular Labour candidate, polls were consistently higher than the average, reaching 80 per cent or more. This was in fact the national average poll for borough constituencies, but due to removals and travelling to work London as a whole polled 10 per cent below the national average in 1892 and 1895, and 5 per cent below in January 1910.[4]

The political system was also weighted in favour of the prosperous by the cost of political life. It is true that this was a declining factor. In the mid-19th century London elections had been exceptionally expensive, commonly exceeding £3,000 for each candidate.[5] After 1885 it was legally limited by a scale which in practice meant between £470 and £770 at the beginning of the period, rising to £1,200 or more by 1910. Members of Parliament had no salary until 1913, and were

[1] E.g. *Londoner*, 19 July 1895, removals in West Islington already 2000 out of 9000; *Daily Chronicle*, 8 October 1900, Bermondsey 3000 out of 11,300; *Daily News*, 21 November 1906, Haggerston 4000 out of 8000; 22 November, West Ham North 5000 out of 15,600; 1 December, Limehouse 2000 out of 6400; 2 December, Wandsworth 10,000 out of 38,500; *Standard*, 15 December 1909, Hampstead 4000 out of 12,000; 25 November 1910, Walworth 3000 out of 8500, etc.

[2] E.g. *London Statistics* 1906–7, p. 27.   [3] See Appendix A.

[4] J. A. Baines, op. cit., and S. Rosenbaum, op. cit.

[5] W. B. Gwyn, *Democracy and the Cost of Politics in Britain*, London 1962, p. 34.

widely expected to contribute as much as £200 a year towards the organisation of their constituencies.[1]

On the other hand, as a result of the Corrupt Practices Act of 1883 there was less opportunity for a very rich man to buy his way to victory through wealth alone. Certainly it was possible for him to spend a great deal of money in registering his supporters, and thereby to impose himself on the constituency. Hume Webster the City accountant attempted this in West Ham South between 1886 and his suicide in 1892. There was also a continuance in some constituencies of indirect forms of corruption. The candidate would be a vice-president and notable contributor to a local charity, which by chance distributed free boots, soup and blankets at the time of the election. In Hammersmith, for example, the defeated Liberal candidate in 1910 complained of 'an under current of corruption in the constituency' which operated 'mainly through the machinery for the distribution of charity, which machinery is for the most part in Tory hands'. It was admitted that the West London Philanthropic Society, of which a leading local Conservative was president, had supplied free beer coupons before the election which were given away during it, and that the Nuts Benevolent Society, of which the Conservative Member was 'only one of the patrons', gave away free boots at the same time.[2] But these activities were marginal, and were the nearest approach to the once prevalent bribery which survived in elections. Even this was avoided by overtly political clubs and organisations such as the Primrose League. At a discussion of the law in 1893 the South Kensington Conservative Association came to the conclusion that 'nothing is more dangerous than "partial" treating, such as selling refreshments at Primrose League gatherings, at a price less than they are provided by a contractor. Drink paid for by a member of the Habitation for a friend who is not, is "treating". Providing entertainment in the shape of music etc. is probably safe, but anything in the shape of meat or drink is dangerous'.[3] In the election instructions issued by agents of both parties in this period the insistence of observation of the law, and particularly on the avoidance of payments for election help, is very noticeable.

As a result it was necessary for a candidate to be supported by a large army of voluntary workers, and in practise this meant that he must both be wealthy and be supported by a political party. A few examples of local magnates still occur: landowners such as Evelyn (Conservative, Deptford) and Carr-Gomm (Liberal, Rotherhithe) or

[1] Ibid., p. 57; cf. C. W. Bowerman and Deptford, Ch. 11.
[2] *West London Observer,* 4 February 1910.
[3] South Kensington Conservative Association executive committee minutes, 3 March 1893.

employers such as Charrington the brewer (Conservative, Mile End) or Pearce the chemical manufacturer (Liberal, Limehouse). But the day of the independent wealthy candidate had gone. In 1885, because of the imperfect Liberal Party organisation, there were still nine independent Liberal candidates opposing the official party nominee. After this, apart from independent labour or socialist candidates, there were never more than two independent candidates at a general election, and the only case in which the independent secured a respectable vote was when the local party was divided between the two candidates.[1]

In the mid-19th century the majority of election helpers had been paid for their services. In London the Member for Hackney, Henry Fawcett, had successfully relied on voluntary canvassing in 1874 and 1880, but this was exceptional.[2] The 1883 Corrupt Practises Act, by limiting the number of paid assistants to a single agent, one deputy at each polling station, and a specified number of clerks and messengers, none of whom were allowed to vote, and by prohibiting payment for the conveyance of voters to the poll, quickly brought into being a voluntary system remarkably similar to that in operation today. Firstly, the constituency Association was constructed on a democratic basis, with individual members subscribing a small annual sum, usually one shilling, grouped in committees in each ward, and managed by a central committee consisting of ward delegates, the officers elected at the annual general meeting of the Association, and certain special delegates. These delegates would represent Conservative or Liberal clubs, and also in some Conservative Associations the Primrose League, and in some Liberal Associations the local temperance societies. After 1885 this 'new and complete system of organisation' was as strongly urged by the central office of the Conservatives as by the Liberals.[3] In addition, supporters were

[1] In December 1910 in Hackney South there were two Liberal candidates, of whom Horatio Bottomley polled 5068 and R. H. Roberts polled 1946. Bottomley, who published the *Sun* and *John Bull*, was a very uncharacteristic Liberal, flagrantly indulging in drink, sex and gambling, and nursing the constituency with horse parades and soup kitchens. This alienated local Nonconformists, who put up the Rev. William Riley in 1906 'to promote national righteousness, political purity, the defence of good citizenship', and in December 1910 a schoolmaster, R. H. Roberts. (Julian Simons, *Horatio Bottomley* London 1955; Rev. William Riley, election manifesto 1906.) No other candidate not standing as an official Liberal Conservative or Labour nominee polled more than 1000 votes in any parliamentary election.

[2] H. J. Hanham, *Elections and Party Management*, London 1959, p. 245.

[3] E.g. South Kensington Conservative Association executive committee minutes 8 June 1866; South West Bethnal Green Conservative and Unionist Association rules, 1899, Hammersmith Conservative and Constitutional Association rules, 1893, and Lewisham Conservative and Constitutional Association rules, 1905, Bull Collection.

enrolled through the Women's Liberal Associations, begun in 1886, and the Dames of the Primrose League, which had been started in 1883. The latter organisation offered the inducement of mock feudal orders and ceremonies, as well as the river steamer outings, annual dinners, and garden parties graced by the aristocracy, which now provided the customary rewards for political services. The number of members of these constituency organisations varied considerably, but the 300 members of the Hammersmith Conservative Association in 1895, with a similar number of Primrose Dames, was a very respectable figure. Although only a nominal subscription was required, most members in fact gave a guinea or more, and a prosperous Association would have an income of between £200 and £500 annually.[1] There were no constituency Associations with a mass membership before the Woolwich Labour Party of the 1900s.

Between elections an efficient organisation carried out as thorough as possible a canvass of the constituency for registration purposes. It is difficult to obtain comparative figures, but in 1900 more than half of the Conservative Associations were reported to be carrying out registration work with thoroughness, while only about five Liberal Associations were really effective.[2] This was a particularly poor period for the Liberals, and in the early 1890s and later 1900s their organisation would have compared less adversely with the Conservatives. From this canvassing a marked register was built up. Before the election poll cards would be sent to supporters. On the polling day canvassers would be sent out to remind supporters to vote, while volunteers at the polling collected voters polling cards and those who had voted were ticked off on the marked register of supporters kept at the party committee room.[3] Lists of those needing conveyance to the poll and of supporters willing to lend carriages or later motor cars were also made before the poll. From the 1890s the Conservative Party developed an effective system for the transference of volunteers and conveyances to marginal constituencies.[4] In a safe constituency like Hampstead the Primrose Dames acted as 'a missionary station

---

[1] E.g. Hampstead Conservative Association reports, 1905 and 1909, £268 and £450 subscriptions, and Fulham Constitutional Registration Association, appeal for £500 a year, 1905, Bull Collection; Woolwich Conservative Association income 1906, £460, *Woolwich Pioneer*, 8 February 1907.

[2] Holland to Gladstone, January 1901, Herbert Gladstone Collection.

[3] E.g. Conservative Central Office leaflet and instructions issued by Conservative agent, Hammersmith, 1895, Bull Collection.

[4] E.g. South Kensington Conservative Association minutes, 12 July 1892, helpers sent to North Kensington, Chelsea, Fulham, etc. and a special committee set up for the 'very difficult work' of canvassing non-resident voters; carriages also sent 1895 from South Kensington to these constituencies, Bull Collection; *London Argus*, 29 January 1898, 'flying squadron' of canvassers for marginal seats, etc.

for the Unionist cause.¹ By 1910 the Conservatives had organised a central clearing house for tracing removals, and a grand scheme of motor cars to convey them to the poll. The Central Office also appealed for 10,000 volunteers for canvassing and organisation, and distributed these to the marginal constituencies.²

It can be seen that in this period elections were fought in a skilled professional manner. The significance of efficient organisation, which reflected as much as created party morale, can of course be exaggerated. After the 1910 elections the Conservative Central Office believed that it had done less well in London 'simply from reasons of defective organisation', and after both 1905 and 1910 there were Conservative reorganisations. Inevitably after defeats the leadership, 'a little winded, and rather irritated ... turns to the investing army, and, addressing the non-commissioned officers, informs them that there is something the matter with their organisation.'³ Even so there is no doubt that the generally superior efficiency of the Conservatives, and the slowness of both Liberals and socialists in recognising the crucial importance of organisation, helps to explain Conservative electoral success in London.

The same rapid exploitation by the Conservatives of new techniques can be seen in the field of propaganda. In 1885 a high proportion of the population was still illiterate, and the outdoor meeting was the most effective method for influencing the electorate. Rhyming slogans which could be chanted by supporters were also widely used. In 1895, for example, the Hammersmith Conservative slogan was:

> Goldworthy's worth his weight in gold,
> Refined, assayed and proved of old;
> And Hammersmith will not be led
> By Steadman in a good man's stead.⁴

But already, although these slogans continued to be used, they were of declining importance. In the 1890s both parties issued a mass of free election leaflets. During the 1895 L.C.C. elections, for example, the Progressive London Reform Union circulated three million leaflets, the Conservative London Municipal Society four and a half million.⁵ In contrast to these efforts the usefulness of outdoor meetings for the major parties was slight, although they continued to

---

¹ *Standard*, 15 December 1909; the local Primrose League had 1500 members.
² *Star*, 8 December 1910; *Standard*, 7 and 12 January 1910.
³ J. Sandars to A. J. Balfour, 19 and 21 January 1910, Balfour Collection; *The Times*, 16 January 1911.
⁴ Election literature, 1895, Bull Collection.
⁵ London Reform Union annual report, 1895; London Municipal Society report, and press cutting 7 December 1895, London Municipal Society Collection.

be important for independent candidates. But even among the socialists there was a growing feeling that more good was done by journalism than by oratory. Robert Blatchford declared in 1897 that 'there are times when meetings are useful; there are cases where open-air speaking does good; but I think open-air speaking often does a great deal of harm. The fact is, oratory has had its day, and is doomed. The new weapon is the Press.'[1]

Blatchford was exaggerating. Until the advent of the wireless it was still essential for a successful politician to have a loud voice. He was also over-optimistic in anticipating that the press would prove the best method of exploiting the new literacy. By 1906 the Conservatives were devoting a far higher proportion of their energies to advertising. Captain Jessel of the London Municipal Society told a journalist in 1912 that he regarded 'hoardings as an infinitely better medium for political advertising than the newspaper. "Everybody sees the hoardings", he says, "and the posters, if cleverly designed, can contain quite as much argument as the average unintelligent voter is likely to understand".' As an example he illustrated a poster in which a man was shown raising a glass of beer, with the slogan 'Municipal Reform means Good Health'. Platform speeches he dismissed as only important in 'keeping up the enthusiasm and fighting spirits' of the election helpers. 'You see exactly the same thing in electioneering that you are, of course, familiar with in business . . . all the paraphernalia of salesmanship or electioneering, as the case may be. The big advertiser calls in the aid of professional experts. . . . The electioneer, if he is to secure the greatest efficiency for his campaign, must do the same.'[2]

These last examples have been taken from local election campaigns. Changes in this field were much more important than in parliamentary elections, for the transition to democracy had scarcely begun before 1885. The system of London local government at that date was still based on the Metropolis Management Act of 1885. The old and originally democratic City Corporation had failed to extend its boundaries with the growth of London. It escaped reform in 1832, and although in 1867 the vote for the Common Council was extended to all £10 ratepayers in the City, the rapid dwindling of the resident population meant that the Corporation remained an archaic system of guilds, livery companies and freemen, with no more than a ceremonial importance in the rest of London. Outside the City the local parochial vestries and the Dean and Chapter of Westminster Abbey were the local authorities. During the 18th and early 19th century most of them delegated their powers for paving, lighting and drainage

[1] *Clarion*, 22 May 1897.   [2] *Printers Ink*, May 1912.

to self-perpetuating bodies of commissioners. The turnpike trusts were consolidated into two Boards in 1826, and in 1834 the Poor Law responsibilities were transferred to Boards of Guardians elected by the ratepayers, with extra votes given to the richer ratepayers. Before 1894 at elections there were no polling stations: the ballot papers were distributed and collected by parish officials. The parish rector and usually the churchwardens were ex officio Guardians. In the area of the future county of London there were 30 Boards of Guardians, with 694 elected and 311 ex officio members (Map 24).

The Metropolis Management Act established a uniform system for the election of vestrymen by the ratepayers. Previously some vestries had been self-electing oligarchies, while others had been open vestries of the entire parish. The smaller vestries were now grouped into 12 Local Boards, composed of delegates from the elected vestrymen, while the 29 larger vestries kept their independence. Part of Woolwich had been given a Board of Health under the 1848 Public Health Act, and this functioned as a vestry in its district (Map 25). The vestries were given powers over the administration of sewers and streets, various health responsibilities, and optional powers to provide housing, baths and washhouses, and cemeteries. The vestrymen elected had to be ratepayers on property of an annual value £40, or in certain poorer districts of £25, and they were elected at annual meetings which any parishioner could attend. Voting was by a show of hands, unless a parish poll was demanded. Polls were not usual, and it was easy for a parishioner without voting qualifications to take part in the vote at the meeting.[1]

In practice, however, the chief problem was not the contested election, but the securing of enough qualified candidates. Even the members of the administrative vestries and boards exceeded 4,000, and there were also those of non-administrative vestries. Consequently it was easy for any publican or house-owner with an interest in preventing the reduction of licenses or the improvement in housing to find a place when he wished. In fact the vestries scarcely used their adoptive powers before the 1880s, and were extremely lax in their health administration, in spite of a number of outstanding medical officers whom they appointed. In 1885, for example, only two vestries were properly attempting to enforce the regulation of numbers in tenements and lodgings. In Clerkenwell, which was subjected to special investigation by the Royal Commission on Housing, 'the two joint dictators of the parish, who had control of the Vestry and its leading Committee, one of them being Chairman of the principal Committee, were, the largest owners in the whole district of Clerkenwell of bad or doubtful property'. Of the 72 vestrymen about

[1] E.g. W. S. Sanders, *Early Socialist Days*, London 1927, p. 72.

30 attended regularly, and of these there were 14 house-farmers 'and 12 publicans who seemed to work very much with them'.[1]

At the same time a Metropolitan Board of Works, composed of delegates from the vestries, with powers over an area practically identical with the future county, was given the responsibility for street improvements and the construction of a sewerage system. In contrast to the vestries it proved an energetic body, although it was suspected of corruption in some of its development schemes. It took over the fire brigade, freed the river bridges of tolls in 1877, promoted the first building regulations, created several new parks, carried out sixteen slum clearance schemes, and built the Thames Embankments and important streets such as Charing Cross Road and Shaftesbury Avenue.

A number of other authorities, such as the Middlesex Quarter Sessions and the Metropolitan Asylums Board, continued to exercise administrative powers in London, and in 1870 another was added by the creation of the London School Board. This Board, which was responsible for starting a universal system of elementary education in London as well as providing further education in some fields, was elected triennially by the ratepayers in eleven divisions, each with between four and seven members. Two of the divisions, Westminster and the City, were small, the remainder extremely large. There were fifty-five members in all. Each elector was able to give as many votes as there were members in his division, and was allowed to plump for a single candidate. The School Board elections therefore offered an opportunity for minority representation (Map 26).

Before the 1880s few of these local elections had been overtly political. In contested elections it was not uncommon for local Ratepayers' Associations to issue lists of recommended candidates, and the Licensed Victuallers' Protection Societies also published recommendations. In Stepney a committee formed in 1884 issued a circular to every 'large owner of property in this district' asking for support.[2] There were also sporadic campaigns by radicals and reformers, generally expressing rebellions by the smaller ratepayers. Consequently radicalism usually took the form of economy. The Bow and Bromley Ratepayers' Association, a radical organisation, in 1878 were 'STRONGLY OPPOSED to the expenditure of £12,000 FOR A NEW VESTRY HALL, Thousands of Pounds for Lawyers Bills, Thousands of Pounds for Surveyors Bills, £20 for Small Pox Hospital! NEXT TO USELESS. Hundreds of Pounds for Turtle Soup, Salmon, Lamb and Green Peas. DINNERS where 36

[1] (Sir Charles Dilke, House of Commons, 4 March 1884) H. Jephson, *The Sanitary Evolution of London*, London 1907, p. 308.
[2] Circular, May 1884, Stepney public library.

Bottles of Champagne WERE DRUNK and 18 Vestrymen WERE DITTO!'[1]

Refreshments and nepotism were typical election issues. The same Association thought 'that the present Vestry will bear a little *fresh blood*, ... all *lucrative appointments* seem to be monopolised by *one family*.'[2] In other parts of the East End religious disputes still provided the most excitement. The churchwardens of St. George's in the East issued a thankful declaration that 'the Protestant Cause has triumphed over the Tools of Jesuitical Tyranny by the Glorious majority of 76 in favour of Messrs Liquorish and Bond, the true friends of the Church and of Civil and Religious Liberty'.[3] Very often the whole system appeared so hopeless that much of the propaganda issued was purely farcical. Electors were invited to the 'THEATRE OF VARIETIES, CABLE STREET. EXTRAORDINARY ATTRACTIONS. THURSDAY, June 12th, In addition to the Usual Programme will be performed the 3rd Act of a NEW COMEDY, entitled FINANCE or the way to help the distressed Stage Manager, Money Takers, Scene Shifters, Bill Posters, Supernumeries, etc., by paying them twice for the work, and supplying them with Refreshments whilst so engaged.'[4] Quizzical posters were issued by 'Anti-Porcine, the Author of "Led by the Nose", not Proboscis, "A Churchwarden's Baby", "Spur On", "Our Needy Relatives", etc.'[5]

At the end of the 1880s, stimulated by the radical campaigns of the *Star*, reform candidates began to stand much more frequently for the vestries and Boards of Guardians, and at the same time the London School Board elections, which had been purely denominational, came to be fought on more political lines with the Nonconformists and Liberal educationists uniting in a Progressive Party. At the same time a series of important changes in the system began.

Firstly, in 1889 the Metropolitan Board of Works was replaced by the London County Council. Its 118 councillors were elected triennially for the parliamentary constituencies on a franchise composed of the householders, freeholders and £10 occupiers of the parliamentary electorate, and in addition including some 80,000 women and peers who had these qualifications, but not including lodgers and those occupying premises provided by their employers. It was thus at first slightly smaller than the parliamentary electorate. At this stage

[1] Bow and Bromley Ratepayers Association election poster, 1878, Poplar public library.
[2] Ibid., c. 1875.
[3] Circular issued by churchwardens of St. George's-in-the-East, c. 1875, Stepney public library.
[4] Election poster, St. George's-in-the-East, 1879, Stepney public library.
[5] Election poster, Poplar, c. 1875, Poplar public library.

the London School Board electorate, at over 700,000, was the widest in operation. In 1900 the London Qualification Act extended the county council vote to all parliamentary electors, and thereafter the L.C.C. electorate was larger than the parliamentary within the county, 826,000 as compared with 690,000 in 1914.

The L.C.C. was the fulfilment of the campaign for a unified London government started by James Firth and his Liberal friends in 1876, who naturally threw themselves with enthusiasm into its first election. L.C.C. elections were thus fought on political lines from the beginning. On the other hand although candidates were selected by the Liberal Associations they preferred in predominately Conservative London to call themselves Progressives, while the Conservative Associations, trusting that the independence of local elections would continue to work to their advantage, gave no overt help to a Moderate Party which was clearly Conservative in inspiration. The elected Council was from the first organised by these two parties each with leaders, whips and party meetings. After two progressive victories the London Municipal Society was formed in 1894, and with Lord Salisbury's declaration that 'we must not be shy of using all our political power and machinery for the purpose of importing sound principles into the government of London', the Conservative Party threw its whole weight into the L.C.C. election. Candidates openly declared their Unionist convictions. In 1898 Joseph Chamberlain urged the Conservatives to 'make it a party fight, gentlemen, based upon party principles, the broad principles which divide us from our opponents'; and although the Progressives attempted after 1895 to conceal their Liberal affiliations through basing their election work on the London Reform Union, the disguise had little practical effect.[1]

The party struggle in the vestry and Guardians' elections, which had been developing in the late 1880s, became much more open at the same time. The principle reason for this was the removal of the property qualifications for candidates and the extension of the vote to all county council and parliamentary electors. The vestry elections remained annual, but the Guardians became triennial. The Liberals formed local Progressive Parties through the London Reform Union which often claimed to be non-political, but the Conservative Central Office offered help in 1894 to any Conservative Association which wished to fight on party lines, and the practice became common.[2]

[1] Gibbon and Bell, op. cit., pp. 90, 595.
[2] E.g. South Kensington Conservative Association General Council minutes, 28 June 1894, statement that the Metropolitan Division of the National Union of Conservative and Unionist Associations would assist constituencies 'who desire to fight municipal elections on party lines'; cf. ibid., 12 December 1890,

Candidates often stood as 'Unionists', parties were formed on the vestries with whips and party meetings to decide on committee nominations and policy, and even where local Ratepayers Associations continued to be overtly responsible for the running of candidates, private lists of recommended Conservatives were circulated.[1]

In 1900 the London vestries were abolished, and replaced by 28 Borough Councils, elected on the same franchise, but triennially instead of annually, with 1,362 councillors replacing the 4,170 vestrymen (Map 27). The boroughs were given mayors and aldermen. At the same time 12 Burial Boards, 187 Boards of Library Commissioners, 10 Boards of Baths and Washhouse Commissioners and 56 Boards of Overseers (who had been responsible for electoral registration), were taken over and their responsibilities given to the new boroughs. They also had powers over street lighting and paving, minor housing schemes, refuse disposal, small open spaces, various minor health powers and optional powers to supply electricity.

The Boards of Guardians continued to be the poor law authorities, and until 1903 the London School Board the education authority. In that year the Education Act for London abolished the Board and transferred its powers to the County Council. The L.C.C. had meanwhile added to the powers which it had inherited from the Metropolitan Board of Works a number of others, principally technical education, increasing health and building control powers, and the operation of the tramway system. Its ambitions to control the water, gas and electricity supply and the port of London were all finally frustrated during the 1900s, and it did not take over the management of the Poor Law and London hospital system until a later date. It

---

[1] Whips and party meetings, e.g. notices issued by two whips to 'the Unionist members of the Clerkenwell vestry' and private printed list of 'Unionist selections for vestry committees', cuttings book, 1896–7, Finsbury public library; 'private' circular issued 30 May 1895 after 'a Meeting of the Unionist Members' of the Poplar vestry, at which 'it was decided to support the following Gentlemen to represent Poplar on the Board of Works. . . . Kindly note that Mr. LOUIS WILLIAMS has been elected as one of the Whips, in place of Mr. BARGE, resigned', Poplar public library; for private lists, e.g. South Kensington Conservative Association minutes, or Bull Collection; for complaints against Conservative lists issued by Ratepayers' Associations, e.g. *Westminster and Lambeth Gazette*, 28 May 1887.

'it was generally the opinion that it was desirable that the election should be fought on strictly party lines' for the L.C.C.; Hammersmith Conservative Association circular, 7 December 1894, 'it has hitherto been the policy of the Conservative Party in this Borough to stand aloof, in a party sense, from Municipal Elections, but, in view of the public declaration of the Radical Party as to their intention of "capturing" the vestries etc., and in fact "sweeping London", and so utilising these Institutions in the interests of Party, it is no longer possible for us to continue to maintain that attitude of neutrality'.

POLITICS AND PARTIES

remained, like the Metropolitan Board, principally concerned with drainage, fire prevention, river embankments, parks, street improvements, health and housing.

During the 1900s local elections were increasingly fought on party lines. There was, however, a new tendency in boroughs where the Labour Party provided a threat for a Municipal Alliance of Liberals and Conservatives to be formed, thus anticipating the future development of national politics. West Ham, East Ham and Poplar had anti-socialist organisations of this kind. There were also Middle Class Defence Leagues formed in some districts, including Hampstead.[1] The party political system was still far from uniform in borough and Guardians' elections, and there were some districts, most notably Stoke Newington, where overt party politics were entirely avoided.

Although none of the local elections produced polling figures generally as high as those in parliamentary elections, the L.C.C. and Borough Council poll was usually approximately 50 per cent. In the vestry elections between 1894 and 1899 it was much lower, and the polls for the Guardians were also generally low, falling to 20 per cent by 1913. It is noticeable that most of the higher polls for Borough Council elections were in middle class districts, and in 1906 every poll of less than 40 per cent was in a working class ward. But just as in the parliamentary elections a strong Labour candidate often provoked an exceptional poll, in local elections there were exceptions to the common working class apathy, notably in Woolwich and Poplar. Even in the Guardians elections these two Boards had polls of 51·5 per cent and 48·9 per cent respectively, compared with an average of 28·1 per cent, in 1907. In borough elections Woolwich frequently exceeded 70 per cent, far more than any other borough. Where important issues appeared to be at stake the apathy disappeared.

This description of local government has ignored the districts beyond the county boundary. Here the Quarter Sessions were the authority until the elected County Councils for Surrey, Essex, Middlesex and Kent were established in 1889. As the suburbs developed, most of them acquired elected Local Boards under the 1848 Public Health Act, and in 1894 these were transformed into Urban District Councils with the combined County Council and parliamentary franchise (Map 27). A few were elected triennially, but in most a third of the councillors retired annually. Some of the suburbs became boroughs, but only West Ham became a County Borough. In

---

[1] Formation of Middle Class Defence League, 19 May 1906, 'to resist extravagance' and 23 June 1906, to support candidates 'to represent their special interests, as had been done in the Labour world', cuttings book, Hampstead public library.

addition there were Boards of Guardians, covering very large areas designated in the rural past of 1834, and School Boards set up under the 1870 Education Act. As the suburbs grew some of the Boards of Guardians and School Boards were divided, further complicating the timing of elections. The powers of the School Boards were transferred to the County Councils in 1902. In a number of the suburbs local elections became party fights, and the School Board elections were fought on denominational lines, but there were rather more districts in which the contests remained individual. Because of the large rural hinterland in each of the counties the elections for the County Councils did not rouse much political interest.

In the earlier 19th century campaigns for the extension of the franchise had been major incidents in political history. In this period this was no longer so, probably because the classes who were wholly or partly disfranchised tended to be poor, socially depressed and thus politically apathetic. Although the programme of radical working men's organisations and later of the Labour Party included adult suffrage, measures of social reform were regarded as of more immediate importance. It was only with the suffragette movement that the franchise itself again became a burning issue.

Women had been given the county vote in 1889, and after 1894 could stand as local election candidates, but even those who were heads of households or property owners were disqualified from the parliamentary electorate by their sex. On the other hand the increased usefulness of women as voluntary election helpers after 1885 helped to fulfil their political interests, and the suffrage movement was unimportant before the formation in 1903 of the Women's Social and Political Union among independent Labour supporters in Manchester. Led by Emmeline Pankhurst, the movement took up its headquarters in London. F. W. and Emmeline Pethick-Lawrence, two Nonconformist London social workers with independent means who had married in 1901, threw their whole weight behind the movement; Emmeline Pankhurst's two daughters Sylvia and Christabel joined their mother, and some militant Lancashire factory girls were planted in the East End. In 1906, with the siege of the house of the rich Hammersmith socialist Dora Montefiore for refusing to pay taxes and the beginning of mass lobbies of Parliament, the militant suffrage movement began. The movement's journal, *Votes for Women*, reached a circulation of 16,000 in 1907, and later 40,000.[1]

In 1908 the democratic constitution of the Women's Social and Political Union was suspended, and Emmeline Pankhurst became the 'autocrat'. A number of supporters, notably the veteran socialist

[1] E. S. Pankhurst, *The Suffragette Movement*, London 1931, p. 223.

Charlotte Despard, withdrew and formed the Women's Freedom League, a smaller organisation, also militant, but democratic. The suffragettes now became progressively more violent, window-breaking, causing disturbances in the House of Commons, chaining themselves to railings in Downing Street, wall-chalking, staging huge outdoor demonstrations, and when imprisoned hunger-striking for release. Very probably a majority of the Liberal Party and of the Labour Party supported the women's claims, but there were a number of outstanding anti-feminists in both Parties and among them was Asquith, the Prime Minister from 1908. Due to his antipathy, although the enfranchisement of women seemed frequently within reach and the militant campaign was suspended during several periods of hope, the measure was delayed until the general introduction of adult male suffrage in 1918. As a result of this delay the movement developed into hysterical violence after 1912. The Pankhursts decided to dispense with the help of the Pethick-Lawrences, who had been made bankrupt in 1912 through damages resulting from window-smashing campaigns. To this was now added arson, picture-slashing, cushion slitting, fuse blowing and acid on golf greens. At the same time Sylvia Pankhurst from 1912 began to build up a more constructive movement among working class East End women, especially in Bow and Bromley where the suffragettes were supported by George Lansbury. In spite of the coolness of many of the Labour leaders, who were not attracted either by the middle class airs or the violent tendencies of most of the suffragette leaders, Sylvia Pankhurst had a considerable following by 1914, when she formed an independent East London Federation of suffragettes. She continued the agitation during the war, with an increasing emphasis on wider social issues.

Except in its effect on George Lansbury's career, and in generally adding to the militant atmosphere which was being produced in the same years by the syndicalist movement and the growth of violence in Ireland, the suffragettes did not affect the main political developments of these years. The political parties were all controlled by men, and although women were more influential in the socialist movement the suffrage issue did not produce important internal struggles among socialists. At most it proved a diversion to women who might have otherwise given their time to the Labour Party.

London politics, as has been shown, was biassed in favour of the wealthier classes. In the mid-19th century this bias had been heavier. This did not, however, mean that before 1885 there had been no attempts by working men to play an independent role in politics. William Newton of the engineers had been an independent Labour candidate at the 1852 general election for Tower Hamlets, the East End parliamentary borough. At the time of the trade union expansion of the early 1870s a Labour Representation League, formed in 1869 and supported by the leading trade unionists of the period, put up parliamentary candidates and six candidates for the first London School Board election, of whom Benjamin Lucraft the cabinet maker was elected. Lucraft was a parliamentary candidate in 1880, and in the 1885 general election three working men standing as Liberals were elected. Sporadic efforts to secure the election of 'a THOROUGH WORKING CLASS REPRESENTATIVE' can thus be found at an early date.[1] For the moment, however, there was little suggestion that if working class representatives were elected their political standpoint would be so distinctive that they could not work within the existing parties. Consequently in 1885 the political choice for the working class lay simply between the Conservative and Liberal Parties.

Between 1885 and 1914 a third choice developed, that of the Labour Party. Because the Labour Party ousted or absorbed the Liberal Party where it rose to dominance, one of the principal concerns of this study is to show why the Liberal Party failed to hold the allegiance of the working class voter. But one of the most important features of the Labour Party was its ability to draw support from formerly Conservative working class voters. Is a concentration on the problems of the Liberal Party justified?

If the London constituencies are grouped on the basis of the social class composition of their electorates, it can be seen quite clearly that even in the 1880s the backbone of the Conservative vote was middle class[2] (Maps 13, 28 and 29). There was never any doubt that the Conservatives were the wealthier of the two parties, and that they had the support of large employers and property owners such as those represented by the London Owners' Committee.[3]

At the same time the Conservatives depended for their electoral success on securing a substantial proportion of the working class vote, and in some elections, such as that of 1900, this share must have been as much as 50 per cent. Unfortunately it is very difficult to prove how this support was held, either in terms of organisations or of issues. Evidence is surprisingly scarce and the historian and political scientist suffer from the general lack of study the 'deferential' worker. It has been observed that deferential and Conservative political attitudes are commonest among craftsmen working in small shops, workers in personal service, and rural immigrants to the

[1] Greenwich Advanced Radical Association poster, 1869, Greenwich public library.
[2] See Appendix A.   [3] *London*, 20 April 1893.

towns. The small scale of London industry, the army of domestic servants and the high proportion of immigrants from the agricultural south and east in its population would lead one to expect a deferential Conservatism in London, and although there is too little contemporary evidence, it tends to support this interpretation.

What is clear is the absence of a Conservative working class movement comparable to radicalism or socialism. Certain trade unions, such as the Watermen and Costermongers, catering for privileged workers and small tradesmen, were regarded as traditionally Conservative, at least until 1906;[1] but they were exceptional, and could not compare with the powerful Conservative cotton unions in Lancashire. Conservative M.P.s with working class constituencies were careful to emphasise that they were 'the True Friends of Labour', and the London Conservative Members frequently received trade union deputations, but such gestures were no more than common political tact.[2] A more vigorous expression of London Conservatism could be found in the anti-union activities of the Free Labour movement, and the bogus unionism of the Kelly-Peters group in Whitechapel which preceded it.[3]

Similarly, although Conservative 'working men' can sometimes be found standing in local elections, they were very frequently insurance agents or self-made men running one man businesses.[4] Even so they were a rarity, and it is significant that they tended to appear, as in Woolwich and Battersea, where a strong labour movement was assisting the Liberals. They appear to be a reaction rather than a spontaneous development. The Conservative agent for Hammersmith in 1897 was paying the election expenses of a working man candidate, and this practice may not have been unusual.[5] Certainly

[1] Watermen, Gosling, op. cit., p. 28, *Daily Chronicle*, 3 January 1906, and *Daily News*, 11 and 15 January 1906; Costermongers, *East London Observer*, 9 March 1901 (Stepney L.C.C. election).

[2] Election leaflets, 1897, etc., London Municipal Society; London Unionist Members Committee minutes, 21 May, 19 October, 3 November 1908, 7 April 1910, 4 May 1911, etc.—deputations from Postmen, National Telephone Company staff, telephone employees ('workmen as opposed to officials'), Cab Drivers, Operative Bakers.

[3] J. Saville, 'Trade Unions and Free Labour', in A. Briggs and J. Saville, *Essays in Labour History*, London 1960.

[4] E.g. Woolwich and Plumstead nominations, *Kentish Independent*, 8 December 1894; Battersea, *South Western Star*, 8 December 1894; Camberwell, *South London Press*, 20 and 27 May 1899.

[5] T. Rutter, 41 Railway Cottages, Willesden Junction to W. Bull, agent for Hammersmith, 28 June 1897, Bull Collection: 'I thank you very much for the kind and generous feeling expressed toward me in your letter of 14th ult. I may state that Mr Payne paid the expenses of election for himself and me on the vestry, and has forwarded me the a/c, with a request, that I will remit half the amount. Will it be convenient to see you at King Street one morning this week

those working men who spoke for propaganda organisations like the Tariff Reform League were professionals, and some of them also worked for anti-trade union organisations.[1]

None of these men became a leading London politician. The Conservative Party's national leaders, while 'entirely in favour' of encouraging working-class parliamentary candidates, in practice believed that it might 'do more harm than good if a working man was selected by the Conservative Party and run with Conservative money. ... The difficulty principally arises from the fact of the Conservative working men outside the Trades Unions not being an organised solid body.'[2] Nor was there a Conservative Labour press outside antiunionism. Thus it is difficult to assess the significance of bodies such as the Working Men's Association which supported Conservative local election candidates in Hampstead in the 1900s, the National Movement of Conservative Working Men in Kensington in the 1890s, or the Unionist Labour League in Lewisham in 1907.[3] They had no recognisable part in the Conservative Party organisation, although the party was anxious to show a minority of working men in its lower ranks; the South Kensington Conservative Association considered adopting a rule in 1890 by which 'at least one working man' from each ward would have been elected to the central committee.[4] It is also difficult to assess the importance of the Conservative clubs, which were being founded as late as 1914, as counters to the radical clubs. Harry Smith, the experienced agent for Bow and Bromley, where the Municipal Alliance claimed a working class membership of 2,000, considered the clubs to be 'in the front rank of their army'.[5] But Charles Booth had found the Conservative clubs in the East End politically lethargic, and not genuinely working class; the members

[1] E.g. *Woolwich Pioneer*, 21 October 1904, *Standard*, 30 July 1908, trade union speakers for Tariff Reform League.

[2] Viscount Chilston, *Chief Whip*, London 1961, pp. 174–8. The Kelly-Peters group were regarded as 'utterly untrustworthy': R. Middleton to Salisbury, 16 July 1885, Akers-Douglas Collection.

[3] Hampstead—26 October and 4 November 1905, cuttings book, Hampstead public library; it was led by G. Buckle, a coster, and J. Dyter, a coffee room keeper, *Hampstead and Highgate Express*, 3 October 1903. Kensington—*Kensington News*, 24 October 1896, 15 May 1897 'practically extinct', but again 15 February 1901. Lewisham—*Kentish Mercury*, 15 February 1907.

[4] South Kensington Conservative Association annual meeting minutes, 12 March 1890.

[5] *East London Advertiser*, 1 July 1911.

---

with reference to it?' Cf. letter on the 1906 general election asserting that Conservatives 'had offered inducements to several labourers in Islington if they would consent to come out as Labour candidates, and so split the working class vote'—*Islington Daily Gazette*, 26 October 1909.

belonged 'mainly to the upper or lower middle class'.[1] There was no London parallel with Lancashire constituencies like Liverpool where the clubs were a self-sufficient and powerful element in the Conservative organisations, supplying a high proportion of the party's officers as well as members.[2]

London working class Conservatism also lacked the Lancashire advantage of a religious issue to provide a distinctive electoral policy. Once again its essential passivity is revealed. The attitudes of a deferential worker, his traditionalism and respect for social superiors, his belief in leadership, could hardly create election issues any more than they could sustain consistent political activity. Most Conservative policies appear as reactions to Liberal proposals; protecting the interests of the Catholics in education, of the liquor trade against temperance reform, of the watermen whose ferries were threatened by Thames tunnels. Although more positive, the demands of Woolwich Arsenal workers for a more aggressive foreign policy and of East Enders for an end to the tide of alien immigrants were essentially labour issues, and came to the front in times of unemployment. Beyond these sectional issues the Conservatives had few policies with which to attract the labour vote, so that East End M.P.s like Claude Hay of Hoxton were forced to challenge the Liberals on their own ground, standing for social reform. The *Daily Chronicle* denounced him as 'scarcely distinguishable from a Social Democrat in his East End utterances';[3] and certainly his electoral speeches indicate once more that working class Conservatism was a reaction, rather than a spontaneous movement.

However radical some Conservatives claimed to be during elections, there is no evidence of Conservative working men who believed that their party might develop into a working class party of social reform. In the case of the Liberal Party there clearly was such a hope after 1885. Consequently the politically active working man was almost always a Liberal or a socialist. Where there is a cause, an opposition will usually be generated; but the real movements in working class politics in this period were the radical movement, the labour movement and the socialist movement; and the most important question was how far they could be realised through the Liberal Party.

[1] Booth, op. cit., I, p. 99.   [2] *The Times*, 16 January 1911.
[3] 28 December 1905: election manifesto, 1906, Shoreditch Public Library.

V

LIBERALS, RADICALS AND LABOUR

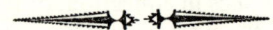

IN the 1880s and 1890s the Liberal Party was faced with a great challenge in London, a challenge which it failed to meet. The mid-19th century middle class electorate had been consistently Liberal, and it was not until 1875 that the Conservative Party secured even a substantial minority representation.[1] By that date the wealthier classes, their principal demands for political reform met, were tending to become more Conservative, leaving Nonconformists as the principal supporters of Liberalism among the middle classes. But with a growing proportion of working class electors it was clearly possible for the Liberal Party to find new causes and ample compensating support. After 1885 the working class were a majority in 38 of the 58 constituencies within the county of London. With a third of the country's population living in chronic poverty there was an obvious need for social measures. Yet in the five general elections of 1885–1900 the Liberal Party, formerly dominant, was able to win only 72 seats to the Conservatives' 218, and in the whole Greater London area the Liberals only twice won more than 10 seats. The loss of London was as serious to the Liberals as that of Birmingham, and a major cause of the long Conservative ascendancy after 1886. The fact that this failure was with a working class electorate, and the internal conflict which was behind it, opened the way for the replacement of the Liberal Party by a Labour Party.

At the same time the socialists were presented with a great opportunity. During these two decades they were replacing radicalism as the typical creed of the politically active working class. The failure of

[1] Between 1832 and 1865 only 7 Conservatives were elected, and in 1835, 1859 and 1865 every London member elected was a Liberal. Subsequent results were: 1868, 21 Liberal, 4 Conservative; 1875, 14 Liberal, 11 Conservative; 1880, 15 Liberal, 10 Conservative.

the socialists to exploit this situation by assisting the development of an independent Labour Party anticipates their similar mistakes and the backwardness of London Labour in the 1900s. Thus for both parties the problems of the 20th century were anticipated and to a large extent set in the last two decades of the 19th century, and especially by the crucial events of 1885–95.

The fundamental cause of the Liberal problem was the need to reconcile its new working class and old middle class supporters. In many parts of the country a gradual transition in the character of the party was made possible by the strength of Nonconformity among artisans and trade union leaders, and in smaller towns by a shared community life. But in London neither of these links existed. The social gulf between the working and middle classes was instead widened by the general religious apathy of the working class, and still more by the bitter hostility between Nonconformity and secularism.[1]

This conflict in fact developed into a political antagonism. In the early 1880s the radical leaders had formulated demands for social legislation for the rural workers, but had found no equivalent 'urban cow'. Land reform was a somewhat unreal issue in a big city. Until the characteristic Labour demands of the 1890s had been suggested by the socialists, the political battles of the secularists served as a cause for the radical London working class. The secularists were only a small, if active group, but the struggle of Bradlaugh to take his seat as an atheist M.P. gave wide attention to their cause, and in 1885 the Working Men's Clubs and Institutes Union elected him as a vice-president.[2] When the Metropolitan Radical Federation was formed, secular societies were allowed to affiliate as representing 'bona fide Radical views'.[3] In the London School Board elections the secularists put up their candidates independently of the Liberals, who supported non-sectarian rather than secular education. Frequent resolutions of the radical clubs in favour of secular education and the abolition of the Blasphemy Laws indicate the widespread working class sympathy for secularism.[4] Finsbury, where the secularists had their headquarters, was significantly early in attacking the middle class monopoly of the Liberal Party. As early as 1879 there were

[1] For evidence of hostility, e.g. *Freethinker*, May 1881; London City Mission, *Socialism amongst the masses and how to deal with it*, 1888. In the 1890s indifference became a more obvious challenge than hostility, but not before; e.g. Booth, op. cit., *Religious Influences*, 7, p. 424.
[2] B. T. Hall, *Our Fifty Years. The Story of the Working Men's Club and Institute Union*, London 1912, p. 89.
[3] *Freethinker*, 7 February 1886.
[4] E.g. *Freethinker*, 7 June 1885, 10 October 1886; Mudie-Smith, op. cit., p. 342.

demands for 'fresh candidates ... from the ranks of labour',[1] and eventually in March 1885 Bradlaugh was adopted as candidate. He stood down, and James Rowlands, a working man and 'advanced freethinker', replaced him.[2] A section of the middle class Liberals seceded to the Conservatives in protest. Similar disputes occurred in many other new constituencies in 1885. G. W. Foote, editor of the *Freethinker*, narrowly missed selection in Walworth.[3] In Hammersmith the radicals had wanted James Beal the veteran municipal reformer as their candidate, but the Liberal Association was in the hands of 'time servers and Whigs', 'meddlesome, narrow-minded bigoted little Bethelites', and passed him over. Eventually a compromise candidate was agreed. 'The hatchet is buried; serene contentment reigns around; the lion and the lamb, the Rev. William Stiggins, of little Bethel, and the Atheistical Socialists, have comfortably nestled together, and are baaing and bleating in one happy fold.'[4]

This religious class friction was accentuated by the separate organisation of working class radicalism and the official Liberal Party. In the past the Liberal dominance had meant that there was little need for an organised party caucus system. As many as five Liberal candidates could stand for a two-member constituency without letting in a Conservative. But even when the Conservative Party became a serious challenge no democratic constituency parties were developed of the kind found in Birmingham and other cities from the 1870s. Before 1885 only Chelsea, where Dilke enlisted the support of a combined committee of the four west London radical clubs, had any kind of popular Liberal organisation, and even here the middle class constituency organisation was a separate body.[5] The strongest Associations were often the most reactionary; the City Liberal Association, the wealthiest in London, according to its one-time secretary depended on bankers and shipowners, 'old fashioned free traders' who 'had never heard or were violently hostile to' social legislation.[6] When a promising agitation for London municipal

[1] *Islington Gazette*, 14 October 1879.   [2] *Freethinker*, 11 July 1886.
[3] Ibid., 21 June 1885.
[4] *West London Advertiser*, (a Liberal paper) 25 April, 23 May 1885.
[5] The Combined Committee consisted of delegates from the Eleusis, Cobden, Progressive and Hammersmith Clubs, and was often represented at radical demonstrations: e.g. *Radical*, 19 February 1881 &c, and Combined Political Committee of the Four Radical Clubs, report for April 1885 (copy in National Liberal Club); in addition there was the Chelsea Labour Association, a weekly meeting of Dilke's trade unionist supporters, e.g. *Labour Standard*, 13 January 1883; and the official Liberal Association. The Chelsea constituency was divided in 1885, but the Association was probably similar to the 'caucus', in which delegates were a mixture of Whigs, tradespeople and working men, described in C. Dilke to J. Chamberlain, 7 May 1886, Dilke Collection.
[6] F. W. Galton, manuscript autobiography.

reform was begun in 1881 with the foundation of the Municipal Reform League, and appeared capable of uniting the wings of the party in a common cause, the Liberal Associations gave its trade unionist organiser 'scarcely any support'.[1] It was their indifference, as much as the violent and unscrupulous Conservative opposition, backed by four Liberal M.P.s who were also City Aldermen, and the timidity of the Liberal government, which caused the failure of the movement. No organised preparation was made for the redistribution and new constituencies of 1885.[2] The London and Counties Liberal Union, set up in 1885, was a purely advisory educational and propaganda body.

In contrast the radical clubs provided a lively focus for working class political enthusiasm. In spite of their regular political lectures the primary function of the clubs was always social, and they never provided party organisation or substantial funds. But in the 1880s their political activity was a rising force, stimulated in turn by the Eastern Question, the agitation against Irish coercion, Henry George's campaign for land reform in 1882–3 and the electoral changes of 1885. The club politicians were fully aware of the distinction of their radicalism, secularist and republican, with its traditions of Paine, the Chartists and the French Commune, from the milder doctrines of official Liberalism.[3] The clubs had their minimum political programme, to which members were expected to subscribe: in the early 1880s it was usually adult suffrage, free education, disestablishment, payment of M.P.s and land nationalisation.[4] As early as 1881 the *Radical* was urging the formation of a new party independent of the Liberals, and it was partly as a response that the Democratic Federation was formed. As the Social Democratic Federation (S.D.F.) it was to become the first English socialist party. It failed to hold the initial support of the clubs, which formed their own organisation in 1884–6. In 1884 club federations modelled on the Chelsea combined committee were formed in Hackney and Finsbury to 'promote and protect the political interests of the working class'.[5] This led to the formation in 1886 of the Metropolitan Radical Federation, to which

[1] John Lloyd, *London Municipal Government: History of a Great Reform 1880–88*, London 1910, p. 12.
[2] 'The redistribution Act turned London upside down. The old organisations, few of which were of a representative character, disappeared, and the new constituencies were thrown upon their own resources': Liberal Central Association, 'Confidential circular, Organising Commission for London', February 1886 (copy at National Liberal Club).
[3] Hostility to official Liberalism, e.g. *Radical*, 18 December 1880, *Radical*, December 1886; Booth, op. cit., Vol. I, p. 99; *People's Press*, 4 January 1890; *Star*, 2 February 1889.
[4] E.g. *Islington Gazette*, 5 May 1884.
[5] Ibid., 8 April, 5 May and 14 September 1884.

clubs and secular societies were affiliated. In 1886–7 the clubs again showed their independence by uniting with the socialists in the free speech struggles against the police suppression of outdoor meetings, culminating in the famous clashes in Trafalgar Square.

Divided between these two wings, the Liberal Party lost its hold on London in the general elections of 1885 and 1886. In 1885 it failed to win the new working class constituencies as it had hoped; in 1886, on the Home Rule issue, it suffered a widespread and disastrous loss of its traditional middle class support. Only ten seats were held. Even in the national Liberal debacle, the failure in London was especially severe. Both elections showed that the Conservative and Liberal Parties were already divided on class rather than religious lines in London, and that the working class voter was the only hopeful basis on which to rebuild the Liberal Party.[1] It was also noticeable that of the ten London members, three were working men, including James Rowlands who had captured East Finsbury from a Conservative— the only Liberal gain in 1886.[2] Already in the summer of 1886 the newly appointed London Liberal organiser, Renwick Seager, was reporting that of the Associations which he had formed those in the East End, 'mainly composed of working men', were 'by far the best'.[3] But his optimism was premature: radical suspicions were not easily laid. When Seager co-ordinated the new constituency Associations into the London Liberal and Radical Union in 1887, the Metropolitan Radical Federation protested vigorously at the usurpation of its title. The *Pall Mall Gazette* in return denounced 'these malcontents' without 'a single penny for any political purpose'.[4]

The Liberal Party was in fact in an impossible dilemma. To win the working class support it needed, it would have to adopt a more radical policy. But radical demands, such as land nationalisation and the abolition of the House of Lords, would have alienated the remaining middle classes. The middle classes could not be dispensed with for two reasons. Firstly, their money was essential to an efficient organisation. Systematic canvassing to put supporters on the register could be crucial to election results, but it was expensive. In analysing the election failure of 1885, a Liberal Central Association circular reported that 'one of the chief causes of this want of proper organisation is the poverty of many of the constituencies... (where) the Liberal Party is composed of working men, who are most willing to contribute

---

[1] See Appendix A.
[2] George Howell, Bethnal Green North East; W. Randal Cremer, Shoreditch Haggerston. Joseph Leicester, who had been elected in 1885 for West Ham South, was among those defeated in 1886. Rowlands was regarded as a working man although a self employed watchsmith (*Star*, 29 April 1891).
[3] *Pall Mall Gazette*, 20 August 1886.   [4] Ibid., 11 January 1887.

voluntary help in person, but who cannot afford to subscribe the necessary money for a permanent organisation'.[1] The very fact that the Home Rule desertions had been a revolt of the wealthy meant that the remaining subscribers were all the more essential. This was in fact the fatal obstacle, as the Fabians were to admit, to any conversion of the Liberal Party by infiltration. 'The swamping of the backward or Whig element in the caucuses by an influx of Socialists or Radicals ought to be the easiest thing in the world. Nevertheless, the moment it is carried beyond a certain point, it is effectively checked by the bankruptcy of the swamped caucus. Political operations cost money; and whereas there is always sufficient to be had from a few rich Liberal subscribers in the district or from headquarters as long as the caucus jogs along quietly in the old Liberal rut, the moment it moves too fast supplies are cut off.'[2]

Middle class supporters were also needed for their votes. Although the franchise was more democratic after 1885 the bias of the electoral system greatly exaggerated their influence. The difficulty in securing the registration of working class lodger voters, the high proportion of removals in working class districts, and the difficulty, especially for those living long distances from their work, of getting to the poll before the booths closed, all made a reliance on working class votes extremely hazardous. A comparison between religious attendance and polling figures suggests that in Bethnal Green, where Nonconformists were a mere 1·3 per cent of the population, they could have been 16 per cent of the poll in 1892. In West Ham they could have accounted for two in every three Liberal votes.[3]

These facts help to explain why throughout this period the essential tone of London Liberalism remained closer to Nonconformity than to working class radicalism. The attempt to transform the Party organisation was a failure. By 1889 the *Star* was denouncing the new Liberal Associations, which Seager had hoped would be representative, as weak, hostile to the radical clubs, and often attended 'by a score of people, who nominally elect about 50 to 150 councillors for their ward'.[4] The Liberal parties on most London vestries and Boards

---

[1] Liberal Central Association, 'Confidential Circular, Organising Commission for London', February 1886.

[2] *Fabian Election Manifesto* (1892), Fabian Tract No. 40.

[3] This is intended to be a suggestive comparison, not an estimate. The figures of male Nonconformist attendance in Mudie-Smith, op. cit., cannot account for those Nonconformist men attending chapel on the survey Sunday who were Conservative voters, or who abstained, or who were not qualified to vote by local residence or property, or who were aged 16–21; nor, on the other hand, for those Nonconformist Liberal voters who were absent from chapel on the Survey Sunday.

[4] *Star*, 2 February 1889.

of Guardians continued, even after the removal of property qualifications in 1894, to be controlled by local tradesmen. The Progressive Party on the School Board remained typically Nonconformist and largely clerical, refusing electoral co-operation with secularist radicalism. Its electoral organisation in 1894, when it at last won control of the Board, was under the nominal Presidency of John Burns, but most 'labour' candidates were clergymen, and the secretary and leading spirit was the great Westbourne Park preacher and later crusader against the Balfour Education Act, Dr. Clifford.[1] The Progressive Party on the L.C.C., with its annual Citizen Sunday and its temperance policy, supported by the election manifestoes of the London Nonconformist Council, led by Nonconformist laymen such as John Benn, Corrie Grant and Passmore Edwards (the last an indispensable financial supporter), was not made very different by the inclusion of a genuine 'labour bench' after 1892. The Progressive Party in 1889 consisted, with the exception of John Burns, of professional and business men, and it remained in their control, ultimately to pass in the years of its decline to the leadership of a Nonconformist clergyman, Scott Lidgett.

Even if it failed to divest itself of this essentially middle class Nonconformist character, the Liberal Party was able to make a remarkable recovery in London at the 1892 election, and this recovery appears to have been based on working class votes. Although the peculiarities of the registration system make accurate comparison difficult, Charles Booth's social survey can be used to estimate the proportion of middle class electors in each constituency. From this it emerges quite clearly that in the 22 constituencies in which over 80 per cent of the electors were working class the total poll, the Liberal vote and the Liberal share of the vote were all higher than in any other election between 1885 and 1900. 17 of them were won. On the other hand the Liberal performance in middle class constituencies, particularly when compared with 1885, was decidedly less impressive. Nor can this result be explained by the Irish support of the Liberals in this election, for, as has been indicated in Chapter Three, the Irish vote was a slight asset.

It has been widely accepted that this labour-based Liberal victory was to a considerable degree due to the tactics of the Fabian Society in infiltrating the Liberal Party and winning support for working class candidates and policies.[2] As we shall see in Chapter Seven,

[1] The 'labour' representatives elected were Graham Wallas and five clergy, Copeland Bowie, Jephson, Carlile, Oxford and Headlam.
[2] The view prevails in Fabian circles, e.g. M. Cole, *The Story of Fabian Socialism*, London 1961, p. 47; Fabian claims are treated with respect by S.

there is very little substance in this view, which has prevailed chiefly through the longevity of its originators, Bernard Shaw and the Webbs. The only Fabian who played a crucial part in these years, Annie Besant, was working in a different direction from the Fabian leaders, attempting to bring socialists and radicals together into an independent political party. Her reputation as a secularist and her ability as an orator gave her an outstanding influence over London radicals and enabled her to unite them with the socialists in the free speech struggles. But as a whole the Fabians chose to work through the Liberal organisation and attempted to recruit radical and socialist members to break down the isolation of the Liberal Associations, thus merely supporting the efforts of Seager, and there is no evidence that they succeeded where he failed.[1] Nor is there any particular issue on which Liberal policy can be shown to be due to Fabian influence.[2] The real motive forces in the Liberal recovery were the *Star* newspaper and the trade union boom of 1889–92.

First published in January 1888 by T. P. O'Connor, the *Star* set out at once to be the paper of the London working classes, and as such it achieved an unprecedented daily circulation—140,000 at once, and by the summer of 1889 279,000. Shaw later claimed that the Fabians promptly 'collared the *Star* by a stage-army stratagem, and before the year was out had the assistant editor, Mr. H. W. Massingham, writing as extreme articles as Hyndman had ever written in Justice.'[3] At times he was willing to admit the claim was an exaggeration, and once he even arranged a lecture to describe the permeation of the *Star* 'and how soon it was checked'.[4] If the Fabians were early in lobbying the *Star* with letters, so was Engels, who found 'that at the *Star* office great weight is laid upon such bombardments with letters from the outside public'.[5] Massingham did not in fact

[1] In addition to the contemporary press, the Fabian Society archives, and the Shaw, Wallas and Passfield Collections are available; the absence of evidence would appear to be conclusive.

[2] Examined at length in A. M. McBriar, *Fabian Socialism and English Politics 1884–1918*, Cambridge 1962; the Passfield Collection, which has since become available, is equally negative.

[3] G. B. Shaw, *The Fabian Society: Its Early History*, London 1892, p. 18: the story is repeated in Briggs, op. cit., p. 346.

[4] Typescript syllabus, 5 June 1896, correspondence with Fabian Society. Shaw Collection.

[5] F. Engels to L. Lafargue, 14 May 1889, Friedrich Engels, Paul et Laura Lafargue, *Correspondence*, Paris 1956, 2, p. 257.

Maccoby, *English Radicalism*, 1886–1914, London 1953, pp. 58–62, 90–91. The Fabian claims with regard to the L.C.C. Progressive Party are accepted by Maccoby, op. cit., pp. 411–12, Halévy, op. cit., pp. 162, 239–41, Pelling, op. cit., p. 96, and Briggs, op. cit., pp. 341–50.

join the Fabians until 1891, and when Shaw wrote political articles O'Connor refused to print them.[1]

The political intention of the *Star* was clear from its first number, and requires no external explanation. It announced 'war on all privilege' and that any policy, even if 'socialistic', 'will be esteemed good or bad by us as it influences for good or evil the lot of the masses of the people'.[2] It rapidly settled for a programme emphasising housing, land reform and progressive taxation. By March 1889 it had added free education and libraries, the humanising of the poor law and prisons, and labour issues such as hours, conditions, and 'work for the workers'.[3] On this programme it hoped to found a new progressive Liberalism, drawing together the Liberal Associations, the radicals, and where possible the socialists. Although the Fabians were scarcely mentioned before July 1888, the activities of John Burns and the rest of the socialist group led by H. H. Champion were reported from the start.[4] Where socialists were damaging Liberal interests they were freely attacked. 'We regard the organisation of London Radicalism as the first great work of the *Star* ... Thanks to our efforts the stupid ostracism of socialists has come to an end; and, on their side, Socialist organisations have abandoned much of the wild talk, the "viewy" aims, the impracticable methods which they had inherited from German sources.'[5]

The *Star*'s first year was one of undoubted electoral progress. It campaigned against the corruption of the London vestries, and at the May elections there were greatly increased polls and notable gains for the reformers on nearly twenty vestries. It then turned to the School Board election. The system of voting allowed each elector as many votes as there were vacancies in each of eleven large divisions, and the separate lists of candidates issued by Nonconformists and secularist radicals in previous elections had resulted in a Conservative Church majority. Annie Besant had already started her own election campaign and was urging the formation of joint democratic committees.[6] The *Star* took this up. 'We hope to see a "Democratic Joint Committee" formed in each School Board division, consisting of representatives from every working men's club, political associa-

---

[1] W. Pope and others, *The Story of the Star, 1888–1938*, London 1938, p. 30.
[2] *Star*, 17 January 1888.
[3] Ibid., 22 March 1889. Maccoby, op. cit., p. 59, prints a much more extreme programme for the *Star*, 8 August 1888, but this is from a letter signed 'S.W.' and not editorial policy. 'S.W.' claimed that the programme had been picked up in the street. If this was part of the stage army stratagem it had no discernible consequences on editorial policy.
[4] *Star*, 17 January 1888; the first prominent mention of the Fabians is ibid. 7 July 1888.
[5] Ibid., 17 January 1889.   [6] *Link*, May-June 1888.

tion, or other popular organisation within the area. The co-operators, the Nationalists, the Socialists, must all be included.'[1] The committees were federated into a Central Democratic Committee. They failed to get the support of the Liberal Associations, in spite of the omission from the *Star* programme of secular education, and eventually with one exception the *Star* recommended only candidates supported by the Nonconformist-controlled Liberal School Board Election Committee. Among these were Annie Besant in Tower Hamlets and Stewart Headlam in Hackney, and both were elected. Although Fabians, both owed their adoption not to permeation but to their position with the radicals.[2] More significant for the future was A. G. Cook, put up by the London Society of Compositors with the intention of influencing the contracts policy of the Board.[3] Together with Headlam and Besant he induced the Conservative Board to impose trade union rates on its contractors, the first public body in the country to do so.

The School Board election was followed in January 1889 by the election of the first London County Council, replacing the indirectly elected Metropolitan Board of Works. The Council's powers were limited and its annual budget was subject to parliamentary control. The Conservatives were probably confident with their easy majority of London M.P.s that the Council, elected on a narrower franchise, excluding the lodger vote, would be politically safe, and they neither anticipated nor answered the vigorous Liberal response to the plan. In August 1888 the London Liberal and Radical Union resolved on a programme based on the demands of the Municipal Reform League in the early 1880s, in turn derived from J. B. Firth's *Municipal London* of 1876.[4] Working class housing was emphasised, and control by the Council demanded of London markets, gas, water, police, hospitals and poor law. The *Star* issued this programme as *Questions to Candidates*, adding as new demands the taxation of land values and 'the prohibition of sweating and the denial of contracts to unfair masters'. 'It is the condition of London question which is to the fore,

[1] *Star*, 12 July 1888.
[2] Annie Besant had failed to work with the Marylebone Joint Committee, which refused to include secular education in its programme. In Tower Hamlets the weaker Liberal Associations, aware of her outstanding popularity among radicals and secularists dropped one of the official Liberal candidates for the division, and she was elected top of the poll. (*Link*, 11 August and 24 November 1888.) Headlam, popular as a land reformer and a clerical sympathiser with secularists, headed the list of candidates chosen by the Hackney Liberal Associations. (*Star*, 18 October 1888.) Since Hackney was the sphere of influence Professor Stuart, the radical leader whom Sidney Webb regarded as the principal opponent of permeation, it was not a likely district for manipulation.
[3] London Society of Compositors annual report, 1889.
[4] *Star*, 15 August 1888.

and must steadily be kept there ... The programme must be wide enough to include the most advanced section of the democracy'—including the socialists.¹ For although the Fabians had not yet realised the possibilities of the reform programme, and produced neither candidates nor literature for the election,² the first argument for municipal socialism had already been published by H. M. Hyndman in his pamphlet *A Commune for London*. At the time of the election he contributed articles to the *Pall Mall Gazette*,³ and four members of the S.D.F. including John Burns stood as candidates.

As part of its effort to rally all possible support the *Star* not only vigorously attacked discreditable candidates selected by the Liberal Associations, and ran a special campaign against former members of the old Metropolitan Board, but successfully worked to secure a straight fight for Burns in Battersea, and in its final list supported three other socialists who were not standing against progressive Liberals.⁴ The reformers had the advantage of a relatively fresh register, and the Conservatives, who deprived themselves of their normally superior electoral organisation by trying to keep the contest on non-party lines, found themselves a minority of 50 in a council of 118. The *Star* followed up the election by insisting that the reformers must keep their pledges. 'The progressive party must know its mind, select its leader, fix its programme ... There must be no weak concessions, no maundering—no parleying.'⁵ By the end of the summer bills for wider powers had been introduced into Parliament. The model labour policy initiated by the School Board was adopted, and pressure from Burns kept the Council to it. By 1891 an ambitious 15-acre slum clearance scheme at Bethnal Green had been planned.

The *Star* had declared after the results that there was 'a great Radical revival going forward, an immense springtide of democratic sentiment'.⁶ There is little evidence for this. The club radicals played a small part in the election. During the years of economic depression of 1884–7 the younger politically-minded working men had been turning to socialism, and as the number of socialist branches in-

---

¹ *Star*, 6 December 1888.
² Professor Briggs (*Victorian Cities*, p. 341) states that *Facts for Londoners* came out 'on the eve of the first elections to the London County Council'. In fact it was only published nine months afterwards. He also writes that in January 1889 after the Progressive victory 'the Fabian Society was almost alone in giving a lead', (p. 348), and appears to suggest that Dilke and a 'Fabian stiffening' (p. 349) were elected with the Progressive Party in 1889. None of these suggestions is true.
³ *Pall Mall Gazette*, 19 January 1889.
⁴ *Star*, 7, 10 and 16 January 1889.   ⁵ Ibid., 19 January 1889.
⁶ Ibid.

creased, so secularism, the spirit of traditional radicalism, declined. Between 1885 and 1889 its London strength was halved. It was no coincidence that the only working man on the first L.C.C. was John Burns, socialist hero of the free speech struggles. There was more truth behind the *Star*'s comment that the other 'socialist candidates are nowhere; but the best and most practicable items in their programme have been taken over by both parties'.[1] The real lesson of the election was that the Progressives, by standing on a thoroughly radical programme, had been able to take the wind out of the socialist sails.

The second motive force of the Liberal recovery, the great expansion of trade union activity set off by the economic boom of 1888–91, was to drive the Liberals further in this direction. There had been notable trade union activity in politics in the 1860s and early 1870s, but the weak London trade unions of the 1880s had not continued these efforts. The London Trades Council had made no serious effort to sponsor Labour candidates, in spite of resolutions in 1883, 1885 and 1888, and the three London Liberal working class M.P.s did not represent significant local trade union interests.[2] While the first Labour councillor in Birmingham had been elected in 1880 and in Sheffield in 1886,[3] the first genuine local trade union candidate elected in London was Cook of the Compositors in the 1888 School Board election.

This situation was transformed by the advent of the new unionism. The Gas Workers' secretary Will Thorne and the Dockers' leaders Ben Tillett, Tom Mann and John Burns were active socialists convinced of the need for working class political action, and the new unions at once entered the political field. In October 1889 the Gas Workers put up two candidates for the Barking School Board, supported by an election committee of 1,600, and celebrated their victory by a torchlight procession of 10,000.[4] A month later in the West Ham Council elections and aldermanic bye-elections four new unionists were elected, including Walsh, the London secretary of the Sailors and Firemen's Union. Lambert of the Canning Town dockers was elected with the Gas Workers' support, top of the poll in the bye-election 'despite the *Star*'s declaration that he had allied himself with the Tories'.[5] Of the other three candidates two stood against sitting Liberals. The third was W. R. Athey, of the General Railway

[1] Ibid., 18 January 1889.
[2] Rowlands was a watch-case maker, a tiny trade; Howell a bricklayer and Cremer a carpenter, important trades but not very well organised in London. Howell did not even belong to the London Bricklayers, while Cremer had quarrelled with the Carpenters (Postgate, op. cit., pp. 222, 336 and 290–2).
[3] Clegg, Fox and Thompson, op. cit., p. 286.
[4] *Justice*, 19 October 1889.   [5] *Labour Elector*, 30 November 1889.

Workers' Union branch at Stratford; after his election the Compositors subscribed to his wages fund.[1] These successes stimulated further candidatures in other parts of London in 1890, and more in the following years. Among those elected was Campion Watson, the General Railway Workers' Union secretary, in North Kensington, J. Cole the Vestry Employees' Union secretary in Camberwell, and Will Steadman the Bargebuilders' leader in Mile End. After a year on the vestry Steadman found 'that as regards labour there is not much to choose between either party', and ran a campaign in 1891 with Tom Mann, securing the election of eleven more labour members.[2] As the number of these candidates increased, more of them can be found standing with Liberal or Conservative support, but from the beginning they generally preferred to call themselves 'labour' candidates. They invariably stood for trade union wages and conditions, and this labour question was frequently raised in vestry elections where there were no labour candidates after 1890. The climax of the movement was reached with the abolition of property qualifications in December 1894, well after the strength of the new unionism had started to decline, and as a result the candidates in most districts failed badly. Even so, in Battersea, West and East Ham, Barking, Edmonton, Walthamstow and the various Poplar and Southwark vestries there was a strong working class element elected, and a small but significant minority on several other vestries.

The pioneers of this labour representation were the Gas Workers, Dockers, Railway Workers and Vestry Employees. In their 1892 report the Gas Workers claimed to have eighteen members elected to local councils and boards throughout the country, and their secretary Will Thorne, himself a West Ham councillor, expressed an 'earnest desire that all Members make the 8 hours a test question in all elections and make no distinction between the two political parties, as from a labour standpoint they are one and the same'. The *Docker's Record* urged similar attitudes. Municipal bodies 'can and must be controlled by the workers themselves. First of all, wherever possible, competent and reliable trade unionists should be chosen as candidates for these different boards, and meetings of an educational and explanatory character should be held, so that a real interest shall be created in the work of the boards. If this cannot be done, then candidates only should be supported who are prepared to support a labour programme . . .'[3]

Although an advance in local labour representation can be found in a number of large towns in these years, in London it was especially rapid. Similarly, although the London Trades Council followed

[1] London Society of Compositors annual report, 1889.
[2] *Star*, 13 May 1891.   [3] *Docker's Record*, October 1890.

Manchester and Liverpool in sponsoring labour candidates, its swing from inactivity to wholehearted political intervention was much more dramatic.

Nearly every Dockers' branch affiliated to the London Trades Council in 1890. Ben Tillett, their secretary, believed it 'ought to be the Workman's Parliament for London',[1] and Tom Mann, the union president, led a reforming group. The affiliations of Compositors, Engineers and Gas Workers helped to treble the Trades Council membership between 1888 and 1891 and to bring it to a militant standpoint. It was reorganised with an effective committee system, a lecture bureau, and a team of experienced leaders able to give effective assistance to an unorganised revolt such as that of the busmen in 1891. In May 1891 it resolved to set up its own political party, a Labour Representation League. It was to have branches and 'a central exchequer for the reception of small regular contributions from the workers of London for the purpose of running and supporting Labour candidates for Parliament.'[2] The League was launched in November, and in spite of Liberal opposition it supported five candidates, including four members of the S.D.F., at the School Board election, and although none were elected their polls were high: over 10,000 in three of the eleven divisions. In March 1892 at the L.C.C. election it issued a manifesto for the labour candidates, including the S.D.Fers, 'irrespective of creed or sect',[3] and among the victorious Progressives nine labour men were elected. The tenth labour man was narrowly defeated, and two of the S.D.Fers polled up to 2,000 votes. Three more labour men were elected among the ten aldermen, including Ben Tillett.[4] The twelve at once formed a distinct 'labour bench', with their own party meetings.

The 'labour triumph' of the L.C.C. election did not result in the

[1] Dock, Wharf and Riverside Labourers' Union Annual report, 1890.
[2] London Trades Council minutes, 14 May 1891.
[3] Ibid., 11 February 1892.
[4] The labour councillors elected were Burns (Battersea), Charles Freak (Bethnal Green North East—Boot Operatives), Fred Henderson (Clapham), F. C. Baum (North Kensington—Upholsterers), Frank Smith (North Lambeth), Ben Cooper (Bow and Bromley—Cigar Makers), W. C. Steadman (Stepney—Bargebuilders), A. Mercer (St. George's in the East—Seamen), Will Crooks (Poplar—Coopers). Tom Chambers (Woolwich—retired engineer) was defeated but elected an alderman, with Ben Tillett and H. R. Taylor (Bricklayers). Edward Cray (Dulwich, S.D.F.) polled 1999, and John Ward (Wandsworth S.D.F.) polled 2724; Ward narrowly missed selection as an alderman (*Star*, 10 March 1892). The labour bench did not apparently include Sidney Webb (Deptford), H. Keylock (Deptford—retired Carpenter), or prominent radicals such as James Tims (Battersea—secretary of the Metropolitan Radical Federation) and Aeneas Smith (Chelsea—Eleusis Club), who were also elected as Progressives in 1892.

formation of a strong independent Labour Party in London. This was partly because the economic boom had ended and trade union activity was contracting. But it was also due to the character of the socialist movement in London. The political activity of the new unionism sprang from the socialism of its leaders. The London Trades Council which set up the Labour Representation League in 1891 had a socialist majority on its executive committee.[1] Seven of the twelve labour members of the L.C.C. were socialists.[2] Apart from the contracts policy, the specific political demands of labour were all taken from the socialists—the eight hour day, the labour exchange and free meals for schoolchildren. But neither of the two dominant London socialist organisations, the S.D.F. and the Fabians, were really interested in the idea of a new party based on the working class rather than on a political creed.

The Fabian Society had grown rapidly in these years; it set up an office with a fulltime secretary, started *Fabian News*, formed a series of active local groups, and reached a London membership of nearly 400 by 1893. The group in Poplar included local trade unionists and took the lead in forming the Poplar Labour Electoral Committee in 1892, a body which in the 1900s helped to form a local Labour party. But apart from this group the Fabians were overwhelmingly middle class in membership. They felt more at ease in the Liberal Associations, where their views were tolerated and their support rewarded by selection as Liberal election candidates. The fear of demagogy and the political wilderness prevented enthusiasm for independent labour politics, and during the 1890s the Webbs in particular were as savage as the Liberals in their attacks on the Independent Labour Party.

In the S.D.F. the principal obstacle was Hyndman, who controlled the party office and its paper *Justice*. He also appears to have been afraid, as a middle class man, of losing his influence in a party based on class rather than political principle. Between 1888 and 1891 the S.D.F., although by far the largest socialist party in London, failed to increase its membership. Some of the leading working class members, including Burns and Mann, were so infuriated by Hyndman's scorn of trade unions that they left the party. Nevertheless, none of the various attempts of the secessionists to form an alternative party in London succeeded. Even when the national Independent Labour Party (I.L.P.) had been established, its London branches could attract the consistent support of no prominent London labour

---

[1] The executive committee in May consisted of H. R. Taylor, Baum, Cooper, Bateman, Hammill, Lyons, Macdonald, Steadman and Pamphilon; all declared socialists except for Taylor, Cooper and Pamphilon.
[2] Burns, Henderson, Baum, Smith, Steadman, Crooks and Tillett.

leader and were riddled with dissensions. London socialists were attracted to the clear political standpoints of Marxist Social Democrats or anti-Marxist Fabians rather than to an undefined middle view. The ground left between the S.D.F. on the one hand and the Liberals and Fabians on the other was a no man's land, the resort of the unstable and outcast, of the anarchists, the Engels entourage and the suspect ex-Tory H. H. Champion; impossible ground on which to found a party.

The unwillingness of the S.D.F. and the Fabians to support an independent Labour Party allowed the Liberals to recover the initiative. The Liberal press was immediately sympathetic to the new unions and supported most of the strikes during 1889. Later it was more discriminating, in the case of the *Star* because of shareholders' revolts in 1890 and 1891. The wave of non-party labour candidates was at first officially resisted; in 1890 the *Speaker*, the new paper of the Liberal leadership, was urging a 'judicial' attitude on the claims of labour[1] and the *Star* opposed some of the first labour candidates in West Ham, where the Council was already under the control of Liberal tradesmen. But the failure of this and of the attempt at the 1891 School Board election to crush the labour vote showed clearly that resistance would only damage the Liberals. The *Star* more usually supported labour men in local elections, claiming them as radicals. By 1891 the *Speaker* was urging that labour candidates with 'breadth of view and intellectual calibre ... should be brought forward and treated as friends', and in February 1892 applauded the central office's 'genuine and unfailing interest in labour representation'.[2] When John Benn in the spring of 1891 began to organise the 1892 L.C.C. election for the Progressive Party he 'conferred with the London Trades Council and the representatives of the Labour Party and as a result the Liberal and Radical Associations cordially joined hands with the Labour candidates.'[3] Ten labour candidates were given straight fights by the Liberal Associations, and all but three relied on the Liberals to organise their election campaign. The Labour Leagues formed at Woolwich and Clapham for the election, the Labour Electoral Committee at Poplar and to a large degree the London Trades Council Labour Representation League thus owed their existence to official Liberal encouragement, and once elected the 'labour bench' of nine councillors and three aldermen was absorbed without difficulty. Unlike John Burns, whose Labour League of supporters in Battersea was able to raise an adequate wages fund, the new labour members were unable to give enough time to be

[1] *Speaker*, 22 February 1892.
[2] Ibid., 7 November 1891, 20 February 1892.
[3] *Pall Mall Gazette*, 8 March 1892.

influential councillors. Most were satisfied with places on minor committees and some like Tillett scarcely appeared.[1] The Council continued to be run by a professional inner circle.

At the general election in the summer of 1892 the Liberals again encouraged a number of labour candidates. The three elected in 1886 stood again. In Battersea John Burns was officially supported by the Liberal Association, and in West Ham South Keir Hardie, who had been adopted by the radical half of the disorganised local Liberal Party in 1890, was eventually secured a straight fight. Havelock Wilson, the Seamen's leader, was the adopted Liberal candidate in Deptford before he decided to stand independently in Middlesbrough.[2]

These electoral arrangements were accompanied by the presentation of election programmes designed to catch the labour vote. At the L.C.C. election the Progressive programme of 1889 was repeated. It had been written up in the interval by Sidney Webb with the addition of one item—the municipalisation of the docks, made topical by the dock strike. The programme for the general election was adopted at the 1891 Newcastle party conference, but the issues of London importance, housing legislation and the taxation of ground values, had already been adopted by the Conference in 1888. The principal labour demand, the legal eight hour day, was rejected, in spite of the fact that at the London Liberal and Radical Union conference in November 1889 the future socialist George Lansbury, then the Liberal agent in Bow and a member of the Bromley branch of the Gas Workers, carried the proposal 'with a fiery honest rough eloquence that held the meeting breathless'[3]—and gave an indication of the political earnestness of the new unionism. There is no evidence that the Newcastle Programme owed anything to the Fabians; the Fabian draft eight hours bill of November 1889 only served to confuse the issue, while the resolutions of June 1889 of some six London Liberal Associations in favour of a modest programme drafted by Webb in 1888 had no discoverable effect. It was not the measures proposed which were remarkable, but the fact that the party was pledged to them as a programme, and this must be regarded as the final triumph of the new approach for which the *Star* had called since 1888. It had imposed with great success the conception of an L.C.C. programme;

[1] McBriar, op. cit., p. 201n.; B. Tillett to J. Burns, 11 December 1893 and 3 November 1896, Burns Collection.

[2] In addition George Bateman stood in the Conservative safe seat of Holborn. For Battersea, John Burns, diary, 7 October 1891. For Deptford, *Speaker*, 20 February 1892. For West Ham, see Ch. 6; according to the *Pall Mall Gazette*, 3 June 1892, 'the Liberal managers have been absolutely neutral'. Lacking official encouragement, efforts to oppose Hardie eventually failed.

[3] *Star*, 15 November 1889.

the same had now been achieved with the national party. But while the Progressives had accepted a new labour policy, the national leaders were less generous, and their success at the 1892 election less complete.

Three years later, decisively defeated at the general election of 1895, the Liberal Party was back in the doldrums, a middle class minority. Of the fourteen seats lost, eleven were in constituencies in which the working class vote was decisive, and the electoral swing against the Liberals was more marked in this type of constituency than where there was a strong lower middle class vote. Of the working class M.P.s, only John Burns survived. How had the Liberal Party lost the labour vote?

The Liberal success had been based on the unifying propaganda begun by the *Star*, political programmes designed to win working class votes, and the support of a new, vigorous and politically conscious trade unionism. By 1895 this combination of forces had disintegrated. The economic prosperity of 1888–91 had been succeeded by a slump and serious unemployment. Many of the smaller new unions had collapsed in these adverse trade conditions, and all of them lost numbers heavily. Since 1890 the Gas Workers had probably lost a third and the Dockers four fifths of their London members. In 1895 the unions were fighting to survive, and had little surplus energy to put into politics. Confidence in trade union political influence, which would have been in any case uncertain in these circumstances, had been further undermined by the widespread failure of the overnumerous working class candidates put up for the local elections in December 1894.

Even if the trade unions had been in a position to play a stronger role in the election, the Liberal Party would have secured none of the wholehearted support which it had in 1892. The voice of the *Star* had been moderated after the shareholders' revolts of 1890 and 1891, and by 1895 its influence was much diminished. The Liberal government had miserably failed to implement its election promises and could offer no solution to the growing unemployment. Instead of responding to working class criticism, and particularly to that of Keir Hardie in the House of Commons, the Liberal leaders made the fatal mistake of denouncing the independent labour leaders. They wholly misunderstood the 1895 defeat. The *Speaker*, for example, argued that the defeat of 1895 was due to the mistake of making promises in 1892. It dismissed the new Independent Labour Party as a 'ridiculous organisation' of 'dreamers and revolutionaries' and advised that independent labour men 'should be taken at their word, and fought instead of courted. ... We only alienate votes by our efforts to please them.' Men like Hardie and Tillett were 'rapidly ceasing to represent working class opinion in any form'.[1]

Unfortunately for the Liberal Party the *Speaker* was wrong. In London it is true that, in contrast to its advances in the north, the I.L.P. was very weak, and after 1894 the Fabian Society, by breaking with the Liberals nationally without committing themselves to an independent party, became an isolated group with a declining London membership. But the S.D.F. grew significantly after 1891. By 1899 there were over forty of its branches in London, and all the best were in purely working class districts. Its influence on the London Trades Council and important unions such as the Gas Workers and the Compositors was considerable. Unemployed agitation was an S.D.F. monopoly. No other party organised as much outdoor propaganda. In London, so far from being the dogmatic bitter sect with little significant support traditionally pictured by historians, the S.D.F. was winning more hard working and idealistic members among working men than any other political movement. By contrast radicalism was in manifest decline. By the late 1890s the secularist movement had disappeared and the radical clubs had almost dropped political lectures.[2] The Metropolitan Radical Federation had lost its vigour. The *Clarion* commented that a rumour that it was to run twelve labour candidates for the 1895 election was 'all moonshine; ... the M.R.F. is being reorganised, and its new chairman, Chant, of Hoxton, is a free critic of the older liberalism; but the Federation leaves the selection and running of candidates to the party caucuses.'[3] There is no clearer indication of the extent to which Social Democracy had replaced radicalism among the politically-minded working class than the fact that the National Democratic League, set up in 1900 to stimulate a radical revival, was obliged to rely for its London secretary on a prominent Camberwell S.D.Fer, and for its national organiser on Jim Connell of Deptford, author of *The Red Flag*.[4]

There were still signs after 1895 that a Liberal Party recovery based on renewed working class support might be possible, in spite of the decay of radicalism. By 1897–8 trade was recovering, and there was a revival of trade union militancy. The fierce resistance of the employers made the long strikes of the engineers and the Penrhyn quarrymen into national struggles, supported by both old and new trade unionists. At the same time there was a revival of political activity, and a notable unity was again shown in the formation of the Workman's

[1] *Speaker*, 5 January, 20 April and 20 July 1895.
[2] E.g. Fabian Society annual report, 1900; Mudie-Smith, op. cit., p. 342.
[3] *Clarion*, 23 June 1894.
[4] *Democrat*, June–November 1902.

National Housing Council, with an S.D.F. compositor as secretary, and the start of the Browning Hall campaign for state old age pensions. Trade unionists standing as Liberals gained seats at parliamentary bye-elections at Walthamstow in 1897 and Stepney in 1898. On the L.C.C. in 1895 the Progressives had kept their majority, by the use of their aldermanic votes: the election result had been a tie. The Conservatives in 1895 were for the first time overtly organised on party lines by the newly formed London Municipal Society, but the Progressives responded by severing their open connection with the Liberal Party, hoping to keep the support of the Liberal Unionists who were thought to vote Progressive, and also securing a partial protection against labour disillusionment with the Liberal government. With the advantage of regular triennial elections on a relatively fresh register, a good administrative record, and the 'labour bench' to secure trade union backing, the Progressives were able to recover most lost support in 1898.

But these were isolated gains. Neither the Progressive movement nor the Liberal Party showed an encouraging picture. The L.C.C. could boast of its tramways in south London, its housing in Bethnal Green, the extension of running water supplies to most houses, and the new facilities for technical education. But these achievements were less impressive than those of the old Metropolitan Board of Works. Neither Liberal nor Conservative governments had given the increased powers demanded by the L.C.C. Gas, electricity, water and the port of London were still in other hands. No real onslaught on the slums had been made. The Progressive Parties on the vestries could show in some cases better health administration, new baths and libraries, even municipal electricity supply, but nobody could still believe that a rapid transformation of London could be achieved through municipal government. There was a notable return to apathy in local elections. The Progressive Parties made no general advance after 1894. Of the 41 local administrative vestries and joint Boards only 9 were controlled by the Progressives in 1898—1 less than in 1895. Of the 30 Boards of Guardians, 7 were Progressive—no advance on 1895. Many of them had a small proportion of labour members, but it was only a large proportion in Battersea, Barking, and some of the Southwark vestries. The Progressive movement was no longer preparing the way for a Liberal recovery at a general election, as before 1892.

More serious still was the decay in the Liberal electoral machine. In the past lack of money had been more of a problem than lack of workers. It could now be seen that both were essential. Because of the migration of the middle classes to healthier residential districts, a party which could not rely on extensive local working class support had to be managed by generally non-resident and thus rarely wholehearted professional and business men. By 1900 only 3 London constituencies had a competent Liberal agent; the Conservatives had 30.[1] The work of registration had been so neglected that the number of constituencies in which lodgers exceeded 15 per cent was allowed to fall from 13 in 1895 to 9 in 1899. Evidently resisting labour demands had not rekindled much middle class enthusiasm. It was hardly surprising that the Liberal Party received another crushing defeat in 1900.

The danger to the Liberals was not merely a long period in the wilderness. The Party might be superseded. Already as a result of local Liberal weakness in two working class districts, Bow and Bromley and West Ham, strong local Labour Parties had been able to develop based on a trade union-socialist alliance and under S.D.F. control. In West Ham the new party captured the Borough Council in 1898 and forced the Liberal tradesmen into a Municipal Alliance with the Conservatives. In both districts the Liberal Party had been so reduced that at the 1900 General Election S.D.F. candidates (endorsed by the new national Labour Representation Committee) secured straight fights against the Conservatives in Bow and Bromley and West Ham South. Here at least the Social Democrats had effectively won the political leadership of the working class from the Liberals. Equally ominous was the situation in Woolwich, a constituency to be won within three years by the Labour Party. In 1900 the Conservative was unopposed. The Liberal Party was rotting at its roots. The prospects of a revival looked even less encouraging than in 1886.

There had been two great changes in these years. The first was the emergence of labour as a new political force, supported by an extended trade unionism, and capable of winning elections for either Liberals or socialists. The second was the decline of secularist radicalism as the typical creed of the politically active working class, and its gradual replacement by the Marxist socialism of the S.D.F. On the other hand there was as yet little room in London for an independent non-socialist Labour Party. It seemed more likely either that the Liberals would remain the principal working class political party or that they would be replaced by the Social Democrats than that both would be ousted. The Liberal Party success in alliance with labour in 1892, and the successful S.D.F.-controlled Labour Parties in Bow and Bromley and West Ham, indicated that either party could make great advances with labour support. But the Liberal Party had ignored the lesson of 1892, remaining in 1900 little less a middle class organisation and little less Nonconformist in tone than it had

[1] L. Holland to H. Gladstone, January 1901, Herbert Gladstone Collection.

LIBERALS, RADICALS AND LABOUR

been in 1880. It was to achieve another recovery in the 1900s, but once again fail to overcome its internal conflicts. In the same way the S.D.F. leadership was to persist in its mistaken opposition to a labour-socialist alliance. It was the inability of either party to adapt, rather than the inherent attractiveness of a non-Liberal non-Marxist Labour Party, which might have suggested the future outcome.

VI

THE SOCIAL DEMOCRATIC FEDERATION

THE story of the foundation of the Social Democratic Federation (the S.D.F.), the first avowedly socialist political party in England, has been recounted in some detail by historians of socialism.[1] It will be sufficient here to say that it resulted from a coincidence of radical dissatisfaction with Gladstonian Liberalism, with the arrival on the political scene of H. M. Hyndman. It is clear from reports in the *Radical* that already some club speakers were urging the need for 'a labour party which should be independent of the Liberal party' and arguing that 'nearly every internal struggle in a country—whether it be Nihilism in Russia, Socialism in Germany, Communism in France, or Radicalism in England—could be reduced to this logical fact—a fight between the profit producer and the profit receiver.'[2] In 1881 the *Radical* began a campaign, very probably suggested by Hyndman, for 'a non-Ministerial Radical party' to be led by Joseph Cowen, the radical M.P. for Newcastle.[3] The first of a series of conferences resulting in the formation of the new party, the Democratic Federation, was held under Cohen's chairmanship in February. But the fact that the Democratic Federation survived, and developed into a socialist party, was because it very rapidly passed to Hyndman's leadership.

A man of independent means, widely travelled, a Cambridge graduate aged nearly 40, Hyndman was temperamentally a radical imperialist Conservative in the tradition of Disraeli, who had been converted to the Marxist standpoint by reading a French translation of *Capital* in 1880. He was to be the undaunted propagandist of English socialism for another forty years, but in spite of his dedication he was

[1] C. Tsuzuki, *H. M. Hyndman and British Socialism*, Oxford 1961; E. P. Thompson, *William Morris: Romantic to Revolutionary*, London 1955.
[2] 18 and 25 December 1880.   [3] 15 January 1881.

always an incongruously unsuitable leader. A natural gambler and adventurer who delighted in political crisis, he totally lacked the personal tact and strategic skill which a successful politician needs. The personal enemies he made included Marx and Engels, William Morris, and the trade unionist socialist pioneers John Burns and Tom Mann. He regarded first the Independent Labour Party and then the early Labour Party with scorn. He opposed the campaign for an Eight Hour Day as a diversion, and denounced the 'First of May folly'. He regarded trade unions as politically unimportant and their leaders as 'the most stodgy-brained dull-witted and slowgoing time-servers in the country'. He opposed both the syndicalists and the suffragists in the 1900s, and suggested that women who struggled for their emancipation as a 'sex question' 'ought to be sent to an island by themselves'. He was a persistent anti-semite, became a violent anti-German, supported Carson and the Ulster Protestants and backed allied intervention against the Russian revolution.[1] In considering the mistakes made by the S.D.F. in London and the eventual failure of Marxist socialism to consolidate its early advances, it is important to remember that it suffered throughout the period from singularly unsuitable leadership.

At first the Federation was a negligible force, with only two branches in 1881–2. It quickly lost the support of the radical clubs when Hyndman's hostility to 'capitalist radicalism' was made apparent. The real socialist revival was set off by Henry George, the American land reformer, whose English campaign tour of 1882 seemed to kindle the smouldering unease with narrow radicalism. This radical 'voice from the Far West of America, a land of boundless promise, where, if anywhere, it might seem that freedom and material progress were secure possessions of honest labour, announced grinding poverty, the squalor of congested city life, unemployment, and utter helplessness.'[2] George's book *Progress and Poverty* sold 400,000 copies. His argument pointed beyond land reform, and stimulated an intellectual interest in socialism, which he certainly never intended. The new atmosphere brought important recruits to the Democratic Federation in 1883 and 1884: William Morris, Dr. Edward Aveling a Darwinian chemist and secularist leader, Harry Quelch a packer in a city warehouse, H. H. Champion a former army officer, and John Burns, born in Battersea of Scots parents, a temperance enthusiast who had been influenced by an old French communard in his engineering workshop. To these should be added three of the initial members, a Scots tailor James Macdonald, a radical

---

[1] Tsuzuki, op. cit.
[2] J. A. Hobson, 'The Influence of Henry George in England', *Fortnightly Review*, 1897.

Nonconformist civil servant Herbert Burrows, and the future unemployed leader Jack Williams, an unskilled dock labourer brought up in a workhouse.[1]

With this nucleus the Democratic Federation was able to expand. Ten branches were founded and outdoor meetings started. Champion became secretary, a weekly paper *Justice* was launched, the object of the Federation was defined as socialism, and a political programme was adopted. Its name was changed to the Social Democratic Federation.

If the S.D.F. did not maintain this rapid progress, it was principally due to a series of splits. First Hyndman quarrelled with Morris and Aveling, and as a result the first rival to the S.D.F. the Socialist League was set up in 1884. Then in 1885, after the scandalous revelation that it had accepted 'Tory Gold' for election candidates, most of the members which it shared with the infant Fabian Society seceded, and a second shortlived rival party, the Socialist Union, was formed. Most serious of all, in 1888 Hyndman broke with Champion and the group of future trade unionist leaders including Tom Mann and John Burns who were to lead the development of independent labour politics. Consequently the S.D.F. grew in a series of forward jolts rather than by steady progress. Its London branches, which until 1895 constituted half its strength, rose to 14 in 1884, and then fell back in 1885; rose to 24 in 1887, and then fell back again; grew more uncertainly to 27 in 1892; then picked up again more rapidly reaching 39 in 1895; fell back again in 1896–7; and then finally resumed progress reaching over 40 by the end of the decade.[2] The rhythm of its growth outside London was similar, except that after 1895 it continued until 1897 and then declined until after 1900.[3] It is revealing that outside London its chief stronghold was Lancashire, where Catholicism provided the same kind of preparation for a doctrinal Marxist socialism as did secularism in London.

It is also noticeable that in its early years, in direct contrast to trade unionism and so to the labour movement in general, the growth of the S.D.F. was most rapid in periods of serious unemployment. From the beginning the Social Democrats assumed the leadership of unemployed organisation and agitation, using it to expose the deficiencies of the capitalist system. Engels, usually a bitter critic of S.D.F. tactics, remarked with approval that 'as the Radical Clubs of the East End take no initiative whatever with regard to the Unemployed, the S.D.F. have no competition, are alone in the field and work this question, which springs up afresh as soon as winter comes

[1] H. W. Lee and E. Archbold, *Social Democracy in Britain*, London 1935; W. Kent, *John Burns: Labour's Lost Leader*, London 1950.
[2] See Appendix B.   [3] Tsuzuki, op. cit., p. 284.

on, entirely to their own liking.'[1] In this their attitude contrasts interestingly with the opinion of Bernard Shaw, that the unemployed were 'as great a nuisance to socialists as to themselves. Angry as they are, they do not want a revolution: they want a job.'[2]

At the beginning the S.D.F. was not a serious electoral organisation. Its parliamentary candidatures in 1885, although in fact bringing nothing but discredit, were intended as propaganda. Hampstead and Kennington, the seats fought, were not even working class constituencies. Four candidates stood in the 1885 School Board election, but only Burrows with his radical reputation secured a good poll. The S.D.F. had little or no electoral organisation in the 1880s. Its organisation committee was simply concerned with keeping branches in existence and with supplying them with speakers for outdoor meetings and indoor lectures. There was a lecture secretary, but no election organiser.[3]

It was because the S.D.F. lived for propaganda that the free speech struggles of 1886–7 against the police suppression of outdoor meetings were fought with such bitterness. Already every branch was conducting street corner meetings in summer, and some all the year. In the winter they turned to political lectures, discussion groups, economic classes, and the branch library, preparing ammunition for summer 'mission stations'.[4]

By the end of the 1880s the S.D.F. was far short of covering most London working class districts. It is noticeable that apart from Bermondsey and Deptford nearly all the strong branches were in relatively newly-settled working class districts, Battersea, Peckham and Wandsworth in south London, and Barking, Canning Town, Tottenham and Wood Green in outer east and north-east London. The East End was particularly weak. The divisions in the socialist movement account for other gaps, such as the failure to maintain branches in Woolwich and Hammersmith.

Even so, the membership of the S.D.F. was clearly drawn from very mixed class groups. At the one extreme were the middle class leaders, at the other the unemployed. According to Annie Besant the Deptford branch consisted 'mostly of the very poor; I should say fully one half of them are men who are out of work each winter'.[5] A skilled engraver found the Clerkenwell S.D.Fers 'a poor lot . . . a sort of gathering of down and outs to discuss their grievances'.[6] But

[1] F. Engels to L. Lafargue, 24 November 1886, Engels and Lafargue, op. cit., 1, pp. 408–9.
[2] *Pall Mall Gazette*, 11 February 1886.   [3] *Justice*, 11 February 1884.
[4] Branch reports in *Justice*. At least seven branches had reading rooms; Graham Wallas conducted an economic class for Southwark S.D.F. (13 October 1888).
[5] *Link*, 24 March 1888.   [6] F. W. Galton, manuscript autobiography.

probably the majority of the early members were less poor than this, and branches often explained their difficulties in working 'as Mr. Booth's newly published book shows, one of the poorest and therefore most apathetic districts in London to spread the propaganda in'.[1] Booth himself found 'the springs of Socialism and Revolution' among artisans rather than the poorer unskilled workers.[2] In Battersea it was in the Shaftesbury Estate, 'chiefly inhabited by superior artisans... that the intelligent portion of the Socialism of the district is chiefly to be found, and the colony represents perhaps the highwater mark of the life of the intelligent London artisan'.[3] Certainly the early working class Social Democrats were frequently self-educated intellectuals. John Burns with his precious collection of books, Harry Quelch 'the greatest intellect bred in and by the working class movement' who learnt French in order to read *Capital* (then untranslated to English) and later taught himself German and Latin, and Tom Mann, vegetarian and teetotaller, in turn a Malthusian and Swedenborgian, amateur violinist, leading spirit of a Shakespeare Mutual Improvement Society, were each leading figures in their branches.[4] It is also noticeable that at this date every branch met in rooms or a coffee bar, and *Justice* opposed an attempt to found a branch meeting in a public house in 1884.[5] It appears that although mixed in composition, the S.D.F. was drawing particularly on the same kind of working men who formed the backbone of London radicalism, and that in the newer suburbs, where radicalism had had less time to become well established, socialism more easily took root.

With the successful conclusion of the free speech struggles, the improvement of the economic situation, the publication of the *Star*, and the advent of the new unionism, the S.D.F. would in any case have faced a crisis in its policy at the end of the 1880s. How was it to profit from the upsurge of working class political feeling without sacrificing its independence? In fact the issue was never really faced, because the supporters of a change in tactics left the S.D.F. Their leader was Champion, who determined in 1887 to 'rescue the Federation from Mr Hyndman' and his wanton vilification and insult to friends'.[6] Champion declared that 'after five years of stormy propaganda there is a distinct slackening of the rate of progress... The whole popular organisation of the movement has hitherto been directed towards the one main end of gaining the ear of the public.

[1] *Justice*, 4 July 1891.   [2] Booth, op. cit., I, p. 177.   [3] Ibid., I, p. 280.
[4] On Quelch: Tillett, *Memories and Reflections*, p. 189, and E. B. Bax (ed.) Harry Quelch, *Literary Remains with a Biographical Introduction*, London 1914; Mann, op. cit., and Torr, op. cit.
[5] *Justice*, 1 November 1884.   [6] *Today*, July and October 1887.

For this have been the processions and open air meetings, the extreme language and denunciation of society, the church parades and banners ... Having secured an audience, something more definite and sustaining must be put before it ... We have got to abandon the mere denunciation of existing society, and to expound the practical plans for reform for the sake of which the whole agitation has been guided.'[1] Champion's most valuable ally proved to be Tom Mann, who provided him with a model practical plan, the compulsory eight hour day. Through Mann John Burns was drawn in, and Champion was able to make contact with other supporters outside the S.D.F. By 1888, when the difficulty of ousting Hyndman had become apparent, Champion felt strong enough to lead his supporters out of the S.D.F. and attempt to build an independent Labour Party on a wider basis. This attempt is discussed in the next Chapter. But there is no doubt that the split, by undermining the confidence of the outstanding leaders of the new unionism, Mann, Burns, Ben Tillett, and for a time Will Thorne, made it impossible for the S.D.F. to profit as it might have done from the advent of independent labour politics in 1889–92.

Equally, there can be little doubt that Hyndman's personality rather than the issue itself perpetuated the split. For example, in 1887 Hyndman himself produced an important contribution to the practical policies advocated by socialists. His pamphlet *A Commune for London* was the first argument for municipal socialism. In addition to the municipalisation of essential services, gas, water, lighting, trams, parks, poor relief, markets, 'and (within limits) education', which had been advocated by James Firth in his *Municipal London* of 1876, Hyndman suggested housing rented at cost rates, free education and the feeding of schoolchildren, municipal supply at cost price of bread, meat and vegetables, the useful organisation of unemployed labour, and a policy of fair wages and reduced hours for council employees. Housing had become part of the general radical programme in the 1880s, but his other additions were innovations. Hyndman's vision of a city council captured 'to lead the way in the great Social Revolution which will remove the crushing disabilities, physical, moral and intellectual, under which the great mass of our city populations suffer at the present time', was new to London socialists. It was perhaps influenced by the success of the French possibilists in Paris in 1887, and by the local election work which had been begun by Champion. Nevertheless the credit for first expounding this approach must go to Hyndman, and the closeness to Champion's attitude only underlines the essentially personal nature of their conflict.

The S.D.F. was in fact able to survive the split largely because it

[1] Ibid., June 1887.

tacitly followed Champion and the new unionists. It was some time before the division became final. When John Burns was elected to the L.C.C. with the support of the Progressives he was still a member of the S.D.F., and even as late as 1892–3 he was in demand as a speaker at S.D.F. meetings and a regular visitor to the Battersea branch.[1] Mann, who resigned after Burns in 1889, remained friendly; Thorne, in spite of the influence of Aveling, does not appear to have considered resigning. John Ward, the leader of the Wandsworth branch and another new unionist, contrived to oppose Burns desertion while keeping his friendship.[2] After the dock strike even the hostility of *Justice* was moderated. Engels noted that 'the violent attacks of *Justice* on Champion, Burns, etc., have suddenly ceased; there is instead a sort of hidden, verschämtes sighing for some sort of universal brotherhood'.[3]

In both election and trade union work in spite of the split socialists of different parties continued to work side by side. Herbert Burrows and Annie Besant, both of whom remained in the S.D.F., organised the matchgirls strike in 1888. They were helped by H. W. Hobart, another S.D.Fer., who was also a prominent assistant of the Dockers and Gas Workers at their earliest meetings. If the Gas Workers were pioneers of independent labour candidatures, the most powerful branches such as Bromley and Canning Town remained the backbone of their local S.D.F. branches. John Ward and Jack Williams formed the National Federation of Labour, James Macdonald and Lewis Lyons led the tailors' agitation. In the dock strike Harry Quelch organised the south side. There was not infrequently friction, especially in the dock strike, when Tillett resented the rivalry of Quelch and Burns allowed a red flag to be seized by the police; but this particular clash was principally caused by the conflict between general unionism and the 'ring fence' policy of the Dockers, and generally the picture is one of co-operation in a common cause.

Equally it is clear that after the split the S.D.F. candidates were as willing as other socialists to run with radical or labour support. Harry Quelch stood twice for the Bermondsey vestry with the radicals, and after his second defeat in 1889 was tried with the radical F. W. Soutter for disturbing the peace.[4] In the London School Board election of November 1888 Annie Besant, John Ward, Harry Quelch and Mrs. Amie Hicks stood as candidates of the Central Democratic Committee. Although Annie Besant alone was success-

---

[1] J. Burns, diary, 6 and 27 March 1892; W. Webb to J. Burns, c. December 1892; and J. Falkner to J. Burns, 2 September 1893, Burns Collection.
[2] J. Burns, diary, 24 September 1888 and 17 February 1891.
[3] Engels and Lafargue, op. cit., 2, p. 342.
[4] *Star*, 14 May 1888, 6 May 1889.

ful, Ward polled over 8,000 votes, and in the same month in the Tottenham School Board election an S.D.Fer without Fabian connections, William Snow, an engineer, was elected. In the first L.C.C. election of January 1889 the S.D.F. put up four members in addition to John Burns, and two of these were supported by the *Star*.[1] The Progressive victory was greeted by *Justice* as 'a greater triumph for Democracy, Social Democracy, than even the most advanced radicals yet understand. No one could have believed beforehand that a programme which, if faithfully carried out for the next two years and a half, will go far to establish a real Commune for London for us to capture.' The victory of John Burns in Battersea was singled out as '*the* feature of the election' and his wages fund advertised.[2]

When the 1891 School Board elections came round the S.D.F. was able to profit from the growing influence of socialists on the London Trades Council. Of the committee of seven which launched its Labour Representation Scheme three were S.D.Fers.[3] At the 1891 School Board election four of the five candidates supported by the Trades Council Labour Representation League were S.D.Fers.[4] The S.D.F. was unlucky that none were elected, for two polled over 10,000 votes. The *Star* did not support them, and was clearly surprised by the results, especially that of S. D. Shallard, in prison awaiting trial for speaking in the World's End free speech fight, at Greenwich.[5] The labour-socialist unity was particularly striking in West Lambeth, the division which included Battersea, where the candidate was the Battersea S.D.F. branch secretary. In significant contrast in Southwark, where Harry Quelch as candidate was opposed by the trade unionist leader Steadman, the lowest poll was recorded.

The S.D.F. candidates for the 1892 L.C.C. election were also supported by the Trades Council. Two of the six were adopted by the local Progressives and polled up to 2,000 in difficult constituencies, and of these two John Ward was nearly rewarded with an aldermancy.[6] At the general election later in 1892 the single S.D.F. candidate provided an instructive contrast. H. R. Taylor opposed the

[1] 10 January 1889.   [2] 26 January 1889.
[3] Will Pearson (Dockers), H. B. Hobart (Compositors) and J. Roy (Gas Workers).
[4] Quelch (Southwark 2203), Rogers (West Lambeth 11,993), King (Chelsea 7114), Shallard (Greenwich 10,109). The polls of those elected were Southwark 7772–5327; West Lambeth 21,560–13,721; Chelsea 15,423–8986; Greenwich 14,913–10,864.
[5] E.g. 28 November 1889.
[6] John Ward (Wandsworth 2724) and Edward Cray (Dulwich 1999)—both difficult constituencies; for the aldermanic elections, *Star*, 10 March 1892: cf. the assertion by M. Cole, op. cit., p. 40, that 'the solitary S.D.F. candidate polled 67 votes only'.

old-style Liberal trade unionist George Howell at Bethnal Green, and although supported by leading radicals as well as socialists Taylor only collected a miserable 106 votes.[1] Labour unity was already vital to socialist election candidates.

Significantly, in spite of the split, the best S.D.F. performance in local elections remained in Battersea. In 1888 the branch had already two vestrymen, a women's section, library, co-operative stores, athletic club, and regular park meetings attracting over 1,000.[2] Although some of the abler members such as William Sanders followed Burns into the Battersea Labour League, set up as his personal party in December 1889, the majority remained loyal, and the two organisations formed a joint committee for local elections.[3] A small S.D.F. party was maintained on the vestry, the custom of free breakfasts for children of the unemployed continued, and the first of all Socialist Sunday Schools begun in 1892.[4] It was not until 1893 that serious conflict between the Labour League and S.D.F. developed.[5]

Until 1892 the Federation was struggling to hold its own. After this its strength increased more rapidly, and this was despite some further secessions—the Deptford branch went over to the I.L.P., and John Ward, after failing in the L.C.C. election of 1892, belatedly followed Burns into the Progressive camp, thereby wrecking the Wandsworth branch. The most encouraging feature was that by 1900 the S.D.F. had succeeded in establishing itself in some of the inner working class districts. Notably strong movements developed in Poplar, Walworth, Camberwell and Lambeth, and good branches in Bethnal Green, Shoreditch and Stepney. There were also active branches in north London. The weakest area remained west London, where the I.L.P. succeeded to some of the position of the former Socialist League. But the advent of the I.L.P. in general proved more of a stimulus than a threat; the S.D.F. was running its own London campaign in 1894, before the I.L.P. campaign began, and a large number of a new branches were founded. Although several proved transient the S.D.F. suffered none of the disastrous defections which wrecked the I.L.P. after the electoral disappointments of 1894–5.

To some extent this growing strength of the S.D.F. was reflected in local elections. In Poplar and West Ham, where the S.D.F. were

[1] Among Taylor's supporters were Cooper and Baum of the L.C.C. labour bench, and Ben Ellis the Peckham radical; *Workman's Times*, 25 June 1892.
[2] *Justice*, 1 August 1885, 4 and 11 August 1888.
[3] *Star*, 30 April 1891.
[4] *Justice*, 2 April 1887 and 16 February 1895.
[5] Opposing candidates were then put up for a bye-election to the L.C.C.; relations so deteriorated that there were free fights in Battersea Park: *Workman's Times*, 22 July 1893.

firmly allied with the trade unions, notable successes were achieved. In Battersea, Camberwell and Lambeth the branches worked with local radicals, and some of their members secured election. But in these districts, and to a lesser extent in Poplar and West Ham, there was a significant contrast between minor local elections and more important contests. In Lambeth, for example, the S.D.F. supported the local Labour Electoral Association, and in 1894 two S.D.Fers were elected to the vestry and one to the Board of Guardians.[1] Yet their candidate, Nelson Palmer, a Fabian, polled a mere 68 votes in the 1898 L.C.C. election. Similarly in Walworth the S.D.F. in alliance with local trade unionists secured the election of two members to the Newington vestry in 1892, but the candidature of George Lansbury for the constituency in 1895 proved a dismal failure.

In general the performance of the Social Democrats at L.C.C. and School Board elections deteriorated sadly after 1891–2. The only important exception was Will Pearson's poll of 12,437 in Tower Hamlets at the 1897 School Board election. Pearson, who was killed in a dock accident in the following year, was one of the outstanding working class socialists of the period. A casual labourer at the docks, he spent much of his time in self-education at the British Museum and taught himself to speak, according to Hyndman, 'as correctly, as naturally, and with as refined an accent and intonation as a thoroughly educated member of society'. He was for several years a touring speaker for the Land Restoration League and was able to rally all the advanced sections to his support.[2] But it was no longer easy to secure such broad backing. The Progressive parties, securely established with their labour members, had no longer anything to gain from the support of militant socialists. The Liberal leadership was in any case now against co-operation. With electoral opinion swinging away from radicalism it was not surprising that independent socialist candidates could win little support. The S.D.F. executive would have preferred abstention from the 1895 L.C.C. election, but could not prevent six candidatures put up by ill-advised branches. *Justice* openly confessed after their defeat that 'they have made a ridiculous exhibition'.[3] Three years later a similar exhibition was repeated.

These candidatures were not entirely wasted, for they served to demonstrate the independence of the S.D.F. which might have otherwise appeared to be compromised by local election compacts. The

[1] *Clarion*, 1 September 1894.
[2] *Labour Leader*, 12 February 1898; H. M. Hyndman, *Further Reminiscences*, London 1912, p. 443.
[3] 9 March 1895: 'The Committee appointed to enquire into the matter practically recommended that, considering the depleted state of branch funds and the indebtedness of many branches, no candidates should be run for the L.C.C. But under the present rules of the S.D.F. such a decision could not be enforced.'

advent of the rival I.L.P. made independence more important. At the same time they served to point out the genuine distinction between Social Democracy and Progressivism.

The S.D.F. had already acquired a special reputation on the unemployment issue, and this was maintained during the 1890s. The I.L.P. formed a joint committee with the S.D.F. in 1895, but left the running of it to the more experienced Social Democrats.[1] The Fabians continued to regard unemployment as a threat rather than an opportunity, and quickly withdrew their delegate from the central Unemployed Organisation Committee formed with the other socialists in 1892.[2] The delegate, Halliday Sparling, had in any case argued a policy scarcely distinguishable from that of the Charity Organisation Society, with relief only granted through a register and work test, restricted to inhabitants of twelve months standing. He opposed the 'irresponsible and indiscriminate provision of meals' and argued that a special relief fund would 'seriously aggravate the disease'.[3] It is not surprising that Jack Williams' mass protest meetings on Tower Hill were more effective in winning socialists than this Fabian reasoning.

To this propaganda the S.D.F. could now add some real achievement. The Social Democrats on the Boards of Guardians, and especially Mary Gray in Battersea, Mrs. Despard the future suffragette in Lambeth, and George Lansbury in Poplar, had an influence out of proportion to their numbers.[4] The *Star* had early included the humanising of the Poor Law in its programme, but the policy does not seem to have been realised before Lansbury's election as a socialist Guardian with Will Crooks in 1893. Lansbury was deeply shocked by his first visit to a workhouse after his election. 'It was not necessary to write up the words "Abandon hope all ye who enter here". Officials, receiving ward, hard forms, whitewashed walls, keys dangling at the waist of those who spoke to you, huge books for name, history etc., searching, and then being stripped and bathed in a communal tub, and the final crowning indignity of being dressed in clothes which had been worn by lots of other people, hideous to look at, ill-fitting and coarse—everything possible was done to inflict mental and moral degradation.'[5] He determined to make the Poplar administration 'a humane agency of help instead of a place of despair', and although the Board was still under Moderate control he

[1] I.L.P. London District Council minutes, 4–24 January 1895.
[2] *Workman's Times*, 24 December 1892.
[3] Ibid., 14 January 1893.
[4] Battersea, *Justice*, 8 December 1894; Lambeth, *Woman Worker*, 17 July 1908.
[5] Lansbury, op. cit., p. 135.

was immediately able to effect notable changes.[1] The diet was improved, the uniform clothing replaced, light work was provided for the old, separate rooms for aged couples, dominoes, chess and newspapers and tobacco for the over 60s, and children were taken out of the workhouse and sent to ordinary Board schools.[2] Although lack of money prevented its immediate realisation, the policy of replacing the casual wards for the unemployed by colonies for training and resettlement was agreed. Lansbury made 'Poplarism' a symbol to both reformers and reactionaries, and gave himself a local standing as 'the friend of the poor' which was unshakeable.

The S.D.F. also acquired a reputation for its attitude to housing. Here again it was persistence rather than originality which counted. Writing in *Justice* in 1889, Harry Quelch described the gloom of a typical working class street, 'long lines of dwelling houses, their dull, smoky yellow brick fronts grim, dirty, unenlivened by any ornament or variety of colour; their treeless, shrubless surroundings perfect Saharas of cheerlessness.' But it was not merely rehousing that he demanded, but better housing. The characteristic improved tenement of the period was in fact no improvement at all. Quelch attacked 'the horrible prison-like "model" dwellings which are being constructed all over the metropolis by four per cent philanthropists. Rearing their grim colourless walls some 70 feet sheer without break or ornament except the windows ... these "models" are the embodiment of all that is cheap and nasty'; the rooms in them were 'no better than pigeon holes.'[3] This concern for housing grew during the 1890s. It was, for example, a principal issue in the municipal battle fought by the S.D.F. in West Ham. At the end of the decade Fred Knee, an S.D.F. compositor, the future first secretary of the London Labour Party, organised the Workman's National Housing Council, with himself as secretary, which carried the campaign through the 1900s. It was supported by trade unionists of all political opinions.

At the L.C.C. elections the Social Democrats contrasted their policies in these and other fields with the limited achievements of the Progressives. There could be no doubt that there was some justification for their criticism. 'We say that from the point of view of the workers of the metropolis the past six years have been well-nigh wasted. The unemployed question has been burked and the unemployed themselves have been snubbed. The housing of the poor has

[1] Guardians election manifesto 1893, Lansbury Collection; *London*, 6 July, 17 August and 12 October 1893.
[2] Guardians election manifesto c. 1896, Lansbury Collection. Most of the changes were supported by the Local Government Board circulars issued in this period, but ignored by the majority of Boards. As a whole, London Boards remained exceptionally conservative: PP 1909 XXXVII, pp. 167, 184.
[3] *Justice*, 23 January 1889.

been systematically neglected ... The payment of members of the Council has never been so much as discussed because the well-to-do Progressives mean to keep the control entirely in their hands. The feeding and clothing of necessitous children—which the Paris municipal Council has brought out in spite of official opposition—has never been so much as mentioned. The establishment of labour exchanges and bureaux—which also the Paris Municipal Council has admirably carried out—has never been attempted.'[1]

On these issues the Social Democrats were undoubtedly more farsighted than the Progressives. Nevertheless the denunciation by the S.D.F. of Progressivism as 'sheer humbug'[2] and the irritation caused by their hopeless candidatures led many observers to regard the S.D.F. as impolitic and small-minded, a hindrance rather than a help to socialism. After the 1892 L.C.C. election William Morris wrote to Bruce Glasier, 'I sometimes have a vision of a real Socialist Party at once united and free. Is it possible? Here in London it might be done, I think, but the S.D.F. stands in the way. Although the individual members are good fellows enough as far as I have met them, the society has got a sort of pedantic tone of arrogance and lack of generosity, which is disgusting and does disgust both Socialists and Non-Soc.'[3]

This view of the S.D.F. hardened with time. R. C. K. Ensor, for example, argued in a report to the Fabians that the I.L.P. was always killed where the S.D.F. was firmly installed, 'not so much by the hostility of the S.D.F. as by the subtle infection of its methods. The qualities which the S.D.F. typically parade,—their impressive contempt for compromises, the easy laxity of their moral standards, their habitual discouragement of all thinking outside an imposingly narrow range,—are qualities which do not appear to appeal much to the average elector; but they are qualities which rival socialists seem to find very hard to compete with without imitating them. The I.L.P. branches where they have been in competition or alliances with the S.D.F. have repeatedly imitated them, and as repeatedly ruined themselves. The classical example of this is West Ham; but others abound.'[4]

Is there any truth in these accusations? Ensor, as a dogmatic and personally puritanical Fabian, might be expected to have taken an extreme standpoint: do the facts support his hostility? Certainly it can hardly be said that the S.D.F. ruined the I.L.P. movement in

[1] Ibid., 16 February 1895. [2] Ibid., 5 February 1898.
[3] P. Henderson (ed.), *The Letters of William Morris to his Family and Friends*, London 1950, pp. 348–9.
[4] R. C. K. Ensor, memorandum on the I.L.P., September 1907, Fabian Society archives.

West Ham, where there had been no I.L.P. movement of importance to ruin. And West Ham alone is evidence that the 'average elector' did not always find S.D.F. propaganda as unattractive as Ensor. In fact there is more reason for believing that the advent of the I.L.P. caused a deterioration in the S.D.F. than that the S.D.F. corrupted the I.L.P. Rivalry provoked the S.D.F. branches into more hopeless propaganda candidatures, and the middle class Nonconformist tendencies of the I.L.P. must have weakened the early attachment of the Social Democrats to temperance. But there is no evidence that as a whole the S.D.F. were drunken and immoral. This accusation is almost certainly due to the different customs of Londoners from the chapel-going provinces which struck socialists like Keir Hardie when they first came to the metropolis. It is safer to believe Annie Besant, who had a wide experience of the London socialists and radicals, and asserted that 'none save those who worked with them know how much of real nobility, of heroic self-sacrifice, of constant self-denial, of brotherly affection, there is among the Social Democrats'.[1]

It was not, however, so surprising that those who had not worked with them had a less complimentary picture of the Social Democrats. This was due to the contrast, noted by Morris, between the 'good fellows' in the branches and the 'tone of arrogance' of the party as a whole. This tone came from the group round Hyndman, and especially from *Justice*. Harry Quelch, the paper's editor, was strongly influenced by Hyndman, and even tended to exaggerate the inflexibility of his views. His sombre and melancholy temperament too often made his argument bitter and humourless. *Justice* lacked the optimistic crusading spirit of the rival *Clarion*, and all too often the contrast between the S.D.F. and the I.L.P. was assumed to be similar.

In fact there was room in the S.D.F. for attitudes very similar to those of the provincial I.L.Pers. Herbert Burrows, who became a theosophist in the 1890s, would speak 'in a semi-devout manner, as if he wished to convey that socialism was his religion'.[2] He warned Hyndman that 'a nation has never yet been converted by negation or a simple policy of destruction'.[3] Will Pearson is another example. Most important of all was George Lansbury.

The son of a railway engineer, brought up as a working class child, but able to set up a small business of his own in the East End, Lansbury had from his early days been a radical agitator. As a boy he was friendly with John Hales, secretary of the First International.

[1] A. Besant, *An Autobiography*, London 1893, p. 302.
[2] Mann, op. cit., p. 92.
[3] H. Burrows to G. Lansbury, 20 June 1895, Lansbury Collection.

He spoke for the railwaymen, took up the Eastern Question and went as a radical delegate to Ireland. In the early 1880s he was deluded by propaganda into emigrating to Australia, and returned, horrified by the unemployment he found there, to campaign against the dishonest advertising which had deceived him. By the late 1880s he had become a socialist, and the nucleus of the socialist movement in Bow had already gathered round him. But he found the break with Liberalism difficult. He was religious by temperament, and had run a Band of Hope with his wife when younger. He was the close friend and election agent of two radical Liberals, Samuel Montagu, M.P. for Whitechapel, and Murray Macdonald, candidate for Bow and Bromley. Both were urging him to go into Parliament himself. Lansbury was offered the Progressive candidature for the vacant L.C.C. seat at Bow and Bromley when Jane Cobden, who was elected in 1889, was disqualified as a woman, but he refused to stand except as a socialist. He finally decided to break with the Liberals after being pushed off the platform at the National Liberal Federation conference for advocating the eight hour day. With typical consideration he stayed on as Murray Macdonald's agent until the election in 1892. Keir Hardie 'came and helped us the night before our poll. The following night we who had become Socialists packed up, left the Liberals, and formed the Bow and Bromley branch of the Social Democratic Federation.'[1]

Had the S.D.F. been as Ensor pictured it, Lansbury would surely have gone straight to the I.L.P. In fact he was the leading figure of the London S.D.F. in the 1890s. Hyndman was now concentrating his hopes of election to Parliament on Burnley, and Lansbury was the S.D.F. candidate at Walworth in 1895. He became organising secretary of the S.D.F. in 1895 and was chairman of the 1895 conference. In his speech to the delegates he described the socialist movement as 'a sacred trust: we are in it because we wish to do our part for the realisation of our ideal; of what matter to us that our enemies sneer and slander us?' He called on them to 'go back to your homes and bear aloft the fiery cross of a new crusade; carry to the oppressed of all classes the message of hope which socialism brings; teach those who are ignorant; cheer those who are downhearted; and play your part as men and women who fight with hope and courage because you know your faith is sure. I do not promise you glory, I do not promise you fame; but I do say that in the days that are coming the memory of the men and women who lived for socialism in these dark days will be revered and honoured.'[2]

The Bow and Bromley branch was conducted in very much this spirit. There were over eighty members. They included E. E. Metivier,

[1] Lansbury, op. cit., p. 76.   [2] S.D.F. Conference report, 1896.

the records secretary, a friend of William Morris who rallied the branch to save Bow church from demolition, and A. A. Watts, a compositor, 'tall and lean' and 'full of book learning', who 'learnt Marx's *Das Kapital* backwards and forwards', and was a strong supporter of the socialist Sunday schools.[1] In contrast to these intellectuals, Charlie Sumner, Lansbury's most loyal friend, who 'knew nothing of economics according to the books' and 'liked a tankard of beer or a glass of whisky and never concealed the fact', brought in the support of the Bromley Gas Workers branch.[2] James MacPherson, the Shop Assistants' general secretary, was also a member. 'We were all in good jobs, all very enthusiastic, and convinced our mission was to revolutionise the world. . . . Our branch meetings were like revivalist gatherings. We opened with a song and closed with one, and often read together some extracts from economic and historical writings.'[3] 'The bond of unity which held us together and never failed was our faith that, out of the seeming hopelessness and despair which a society based on riches and poverty creates, a nobler, more enduring civilisation would be built. We were enthusiasts because we were certain of victory.'[4]

This crusading atmosphere could have been found in many branches. T. A. Jackson, a book-hungry compositor of an extreme revolutionary disposition, who joined the S.D.F. in 1899, remembers the 'deep passionate earnestness, the intense conviction, and the fervid exaltation' of the S.D.F. 'There was an evangelical fervour about the agitation which was, on its emotional side, exalting to a degree.' Jackson describes a normal branch meeting: 'The customary routine was, after the "minutes" and correspondence, to fix arrangements for the Sunday propaganda meetings, and for any weekday meetings there might be. The life-activity of the branch centred around these propaganda meetings . . . Some comrade would establish himself as a local favourite and he would take the "stump" as a matter of course . . . (Speeches) usually took the form of a general statement of Socialist aspirations, a general criticism of capitalism and its evils, and a special application to current happenings, particularly the doings of the local Borough or Town Council. A well-established speaker, with a regular following would give an account of the latest meeting of the Local Authorities with a running commentary on the manifest wickedness of each member.' 'There were few Sundays on which I did not speak twice to as many as six times. More than once I have made my way across London from

---

[1] Metivier: Lansbury, op. cit., p. 171; Watts: G. Lansbury, *Looking Backwards—and Forwards*, London 1935, pp. 196–7.
[2] Lansbury, *My Life*, p. 70; *Looking Backwards*, p. 193.
[3] Lansbury, *My Life*, p. 78.   [4] Lansbury, *Looking Backwards*, p. 237.

North to South—from Tottenham or Wood Green by way of Finsbury Park, Highbury Corner, Clerkenwell Green and Kennington Triangle to Clapham Common or even Tooting Broadway—snatching a bite and a sup as the opportunity served. Several weeknights would be used for discussions and study-classes. And, be it noted, I was by no means unique in this frenzied activity.'[1]

Socialism for these indefatigable propagandists was more than a creed; it was a way of life. The good branch provided friendship, intellectual stimulation, amusement. A music hall turn was a useful talent in an S.D.F. leader. At a Hoxton branch concert 'Hunter Watts was in the chair and amused the audience very much by singing a selection from Madame Angot in French'.[2] Branches often combined to form classes and clubs. Economic classes were often 'formed by the members individually, usually from different branches as they got to know each other in club-rooms and places of resort, and we could find a comrade qualified and willing to act as a tutor.'[3]

A typical club was the North London Socialist Club, formed in 1896 'to promote unity amongst the socialists by providing a centre for social intercourse and propagandist work'. At first teetotal, it found a bar financially necessary after three years. Lectures were given by 'persons of different schools of thought in the movement', and the library took all the main socialist weeklies. Room was provided for I.L.P. and S.D.F. branch meetings, the I.L.P. choir, the Clarion Debating Society, the Gas Workers branch and slate club, and for a Socialist Sunday School. Entertainments varied from a musical evening by 'the Bradford Church comrades' and an amateur art exhibition to traditional children's Christmas parties. The strongest influence in the club was that of the S.D.F., and some members of the Finsbury Park branch later to be expelled as impossibilists arranged for the library to take the American Socialist Labour Party paper *People*. It was a small club, with just short of 100 members; but it is in a small association such as this, or in an S.D.F. branch, rather than in the columns of *Justice*, that the real spirit of the socialist movement is to be found.[4]

The extent to which this socialist movement was replacing traditional radicalism has been suggested earlier. By 1900 there were two parts of London in which the S.D.F. had already advanced far enough to break the grip of the Liberal Party. The first was Bow and Bromley. Before 1900 the Poplar Local Board was composed of delegates from the three vestries of Bow, Bromley and Poplar. In

[1] T. A. Jackson, *Solo Trumpet*, London 1953, pp. 54–57 and 78.
[2] *Justice*, 14 October 1893.   [3] Jackson, op. cit., p. 60.
[4] Minutes of North London Socialist Club, 1896–9.

THE SOCIAL DEMOCRATIC FEDERATION

Poplar the S.D.F. had no branch, and the firmly established Labour Electoral League under Will Crooks' leadership fought most elections in alliance with the Liberal Association. In Bromley the S.D.F. had more influence, and the strong Gas Workers branch ran straight Labour candidates at local elections in conjunction with the socialists. Bow was the socialist stronghold. The S.D.F. first made their mark on the Guardians. Lansbury was elected in 1893, and two other S.D.Fers in 1894. Lansbury soon became the dominant personality on the Poplar Board, for a few months acting as its chairman, and elections were fought in alliance with the Progressives who accepted his policies. On the vestries, which had between them over 200 members, the S.D.F. found it harder to make an impression. In 1894 and 1896 the Liberal Associations reluctantly agreed at the last moment to run with the socialists in Bromley and in Bow, but the socialist difficulty in finding sufficient candidates meant that their representation remained minimal.[1] In 1897, however, the Liberal Association made the mistake of refusing co-operation with the socialists, and in a three-cornered battle in Bow were caused serious losses. In 1898 the S.D.F., trade unionists and progressives again combined on an 'advanced programme' and seven S.D.Fers were elected to the vestry.[2] This foothold was made more important by the fact that the S.D.F., according to Lansbury, 'modelled ourselves on Will Thorne and his West Ham colleagues' and allied with the labour men on the vestry.[3]

The full extent of the socialist advance was made clear by two parliamentary elections in 1899 and 1900. Both were fought against the full tide of wartime Conservative feeling, and both were fought on an old register. The first was the bye-election of October 1899. The Liberal candidate, Harold Spender, was not only anxious to avoid a three-cornered fight with Lansbury. 'The fact is I want your help and not only your neutrality . . . This election shall not prejudice the general election, and if impartial judges are of opinion in the future that you better represent the progressive forces of the place, I will stand aside . . . If you would take me to your gas-workers and let me speak with you and by your side, then the situation would be clear, and we should be united against the jingoism of the moment.'[4] Spender secured a straight fight, and with Renwick Seager as his agent the full Liberal Party machinery was put at his disposal. He was defeated by 4,238 votes to 2,123. Following this humiliation the Bow and Bromley Liberal Association appears to have disintegrated, and Lansbury was in turn given a straight fight in the General Election of

[1] *East London Observer*, 15 December 1894, &c.
[2] *Labour Leader*, 4 June 1898.   [3] Lansbury, *My Life*, p. 163.
[4] H. Spender to G. Lansbury, October 1899, Lansbury Collection.

1900. He stood as a Socialist and Labour candidate, endorsed by the new national Labour Representation Committee. In spite of the inferior election organisation at his command, Lansbury was able to reduce the Conservative majority on a higher poll. In more favourable conditions Bow and Bromley could clearly be won by a socialist.

The success of the S.D.F. was more impressive in West Ham. Here the socialist leader was Will Thorne. A tough militant Midland-born worker whose family had been brickmakers, gas-stoking during the slack winter season, Thorne had wandered the country as a young man working with the navvies on railway construction. He found himself influenced by 'these big-hearted carefree men ... an independent type, with the spark of rebellion glowing bright within them.'[1] Eventually he returned to gas-stoking, and in 1882 settled in West Ham. He was a keen boxer, 'slight and fine-drawn ... straight from the retort house with the mark of the fiery place burnt into his features. Round his eyes were dark rings of coal grime.'[2] In later years, condemned to the sedentary life of a trade union official, he developed a well-fed complacency, but in the 1890s he was a fighting leader of real ability. His power was based on the Gas Workers' Union which he formed in 1889. The union, which had a strong grip on London as a whole, had one of its biggest branches in the Canning Town district of West Ham. Even at its weakest point in 1896 there were 1,400 union members in West Ham.

West Ham South had become a Liberal-Labour constituency in 1885, and although the seat was lost to the Conservatives in 1886 there remained a faction among the local Liberals who were unwilling to accept a middle class candidate. For most of the period up to the 1892 general election there were rival prospective Liberal candidates. One of these was the wealthy Hume Webster; the other, from 1889, was Keir Hardie. A three-cornered fight was avoided only when Hume Webster committed suicide, and his supporters were unable to find any potential candidate but the former Liberal-Labour member Joseph Leicester, who was forced to withdraw when it became clear that the general feeling favoured Hardie.[3] Hardie was then elected as

---

[1] Thorne, op. cit., p. 35.   [2] Sanders, op. cit., p. 51.

[3] The meetings of the rival groups and their disputes are reported in the *Stratford Express*. Webster first appeared on the scene in December 1886, and because of the difficulty of working through the existing Liberal and Radical Federation created a new West Ham Liberal Association in his own support. He then proceeded with a steady canvass by paid workers, won over several clubs through donations and gave money towards founding others, and kept efficient registration work going. He failed to win over most leading Nonconformists, and especially at first tended to rely on supporters from North West Ham at his meetings. He was weak in the riverside dock district. The rival group at first adopted W. Morgan, and then a manufacturer Spencer Curwen,

the first London independent Labour M.P. Meanwhile progress was being made at local elections. The first victories of the Gas Workers were in 1889. Thorne himself was elected a councillor in 1891, and by 1892 there were seven councillors described as Labour members. Two Labour men were elected to the School Board in 1892, and others to the Guardians.

These early victories were followed by a severe set-back. The factions within the local Liberal party began quarrelling over Hardie's independent line in the House of Commons, and unsuccessful attempts were made to find a rival candidate.[1] Hardie's defeat in 1895 was partly due to a deterioration in election and registration work since 1892, but also to the active opposition of the anti-Parnellite section of the local Irish and the Temperance Union.[2]

At the same time on the West Ham Council difficulty was caused by the disorganised party situation, in which there was no separately organised labour party. There was also a new friction within the socialist movement caused by the formation of the I.L.P., which drew on some of Hardie's Liberal supporters. The dangers of division led to the formation of a United Socialist and Labour Council, with representatives of the Trades Council, S.D.F., I.L.P. and Christian Socialists. Although the first list of candidates which it adopted appear to have been identical with that proposed by the S.D.F., there was at first some resistance from an extreme wing of the branch and one S.D.F. candidate stood independently in 1894.[3] After that its

[1] E.g. *West Ham Guardian*, 27 October 1894; *West Ham Herald*, 13 July 1895.
[2] *West Ham Herald*, 20 July 1895.
[3] Ibid., 8 and 22 September 1894; *Labour Leader*, 10 November 1894.

---

who was supported by the Nonconformists, a section of the clubs, leading radicals such as Dr John Moir and Alderman Harry Phillips, and most of the Liberals on the town council. By 1889 Webster's persistent canvassing was beginning to win results in the dock district, and his gift of £150 in the dock strike, in contrast to the indifference of Curwen who was abroad, converted Phillips, who was a prominent advocate of the new unionists. At the same time the first labour candidates stood in the local elections, not without opposition from other Liberals. Curwen withdrew in January 1890, and his supporters then brought forward Keir Hardie as 'a strict labour candidate' (*Stratford Express*, 19 April 1890). Those who had openly committed themselves to Webster, such as Phillips and Councillor Walsh the London secretary of the Seamen, found themselves in a difficult position; they argued that although 'in favour of labour representation' they had 'yet to be convinced that it was safe to run a labour candidate in South West Ham, who was half a labour candidate and half a socialist' (*Stratford Express*, 21 March 1891). In spite of his financial disadvantage, Hardie established himself as a dangerous rival to Webster, and when Webster committed suicide in January 1892 Phillips refused to support the adoption of another Liberal. Hardie now had the backing of the majority of both Nonconformist and trade unionists, and the attempt of the dissidents to run Joseph Leicester was a complete failure.

authority was respected. It decided on the wards to be contested and endorsed the candidates, who if elected were to form 'a separate party' on the Council.¹ Thorne was re-elected as the only independent councillor in 1894. The 'old Progressive party' rapidly became overtly hostile, and two former radicals with socialist sympathies, Saunders Jacobs a local solicitor and Percy Alden the warden of Mansfield House, came over to the Labour Party. On the other hand some of the earlier labour councillors remained hostile to independence. By 1896, however, there was a Labour Party of seven in a Council of thirty-six.

At this point an unusual and able election organiser was roused to action. J. J. Terrett came from a Forest of Dean family with a 'reputation for rather wild and adventurous careers', was educated at the Brewers' Company School, where he proved as unruly as intelligent, and then travelled in South America, before throwing himself into the new unionist and socialist movement in 1889. Despite the adoption of the pseudonym A. G. Wolfe for lecturing purposes he found himself out of work and 'lived like a Spartan'.² In 1892, although under age and unqualified he organised a strikingly successful labour-socialist alliance resulting in the election of eight candidates including himself to the Newington vestry. Shortly afterwards he married, and spent two years as an itinerant socialist and Fabian lecturer in the provinces. He returned to settle in West Ham in 1895, but kept out of politics until 1897. Terrett then worked up a big campaign as election organiser, gaining four seats in 1897 and eight more seats in 1898. The Engineers, who were embittered by their strike defeat, threw their important local influence behind the socialists. The remaining labour Progressives decided to support the Labour Party in the aldermanic elections, and two further gains were made in the consequent bye-elections. As a result a Labour Party of twenty-five, of which over half were socialists, was formed. 'The group always met before the Council meetings to discuss the agenda and to decide their policy on particular points.'³ 'Each member of the group agrees to abide by the decisions of the majority of the group, unless exemption has been claimed and given—as it has been, for instance, on a religious question. No member can put a motion on the agenda paper of the Council without the consent of the group; nor, without such consent, can any member engage in a public correspondence so as in any way to pledge the Labour Party.'⁴ This Labour Party, in its procedure and constitution very like the typical

---

¹ *West Ham Herald*, 6 October 1894.
² *Social Democrat*, August 1899.
³ Howarth and Wilson, op. cit., p. 314.
⁴ H. Legge, 'Socialism in West Ham', *Economic Review*, 1899.

Labour Party of the future, the first in the country to control a town council, was the achievement of the S.D.F.[1]

The policy of the Party was much as it would have been if controlled by I.L.Pers or Fabians. The first priority was taken to be the slum housing. More sanitary inspectors were appointed, and a house to house inspection carried out for the first time; although opponents claimed 'in their zeal to exterminate the insanitary landlord, the socialists persist in ignoring the insanitary tenant'. Two new baths and wash-houses were built. Plans were made for 500 council houses, houses for widows and widowers, and municipal lodging houses, known as workmen's hotels. The Council applied for a loan to build 300 further houses when these were finished. A works department was created and given a large initial contract to build a hospital. The local libraries were opened on Sundays, and more branches proposed. More music was provided in the parks, and free winter concerts started. An unemployed register was opened, and the men put to work planting trees. Council employees were given an eight hour day, a 30/– minimum wage, Mayday and a fortnight's holiday. Scholarships to the Technical Institute were founded. Negotiations were opened for the purchase of the local gas and water supply, and tramways. Municipal laundries, dispensaries and insurance were proposed.[2]

The reaction to this enlightened policy, and to the consequent increase in the expenditure, was the formation of a West Ham Municipal Alliance, 'absolutely non-political, non-partisan and non-sectarian', with an alleged interest in 'fair conditions of labour' and 'proper sanitation' in houses and streets, 'to raise the standard of the administration' and 'to prevent wasteful and illegal expenditure'. It was led by 'that uncompromising teetotaller and Nonconformist, the

---

[1] Ibid., and *Labour Leader*, 11 November 1899.

[2] S.D.F. councillors were never more than a small group. In 1898–9 Labour supporters seem from press reports to have divided as follows: 5 outside the Labour Group, led by Athey, a Liberal railwayman; 9 non-socialist Labour Group members, notably Alden and four middle class aldermen elected by the group in 1898; 16 socialist Labour Group members, of whom 8 belonged to the I.L.P. and the remainder probably to the S.D.F. But of the 16 only 5 had sat before 1897: two I.L.P. Liberals (Ward in 1892 and Jacobs in 1893), and three Labour men—Thorne in 1891 (S.D.F.), Godbold in 1896 (I.L.P. and S.D.F.) and Hayday in 1896 (S.D.F.; the only socialist alderman). Of the socialists, the most powerful were thus S.D.Fers. This was reinforced by the fact that Thorne and Hayday were the most powerful trade unionists on the council, while five of the I.L.P. members (including Godbold, Ward and Jacobs) were middle class men, and as such less influential than Alden and the senior aldermen. The Labour Group was the product of S.D.F. trade unionism and electioneering, middle class sympathy and labour solidarity, with the first as the creative force, but only a minority in its constitution. (*Stratford Express*, 12 and 26 November 1898, 18 November 1899, &c.)

treasurer of the Liberal caucus'. Although this combination of frightened ratepayers and businessmen did not oust the socialists at their first attempt in November 1899, they made sufficient gains to make progress impossible. Angry scenes were provoked in the Council, where Labour councillors found that the Alliance 'treat you like dirt unless you are inclined to be submissive'. Labour supporters who did not belong to the Group added to the bitterness, and the local press exploited every incident. Landlords started to raise the rents, and blamed the Council, although in fact the rates—despite the increase in expenditure—had been reduced. Every difficulty was made to prevent the purchase of housing sites in the crowded borough. The 'reckless' increase in expenditure was incessantly attacked; the presence in the borough library of the *Freethinker*—although it had been there before the socialists—was discovered and denounced; the voters were called to end the 'manipulation by caucus' and undemocratic 'packing' of Council committees. The Alliance propaganda resulted in increased polls at the elections, and the Labour Party was dislodged in 1900.[1]

A month before in the general election Will Thorne had been given a straight fight as a Labour and Socialist candidate by the moribund Liberals, but had failed to recover the seat or even to reduce the Conservative majority. These two defeats showed the weakness of the S.D.F. when challenged by well-organised anti-socialist forces. The S.D.F. was not unaware of its vulnerability. When Lansbury was appointed as S.D.F. organiser Hyndman told him it would be 'a great mistake if you overdo your voice. What we need now is organisation and discipline more than agitation.'[2] Lansbury wrote a series of articles in *Justice* arguing that the S.D.F. must 'show that not merely are we the talkers, but that we can organise and work'.[3] But before 1900 only one branch can be shown to have attempted registration work.[4] In West Ham the register had scarcely been touched since Hume Webster's death, and had become 'little else but a Tory roll'. Of a possible 2,000 lodger voters only 99 were on the register. These should have been the backbone of the Labour vote. Similarly at the election only two wards were properly canvassed, and these produced big majorities for Thorne. Silvertown and Tidal Basin, which had been Hardie's strongest areas, were not properly worked and polled poorly.[5] West Ham South might have been won for

[1] Legge, op. cit.; F. H. Billows, 'Socialism in West Ham', *Economic Review*, 1900; *Stratford Express*, 18 November 1899.
[2] H. M. Hyndman to G. Lansbury, 25 August 1895, Lansbury Collection.
[3] 27 October 1895.
[4] Kentish Town, who said at the 1896 S.D.F. conference that they had appointed a registration agent.
[5] J. J. Terrett in *Justice*, 3 November 1900.

Labour even in 1900 if the S.D.F. had had the necessary electoral skill.

After these defeats, stung by a hostile series of articles in *The Times*, Terrett wrote an interesting defence of the West Ham socialists. He described the town, a 'dismal smoke-and-fog becursed marsh', 'the atmosphere blackened with smoke and poisoned with the noxious fumes of chemicals, and the stench of bone-manure and soap-works, and the only sounds to be heard are the shriek of railway engines and the mournful foghorn hoots of the steamboats coming up the river.' In this depressing setting the Labour Party represented 'a Renaissance of the civic ideal'. In its work 'Oxford M.A. and general labourer alike gave the best and the highest that was in them to the service of a generation but as yet half-awakened'. The typical socialist was a thinker, a trade unionist, 'who has read his Morris, digested his Ruskin, and possibly gone on an empty belly to buy his Carlyle, Kingsley or Marx', and was not likely to be hoodwinked by *The Times*. Terrett was surprised that *The Times* had not attacked the 'extravagance' of the council in making a footpath on the Northern Outfall Sewer. 'Only think! If a sufficiently highly coloured picture had been drawn of the working man, rolling in ill-gotten gains, attained by the ruthless spoliation of "those classes who form the backbone of the community", recreating himself by promenading along this embankment with a gasworks on his right, a sewage pumping station on his left, two chemical works behind him, and a soap factory in front, there can be no doubt that the appeal to Parliament "to take note of facts" rather than "cling indolently to theories" would have been supported with a forcible illustration that must have carried irresistible conviction to the minds of the lethargic legislators of Palace Yard.'[1] The S.D.F. had lost a round in the struggle, but there was no reason for doubting its continued vitality. On the contrary, the West Ham achievement showed its potential power within a Labour Party. But would *Justice* change its tune in time?

[1] J. J. Terrett, *Municipal Socialism in West Ham, A Reply to the Times*, London 1903.

VII
THE SOCIALIST LEAGUE, THE FABIANS AND THE INDEPENDENT LABOUR PARTY

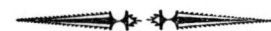

ALTHOUGH the S.D.F. was always the largest of the London socialist societies it was only in its infancy that it had no rivals. Partly because of personal incompatibilities and partly because of theoretical and tactical differences, there were always after 1884 two or more alternative socialist parties fighting for influence in London. The divisions among the socialists were a handicap, not only because they wasted energy, but because they tended to exaggerate the differing emphases of the groups within the movement.

This tendency is especially striking in the first serious rival to the S.D.F., the Socialist League. The two organisations were at first very similar in character. The League, like the S.D.F., lived for its outdoor propaganda. Its membership was a similar mixture of middle class men like William Morris and Edward Aveling, and working class intellectuals like Robert Banner, a bookbinder and 'workman economist',[1] and Joseph Lane, an individualistic East End pioneer. The Socialist League had only three areas of any strength; Woolwich, where Banner was active, Bloomsbury, where Aveling and Eleanor Marx were supported by some of the German communists in Soho, and Hammersmith, centred upon William Morris. The Hammersmith branch was the best, with over 120 members, and offshoots in Fulham, North Kensington and Acton. Although the League was able to start with some East End branches brought in by Joseph Lane these did not long survive. Consequently there was little geographical friction with the S.D.F. and the two organisations were soon 'jogging on alongside each other without collision'.[2] The S.D.F. in fact was

[1] H. W. Lee and E. Archbold, *Social-Democracy in Britain*, p. 80.
[2] F. Engels. to L. Lafargue, 8 March 1885, Engels and Lafargue, op. cit., 1, p. 272.

unable to re-establish itself in West London and Woolwich for over a decade after the disappearance of the League.

The differences of political theory within the Socialist League were at first even wider than within the S.D.F. There were orthodox Marxists, such as Aveling and Eleanor Marx herself, with the support of Engels in the background. William Morris and Joseph Lane, although strongly influenced by Marxism, were from the start inclined to anti-political anarchism. Thomas Binning of the Compositors and John Mahon, an Edinburgh engineer, were more responsive to the importance of trade unionism. At first the League was able to reconcile these various groups by confining its activity to socialist propaganda, but by 1888 the Marxist group felt that political activity had become necessary. After the annual conference had decided against parliamentary candidatures, the Marxists and trade unionists seceded, taking with them the Bloomsbury and Woolwich branches. William Morris now found himself in the power of the anarchists within the League, and to an increasing extent of young anarchists with a taste for violence. When he was voted out of control of the League's journal *Commonweal* at the 1890 conference the Hammersmith branch seceded, forming the Hammersmith Socialist Society, and by 1891 the League had dissolved into a series of small anarchist groups.

The Fabian Society showed a similar crystallisation in a very different direction. It emerged from a small religious drawing-room group in 1884, and until 1888 it was little more than a discussion group itself. It published seven pamphlets in its first five years, and some of its members were in frequent demand as political lecturers by clubs and socialist branches, but it cannot be said to have had much collective political influence or any defined political standpoint. The early members were a mixture of Marxists and radicals, and many of them also belonged to the S.D.F. including the first Fabian Society secretary Frederick Keddell and its first treasurer Hubert Bland. Even in the later 1880s Annie Besant belonged to both societies. Bernard Shaw was a Marxist when he joined in September 1884; Sidney Webb and Sydney Olivier, two young civil servants, and Graham Wallas, then a Highgate schoolmaster, who all joined in 1885–6, were milder socialists who had reached their new convictions through Liberalism and social conscience. Stewart Headlam was a radical clergyman who never came closer to socialism than land reform. There was even an anarchist section among the members led by the wife of a wealthy stockbroker, Mrs. Charlotte Wilson. The true basis of the early Fabian Society was not a political creed, but a desire to discuss socialist ideas.

To some extent this early variety among the Fabians survived. Because of its role as an intellectual discussion group and because of its publications the Fabian Society was able to attract both Liberals and revolutionaries into its membership right up until 1914. But in common with the S.D.F. and the Socialist League it found a need to clarify its standpoint in the later 1880s. It is not surprising that this clarification produced an anti-Marxist theory and the comforting new political tactic of permeation. From the beginning the Fabian Society was overwhelmingly middle class in membership, and consequently frightened of the idea of the class struggle. The Fabians could find little hope for the future through the working classes. The very poor, the unemployed, were a danger, a threat of violence, a 'bear-garden';[1] the more prosperous were 'struggling up slowly from mere squalor and ignorance to middle class respectability'. The working class, in Bernard Shaw's view was 'not going to unite with the proletarians of all lands: it objects to foreigners. It is not going to make a revolution, because it knows too well what a working man is like when he throws off restraint. It is infinitely more insular and more attached to law and order than the old Whig cosmopolitan or the old Tory sportsman.'[2] It must have been a relief to many of the early Fabians when the free speech struggles showed how easily the police could break up an unarmed demonstration. Certainly they could feel, as middle class men, stockbrokers, civil servants and clergy, that they would have more to contribute to a socialism achieved through administrative reform and political persuasion than to a revolutionary upheaval.

The new Fabian doctrine, with its gradualist vision and its economics based on Jevons instead of Marx, was worked out in a series of discussions in 1888 and published in *Fabian Essays* in 1889. As a positive theory of economic exploitation Jevonian Fabianism was soon forgotten, although it served to discredit Marxism and to make the gradual achievement of socialism without the class struggle seem more convincing. There is no evidence that the new doctrine was ever widely held among socialists. Rather, its importance was in excusing those who dislike Marxism from the need to master its theory, and in providing a justification for many who wished to consider themselves socialists but not revolutionaries.

The new political tactic, the permeation of the existing political organisations rather than the creation of an independent socialist party, was the essential counterpart to the theory. The first Fabians had been divided between those who supported the S.D.F. and those,

[1] Halliday Sparling in *Workman's Times*, 14 January 1893.
[2] G. B. Shaw, 'The Political Situation', lecture to the Fabian Society, 1895, Shaw Collection.

like Webb, Headlam and Wallas, who preferred to remain with the Liberals. For civil servants and schoolmasters the preoccupation of the S.D.F. with outdoor meetings must have been a strong deterrent, and most of the Fabians who had joined the S.D.F. were quick to take the chance to disown it after the Tory Gold scandal of the 1885 election.

That the Fabians did not at once decide on permeation was due to the intervention of Annie Besant, who joined the Society in 1885. She was their best known early member, the secularist and radical colleague of Bradlaugh, one of the great political orators of the period. She made two unsuccessful attempts to convert the Fabian Society into a political party, first through a scheme of 1886 to form branches of the Society, and then in 1887 through the formation of a separate Fabian Parliamentary League. Both these efforts failed through the lack of support of the leaders of the Society. After this Annie Besant joined the S.D.F. and became its election treasurer. In the year of her greatest success, 1888, when she organised the matchgirls strike and was elected as an avowed socialist to the London School Board, she had already been defeated in her plans for the Fabian Society. But even so, by lending her name to the Fabians, Annie Besant more than any other member gave the Fabian Society its first reputation.

Eventually, after 1890 when she herself had been converted to theosophy and had withdrawn from politics, the Fabian Society expanded in the way that she wished. This expansion was made possible by the association of the Society, chiefly through Annie Besant, with the new unionism, and by the fortunate coincidence of the issue of *Fabian Essays in Socialism* with the upheaval of 1889. Although trade unionism is ignored in *Fabian Essays*, the socialist convictions of the new unionist leaders created a public demand for socialist literature, and quickly pushed the sale of the essays up to 25,000 copies, more than all the socialist tracts of the 1880s.[1] The Fabians were also able to take advantage of the unexpected Progressive triumph in the first L.C.C. election, in which they had taken no part, by publishing *Facts for Londoners* in the autumn of 1889. Equally cleverly they shortly afterwards brought out a draft *Eight Hours Bill*, thus staking their claim in the eight hours agitation. As Engels was bitterly to remark, the Fabians were astute 'careerists who have understanding enough to realise the inevitability of the social revolution; but not trusting this gigantic task to the crude proletariat alone, they are gracious enough to stand at the head of it.'[2]

At the same time, with the disintegration of the Socialist League

[1] M. S. Wilkins, 'The Influence of Socialist Ideas upon English Prose Writing and Political Thinking, 1880–95', Cambridge Ph.D. thesis, 1957, p. 170.
[2] Quoted in *Lenin on Britain*, London 1934, p. 77.

and the failure of the group led by H. H. Champion, the Fabians became until the formation of the I.L.P. in 1892 the only alternative socialist party to the S.D.F. Late in 1889 Edward Pease, one of the original Fabians, a Quaker stockbroker who had moved to Newcastle in 1886 to live as a working cabinet-maker and had there become involved in the new unionism, returned to London to set up an office as fulltime paid Fabian secretary. A young Cambridge graduate, W. S. de Mattos, was taken on as a paid lecturer and *Fabian News* was started in 1891. A recruiting campaign was organised in Lancashire. The national membership rose from 173 in 1890 to 640 in 1893, of which 399 were London members. The new members came from various sources. Some were former Socialist Leaguers like Robert Banner, others active S.D.Fers like Fred Knee, new trade unionists like Will Crooks or radical clergy like Arthur Jephson. An important group were future I.L.Pers, among them Frank Smith, Keir Hardie and Margaret McMillan. It is hardly surprising that the new north-country Fabian branches and London Fabian groups showed an equally diverse political complexion.

The London Fabian groups were more important as a link in the origins of the I.L.P. than as part of the development of the Fabian Society, and their activity is therefore described later. But it is important to remember that at the point when the Fabian leaders became convinced of the efficacy of permeation, they had behind them a vigorously developing Society, even though its expansion was not based on their own political standpoint.

Most of the early middle class socialists had hoped to carry radicals and Liberals with them. William Morris had been treasurer of the National Liberal League in the early 1880s, Hyndman had formed the Democratic Federation with the support of the radical clubs, and the early Fabians can be found carrying socialist motions in suburban Liberal clubs. But alone of English socialists the Fabian leaders clung to the belief until as late as 1910 that socialism could be most easily achieved through one of the existing political parties. Why was this?

Principally it was because for the Fabians there was far more personal satisfaction to be found in working through the Liberal Association than through a working class party with little immediate prospect of political achievement. It is noticeable that, although the Fabians lectured frequently to the radical clubs, very few of them—Annie Besant and Graham Wallas are the chief exceptions—practised permeation in the working class organisations. The chosen fields were rather the National Liberal Club, the political dinner party, the constituency Association.[1] Here the Fabians found a socially sym-

---

[1] In 1892 50 Fabians, including half the Fabian executive committee, belonged to the National Liberal Club; Wilkins, op. cit., p. 179.

pathetic atmosphere, in which their opinions were tolerated and their support rewarded by minor office. Here their ability was appreciated. As Shaw reminded a Fabian gathering in 1895, 'It is far better to be an official Liberal ... and to do something, than to be an uncompromising Social-Democrat and do nothing'.[1]

In order to prevent permeation from appearing as mere self-interested opportunism, a legend of political achievements was developed. Some of them, such as the claim to have been responsible for the radical policy of the *Star*, were already current by the early 1890s;[2] others did not reach their full fantasy until the 1900s or later. The author of these stories was usually Bernard Shaw. There were times throughout his career when Shaw was willing to admit that 'the Liberal party is in the dust'.[3] He even organised a conference in 1896 to 'describe the permeation game' and 'to show how it all breaks down at a certain point because the parties in power are neither Socialists nor members of the working class working unconsciously towards Socialism in the pursuit of their own interests.'[4] But more commonly Shaw, intoxicated by the brilliance and audacity of his own inventions, went 'uncompromisingly for permeation', 'forcing the fighting as extravagantly as possible'.[5] His is a devastating example of the historical fraudulence that can be purveyed by scintillating rhetoric. For however often Shaw must have been seen to be openly lying, the impression of Fabian influence that he was trying to create was widely accepted, and is still widely accepted today.

One of the best examples of his technique was his lecture, *The Fabian Society: Its Early History*, given before an admiring audience of provincial delegates in 1892. On this occasion he claimed that among the papers which the Fabians had managed to 'induce ... to give a column or two to Socialism', were the *Star*, the *Manchester Sunday Chronicle* and the *Clarion*. The truth about the *Star* has been already recounted. The other two papers owed their socialism entirely to Robert Blatchford, who wrote angrily to point out that the London 'Fabian Society never had a word in it. Why should they? Claim as much credit as you please, advertise your own work as much as you please, but let us possess our own souls in peace.'[6] Shaw

[1] G. B. Shaw, op. cit., 'The Political Situation'.
[2] E.g. *Scottish Leader*, 4 September 1890; *Workman's Times*, 16 October 1891.
[3] G. B. Shaw to anon., 16 December 1890, Wallas Collection.
[4] Typescript syllabus, 5 June 1896, correspondence with Fabian Society, Shaw Collection.
[5] G. B. Shaw to E. Pease, 11 January 1893, ibid.
[6] R. Blatchford to E. Pease, 14 August 1892, Fabian Society archives. Blatchford was president of the Manchester Fabian Society which did not share the political approach of the London Fabian Society.

dropped that story, but two others put forward on this occasion were much developed over the years. These were the claims to have permeated the Liberal Associations and thereby to have caused the adoption of the Newcastle Programme and the Progressive policy of the L.C.C. The work of permeation, Shaw suggested, had begun in 1886 and continued until 1890 when the Fabians were 'found out'. It is of course true that many Fabians remained within the Liberal Associations in these years and Webb was elected to the London Liberal and Radical Union committee in 1889. But their influence is more difficult to demonstrate. On this occasion Shaw was content to point to the election programmes, which were 'full of ideas that would have never come into their heads had not the Fabian put them there'. Yet in fact Dr. McBriar's close examination of these programmes shows that they were not novel departures, and not a single item in them can be attributed to Fabian influence.

Shaw later developed evidence. The basis of the Newcastle Programme, it was asserted, was a very moderate and unoriginal leaflet, *Wanted a Programme*, which Webb had privately circulated in 1888.[1] But this advocated a much less advanced programme than that suggested by the *Star*, so that the fact that in 1889 six Liberal Associations passed resolutions in its support can hardly be regarded as in any way significant. The programme did not include the eight hour day, the most important new issue of the period. One of the Associations which accepted it was South St. Pancras, at the suggestion of Shaw himself. Thus, according to Shaw's final version, 'the first Fabian Socialist program on which a General Election was fought and won in 1892 was drafted by Sidney Webb; but it was called the Newcastle Programme and put forward as the program of the Liberal Party. It was in fact fobbed on it by me at an obscure meeting of an obscure branch of the Liberal Association in a speech of which the reporters and the Liberal Parliamentary candidate who seconded me (the whole audience) did not understand a single sentence.'[2]

Although the Progressive election victory and policy of 1889 owed nothing to the Fabians, Shaw was prepared to suggest even as early as 1892 that Webb had had a hand in it. Here again in time he concocted evidence. In 1915 he was writing that 'the Fabians had been the first to grasp the opportunity offered to practical socialism by the possibilities of municipal enterprise' (forgetting Hyndman), and that in 1889 'they circulated leaflets suggesting questions to county councillors'; 'the candidates for the new bodies, having no

[1] E.g. S. Webb to E. Pease, 4 June 1915, Fabian Society archives, and E. Pease, *The History of the Fabian Society*, London 1916, p. 111.
[2] G. B. Shaw and others, *Fabian Essays*, Jubilee edn, London 1948, p. 208.

platform and no traditional policy to fall back on, snatched at the program thus adroitly suggested', which 'suddenly took shape in London as Progressivism'.[1] There was, of course, a very clear traditional policy, which was adopted by the London Liberal and Radical Union and the *Star*. It was the *Star* which published *Questions to Candidates*. Yet Pease suggested in his *History of the Fabian Society* that it was a Fabian publication,[2] although omitting it from his list at the end of the book. In fact the Fabians did not issue election literature of this type before 1891–2. As time passed Shaw was able to confuse the two elections of 1889 and 1892 and assert that in 1889 'the new London County Council, finding itself without a programme, had one imposed on it by Webb's Questions for County Councillors, which filled the vacuum, and launched the Fabian Progressive Party in municipal London'.[3]

Probably as he grew older Shaw began to believe his own stories. Perhaps Sidney Webb always believed them. Webb was a strangely unlikely figure for a political leader; a short, rough-haired man, with a wide forehead, prominent reddish eyes, swollen lips, a bad complexion, and a protruding behind.[4] The son of a London shopkeeper, he had become a professional civil servant. He was undoubtedly able and industrious, but unimaginative. Shaw supplied most of his original ideas. He could get through any book almost as fast as he could turn the leaves, and no doubt suffered from the speed with which he read. He dismissed Volume One of *Capital* as irrelevant in

[1] 'Fabianism', *Chamber's Encyclopaedia*, London 1924; the manuscript, dated 19 May 1915, Shaw Collection.

[2] Pease, op. cit., p. 79.

[3] *Fabian Essays*, 1948, op. cit., p. 209; cf. B. Webb, *Our Partnership*, London 1948, p. 60. A more recent distorted version of this claim may be found in M. Cole, *The Story of Fabian Socialism*, p. 40.

[4] B. Webb, diary, 14 February 1890, her first impression, 'a remarkable little man with a huge head and a very tiny body, a breadth of forehead quite sufficient to account for the encyclopaedic character of his knowledge. A Jewish nose, prominent eyes and mouth, black hair, somewhat unkempt, spectacles . . . His pronunciation is cockney, his H's are shaky, his attitudes by no means eloquent—with his thumbs fixed pugnaciously in a far from immaculate waistcoat, with his bulky head thown back and his little body forward he struts even when he stands, delivering himself with extraordinary rapidity of thought and utterance and with an expression of inexhaustible self-complacency'; ibid., 26 April 1890, 'his tiny tadpole body, unhealthy skin, cockney pronunciation, poverty, are all against him'; cf. Oscar Bailey in H. G. Wells, *The New Machiavelli*, London 1913, p. 205, 'a short sturdy figure with a round protruding abdomen and a curious broad, flattened, clean-shaven face that seemed nearly all forehead. He was of Anglo-Hungarian extraction, and I have always fancied something Mongolian in his type. He peered up with reddish swollen-looking eyes over gilt-edged glasses that were divided horizontally into portions of different refractive power, and he talked in an ingratiating undertone, with busy thin lips, an eager lisp and nervous movements of the hand.'

an hour, according to Shaw.¹ 'I do not number my hours of work, because I do nothing else. I see no friends, save in the work. I have not read a book for months. I have not been to a theatre or concert or picture gallery in London for years.'²

No doubt Sidney Webb's relentless industry would have made its mark in any field, but without Shaw's puffing he would hardly have so rapidly acquired a reputation for political influence. Already when his future wife, Beatrice Potter, met him in 1890, Webb had 'the conceit of a man who has raised himself out of the most insignificant surroundings into a position of power—how much power no one quite knows. This self-complacent egotism, this disproportionate view of his own position, is at once repulsive and ludicrous.'³ Even so, Beatrice soon found him an agreeable companion in socialist research work; the relationship deepened into love, and in 1892 they married. Her income gave them independence. At the same time her influence turned Webb towards a new type of permeation. She at once advised him to drop the 'bribe and threat' tactic of offering the Liberal leaders victory if they conceded a socialist election programme.⁴ Instead it was necessary to penetrate 'the inner circles that really *do* the government of England. Politics in England are too much of a fine art for men without technical skill to succeed. . . . (A man) must be socially *self-sufficient*: he must be fully aware of class differences but not subservient to them. . . . He must possess social charm.'⁵

Beatrice did not want Sidney to become a full-time Parliamentarian. She would see less of him, and she would be less able to play the central political role for which she was so suited. A tall, impressively handsome woman, an imaginative and fascinating conversationalist, it was easy for Beatrice to convince herself that political influence was exerted at the dinner-table rather than on the platform. The fact that she was an extraordinarily erratic judge of character helped this illusion. Keir Hardie, for example, she wrote off in 1895.⁶ At the same time she exaggerated her own powers. In 1895 she undertook to reorganise the London Reform Union herself, with the comment that the committee 'is very "plastic", feel pretty confident I could get them to do anything I want.'⁷ She could not.

Encouraged by Beatrice and by Bernard Shaw, Sidney Webb became the hero of the Fabian legend. His increasing self-deception is clearly shown in his relationship with the L.C.C. Progressives. The

---

[1] M. Cole (ed.), *The Webbs and their Work*, London 1949, p. 4.
[2] S. Webb to B. Potter, 6 April 1891, Passfield Collection.
[3] B. Webb, diary, 26 April 1890.
[4] B. Potter to S. Webb, summer 1891, Passfield Collection.
[5] B. Webb, diary, 24 January 1897.   [6] *Our Partnership*, op. cit., p. 127.
[7] B. Webb, diary 9, April 1895.

first sign of Fabian interest in the L.C.C. had been the publication of *Facts for Londoners* in the autumn of 1889. This was followed by a series of articles by Webb in the *Speaker*.[1] The sudden death of James Firth in 1889 had deprived the Progressives of their best propagandist, and the Liberal Party, impressed by Webb's presentation of the Progressive programme, decided in 1890 to reprint the articles as a pamphlet. Webb already had a very fantastic view of the project. 'If this comes off (and it is a secret as yet) it will mean a wonderful change in the Liberal programme and way of looking at things.'[2] In fact the pamphlet was dropped, but Webb decided to amplify and republish the articles as a book, *The London Programme*. He now believed himself to be a pioneer, doing what the London Liberal leader Professor Stuart 'ought to have done long ago, viz. actually write down what the London programme is'.[3] The book proved a success. It added one item to the Progressive programme, the municipalisation of the docks, made a topical issue by the dock strike. In the words of a reviewer, it 'traversed ground familiar to readers of the Star'.[4] But Webb had forgotten this, and when the Progressive party reasserted its programme for the 1892 election, he called it 'from beginning to end a "Fabian" manifesto'.[5] When Stuart wished to alter the draft, Webb felt 'he is obviously *following* me now, so that I can well afford to be generous'.[6] Meanwhile with the prospect of marriage and a secure income, Webb decided to leave the civil service and secure a seat on the County Council. After some negotiation he was adopted as a Progressive at Deptford. He greeted the Progressive triumph as a 'simply gorgeous justification of Fabian electioneering' which ought 'to convince the provincials that our game is the right one—and also to give us the control of London politics for the next three years'.[7]

Of course the 1892 victory was the final climax of the policy advocated by the *Star*, and in the most significant feature of it, the adoption of ten labour men as Progressive candidates, the Fabian Society played no part.[8] Certainly it is true that five of these labour

[1] 12 July 1890 &c.
[2] S. Webb to B. Potter, 17 October 1890, Passfield Collection.
[3] 14 March 1891, ibid.   [4] *Star*, 2 February 1892.
[5] S. Webb to B. Potter, 15 November 1891, Passfield Collection.
[6] Ibid., 20 November 1891.
[7] S. Webb to G. Wallas, 6 March 1892, Wallas Collection.
[8] Although there is plenty of evidence of Webb's own negotiations (e.g. S. Webb to Fenton, 3 and 4 March 1891, S. Webb to B. Potter, 14 March, 27 August, 7 September, 16 September, 20 October, 2 November, 11 November, 15 November, 8 December, 9 December, 10 December 1891, Passfield Collection), there is no evidence either in the Passfield Collection or Fabian Society archives of any Fabian intervention in favour of the adoption of labour candidates by the Progressives.

candidates had joined the Fabian Society in 1891–2, during its period of expansion, but they were in no way involved in the permeation schemes of the Fabian leaders.[1] Webb was the only typical Fabian who stood in 1892. Once elected he was admitted to 'that little circle of a dozen committees who practically run the L.C.C.'[2] He became the Progressive expert on education, and in that role was responsible for the considerable educational achievements of the Council in the next ten years. But it is important to notice that Webb did not align himself with the socialists who demanded a universal free secondary education, and was content to build a very narrow 'scholarship ladder'. It is also significant that the committees which were pursuing policies which could be described as 'municipal socialism' were led by orthodox Progressives like John Benn and W. H. Dickinson. But in spite of all the protests of the Progressives, this did not prevent the legend of Fabian influence on the Council's policy from growing steadily over the years, reaching a climax at the time of the great defeat of the 1907 election.

Webb and Shaw were not able to convince the Fabians of the merits of permeation without encountering some resistance. The influx of new members with different views brought more than one serious challenge before 1893. In December 1890 Shaw warned Webb that 'the seismological signs indicate that we are all spoiling for a fight. What is more, the revolt is going to be against the Webbite opportunism.' Shaw himself was ready to change tactics, and 'proclaim ourselves, not an advanced guard of the Liberal party, but a definitely Social-Democratic party'.[3] But the revolt came to nothing. A year later, when 'the younger impatient element' wanted 'to throw the whole movement entirely into the Labour Party', Webb's resis-

---

[1] Frank Smith and Will Crooks were elected to the Fabian Society on 27 January 1891, Baum before October, Henderson on 8 December 1891, Steadman on 23 February 1892. Of the aldermen elected, Tillett was a Fabian elected on 24 March 1891. Burns joined in June 1893, Cooper in January 1897 (Fabian Society executive committee minutes). There were thus six Fabians on the labour bench, but they were all involved in the independent labour movement. Frank Smith and Henderson had tried to form independent parties themselves; Baum was secretary of the Trades Council Labour Representation League; Tillett was standing for Bradford in the General Election as an independent socialist; Crooks and Steadman had both created their own local parties, and were at this time hostile to both Liberals and Conservatives, e.g. Crooks at Guardians election meeting, *Workman's Times*, 11 March 1893, 'I want both political parties to take this as a declaration of war', and Steadman, 'that as regards labour there is not much to choose between either party', *Star*, 13 May 1891. Progressive co-operation, and their consequent realisation of dependence, changed their attitudes.

[2] B. Webb, diary, 1 December 1892.

[3] G. B. Shaw to anon., 16 December 1890, Wallas Collection.

tance was again very successful.[1] Consequently in 1892, during the formation of the I.L.P., the Fabians were declaring that a genuine working class party was not a practical possibility.

The most formidable challenge to permeation came with the election of a Liberal government in 1892. Even if a radical programme could be imposed on the Liberal Party, a Liberal government would not necessarily enact it.

The first Fabian reaction was to create a pressure group partly within the Liberal organisation, based on the L.C.C. Progressives. In October 1892 the London Reform Union was formed with Tom Mann as secretary and other trade unionists on its committee. But it soon became clear that it would have little independent influence. Its new journal, *London*, confined its interests to municipal matters, and the twenty-three branches formed in the constituencies were from the beginning led by Liberal M.P.s, councillors or clergy.[2] Mann ceased to be full-time secretary in the summer of 1893.

The Fabians then suddenly decided to abandon permeation and support an independent Labour Party. They were inspired to this step partly by frustration with the Liberal government and partly by the decision of the T.U.C., which in fact proved abortive, to start a political fund. In the autumn of 1893 they issued a vehement attack on the Liberals, 'To Your Tents, Oh Israel!'[3] It produced an outcry among the Liberals and some resignations from the Society, but it did not produce a new labour party, and the Fabians were careful to avoid committing themselves to the I.L.P. Among those who resigned was Massingham, who wrote to Webb 'embittered by the levity and recklessness of the whole movement'. 'I have been a permeator all my days, a collectivist Radical working on journalistic lines, and that I remain. It is Fabianism which is changed and I who remain the Fabian.'[4]

After this failure, which gave more evidence of the limits of influence through permeation, the Fabians turned to the London Trades Council and through Fred Hammill attempted to revive its Labour Representation League.[5] This too came to nothing.

---

[1] S. Webb to B. Potter, 11 and 12 December 1891, Passfield Collection.
[2] London Reform Union Annual Report, 1893.
[3] Webb wanted 'a strong tract showing up the Liberal party' (S. Webb to G. Wallas, 12 September 1893, Wallas Collection). The new statement was first published as an article in the *Fortnightly Review*, November 1893, and separately published as part of Fabian Tract No. 49, *A Plan of Campaign for Labour*, 1894.
[4] H. W. Massingham to S. Webb, 3 November 1893, and to G. B. Shaw, 20 October 1893, Passfield Collection. Rev. Arthur Jephson, Headlam's School Board colleague, was among the members who resigned.
[5] Fabian Society executive committee minutes, 15 December 1893 and January 1894.

These three defeats brought to an end the grander political ambitions of the Fabian Society for the time being. Permeation was resumed, but without a plan of campaign. Individual Fabians co-operated with Liberals in local politics. Webb remained important with the L.C.C. Progressives, and continued to cultivate the political leaders of both national parties who could be persuaded to dine. The temporary abandonment of permeation did not prevent the continuance of an acutely hostile attitude to the I.L.P. through the 1890s. It was only in 1899, when the I.L.P. set up a joint Local Information Bureau with the Fabians that any sign of the future warmth between the two parties can be found.

In the later 1890s the Fabians were in fact a declining group of diminishing influence. With the decay of working class radicalism their most useful work, the lectures to working men's clubs, had 'almost ceased'.[1] After 1894 their London membership began to fall slowly. The more important working class members who had joined in 1890-3, including Keir Hardie, Frank Smith, Tom Mann and Fred Hammill, went over to the I.L.P. by 1894. Will Crooks who remained a Fabian and Ben Cooper, another L.C.C. Labour member, who joined in 1897, were comparatively minor figures. At the same time some of the best middle class members had also gone. Annie Besant resigned as early as 1890 when she became a theosophist; Olivier was abroad, although he remained a subscriber until the Fabian Society refused to declare against the Boer War. This incident, together with the Fabian policy over the Conservative Education Bills, was to alienate other members, among them Wallas and Headlam. Thus the Society became more and more exclusively controlled by the Webbs, sharing their political attitudes. It was still an important discussion group, although even here it had rivals, such as the Rainbow Circle, of which Ramsay MacDonald was secretary and J. A. Hobson, C. P. Trevelyan, Herbert Samuel and Percy Alden were members, playing quite as great a part in the development of ideas on social policy and better placed to work for their adoption.[2] When the Webbs went on a foreign tour in 1898 Charlotte Shaw wrote to Beatrice Webb that the Fabian Society 'now consists of a parcel of boys and old women thinking they are making history, and really making themselves ridiculous', and on her return, writing her diary, Beatrice herself recognised that they were now 'far removed from political influence'.[3]

[1] Fabian Society annual report, 1900.
[2] L. A. Clark, 'The Liberal Party and collectivism 1886-1906', Cambridge M.Litt. thesis, 1957, p. 52. Ten of its 25 members were elected M.P.s in 1906.
[3] Charlotte Shaw to B. Webb, 6 November 1898, Passfield Collection; B. Webb, diary, 10 October 1899.

What in fact had been the political influence of the Fabians in these years? It seems unlikely that their able and extensive advertising of socialism had not increased the apparent importance of the movement. At the same time they had confused the boundaries between radicalism and socialism, making it easier for socialists to work with radicals and radicals to be drawn into the socialist movement. But if the Fabians realised that the uncompromising isolationism favoured by some of the early socialists was self-defeating, they failed to evolve a workable alternative, and they proved a serious obstruction to those who could see a way through the formation of an independent Labour Party.

Because neither the S.D.F. nor the Fabians supported the formation of an independent Labour Party, the attempts made to form a Party of this kind in London before 1892 made little progress. The picture is generally of three groups, stemming originally from the S.D.F., the Socialist League and the Fabians, creating a large number of similar small but not very significant organisations.

The first group was based on the former S.D.Fers led by H. H. Champion.[1] Champion's plan was to work through the Labour Electoral Committee set up by the T.U.C. in 1886. In 1887 it developed into a Labour Electoral Association and he was able to concentrate his efforts on the Metropolitan Section. At the end of 1887 he started a policy of questioning bye-election candidates on specific policies, especially the eight hours question, and in January 1888 he announced himself as a candidate at Deptford, only withdrawing when the Liberal had made some concessions. It was Hyndman's repudiation of Champion at Deptford which made him break with the S.D.F. In June 1888 he launched a new monthly, the *Labour Elector*, which was successful enough to become a weekly in November. Now denouncing the Labour Electoral Association as 'a mere pander to the capitalistic Liberal Party', Champion induced the Metropolitan Section to secede and become a 'separate distinct independent labour party'.[2] This new party did not come to much. A branch was formed by Robert Banner at Woolwich, and at its conference in November 1889, when an impressive committee was elected, and it was decided to form 'a branch of the distinct independent labour party in every constituency', but it does not appear that other branches were formed.[3]

Meanwhile the *Labour Elector*, which was put under the management of a committee in 1889, had come to represent a stronger

[1] H. M. Pelling, 'H. H. Champion: a pioneer of labour representation', *Cambridge Journal*, 1952.
[2] *Labour Elector*, 15 November 1888.   [3] Ibid., 30 November 1889.

political group. Burns, Mann and Ben Tillett were on the committee, with Keir Hardie, whose paper the *Miner* was absorbed by the *Labour Elector*, and Will Thorne, who made it the official organ of the Gas Workers. Thorne brought Champion into closer contact with Aveling and Eleanor Marx and won him the qualified support of Engels. 'If our lot here—I mean Champion especially—don't make mistakes, they will soon have it all their own way. But I confess I cannot have full confidence in that man—he is too dodgy.'[1]

In spite of its promise, the Championite group melted away without achieving anything. Because Champion's personal contacts were with Conservatives rather than Liberals, his trade unionist allies were uneasy about his intentions, and refused to follow him in his attacks on Liberals and Progressives as 'mere party hacks and at bottom the most treacherous enemies of the working class'.[2] In April 1890, finding himself without the confidence of his committee after an attack on a radical journalist, Champion decided to abandon his plans, closed down the *Labour Elector*, and sailed to Australia.[3] He did not return to London until late in 1891.

His disappearance left his group without any co-ordination, and they soon went their separate ways. Thorne and Aveling turned to the first Mayday scheme. Mann ran for the secretaryship of the Engineers and set about reforming the London Trades Council. Tillett was fully occupied by the Dockers' Union. Hardie began to work vigorously for his election to parliament in West Ham, and John Burns pursued his similar ambition in Battersea.

Undoubtedly the one man among the Championites who could have led them to an independent labour party at this time was Burns. His election to the L.C.C., followed by his dramatic role in the dock strike, had given him, as the *Star* warned, a great opportunity. 'If he neglect it, he will have lost one of the greatest moments of his life for advancing the cause of labour.'[4] Supported by a Wages Fund raised from trade unions and from his local supporters who were now organised in the Battersea Labour League, Burns was in a position of unequalled independence among labour leaders, able to devote his whole time to political and trade union work. As a councillor he had quickly established himself as a spokesman for labour and a leader of the radicals. He led the demand for open meetings and evening sittings, spoke several times on housing, proposed the socialist scheme for a London Labour exchange, and by persistent interven-

[1] Engels and Lafargue, op. cit., 2, p. 342.
[2] *Labour Elector*, 1 March 1890.
[3] *Workman's Times*, 10 December 1892.
[4] 28 September 1889.

tion secured the excellent labour policy and trade union contracts clause of the L.C.C.[1]

Burns failed to use his opportunity. The reason was in just those qualities which secured him such initial success. He had a compelling ambition which had alone enabled him to rise out of the appalling poverty of a slum childhood in Lambeth, the sixteenth child of a Scots engineer who had apparently deserted his family. Because of this ambition, helped by a ready mind and an early passion for books, and above all a fluent tongue and a powerful voice, he was able to assert himself. His self-dramatisation, his straw hat and stories of his childhood, his love of applause and flattery, were the essential equipment of an orator. In an age of outdoor meetings without microphones a voice as powerful as Burns' was bound to make its mark. 'Get your back to the wind,' he advised would-be imitators, 'so that your voice carries. If I was doubtful about the direction of the wind, I threw a few tiny pieces of paper into the air, and then manoeuvred my audience into the position I wanted them to be in.'[2]

A talent for speech-making had been enough to make him the hero of the free speech struggles, the first socialist county councillor, the best-known of the new unionists. But after this other characteristics began to tell against him: egotism and self-deception, with chronic suspicion of rivals and critics. In 1888 local government had been the limit of his ambition; he was 'not anxious to go to Parliament. . . . Membership entitles one to perpetual boredom or worse.' But by 1891 he had decided that vestrymen were 'a lot of drivellers wasting valuable time and public money'. He developed magnanimity. At the 1892 election he recorded that he had addressed his constituents 'in splendid form, roused their sentiments and imagination for a future London. Heartily yea pathetically received.' Once elected a member he found canvassing a little degrading, but 'it is wise after all the work I have honestly done for these folk to wait upon them in this style'.[3] More and more he saw himself a father figure to his Battersea constituents, noting in his diary his own good deeds.

At the same time he discarded all his earlier associates. First he had decided to work with Champion, 'leaving Hyndman, Morris, Aveling and Co to fight out their quarrels themselves'.[4] In 1889 he parted with the Battersea S.D.F. In 1890 he pushed out Champion. In 1891 he alienated the Dockers' Union and broke off his friendship with

---

[1] W. Saunders, *History of the First London County Council*, London 1892, p. 8 (index).
[2] Kent, op. cit., p. 17.
[3] J. Burns, diary, 4 June and 5 July 1888; 25 February 1891; 28 February 1892; 2 February 1898.
[4] F. Engels to L. Lafargue, 21 May 1887, Engels-Lafargue, op. cit., 2, p. 41.

Tom Mann.[1] At the same time he refused to work with Keir Hardie and the I.L.P. After their election as M.P.s he much resented Hardie's assumption that they should sit in opposition.[2] He turned up in a new suit rather than a cloth cap.[3] Once in parliament he was soon exchanging compliments with Gladstone, dining with Haldane, spending country weekends in Sydney Buxton's Norfolk mansion.[4] He convinced himself that it was easier to influence those in power by acting as 'candid and independent friends' than by 'party making, manifesto issuing and "spread eagling" '.[5]

It was one of the difficulties of the London independent labour men that until John Burns finally committed himself to the Liberal government by joining the cabinet in 1905 to many he remained 'labour's leader both at St. Stephen's and Spring Gardens'.[6] After the 1895 defeat he was in fact the only London labour M.P. Had he wished he could at any time have taken his place at the head of the independent labour movement.

The second independent group was that of the former Socialist Leaguers. Aveling and Eleanor Marx had started as early as 1887 a 'campaign among the East End Radicals to engage them to cut loose from the Great Liberal Party and for a working men's party after the American fashion'.[7] Encouraged by Engels, this East End work enabled them to win in 1889 their position with the Gas Workers, and the permanent gratitude of Will Thorne for their assistance in his first administrative efforts.[8] Eleanor Marx was also active in other new unions. Meanwhile the Bloomsbury branch of the Socialist League, to which she and Aveling belonged, had seceded to become the Bloomsbury Socialist Society. It worked with the local Democratic Committee in the 1888 School Board election, and put up a candidate for the L.C.C. who was supported by the *Star*.[9] Advised by Engels, Aveling decided to draw these two fields of activity together in the eight hours movement and the grand demonstration on 1 May 1890 which had been called for by the Marxist Internationalist Congress of 1889. 'The Hyndman lot *dare not oppose* it', wrote

---

[1] T. Mann to J. Burns, n.d. 1891, A. Cunninghame-Graham to J. Burns, 28 November 1891, and J. Burns to B. Tillett, 17 October 1891, Burns Collection.

[2] J. Burns to A. Cunninghame-Graham, 29 July 1892, Burns Collection.

[3] Kent, op. cit., p. 51.

[4] Ibid., p. 57 and 65; R. Haldane to J. Burns, 17 and 22 July 1892, and S. Buxton to J. Burns, December 1893, Burns Collection.

[5] J. Burns to A. Cunninghame-Graham, 29 July 1892, Burns Collection.

[6] F. W. Soutter to J. Burns, 30 November 1898, Burns Collection.

[7] F. Engels to Lafargue, 21 March 1887, Engels and Lafargue, op. cit., 2, p. 25.

[8] W. Thorne, op. cit., p. 117.

[9] *Link*, 30 June and 11 August 1888; *Star*, 9 January 1889.

Engels; 'if they do, they ruin themselves; if they don't, they must follow in our wake'.[1] A committee was formed, meeting like the Bloomsbury Socialist Society at the Communist Club in Tottenham Street, with Aveling as chairman and delegates from the Gas Workers and other new unions and 'the Radical Clubs worked for the last two years by Tussy'. Engels considered that the committee could 'gradually expand into a central body not only of the Eight Hours Bill but for all other revendications' and predicted that 'the sects will soon be put before the dilemma either to merge in it and the general movement or die out.'

The first Mayday demonstration of 1890 was undoubtedly a triumphant success. The S.D.F. attempted to squeeze out Aveling's committee by persuading the Trades Council at the last moment to organise its own demonstration, but as it was unable to secure a monopoly of the platform the two bodies co-operated. Engels 'heard again, for the first time since forty years, the unmistakable voice of the English Proletariat ... England at last *is* stirring, and no mistake.'[2] But although the Mayday demonstration became an annual event of the 1890s, a striking demonstration of the common purpose of the socialists (in spite of the repeated efforts of the S.D.F. to prevent the Trades Council from co-operating with the Eight Hours Committee), it failed to develop into anything more than a holiday of brass bands and banners.

The trade unionist group of Socialist Leaguers who seceded with Aveling and Eleanor Marx in 1888 formed another organisation, the Labour Union. In its political programme this was 'a clear blueprint for the I.L.P.', and J. L. Mahon, its founder, had been in contact with both Champion and Keir Hardie.[3] A branch was formed in Hammersmith, but its main centre was in Hoxton. Supporters included Robert Banner, Thomas Binning the compositor, and Fred Henderson of Norwich Socialist League. Despite its political intentions the Labour Union was chiefly active in trade union work. Its practical influence was broken by a disastrously mismanaged postmen's strike in 1890.

Fred Henderson, undaunted by this experience, became a Labour-Progressive candidate for the L.C.C. in Clapham, next to Burns' constituency, and formed a Labour League of his supporters. He also started a paper, the *Labour Leader*, through which in 1891 he attempted to form a new party by calling for subscribers to write in.[4] Its circulation was too small for success. He was elected to the L.C.C. in 1892,

---

[1] Engels and Lafargue, op. cit., 2, p. 312.   [2] Ibid., 2, p. 380.
[3] E. P. Thompson, op. cit., p. 614.
[4] H. M. Pelling, 'Origins and Early History of the Independent Labour Party, 1880–1900', Cambridge Ph.D. thesis, 1951, p. 90.

but his London political career was shortly afterwards abruptly ended by a personal indiscretion.

There was one other offspring of the Socialist League, the Hammersmith Socialist Society. It continued a vigorous outdoor propaganda, and although remaining officially neutral in elections most of its active members worked for socialist and labour candidates when possible. The S.D.F. had no organisation in Hammersmith, and relied on its help in School Board elections.[1] Charles Kitching, a member of the Society, was the leading spirit in the Hammersmith and District Labour Council,[2] while others helped to set up a Fabian group in the district. At the 1892 L.C.C. election even William Morris was 'pleased on the whole' with what he thought was 'certainly the result of the Socialist movement'.[3] Copies of Fred Henderson's *Labour Leader* were sold at outdoor meetings, and he was invited to lecture on 'an Independent Labour Party'.[4] Even the stronghold of socialist purism appeared ready to welcome the I.L.P.

In addition to these independent organisations there were the London Groups of the Fabian Society, which between 1891 and 1893 were more vigorous than at any other period. There were ten active Groups.[5] All of them met regularly for political discussion, and most organised lectures, kept a watch on the local press, and attempted to permeate their local Liberal Associations. Some put out tracts of their own.[6] But they went far beyond these discreet Fabian activities. Five Groups organised outdoor meetings, including the well-known Poplar Dock Gate meetings. In Poplar, Hackney and Willesden they played an important role on the local committees for organising the unemployed, and protested angrily at the withdrawal of the Fabian delegate from the central committee.[7] Equally surprising was their interest in Labour Churches. In character these Fabian Groups anticipated the later I.L.P. branches, and in fact the Hampstead Group founded the Willesden I.L.P. in 1892 and worked very closely with the Kilburn I.L.P., which sent a Fabian delegate to the 1893 annual conference.[8] The Sunday meetings of the North Western

[1] Hammersmith Socialist Society minutes, 9–30 October 1891.
[2] Ibid., 20 June 1886, 23 January 1892; *Workman's Times*, 1 April 1893.
[3] P. Henderson (ed.), op. cit., p. 349.
[4] Hammersmith Socialist Society minutes, 9 October and 11 December 1891.
[5] Poplar, Hackney, Hampstead, Northern (Islington), North Western, Hammersmith, South Western (Chelsea), Southern (Wandsworth), South Eastern (Woolwich) and Central (Working Men's College). Their activity is reported in *Fabian News*.
[6] E.g. Hammersmith Group, circular to clergy, *Fabian News* August 1894. Northern Group, *Socialism for Tramwaymen, Fabian News* July 1891.
[7] Fabian Society executive committee minutes, 27 January 1893; Hackney Fabian Group minutes, 9 January 1893.
[8] *Fabian News*, December 1892, September 1893.

Group in Hibernian Hall, with 'music recitations and Socialist speeches', would have appealed strongly to a future I.L.Per.[1]

It is chiefly the diversity of these Groups which marks them out as Fabian. In Woolwich they worked with the S.D.F., the Labour League and the Tenants Defence League; in Penge they founded a Women's Liberal Association.[2] The Hackney Group permeated the local Liberals, joined the Progressives on the vestry, started the local I.L.P. branch, when it showed its political independence seceded, and helped to form an S.D.F. branch in Leytonstone and a Ratepayers Association in Buckhurst Hill.[3] The Poplar Group drew in the East End trade unionists, including Will Godfrey of the Carmen, Steadman and Tillett, and took the lead in organising the Poplar Labour Electoral Committee which ran Will Crooks for the L.C.C. in 1892. The Committee's first secretary and treasurer were Fabians, and it later developed into the Poplar Labour League.[4]

These Groups played a stimulating role in the London socialist movement for two years. Once the I.L.P. had been formed they relapsed into unimportant discussion societies; four survived in 1896, and two were still meeting in 1899.

All these organisations which in some sense anticipated the Independent Labour Party had been formed by socialists and were responding to the impact of the new unionism, the wave of labour candidates and the interest in Labour issues at local elections all over London. The committees formed to run these candidates formed yet another set of fore-runners of the Independent Labour Party. In some cases candidates were simply put up by the local trade unions; in others they were adopted as Progressives at conferences of trade union, temperance and club delegates. But in several districts an independent Labour League was set up to run labour candidates, even when the candidates were run with the Progressives. The first was Burns' Battersea Labour League; others followed in Woolwich, Chelsea, Hackney and Stepney. In Poplar and West Ham there were similar Labour Electoral Committees, and there were other less securely established organisations. In Woolwich, West Ham and Hammersmith local Trades and Labour Councils were formed which promoted labour candidates.

Corresponding to these local electoral bodies was the London Trades Council Labour Representation League. This was a striking example of the difficulty of forming a new party in London on the

[1] Ibid., October 1891. [2] Ibid., July 1891, June 1891.
[3] East London (Poplar) Fabian Group minutes, 1891; Hackney Fabian Group minutes, 1891–3; *Clarion*, 8 December; *Labour Leader*, 4 May 1895.
[4] Poplar Fabian group minutes, and report 30 March 1892; Haw, op. cit., pp. 76–77.

basis of a trade union election committee. It started with immense success. The five candidates which it supported at the School Board election in 1891 against the Liberals put up remarkably good performances, and at the L.C.C. election in 1892 nine of its candidates were elected with the Progressives. Yet the League came to nothing. There were two reasons for this. Firstly, it was based upon individual subscriptions rather than trade union affiliation. A highly organised Labour League like Battersea could raise a substantial fund in support of a single member, but a loosely organised League covering the whole of London was financially impotent. In April 1892 the League had seven branches, of which only Islington was vigorous, and its total membership came to 340.[1] Consequently it had less collective financial hold on the Labour members, most of whom badly needed money, than the local Leagues on their individual members.

Secondly, it had no coherent political standpoint. It represented a balance between the Social Democrats and the Liberal-Labour men on the Trades Council. Tom Mann and Fred Hammill, who had been the leading advocates of independent labour on the Council, had dropped out of its political work during 1891, and there was thus no middle group.[2] The League's programme combined a typical labour programme with the labour exchange and free school meals policies of the S.D.F. But the compromise was severely strained at elections. In the School Board election in fact Steadman refused to support Harry Quelch against a Liberal candidate, and at the L.C.C. election Ben Cooper nearly succeeded in committing the League to supporting the Progressives who were running with Labour candidates.[3] The labour victories were due to this willingness of the Progressives to run with ten labour candidates, so that after their election the labour members were inevitably drawn closer to the Progressives. But in June 1892 H. R. Taylor carried a motion at a general meeting of the League, despite 'threats of dissension and secession', by 21 votes to 20, 'that no member of the League shall be allowed to speak on behalf of any candidate who does not approve the whole programme of the League, and whose candidature has not been approved of by the Executive'.[4] No doubt such a rule would have been necessary to make the League into an independent party, but since the inclusion of the nationalisation of all the means of production had been added to

[1] *Workman's Times*, 30 April 1892.
[2] Mann withdrew from the Council (London Trades Council minutes, 23 July 1891) due to overwork; Hammill became fully occupied by the organisation of the busmen.
[3] London Trades Council minutes, 3 December 1891 and 11 February 1892.
[4] *Workman's Times* 11 June, 1892.

the programme in April, the effect of the motion was to make the League exclusively socialist.[1] The League thus ended its effective existence, openly split in two political halves.

It is unlikely that without the intervention of the provinces the political problem of forming an independent Labour Party in London could have been overcome. But in the spring of 1891 Joseph Burgess, the apostle of independent labour in Yorkshire, had moved his paper the *Workman's Times* to London, hoping to build up a circulation and influence in the metropolis comparable to that which it already had in the north. At first Burgess saw the best political chance in supporting the Progressives, and he greeted the 1892 L.C.C. election as 'nothing less than a revolution in politics'.[2] At the end of April he took on the treasureship of the Trades Council Labour Representation League, and at the same time he issued his appeal for subscribers to an independent labour party through the *Workman's Times*. He clearly hoped that in London the basis of this would be the League. But his difficulties were shown at the general election. He issued an appeal for Burns, Hardie, H. R. Taylor of the S.D.F. who was opposing the veteran Lib-Lab George Howell, and Ben Ellis of the Brushmakers, a labour radical in another three-cornered fight. He offered to guarantee £100 each for them.[3] He ignored three other S.D.Fers opposing Liberals and two Fabians standing as Liberals, although these were supported in the list published by the *Clarion*, the new socialist weekly just started in Manchester.[4] Frank Smith in Hammersmith and Ben Jones in Woolwich, labour candidates with Liberal support, were not given any attention before the election. Yet although the election resulted in the return of both Burns and Hardie, and was acclaimed by the *Clarion*[5] as another 'labour triumph', Burgess can hardly have failed to notice the contrast between the candidates supported by the Liberals and those, whether socialist or not, who opposed them.

Burgess called a preliminary meeting of the London I.L.P. at the Democratic Club in June 1892, and a committee was formed. The danger of 'the movement running . . . into mere sectional and local lines' was discussed.[6] Certainly the sectional groups can be readily distinguished. There was a group of S.D.Fers in South London who favoured a more flexible election policy and had worked with Ben Ellis at the general election; they were headed by James Dobson and Nelson Palmer, who had both also joined the Fabian Society. Fred Henderson brought in his Clapham Labour League. There were

[1] Ibid., 30 April 1892. [2] Ibid., 12 March 1892. [3] Ibid., 25 June 1892.
[4] 23 April 1892. [5] 9 July 1892.
[6] I.L.P. London District Council minutes, 13 June, 8 August 1892.

hopes of securing the Islington and Chelsea branches of the Labour Representation League. In Hoxton the dormant Labour Union group had revived, and were forming a branch.[1] Former Socialist Leaguers in Hammersmith also founded a branch.[2]

In addition, there was a new brand of Nonconformist-toned socialism which had been rare in London. In Limehouse Margaret McMillan and Paul Campbell, the son of a Scottish minister, were attempting to start a Labour Church.[3] There was also Keir Hardie himself, and his new friend Frank Smith.[4] Frank Smith had been in business as a Chelsea art-furnisher before becoming a Salvation Army missioner. His mission experiences made him a social reformer, and he was the joint author and first executant officer of General Booth's great social scheme of 1890, *In Darkest England and the Way Out*. But Booth's interference and political suspicions forced him to resign. He set up a Labour Army, a political version of the Salvation Army, with a successful paper, the *Worker's Cry*, which reached a circulation of 20,000. In 1892 he was elected to the L.C.C. as a Labour-Progressive for Hammersmith. Afterwards he found room in his house for Hardie, and became his personal secretary and 'most trusted and confidential friend.[5]

During the next few months the political variety of the I.L.P. continued to grow. Fabian Groups formed branches in Hackney and Kilburn, and a Fabian became branch secretary in Deptford.[6] The Bloomsbury Socialist Society applied for affiliation,[7] and although rebuffed branches were formed in Marylebone and St. Pancras in which its former members were dominant. Aveling also helped to start a West Ham branch after Hardie's election through his connection with the Gas Workers.[8] Robert Banner was reporting to be forming a 'powerful branch' in Woolwich.[9] A Fabian teacher formed a Paddington Socialist Society in association with the I.L.P., while the Chiswick Progressive League was claimed as an 'I.L.P. branch in disguise'.[10] Burgess may well have believed that he was uniting all sections of the London movement.

[1] *Workman's Times*, 22 October 1892.   [2] Ibid., 23 July 1892.
[3] Ibid., 18 February 1893. Paul Campbell: *Labour Leader*, 21 November 1918.
[4] E. I. Champness, *Frank Smith, M.P.*, London 1943.
[5] J. Clayton, *The Rise and Decline of Socialism in Great Britain, 1884–1924*, London 1926, p. 79.
[6] F. E. Green: *Workman's Times*, 4 February 1893; previously secretary Woolwich Fabian Group: Fabian Society executive committee minutes, 21 April 1891.
[7] *Workman's Times*, 4 February 1893.
[8] I.L.P. London District Council minutes, 30 January 1893.
[9] *Workman's Times*, 17 September 1892.
[10] Fabian Society executive committee minutes, 14 July 1893; *Workman's Times*, 16 September 1893 and 4 March 1893.

In fact he was treading a narrow plank and was to lose valuable supporters on both sides. The S.D.Fers in south London failed to persuade the S.D.F. to unite with the I.L.P. in election work and the Camberwell branch broke up.[1] The St. George's branch seceded to the S.D.F., Ben Ellis had become disillusioned earlier when the I.L.P. refused to affiliate radical clubs 'agreeing with the principles of the party'.[2] The Clapham Labour League disaffiliated when Fred Henderson returned to Norwich and the Streatham branch disappeared with it. A bitter dispute developed in Deptford between the I.L.P. branch and the Fabians, led by Sidney Webb's election agent B. T. Hall.[3] Of the thirteen officers and members elected to the London committee in December 1892, six had been lost by July 1893. There was no longer a proper secretary, and there was not even enough money to issue notices for the delegate meeting in April.[4] It was fast becoming clear that in an atmosphere of increasing hostility from Social Democrats, Fabians and Lib-Labs, few prominent London labour leaders were prepared to commit themselves to the I.L.P. Frank Smith was the only labour member of the L.C.C. who remained an active supporter. Ben Tillett, Tom Mann and Fred Hammill, all of whom were themselves prepared to run as independent labour candidates in the provinces, refused to commit themselves to the London I.L.P.

When challenged by Burgess to explain this attitude, Hammill answered that it was 'because of the characters that were already in it'.[5] It was certainly true that because the better labour leaders stood aloof, the less desirable recruits to the I.L.P. were all too prominent in London. The only genuine Londoner elected to the I.L.P. National Council at its first conference in January 1893 was Aveling, and by this date he had ceased to be an asset to any party. For all his intellectual brilliance he seems to have been absolutely devoid of any sense of morality. He was notorious for his unscrupulous financial fraudulence, often extracting money from socialists far poorer than himself and using it to pay for his infidelities to Eleanor Marx, who had sacrificed her public reputation to live with him in a free marriage. Although the ultimate tragedy of their suicides was yet to come, his character was already well enough known. In addition the discredited Labour Union leaders of the postmen's strike, Mahon, Donald and Binning, were active London members of the I.L.P. In

---

[1] *Workman's Times*, 6 August 1892; I.L.P. London District Council minutes, 24 April and 19 June 1893.
[2] Ibid., 19 December 1892 and 23 January 1893.
[3] *Workman's Times*, 1, 8 and 22 April 1893.
[4] I.L.P. London District Council minutes, 10 April 1893.
[5] *Workman's Times*, 23 September 1893.

the background was Champion, who had returned from Australia in 1892 and restarted the *Labour Elector*. The money which Burgess had guaranteed in the general election came from Champion,[1] and Burgess was at first sufficiently unaware of the dangers of this association to try to defend Champion's reputation.[2] But Champion was unable to prevent the creation of a central election fund by the I.L.P. first conference and his interview with the London I.L.P. committee was equally unsuccessful.[3] In March 1893 he was repudiated by the I.L.P. National Council and in the following year he returned to Australia. But his henchman remained entrenched in the London I.L.P.[4] There was also another active member with an undesirable past, H. B. Samuels of Kilburn branch, a Socialist League anarchist who was suspected of dabbling in explosives.[5]

During the first months of the I.L.P. the Fabians and S.D.F. had been uncertain in how to treat the new rival, but by 1893 they had decided on open hostility. Webb declared the *Workman's Times* to be impossibilist 'and the less we have to do with it the better', while Shaw denounced the I.L.P. as 'nothing but a new S.D.F. with Champion instead of Hyndman'.[6] When Shaw and de Mattos appeared at the first I.L.P. conference in Bradford, having previously declared that the Fabian Society would not merge with the I.L.P. and that its policy of permeation was alone practical, 'a shudder ran through the assembly' and 'prompt steps were taken to purge the precincts from the unclean permeation of our presence'. Their credentials were only accepted by the narrow majority of two votes.[7] Bitterness was also increasing with the S.D.F., which at first advised the I.L.P. 'in no carping or cavilling spirit' that their efforts were bound to fail, and then with scarcely disguised pleasure began to 'wonder what the I.L.P. is really coming to. It doesn't seem to be worth a cent anywhere in London.'[8]

---

[1] G. B. Shaw to S. Webb, 12 August and 22 August 1892, Passfield Collection.

[2] *Workman's Times*, 10 December 1892.

[3] I.L.P. London District Council minutes, 3 October 1892: Champion 'made a brief statement as to his position and policy. Some desultory conversation took place between Mr. Champion and the Committee ... and the general feeling was that the interests of the I.L.P. would be best served by Mr. Champion securing a mandate from some Metropolitan constituency, and attending the Council as a recognised and responsible delegate.'

[4] F. V. Connolly, secretary of the Clapham Labour League, was also said to be one of Champion's 'paid agents': *Workman's Times*, 30 September 1893.

[5] I.L.P. London District Council minutes, 18 and 25 October 1895.

[6] S. Webb to G. Wallas, 9 September 1892, Passfield Collection and G. B. Shaw to G. Wallas, 20 September 1892, Wallas Collection.

[7] *Workman's Times*, 28 January 1893.

[8] *Justice*, 21 January and 13 May 1893.

Already in January 1893 Burgess was beginning to lose heart. 'London is a dreadfully hopeless place.' 'We labour and labour here, but it is but rarely we are encouraged by such signs of progress as can be more readily detected in smaller towns.'[1] There was indeed little reason for hope. Of the fourteen London branches recorded in 1893, only eight were alive at the end of the year, and of these one was a Fabian branch of permeators and four were under the influence of Aveling and the ex-Labour Union group. Burgess could not even win a sufficient London circulation for the *Workman's Times* to act as an effective organ of the party.[2] The contrast with the enthusiastic support in the industrial north for the new party, which was to win 10,000 members in two years, could hardly have been more striking. In July he decided to abandon the task and return to Yorkshire.

Although for the moment the force from the provinces had been insufficient to reconcile the London socialists, the I.L.P. had been successfully established as a national party, and its failure in the metropolis was not accepted without further efforts. Tom Mann became national I.L.P. secretary in the spring of 1894, and with Hardie he made London his special responsibility.[3] The London committee, which had stopped meeting, was called together again, and a series of campaign meetings arranged. Fred Hammill now decided to support the I.L.P., and with Mann and Hardie addressed a series of grand meetings, accompanied by bands and choirs, with the campaign slogan of 'London for Labour', which were intended to build up to the local elections under the new wider franchise and candidates qualifications of December 1894 and the L.C.C. election of March 1895. At first all seemed to be going well, and just before the L.C.C. election a peak figure of thirty-four London I.L.P. branches was reached.

This sudden and impressive increase proved transitory for two reasons. Firstly, the I.L.P. continued to harbour disreputable characters. Ultimately the three most difficult members, Aveling, Mahon and Donald, were expelled, but not without causing much difficulty. The St. Pancras branch had to be dissolved and reformed, while the Marylebone branch found after the expulsion that 'the weekly meetings were recriminatory' and 'members did not turn up in sufficient numbers to make a business meeting and that progress was most unsatisfactory'.[4] At the same time the Hoxton Labour Union men left the I.L.P. and the Hoxton branch disappeared with them. H. B. Samuels was forbidden to hold office or lecture for a year, with

---

[1] *Workman's Times*, 28 January and 4 February 1893.
[2] Ibid., 10 June 1893.   [3] *Labour Leader*, 31 March 1894.
[4] I.L.P. London District Council minutes, 14 and 28 September and 5 October 1894.

the result that the Kilburn branch changed its name and refused to be deprived of his services.[1] Sorting out these personal disputes proved a full-time occupation for the London I.L.P. committee and it was unable to give proper assistance to the campaign. At the October delegate meeting a vote of censure was carried, with the hope that 'the future Executive will pay more attention to organising the branches in the London district and less in bickering and narrow-minded debates concerning rules and regulations'.[2] When the hope was not fulfilled the committee's secretary resigned on the insistence of his branch.[3] Frank Smith, who was elected in his place, did not bother to attend a meeting until May 1895, and went on a long American journey with Hardie shortly afterwards. The campaign had failed to produce the nucleus of leaders who were needed to hold the London I.L.P. together.

Nor could it fairly claim to be causing a kind of moral revival, 'getting at men whom the ordinary religious professor fails to touch', so that they were 'giving up liquor, keeping better hours, making home brighter', as the *Labour Leader* suggested.[4] It is true that the I.L.P. contained a middle class element which approved this moral line. In West Ham, for example, the I.L.P. conference delegate of 1895 was a clergyman, and its most notable workers a commercial clerk and a Congregational nursing sister.[5] But there is no evidence that they made converts. Indeed they probably irritated many of the Social Democrats, who had supported temperance in the 1880s, into upholding the virtues of the public house. Will Thorne, for example, gave up the pledge at this time, and the Canning Town S.D.F., which had been meeting in a Temperance Bar, was accused by the *Labour Leader* of criticising Hardie with a speaker who 'three times in the course of the argument' 'went into the pub and refreshed himself'.[6] This sort of self-righteousness was hardly wise in a party with as many black sheep as the London I.L.P.

The second reason for the difficulties of the I.L.P. was the unsolved problem of election policy. The branches in Hackney, Hampstead, Hammersmith and Poplar were strongly influenced by the Fabians, and the Wandsworth and Ealing branches were also involved with the Progressives. The Woolwich branch, and especially Robert Banner, was fiercely attacked for working with the local Trades Council and

[1] Ibid., 6 and 19 December 1895.   [2] Ibid., 19 October 1894.
[3] Ibid., 7 December 1894 and 4 January 1895.
[4] 25 August 1894.
[5] Rev. Tom Warren, Ben Gardiner and Edith Kerrison.
[6] Thorne, op. cit., p. 54; *Justice*, branch notices, 1890; *Labour Leader*, 23 June 1894; cf. Jack Jones, *My Lively Life*, London 1928, pp. 150–1, a characteristic later West Ham Speaker, attacks 'the cloven hoof of intolerant Puritanism ... The public house is the working man's club.'

supporting Ben Jones at the general election.[1] Other branches, notably Deptford, North Kensington, South West Ham and St. Pancras, pursued a policy of co-operation with the S.D.F. against the Progressives. Some branches, such as Chelsea and Peckham, were divided, and unable to do election work.

The S.D.F. were not always quick to respond to the I.L.P. desire for mutual friendship. As the *Labour Leader* conceded, 'the S.D.F. is the fighting organisation of the metropolis', and local S.D.Fers frequently felt that 'the S.D.F. was filling the bill so completely in that part of London that there was no room for the I.L.P.'.[2] Even so the I.L.P. preferred to work with the S.D.F. rather than the Fabians at the 1895 L.C.C. election. A special conference decided to vote only for socialists, and eight I.L.P. candidates were put up, and four S.D.Fers supported. The election manifestoes vigorously attacked Fabianism and 'the specious pleadings of the Socialist and Labour members of the Progressive Party'. 'It is not reform we are after so much as revolution. . . . Municipalisation of waterworks, tramways, gas-works, minimum wage of 24/– a week and trade union conditions are good things in their way, but they are not good enough to turn true socialists aside from their aims. . . . The I.L.P. cannot afford to get dragged into dangerous alliances for the sake of patching up the world as it is.'[3]

This policy produced a head-on clash with the Fabians. Beatrice Webb had foreseen this difficulty. 'The I.L.P. with its lack of money, brains and, to some extent, moral characteristics, is as yet more a thorn in the side of the Liberals than an effective force on our side. . . . At present there is no chance of it being more than a wrecking party, to some extent contradicting the permeating policy of the Fabians.'[4] Early in 1895 Hardie, Mann and Frank Smith were invited to dinner to discuss the situation; Beatrice found 'Tom Mann reverting to the old views of the S.D.F.' and 'Hardie, who impressed me very unfavourably, deliberately chooses this policy as the only one he can boss . . . I do not think the conference ended in any understanding'.[5] Tom Mann wrote in the *Clarion* that the Fabians were 'buttressing up the Liberal Party', and at a rowdy Fabian meeting in February Hardie said that 'the power which will be responsible for the continued existence of the Liberals will be the Fabian Society'.[6] Most of the remaining Fabians in the I.L.P.

[1] I.L.P. London District Council minutes, 11 October 1895.
[2] *Labour Leader*, 7 July and 22 September 1894.
[3] I.L.P. London Divisional Council minutes, 3 and 25 February 1895; *Labour Leader*, 2 February 1895.
[4] *Our Partnership*, op. cit., p. 117.
[5] Ibid., p. 122.
[6] *Clarion*, 16 February and 29 January 1895.

branches seceded during or after the election, with the result that the Hackney branch was left in chronic debt, and three others disintegrated.[1]

The L.C.C. election, following the failure of the I.L.P. candidates to make any impact in the local elections in December 1894, was a humiliating defeat. Beatrice Webb, with apt satisfaction, recorded that the I.L.P. 'has shown the smallness of its influence wherever it has run a candidate'.[2] The *Labour Leader* tried to console itself with the Progressive losses. 'The I.L.P. has good reason to be satisfied with the result of the election . . . Progressivism in London is as much a discarded force as Liberalism is.[3] But to the ordinary party member such brave talk could hardly conceal the fact that while the Progressives had survived in power, only one candidate, Jack Elliott who had secured strong labour support in Deptford, secured even a respectable poll. The poor performances of first-rate candidates such as Pete Curran of the Gas Workers and Fred Hammill must have come as a deep shock.[4]

Following the defeat of Keir Hardie in the general election in the summer of 1895, the London I.L.P. withered away. The number of branches fell steadily. Apart from Deptford and West Ham local election efforts were a complete failure. It proved impossible to secure continuity in the officers of the London district or to organise a proper supply of speakers for outdoor meetings. The dispute on election methods continued to cause internal bickering. The *Labour Leader* admitted the 'stagnation which has enveloped us'.[5]

The years in which the I.L.P. had attempted to establish itself were difficult for labour politics. The return of unemployment, the decline in trade union strength, the disillusionment with the 'labour triumphs' of 1892, made it hard to kindle enthusiasm or even find a foothold. But the London I.L.P. did not pick up with the revival of labour politics at the end of the decade. At the 1898 L.C.C. election it combined attack on the Progressives with an attempt to secure straight fights for its candidates.[6] Only Frank Smith was returned, once more as a Progressive, and Beatrice Webb happily commented that 'the I.L.P. has collapsed in London'.[7] The London committee could not even raise the money to pay its election debts.[8] Three branches dissolved to join the S.D.F., and the Marylebone branch

---

[1] Hackney, I.L.P. London District Council minutes, 23 October 1895; Wandsworth, Chelsea and Ealing disintegrated.
[2] B. Webb diary, 5 March 1895.   [3] *Labour Leader*, 9 March 1895.
[4] Elliott polled 1255 (against Sidney Webb's Progressive partner, who was thereby defeated); Curran 391 and Hammill 147.
[5] *Labour Leader*, 9 January 1897.
[6] E.g. ibid., 5 February 1898.   [7] B. Webb diary, March 1898.
[8] *Clarion*, 23 July 1898.

led a breakaway attempt to negotiate directly for fusion with the S.D.F. executive.[1] At the beginning of 1899 there were sixteen remaining branches, of which six were unsound. Lack of rapid success had also affected the national I.L.P. after 1895, but the 7,500 paying members it had held provided a firm foundation. Scarcely 500 of these can have been in London. Nor was there any sense of the 'movement' which gave the I.L.P. its strength in the north. The Labour Churches had failed. The *Clarion* had a relatively small circulation, and there were only 5 of the 65 Clarion cycling clubs in the London area.

London was still the preserve of the Fabians and the Social Democrats, whose hold was stronger in 1899 than it had been ten years earlier. In order to avert the discredit of annihilation, which was clearly threatened, the I.L.P. National Council decided to appoint a paid London organiser, and sent him along to make friends with Pease and the Fabian Society office.[2] Survival was to be secured at the cost of electoral independence. The London I.L.P. had been a complete failure.

[1] I.L.P. reports to Head Office 1898, with I.L.P. National Council minutes, 20 January 1899.
[2] J. K. Hardie to E. Pease, 22 February 1899, Fabian Society archives.

VIII

THE LIBERAL REVIVAL AND AFTER

In 1900, the year in which the future Labour Party was founded as the Labour Representation Committee, Liberal fortunes in London had also reached their nadir. Apparently deserted on the one hand by the new leaders of Labour and on the other by its former middle class supporters, short of funds, badly organised, denounced as unpatriotic for its attitude to the Boer War, the Liberal Party was lucky to survive the General Election with 8 London M.P.s out of 73. The final eclipse of Liberalism might well have appeared a reasonable prediction. Yet the 1900s were to see a Liberal revival which easily out distanced that of 1892. Moreover, in terms of parliamentary seats the Liberal revival was more striking in London than in any other region. How was this achieved?

49 seats were won in 1906, and 31 and 35 in the two elections of 1910. It is quite clear, both from the distribution of the seats and from an analysis of the voting figures, that Liberal support had increased among all social classes. In 1906 the Conservatives were almost ousted from the predominantly working class constituencies, holding only 2 of 27. The Liberal share of the working class vote rose to over 60 per cent, 5 per cent above the previous record of 1892. In 13 constituencies with over 90 per cent working class electors, nearly half the electorate went to the poll to vote Liberal, as against a third in 1900. Some of this increase came from the higher poll, but this poll was itself due to Liberal enthusiasm; the Conservative vote actually fell despite it.

The Liberals were less successful in middle class constituencies. Nevertheless in some ways their performance in these was still more remarkable. In the 18 constituencies with 40 per cent or more middle class electors, their share of the vote rose from 32 per cent to 45 per cent and the proportion of the electorate voting Liberal rose from under a fifth to nearly a third. The growth of Liberal support was in fact slightly larger than in the working class constituencies, and although this is partly explained by the apathy of Liberals in hopeless seats in 1900, it proves that the Liberal advance was on an extended social front. Five of these eighteen middle class constituencies were in fact captured by the Liberals, and outside the L.C.C. boundary there were other gains in middle class suburbia. The Liberal victories in Chelsea, Greenwich, North Hackney, Harrow and Brixton show that in some areas the Liberal share of the middle class vote must have been a majority. This had not happened in 1892, although it had been relatively frequent before 1885.

At first sight it might appear that the elections of 1910 reversed this trend in Liberalism towards a wider social basis of support. Only one Liberal seat in the middle class group was held, while in December 1910 the Conservatives still had only 3 of the 27 predominantly working class constituencies. In fact the majority of lost Liberal voters must have been working class, for while the percentage of electors voting Liberal fell in working class constituencies it rose in middle class constituencies. This is partly due to working class movement into suburban constituencies, but even where this was not happening the Liberal vote was strikingly well maintained. The Conservative gains were due to better organisation and renewed enthusiasm, reflected in a much higher poll, rather than to a strong swing in middle class party allegiance. It was also noticeable that the Liberals lost less of their gains of 1906 in London than in the Midlands and South as a whole.

The Liberal Party had apparently thus achieved the impossible: in a period in which class interest was increasingly important in politics, it had re-asserted itself as a classless party of reform.

Below the surface, however, different currents can be seen. In London as in the country as a whole Liberalism in the 1900s was a coalition of interests rather than a creed, and it was not easy to hold together. If it was to survive the challenge of Labour to represent the working classes, Liberalism must be firmly rooted in local organisations and not merely be a Party for fighting General Elections. In 1906 and 1910 the Liberal Party had exceptional advantages, which would not have continued, even if there had been no First World War; advantages which in some respects exceeded those of 1892.

The first short-term advantage of the Liberals was the Irish vote. This was not of great importance, for only in St. George's in the East were Irish voters as much as 20 per cent of the electorate in 1910. But the Irish formed an element in the riverside constituencies which, so long as the Liberal Party offered the best hope of Home Rule, might be drawn upon in General Elections. Once Home Rule was won, they would almost certainly be lost. As Catholics, they supported

Conservative policy on the education question. As trade unionists, 'they were labour men and had the cause of labour at heart'.[1]

The second special advantage was that the Liberal Party had once again become the active vote of the Nonconformist middle classes. Enraged by the Conservative Education Acts of 1902–3, which forced them to support church schools through the rates, many Nonconformists who had drifted away from the Liberals in the 1880s and 1890s returned to their old political allegiance. In local elections many Free Church ministers and school teachers decided to stand as candidates.[2] At the 1906 General Election local Free Church Councils issued manifestoes in support of the Liberals. Former Unionists, including the President of the Baptist Union (in Islington), came forward to sign Liberal nomination papers, daily election prayer meetings were held in Fulham, and many reports came from constituencies that 'the Liberal Party expect the solid vote of local Nonconformity, which they have not succeeded in gaining at previous elections'.[3] The Nonconformist vote is hard to estimate, but it must have helped to turn the balance in many constituencies, and in a few, such as Brixton, East Islington and North Hackney, it is the most convincing explanation for the Conservative defeat.

The Nonconformists were of vital importance to the Liberals not just for their votes. The Liberal Associations still relied for their funds on middle class subscribers. The Associations had no other means of stability while the political funds of the trade unions were given to the Labour Party.[4] Thus the education issue, by bringing back many middle class Nonconformists to Liberalism, greatly

[1] At a Catholic meeting in Bermondsey, which supported the Progressives rather than the I.L.P., *South London Press*, 24 September 1909.

[2] E.g. Lambeth, where five Free Church ministers stood, and 'the anti-Education Act movement was worked for all its worth', *Brixton Free Press*, 30 October 1903; Willesden, where of 11 Progressive candidates, 9 were described as Nonconformists, *Willesden and Kilburn Chronicle*, 18 March 1904.

[3] *Daily Chronicle*, 13 January 1906; *Fulham Observer*, 19 January 1906; *Daily News*, 11 January 1906.

[4] Very few financial statements of Liberal Associations have survived. The Dartford Liberal Association reports and balance sheets, 1902–8, are in Dartford public library. It was decided on 9 October 1902 'that a Liberal Labour man would secure the largest amount of support', and Rowlands was suggested. Before his adoption he addressed 'representative meetings of organised labour in Erith and other labour districts' and inquiries were made about funds (undated newspaper cutting of 1903, cuttings book, Dartford public library). Rowlands was elected M.P. as a 'Liberal and Labour candidate'. The subscription lists show that nothing was received between 1902 and 1908 from any trade union branch or Trades Council. Of the £204 subscribed in 1902–3, £100 came from the Liberal candidate of 1900. In 1903–4 ordinary individual subscriptions produced £208, donations and extra subscriptions £113. The pattern in subsequent years was similar.

assisted the reorganisation of the Liberal electoral machine which took place after 1900. But it is hard to see how the Liberal Party could have held their support for very long. Once their special demands were satisfied or, as in fact happened, proved impracticable, they were likely to become once more alienated by Liberal policies on Irish or labour issues.

The working class vote was the third and most important Liberal advantage—as it had been in 1892. This time it was secured by three means: by special election issues and promises, by a political arrangement with the Labour Representation Committee, and by an improved party organisation.

The Liberal Party was particularly fortunate that in 1906 and 1910 it was presented by its opponents with General Election issues which made an election programme designed to appeal to the labour vote unnecessary. In 1906 the Conservative Party challenged the policy of Free Trade and cheap food imports. In 1910 the supremacy of the House of Commons and the right to tax landed estates were apparently at stake. The revival of these questions gave old style radicalism a political relevance which it would have lacked in a General Election fought on unemployment or social reform. They provided a platform which could win working class votes without alienating the middle classes. Thus Conservative tactics helped to conceal the weakness of Liberal policy and to reinvigorate working class Liberalism.

In addition in 1906 the depressed state of the economy was to the Liberal advantage. Their long years of opposition had effaced the memory of the Liberal failure to deal with unemployment in 1892-5.

The Liberal Party was also able to secure the electoral support of the trade unions. This had its limitations during economic depression, for although the broad advance of 1889-91 had been held, membership in 1906 and 1910 was well below the peak figures of those years. The full power of trade unionism was only to be revealed by the expansion after 1910. Trade unions were nevertheless an important influence, and because of the simplification of General Election issues into a choice between alternative governments, the Taff Vale decision was as of much immediate benefit to the Liberal Party as to the Labour Representation Committee. Only a Liberal government could restore quickly the vanished legal protection of trade union funds. Similarly the Osborne decision of 1908-9, depriving trade unions of the right to levy their members in support of the Labour Party, could only be reversed by Liberal legislation. Consequently even in 1910 some of the most influential London trade unions affiliated to the Labour Party, the Dockers, Stevedores and Compositors, can be found sending strong messages of support to the Liberal press.[1] This

[1] *Daily News*, 14 January 1910 etc.

willingness to support both Labour and Liberals was helped by the fact that until 1908, when the Miners' M.P.s joined the parliamentary Labour Party, there were as many trade union M.P.s sitting with the Liberals as with Labour. The Railway Servants' secretary was a Liberal M.P. until 1909 and their London district council was noted for its Liberal-Labour standpoint. The Engineers were represented in the Liberal Government by John Burns. And even where this could not sway the official attitude of the union, local branches could declare their support for the Liberal candidate. Some Liberals made use of these messages in their election manifestoes; in 1910 one Liberal claimed the support of the Compositors, Bookbinders, Bootmakers, French Polishers, Carmen and Costermongers.[1]

The limited strength of the trade unions meant that in 1906 and 1910 their moral support was almost as effective in a General Election as direct affiliation. In 1910 even the funds which they could provide were threatened by the Osborne decision. Moreover after 1910 the more militant trade union leaders, disappointed by a Labour Party closely tied to the Liberals, were diverting much of their energy to industrial rather than political action. The syndicalist movement drew immediately on socialist and Labour Party rather than Liberal-Labour trade unionists. The *Daily Herald* under George Lansbury, with its support of 'rebel' rather than Labour candidates, had a similar effect after 1912. Thus right up to the end of this period the trade union support given at elections to the Liberal Party was comparable to that given to the Labour Party.

This situation was unlikely to continue. The dramatic growth of trade union membership after 1910 meant that the trade unions could provide the Labour Party with a more substantial and more secure financial foundation than the uncertain subscriptions of middle class Liberals. A stronger Labour Party was more likely to be independent, and thus to attract back the energy of those militant trade unionists diverted by syndicalism and the *Daily Herald*.

In a similar way the advent of the Labour Party at first benefited the Liberals. Once Labour was separately organised, creating its own loyalties and interests, the ultimate outlook for Liberalism was bleak. The Liberals must either challenge Labour, thus alienating working class support, or help the growth of Labour as an ally, fostering the cuckoo in the nest. They chose the second course with results which, although in the long run fatal, were immediately wholly fortunate. The Labour alliance was far more effective in securing working class votes than radicalism had been before 1900.

[1] Election manifestoes, January and December 1910. Shoreditch public library. cf. *St. Pancras Chronicle*, 2 December 1910, Martin, Liberal candidate East St. Pancras, claims support of eleven trade unions.

The electoral arrangement with the Labour Representation Committee in 1906 has recently been fully described. It has not, however, been noticed that in London the 'principal beneficiaries' of this arrangement were the Liberals rather than the Labour men.[1] Only two Labour candidates were secured a free run, in Woolwich and South West Ham. In neither constituency was the Liberal Party capable of putting up a serious candidate. Woolwich had been considered a Conservative safe seat until the Labour Party was organised in 1902-3, and South West Ham had been fought by an independent Labour candidate since 1892, and before that by a Lib-Lab. The Liberal organisation had to all practical intent disappeared in both constituencies, and the local Free Church Councils supported the Labour candidates.

The third official Labour candidate was in Deptford. Here C. W. Bowerman, Secretary of the Compositors, had been selected in 1903, and made it clear that he 'had always been an active voter in the Liberal and Radical interest' and, although a Labour candidate, would support a Liberal government.[2] So far from trying to secure him a free run, the Liberal Central Office decided to 'push the idea' of Herbert Vivian, a 'Tory Democrat Free Trader' who had come over to the Liberals.[3] In spite of Labour objections it was still supporting Vivian at the beginning of 1905.[4] It was only on the very eve of the election, when it was obvious that Bowerman had won over even the local Free Church Council, that a leading article was published by the *Daily Chronicle* asking Vivian to withdraw.[5] He refused, and was endorsed by the Liberal whip with the somewhat tardy observation that 'it is always a matter of much regret to me when any friction or conflict occurs between the Liberal and Labour parties'.[6] Even *Reynold's Newspaper* which described the Labour candidates as 'the prime fruit and flower of the British working class', could offer Bowerman no more than a friendly neutrality.[7] Yet in spite of this Bowerman was elected by a decisive majority, with the official Liberal at the bottom of the poll with a mere 6 per cent of the votes.

Of the other seats on Herbert Gladstone's list, two were regarded as Labour constituencies in the early stages, Central Finsbury and Hammersmith. Steadman was adopted in the former, where the

[1] F. Bealey and H. Pelling, *Labour and Politics 1900–1906*, London 1958, pp. 268, 288.
[2] *Kentish Mercury*, 16 October 1903.
[3] H. Gladstone, interviews with Rev. Lyon Turner, 27 March 1904, and W. H. Dickinson, 9 May 1904, Herbert Gladstone Collection.
[4] Ibid., interview with H. Vivian, 27 April 1905.
[5] 30 December 1905.   [6] *Daily Chronicle*, 2 January 1906.
[7] 14 January 1906.

Liberal Association had been for some years defunct.[1] Eventually he refused to sign the Labour Party constitution, and was elected as a Liberal. In Hammersmith the Liberal Association was weak and divided between Labour men and Nonconformists. A Labour candidate, George Belt, was adopted in 1904, but a section of the Liberals would not consider supporting him. The Liberal Association had no funds, but the Central Office came to their assistance and George Blaiklock was adopted against Belt.[2] Had the Labour Party officially supported Belt the issue would have been uncertain, for the President of the Liberal Association had resigned to campaign for Belt.[3] But Ramsay MacDonald had objections to Belt's private life and succeeded in convincing the Labour Party national executive that such a 'moral scalliwag' was not 'a fit and proper man to represent a constituency in the House of Commons'.[4] Blaiklock made the most of the situation but he failed to capture the seat; the Labour poll, although only 8 per cent, was enough to deny him victory.

Ten other seats were listed, two as Liberal-Labour and eight as possible three-cornered fights. The Liberal candidate secured a free run in every case, and won nine. Only one had been Liberal in 1900, and there is no doubt that several of them could have been as easily won by Labour candidates.[5] Deptford and Hammersmith

[1] (The London Municipal Society's cuttings books contain a series of descriptions of Liberal organisation, said to come from the *Daily Chronicle* of July-November 1902. From internal evidence they must date from 1902 or 1903, but I cannot trace them in any Liberal daily for that period. They are referred to as *L.M.S. D. Chron.*) *L.M.S. D. Chron.*, 18 October 1902.

[2] Herbert Gladstone, interview with Blaiklock, 6 February 1905. Herbert Gladstone Collection.

[3] *West London Advertiser*, 4 November 1904.

[4] J. R. MacDonald to R. Davison, 23 March 1905, Labour Party correspondence.

[5] The seats were Tottenham and Haggerston Liberal-Labour; North Lambeth, Walthamstow, North West Ham, Dartford, North Kensington, North Paddington, Stepney and St. George's in the East. Tottenham was a growing working class suburb, still to some extent non-political in local politics (for which it was divided into Tottenham, Edmonton and Wood Green), but with a socialist Labour Party which was remarkably successful in Council elections after 1902. Haggerston was an old Liberal-Labour seat held by Randal Cremer. North Lambeth was a very poor constituency in which the sections of the Liberal Party had always tended to friction. Walthamstow was a new working class suburb; in 1903 the Labour men had broken with the Progressives and selected A. E. Holmes, the organiser of the London Society of Compositors, as Labour candidate; Holmes would have certainly run as an official Labour candidate if he could have secured adequate financial support (P. Campbell to J. R. MacDonald, 24 February 1904, Labour Party correspondence). North West Ham was an area of clerks and artisans, in which the only strong trade union influence, the Stratford railwaymen, were 'not by any means inclined towards our platform' (Labour Party National Executive Committee minutes,

suggest the extent to which the Liberals gained from the electoral arrangement.

In the two elections of 1910 there was little change in the situation. In Bermondsey a three-cornered fight had occurred at a bye-election in November 1909. It was a difficult constituency for Labour, because the local I.L.P. branch had only been in existence for a few months and had no strong trade union backing. Dr. Alfred Salter, the Labour candidate, was a man of strong personality and local popularity who had been elected to the L.C.C. for Bermondsey in 1907 as a Progressive and come over to independent Labour in 1908. The I.L.P. may well have hoped that he would secure a straight fight; certainly the early canvassing suggested that he would poll most of the radical vote, and he had strong support in the chapels. The Liberals put up Spencer Hughes of the *Morning Leader*, and the whole influence of the Liberal daily press, the *Daily News*, the *Daily Chronicle*, the *Morning Leader* and the *Star*, supported by the best election agents from all over London, was concentrated on proving that 'a vote for the Labour nominee was a vote wasted'. During the last week before the election the window-cards displayed in favour of the Labour candidate were widely replaced by Liberal cards, and among those who voted against Salter were two of the electors who had signed his nomination forms and a parson who had sent a telegram of support to his adoption meeting.[1] The result was a Conservative victory, with Salter in third place. The I.L.P. National Council decided not to support another fight at the General Election, and Salter accepted the need 'to settle down to steady spade work for several years and then try again'.[2]

Similar restraint was shown by the Labour Party in a number of

[1] *Labour Leader*, 5 November 1909.
[2] I.L.P. National Council minutes, 26 November 1909; A. Salter to R. C. K. Ensor, 10 December 1909, Ensor Collection.

---

27 June 1911). Dartford was a large Thames-side constituency, still largely rural, but with small towns dependent on heavy industry, of which Erith had a vigorous Labour Party. North Kensington was an unusual mixture of wealthy residential and poor working class districts, captured by a Liberal candidate who was enthusiastically supported by the Labour men in 1892, but fatally split after the candidate of 1900 had alienated the 'Labour and pro-Boer Party' (*West London Observer*, 21 September 1900); in local elections after 1900 the local Liberals allied with the Conservatives against Labour candidates, and a strong Labour Party developed. North Paddington was a similar constituency, but with less Labour activity. Stepney was a working class constituency in which the Liberal Association was defunct, and the only Progressive body was the Stepney Labour League (*L.M.S. D. Chron.*, 24 October 1902); it was held by the Conservatives even in 1906. St. George's in the East was a working class constituency with a strong Irish element and a good Liberal Association.

other constituencies both in 1910 and in subsequent bye-elections.[1] No doubt much of this restraint on the Labour side was merely prudent, but the feeling that it was preventing the growth of the party was not confined to the wilder rank and file. At the I.L.P. National Council Keir Hardie argued strongly in favour of contesting more London seats.[2]

In fact there was only one more official Labour candidate in 1910, George Lansbury at Bow and Bromley. Stopford Brooke, son of the famous Unitarian preacher, had won Bow and Bromley for the Liberals in 1906 in a straight fight, Lansbury having decided instead to run as an unofficial Labour candidate in Middlesborough against the Lib-Lab Havelock Wilson. Lansbury would have probably returned to Bow and Bromley, which he had fought in 1900, in any case, for his local popularity was exceptional. His decision to fight the seat was made in 1907 after the attacks of the Local Government Board under John Burns on the Poplar Poor Law policy. Brooke does not appear to have intervened in the matter, and Sydney Buxton, the Liberal member for Poplar, while personally sympathetic to Crooks and Lansbury and 'very sorry indeed for all the worry and anxiety' could take no 'responsibility for the amount of out-relief that was given. I never disguised my view in Poplar, at the time, that the relief was given far too lavishly.'[3] After this a three-cornered fight in Bow was almost inevitable, and the only difficulty made by the Labour Party over Lansbury's endorsement was his wish, eventually dropped, to run as a 'Labour and Socialist' candidate. In January 1910 he forced the sitting member into third place, and although the Conservative was elected the votes showed that Lansbury had drawn support from both parties—as the wide variety of his support also suggested. The Liberal decision not to contest the seat in December 1910 was made after strong pressure from the Central Office.[4] It was wise, for Lansbury would have very probably won the seat in any case. Lansbury had had 4,000 promises of support in January, enough to win, and the Liberal would no longer be able to erode them by the cry that a vote Labour was a vote wasted.[5]

There can be little doubt that the electoral agreement with Labour proved a great advantage to the Liberals. In all these elections, where

---

[1] Hammersmith was not fought again, and after official discouragement North Lambeth, North West Ham and Walthamstow were also abandoned. Grayson's candidature for Kennington in December 1910 was not sanctioned by the I.L.P. National Council. (Labour Party National Executive Committee minutes, 7 October 1910, 26–27 June 1911.)
[2] I.L.P. National Council minutes, 2 May 1910.
[3] S. Buxton to G. Lansbury, 30 July 1906, Lansbury Collection.
[4] *East London Observer*, 3 and 6 December 1910.
[5] *Labour Leader*, 28 January 1910.

sacrifices were made they were made by Labour. As had been aptly remarked by a speaker at Deptford in 1904, the Liberals were friends of Labour only as long as Labour took the back seat.[1]

The third means by which the Liberal party secured the working class vote was simply efficient organisation. After the defeat of 1900 the Liberal Central Office decided to intervene. It was found that the London Liberal and Radical Union had no general scheme of organisation and there was a 'complete absence of information concerning the present financial condition and political organisation' of the constituency parties.[2] The Union had some political vitality, but 'as an organising body it lacks cohesion, precision and concentration and effectiveness. It depends for its direction too much on men elected for political opinions on this or that question rather than on men primarily organisers and workers. Unpaid men without direct responsibility cannot be persistent and effective workers. ... Its authority (is) not admitted by all constituencies. Constituencies constantly come direct to Parliament Street.'[3] This 'incompetent' body was therefore abolished, and replaced by a purely propaganda body, the London Liberal Federation, with John Benn as its secretary.[4] The essential responsibility for supervising organisation was transferred to Renwick Seager at the Central Office under the direction of Herbert Gladstone. Gladstone assumed an influential role in interviewing and recommending prospective candidates, with the power to give the financial assistance which was needed in a growing number of cases. Candidates had previously been introduced to constituencies by the Union, and 'all their candidates or recommendations are moneyed men, and as a rule, of a class that a large section of the Labour Party will not support. ... The Labour vote is the backbone of the Liberal Party, but owing to the large number of unsuitable candidates that are forced upon constituencies ... this vote is becoming daily more and more estranged.'[5] After 1900 the system of introductions was not abolished, but Gladstone took a special interest in finding suitable constituencies for socially conscious less wealthy candidates such as Charles Masterman and Percy Alden. By 1903 he was able to boast that 'London is far better off for fixed candidates than has ever been the case (so far as I know) so soon after a General Election'.[6]

[1] *Kentish Mercury*, 18 November 1904.
[2] 'Memorandum on the London constituencies,' 46105, Herbert Gladstone Collection.
[3] London Liberal and Radical Union 'relationship to Whips Office', ibid.
[4] H. Gladstone to J. M. Poulton, 31 January 1903, and to Lord Tweedmouth, 20 June 1901, ibid.
[5] F. O. Prince to H. Gladstone, 26 March 1900, ibid.
[6] H. Gladstone to J. M. Poulton, 31 January 1903, ibid.

The state of constituency organisation in 1900 was very serious. The Conservatives had more than 30 full-time qualified agents in London. There were only five full-time Liberal agents, and of these 'three only are competent men. The Party could not afford paid canvassers for registration, and in most districts the Associations were too weak to carry out registration work through voluntary assistance and as a result it was 'pitiably neglected and mismanaged'.[1] In many of the register courts the Liberals were unrepresented. Removals, which could often exceed 25 per cent of the electorate annually, were not traced; there was no central London clearing house. In some working class constituencies, including Woolwich, Central Finsbury, Bow and Bromley, Stepney and Walworth, there was no Liberal Association of any kind; in most it was struggling.[2] Where there was a good agent the Association executive might be holding regular meetings, but only in Bermondsey and East Finsbury was it reported that regular ward meetings were being held.[3] Deptford, regarded as 'strong and active', with an experienced agent in F. W. Galton, had a total membership of 250, although the Association was meant to be composed of 400 delegates.[4]

The key to the situation was finance. If a proper agent could be provided in each working class constituency the Associations could be kept going. South-West Bethnal Green is an illustration. In 1903 no ward meetings had been held for 'a long time' and the Association had no regular meetings, although it had 300 members; E. H. Pickersgill was 'to be the candidate but not yet selected'. There was 'no hope for the division unless a paid agent employed all the time'.[5] Central Office agreed to spend £150 at once on organisation, and £400 in the General Election.[6] The seat was recovered in 1906. As a concession to trade union feeling the Association was renamed the 'Liberal and Labour Association', a tactic adopted in a number of constituencies, but it remained, in spite of a genuine local attachment to radicalism, essentially a creature of external forces. In the selection of candidates, for example, it was not allowed to make its own choice.[7] When the sitting member retired in 1911 Charles Masterman was forced on the constituency with such abruptness that a minority of Liberals seceded to form a Labour Association, and although

[1] Report by Lionel Holland c. January 1901, ibid.
[2] *L.M.S. D. Chron.*, 8 November, 18 October, 24 October 1902.
[3] Ibid., 18 October, 27 July 1902.
[4] Ibid., 11 October 1902.
[5] Interview with T. Wiles, 3 March 1903, Herbert Gladstone Collection.
[6] Interview with Pickersgill, 16 March 1904, ibid.
[7] E.g. the 1911 incident, Sir P. Harris, *Forty Years In and Out of Parliament*, London 1947, pp. 47–48. Harris describes his own adoption as L.C.C. candidate, pp. 36–38.

Masterman held the seat by a narrow majority he lost it at a second bye-election caused by his promotion to the Cabinet in 1914. There was thus a limit to the extent to which Liberalism could be sustained by money, but money could be very helpful within that limit.

There is no doubt that as a result of Central Office efforts London organisation was greatly improved. Although occasional reports continued of Associations in working class constituencies becoming defunct,[1] there is no reason to doubt the claim made in 1910 that there was an organisation in every London constituency, even including Woolwich.[2] The regular annual subsidy of £1,000 for registration work, and the larger special organisation and election grants, had had their effect.[3] The increasing efficiency of Borough Councils in carrying out registration work was at the same time reducing the task to be carried out. Nevertheless it cannot be said that the basic problem of Liberal organisation had been solved. It was freely admitted in the *London Year Book* of 1911 that there were many wards without sufficient Liberals to form a committee, and that only in 'well to do suburban areas' were the Associations self-supporting. Working class constituencies were still unable to provide enough workers at elections. In 1906 St. George's in the East was regarded as a remarkable exception in that canvassing was 'carried out not by imported canvassers from other districts but by working men'.[4]

In the 1880s the weakness of the Liberal Associations had been to an important extent caused and compensated by the strength of the radical clubs. This could no longer be said in the 1900s. The Metropolitan Radical Federation still existed, meeting monthly in one of the clubs for political discussion and entertainment, but its proceedings were no longer regarded as significant and rarely reported in the press.[5] The Hackney Political Council claimed to represent 3,000 club members, but its insignificance was shown in 1910 when it advised members to abstain at the L.C.C. election: the Progressives gained two seats.[6] These organisations could no longer speak for the Labour vote. Certainly Liberal candidates sometimes regretted the lack of a club to help in elections,[7] and occasionally in the growing

[1] E.g. Whitechapel; *East London Observer*, 27 March 1905.
[2] *Daily Chronicle*, 28 November 1910; Woolwich Liberal and Radical Association was refounded 19 July 1909, and could claim one dissident Labour councillor and two Nonconformist clergy but little local influence—*Woolwich Pioneer*, 23 December 1910.
[3] Registration grants, 46105, Herbert Gladstone Collection.
[4] *Daily Chronicle*, 13 January 1906.
[5] Reports of Metropolitan Radical Federation meetings at Woolwich Radical Club, *Woolwich Pioneer*, 21 July 1905 and 26 February 1909.
[6] *Hackney and Kingsland Gazette*, 28 February 1910.
[7] *Fulham Observer*, 11 March 1910.

working class suburbs a new political radical club was founded. The East Ham Progressive Club, for example, was founded in 1903. It assisted in registration and education work, arranged some public meetings (including outdoor meetings in 1905), and in return was generously subsidised by the Liberal M.P. for the division.[1]

More frequently the Liberal allegiance was a largely formal survival from the past. Members of the Eleusis Club still had to sign belief in adult suffrage, secular education, old age pensions, land nationalisation, disestablishment and abolition of the House of Lords, but after 1900 the former Chelsea radicalism was replaced by a rich man's Liberalism.[2] The St. Pancras Reform Club had a Political Committee and was nominally affiliated to the Metropolitan Radical Federation until 1909. In 1910 as a result of election excitement there were discussions in the club on the Tariff Reform issue, and some of the members were disturbed to find there were overt socialists and Conservatives in their ranks. But efforts to expel these members were frustrated by the club committee and older members maintained that in the previous fifteen years they 'had never before heard politics discussed in the club'.[3]

Where a radical club remained strongly interested in politics, it was as likely to support the Labour Party as the Liberals. In Woolwich, Deptford, Hammersmith and Bow and Bromley the clubs, although retaining the title of Radical or Liberal, were affiliated to the Labour Party and supported it against the Liberals in three-cornered conflicts.[4] Even in East Ham the club can be found subscribing to Will Crooks election fund, negotiating with the I.L.P. branch, providing accommodation and holding meetings with the local Labour League, and even sending delegates to the East Ham L.R.C. at a time when Labour candidates were opposing Progressives at local elections.[5]

[1] East Ham Progressive Club minute book, 1903–9; 4 January 1907, cheque for £1000 from Sir John Bethell, M.P., for building fund.

[2] Eleusis Club, *Labour Record*, May 1905; the candidate for Chelsea in 1900 was James Jeffrey of the Eleusis, chairman of the Metropolitan Radical Federation, from 1906 E. J. Horniman, who contributed £28,000 to Liberal funds in 1900, 28 September 1900, 46058, Herbert Gladstone Collection.

[3] St. Pancras Reform Club minute book, 1908–12; especially 28 January and 14 February 1910.

[4] Woolwich and Deptford, Chapter 11; Hammersmith, see e.g. *West London Advertiser*, 30 November 1900, and Blaiklock's speech after his defeat—'There was a club in the borough to which Liberals ought to give attention—a club which became the centre of disaffection and hostility to the Radical cause'— *West London Observer*, 26 January 1906; Bow and Bromley, e.g. reception of Lansbury at Bow and Bromley Progressive Club, *East End News*, 7 February 1911.

[5] East Ham Progressive Club minute book, 5 March 1903, 12 March 1903, 28 April 1905, 3 April 1907, etc. There is no evidence that the club ever sup-

Radicalism in the 1900s was increasingly an outdated political concept. This was probably why the attempt of *Reynold's Newspaper* to revive it in London in 1900–2 proved a surprisingly abrupt failure. It was mere verbal play to pretend, as *Reynold's* wished in 1906, that 'the new Liberal Party is a Radical and Labour Party, or it is nothing. The word "Liberal" is a convenient nickname.'[1] The three real political elements were Labour, Socialist and Liberal. The good fortune of the Liberal Party in the 1900s depended on the coincidence of the revival of both Nonconformist and Labour support, and both these revivals, as we have seen were based on temporary situations. If the Liberals suffered another political eclipse they would have to meet the challenge of a Labour Party of new political and financial strength. Liberalism was a big political tree, but were its roots strong enough? To survive as the principal political party of the working class, it must become a live working class political movement. Was 'the strength of working-class Liberalism' in London noticed in one recent history of the Labour Party a reality?[2]

The decay of radicalism and the parasitic character of Liberal Party organisation in working class constituencies strongly suggest that the working class roots of London Liberalism were no longer reliable. An examination of local elections points to similar conclusions. It is possible, in fact, to see some trees toppling.

After 1895, while the Conservative Party officially intervened in local elections the Liberal Party in theory abstained. Nevertheless in most parts of London local elections were fought on party lines, and an attempt was made to unite Nonconformists and Labour men in a Progressive Party similar to the Liberal Party, and organised by the same people. Because issues were less important and candidates more numerous than in a General Election, these Progressive Parties were more directly responsive to the political undercurrents of the period.

In the early 1900s the most successful Progressive Party was on the L.C.C. In power since 1889, securing trade union support through its 'labour bench' and fair labour principles, justly proud of its improvements in London housing and the tramway system, holding Nonconformist allegiance through its temperance policy, the Party had been returned in the 1904 election by an overwhelming majority. Yet in 1907, a bare year after the General Election triumphs of the Liberals,

---

[1] *Reynold's Newspaper*, 28 January 1906.
[2] Bealey and Pelling, op. cit., p. 268.

---

ported a Labour candidate against a Progressive, but in addition to sending delegates to the East Ham L.R.C. a number of committee members belonged to both bodies (27 August 1906).

it was crushed. In spite of a strong recovery in 1910, it was never again able to secure a majority on the Council.

There were a number of causes for this defeat. The Labour Party was no longer content with an ageing and dependent 'bench' to represent its interests, and decided to fight independently. The Progressives failed to come to an electoral arrangement as in previous elections, and the hostility produced by three-cornered fights weakened their working class support.

Much more serious was the discontent of important Nonconformists. The L.C.C. had taken over the London education system from the School Board after the 1904 election, and decided to administer the new Education Act fairly and not to discriminate against voluntary schools which were genuinely attempting to bring their buildings up to the required standards. Many Nonconformists had hoped that the Council would refuse to administer the Act, or at least adopt a stern attitude to inadequate church schools. The Congregationalist *British Weekly* was open in its hostility to the Progressives, denouncing them as 'men who have betrayed the first principles of Nonconformity. ... Their policy has been of late tyrannical, extravagant and illiberal in the highest degree. We should view with the utmost satisfaction their complete defeat.'[1]

There was corresponding dissatisfaction among Roman Catholics, who suspected that the Progressives with a Liberal government in power would attempt to revoke the 1903 Education Act. The Liberal *London Catholic Herald*, which had previously supported the Progressives, declared itself 'disgusted' by an L.C.C. policy influenced by the Nonconformist leader Dr. Clifford, and advised 'Catholic and Irish Electors! Pledge yourselves to no party. ... Keep aloof, and organise.' It demanded assurances of the Progressives, warning them that 'we are now at the parting of ways'. As the election approached it declared itself satisfied by Progressive assurances, but a central Irish and Catholic election committee had already been set up, and in St. George's in the East two Catholics went to the poll as Independent Progressives.[2] Their intervention gave one seat to the Municipal Reform (Conservative) Party. In other constituencies the advice given by many of the clergy to vote against the Progressives must have been more influential than in previous elections.

The most decisive factor in the election was the success of the Conservative organisation in producing a mass revolt among London ratepayers. English local authorities, because of their exceptional reliance on a single source of income, are particularly vulnerable to this kind of movement. There had been an inevitable tendency, as the

[1] *British Weekly*, 27 September 1906.
[2] 9 November and 7 December 1906.

responsibilities of the L.C.C. increased, for rates to rise. This tendency was exaggerated by the transfer of education from the School Board. Suspicions of unnecessary extravagance by the Progressive Parties on the Guardians had been aroused by the Local Government Board attacks on the Poplar Board, and the failure of the L.C.C. Thames steamboat scheme to make a profit (due to bad weather) was used against the L.C.C. Progressives. With a Liberal government in power there was at least an opportunity for Progressive plans to take over the Port of London and to start a massive electricity scheme, as well as perhaps earlier designs to control water, gas, markets and health, to be realised. There was an obvious danger of a rapid rise in rates, which would inevitably hit the less prosperous classes most seriously. At the same time there was a very serious threat to many powerful interests. Large landlords were frightened of the taxation of ground rents, railway companies of competition from L.C.C. trams, insurance companies of municipal insurance, the electric and dock companies of L.C.C. takeovers. For the first time the Conservatives fought the London local elections with as much, if not more, energy as at a General Election. The threat was anticipated as early as 1905. A campaign against rising rates was launched at a conference with the Duke of Norfolk, one of the largest London landlords, as chairman. Supported by the Industrial Freedom League and the London Municipal Society (the Conservative election organisation), a Central Federation of Ratepayers' Associations of London and Greater London was formed to fight extravagance.[1] Special appeals were issued for funds, and met with obvious success. The 'educational campaign' began in July 1906, with meetings in halls, parks and street corners, 'converted working men', sandwich boards, and a brilliant poster campaign, backed by the full efforts of the Conservative press.[2] While the Liberal electoral machine was 'weary and depleted' by the effort of the General Election, and hoped to win the local elections as before on a minimum expenditure, on the Conservative side 'money was poured out like water'.[3]

The Liberals were stunned by the vigour of the Conservative campaign, and somewhat lamely denounced its 'frantic personal abuse' and 'methods of America'.[4] In one case it was proved that working men marching in a demonstration against the steamboats had been hired at 4/- a day through the labour exchanges.[5] It could be inferred that some of the 'converted working men' had succumbed to similar inducements. But there is no doubt that the secret of the

[1] *Municipal Journal*, 14 April and 26 May 1905.
[2] London Municipal Society, annual report 1906; *Star*, 1 November 1906.
[3] *Star*, 3 November 1906.   [4] *Daily News*, 4 March 1907.
[5] *Star*, 23 February 1907.

THE LIBERAL REVIVAL AND AFTER

campaign, apart from its scale, was the brilliance of its cartoons and slogans. The menacing top-hatted figure spitting 'Ratepayers! It's YOUR money we want' was only one of many effective posters. There were pictures of 'The Progressive Progress' as a march towards a cliff, the ratepayer as a harmless insect wooed by a spider, 'A Socialist Stew, a very Poplar receipt', and various scenes from 'The Progressive Rake's Progress'. The Progressive leaders, McKinnon Wood and Cornwall, were seen together pushing a huge snowball with a figure crushed inside. 'Go on pushing, Wood, we have made it a whopper.' 'Yes, I know, but have you any idea where Ratepayer is? It's his field, you know, and I haven't seen him for some time.' Perhaps most winning of all was a gruesome sheep-shearing scene, with the following pathetic lines:

> Shorn already, very fully,
>   And unmercifully fleeced
> Of his coat, rich warm and woolly,
>   All his joy in life has ceased,
>   And in anguish wildly bleating
>   At this very painful meeting
> 'What again?' he bleats, that melancholy bleat.
>
> With a body bare and bony
>   And an aching heart within,
> Oh, his path is cold and stony,
>   But his persecutors grin.
>   'Wool, more wool!' he cries, 'Why, blow it,
>   I can get no chance to grow it!'
> 'Then,' they answer, 'we shall have to take your skin!'[1]

The most important effect of this propaganda was to bring out large numbers of voters, particularly women, who had not voted in previous elections.[2] The Conservatives also claimed to have won many votes from latchkey voters enfranchised by the Devonport decision, an impression possibly due to the young middle class men in this category. The Progressive vote, although slightly increased in nearly all constituencies, was far short of the Liberal vote at General Elections, while the Municipal Reform party were able to turn out every Conservative voter, and in middle class constituencies even slightly to exceed their General Election poll.[3]

[1] London Municipal Society poster collection.
[2] Chiozza Money argued that in North Paddington, where previously few women had voted, 2200 voted, only 1 in 500 supporting the Progressives—*Daily News*, 5 March 1907. Most newspapers mentioned the women's vote. The London Municipal Society secretary said that 100,000 women had voted, mostly Conservative—*Globe*, 4 March 1907.
[3] See Appendix A.

THE LIBERAL REVIVAL AND AFTER

Threatened by defections on both fronts, the Progressive Party had neither the organisation nor the political conviction to answer the middle class revolt. Its catastrophic defeat was a serious warning of the difficulties which would face a broad-based Liberal government carrying out a radical social policy.

The Progressive Parties on the Borough Councils were much less successful than the L.C.C. Party in combining the various Liberal elements, and never met with such general success at elections. Even in 1903, when the Liberal revival was well under way, only 10 of 28 boroughs were controlled by Progressive Parties.[1] The only majorities to withstand the Conservative onslaught in 1906 were Battersea and Bethnal Green. In 1909 four Councils, and in 1912 three, had a Progressive majority. The only Council which remained Progressive throughout the 1900s was Bethnal Green; Battersea and Southwark were each held in four of five elections, but no other Council more than twice.

The Party at Bethnal Green was an unusual survival. Although one of the poorest parts of London, Bethnal Green had an exceptionally stable population with the highest proportion of London-born inhabitants in the whole county. The local industries, furniture and boot-making, were still small-scale craft trades. These two facts help to explain its old-fashioned radical politics. The Progressive councillors were almost all small tradesmen, and before 1912 there was no attempt to infuse a labour element.[2] The policies of the party were equally old-fashioned. In 1912 there was still only one public baths in the borough, although the Baths Act had been adopted in 1895, no free library, and no municipal electricity, although a provisional order for this had been obtained in 1899.[3] The Board of Guardians, which was also Progressive-controlled, continued to pursue the policy of refusing relief outside the workhouse.[4] Bethnal Green was not so exceptional in the backwardness of its Progressive policies. Of the five Councils which gave their employees a paid holiday, only one was Progressive-controlled.[5] In half the six boroughs with the lowest

[1] In the *Reformers Year Book*, 1904, 14 Progressive Councils were claimed. This figure was reached by counting one Labour Council (Woolwich), one Council in which Labour held the balance (Poplar), one Council in which independents held the balance (Greenwich), and one Council controlled by a 'Non-political and Progressive Committee' of independents (Hampstead).

[2] Professions of candidates, *East London Observer*, 2 October 1909. Labour candidates stood independently in 1912, and the first Labour councillor was elected at a subsequent bye-election—*Daily Herald*, 20 June 1914. He was the future Communist Mayor, Joe Vaughan.

[3] *Daily Herald*, 8 October 1912; *Municipal Journal*, 13 July 1900, 2 December 1904.

[4] *Municipal Journal*, 10 March 1905.

[5] Ibid., 12 May 1905.

number of sanitary inspectors in proportion to the population in 1904 the Progressive Party was either in control, or could secure a majority with Labour support.[1] The attitudes of the Progressive tradesmen of Bethnal Green were thus paralleled in other parts of London. But their political success was unique, and due to a social and industrial situation which could not assist Liberalism elsewhere.

Battersea and Southwark were much more encouraging. Both Councils had good labour policies, high proportions of sanitary inspectors, an excellent provision of public baths and libraries, and municipal lighting schemes. Battersea in addition had built housing, supplied municipal milk, and ran a series of winter concerts. It took the important step in 1901 of appointing a special registration officer and consequently had an exceptionally high proportion of the population registered as electors, an added advantage to the Liberal Party.[2] In both boroughs the basis of electoral success had been an alliance with local trade unions and Trades Councils. In Southwark a quarter and in Battersea rather more than half of the Progressive candidates and councillors were artisans.[3]

It would be unwise, however, to exaggerate the solidity of the Progressive alliance in these boroughs. In both cases the Progressives were helped by the local Irish, although there was some Catholic bitterness in Southwark in 1906–7.[4] Even so the Labour alliance was precarious. In Southwark the number of Labour and Socialist candidates was increasing, and in 1906 the Trades Council affiliated to the Labour Party. The Trades Council succeeded for the moment in combining this affiliation with its old Liberal allegiance, but by 1912 there were clear signs of a growing rift. Most working class candidates were now standing independently of the Progressives, and the Trades Council had attempted to join the independent Labour Electoral Association for the L.C.C. elections of 1913. Its delegate, Charles Jesson, a member of the I.L.P., claimed that he had been elected to the L.C.C. as an independent supported by the Musicians Union 'and he did not receive a penny piece from the Progressive forces neither did he receive their party whip'.[5] It was admitted that he had worked with the three Labour members, but he had refused to join their Party, and on this account he was obliged to withdraw from the meeting. If it was not to make itself absurd the Trades Council

[1] Ibid., 4 November 1904.
[2] Ibid., 14 September 1900, 12 April, 14 June, 22 November 1901.
[3] Professions of candidates, *South-Western Star, Battersea Mercury, South London Mail, South London Chronicle* and *Southwark Recorder*, pre-election issues.
[4] *London Catholic Herald*, 18 January 1907, etc.
[5] Report of London Labour Electoral Association conference, Deptford Labour Association Executive Committee minute book, 30 April 1912.

would have to commit itself more explicitly to either the Liberal and Labour Party, and local labour opinion seemed to be moving towards the latter.

In Battersea the Progressives were held together only by the influence of John Burns. Burns could have led the borough into the Labour Party. With a majority of the Progressive councillors working class, a strong local socialist movement, a Trades Council in favour of the Labour Representation Committee, his personal supporters organised in a Labour League rather than a Liberal Association, and his most experienced organiser William Sanders shortly to become London I.L.P. secretary, it would have been easy for Burns to have joined the Labour Party in the House of Commons. Until 1906 the socialists worked with the Progressives in Borough Council elections. There was a sharp split between the middle class Progressives and the Trades Council over the selection of candidates for a bye-election in 1901. Burns persuaded the Trades Council to adopt another candidate, warning them 'of the disproportionate power and influence the labourers had', and subsequently 'rubbed in with some effect the West Ham condition and our approaching it unless reformation occurred'.[1] Nevertheless the candidates at the 1903 Borough Council election were again predominantly working class, and included no militant dissenter, nothing for the 'great temperance party'. Some dissatisfied Nonconformists ran as an independent Progressive 'Third Party'.[2] Burns was worried by this (although it did not prevent an easy Progressive win) and decided to prevent the Trades Council, which had affiliated to the Labour Party in 1902, from moving any further towards independence. At a series of meetings he 'faced them, broke them up with volleys of good tempered chaff helped by interruption, dissolved them'.[3] The Trades Council continued to send delegates to local Liberal organisations, and early in 1906 disaffiliated from the Labour Party.

Although Burns joined the Liberal cabinet in December 1905 this did not end the trouble. At each Borough Council election from 1906 the Progressives were opposed by the socialists, and were significantly less successful than previously. A Battersea Labour Party was formed in 1908, affiliated to the national Labour Party, and supported by the leading Progressive Trade Unionists and the I.L.P. At the Borough Council election of 1909 it ran its own candidates independently of the middle class Progressives, and the Conservatives captured almost every seat on the Council. Shaken by this disaster, the alliance was patched up and the Council recaptured in 1912. For

[1] J. Burns, diary, 23 October and 7 December 1901.
[2] *Battersea Mercury*, 10 October and 12 September 1903.
[3] J. Burns, diary, 20 October 1904, 25 February 1905.

the moment, with Burns in the cabinet, Battersea would remain loyal to Liberalism. He was able from 1905 to rely for constituency organisation on the Liberal and Radical Association, which he kept out of debt with a generous subsidy from his ministerial salary.[1] But without him the Liberal future was very doubtful.

There was no other successful trade union-Progressive party in London. In most districts, whether or not a local Labour Party existed, a small number of working class Progressive councillors could be found.[2] Very often these councillors had been elected as Labour men, and subsequently decided that it was easier for election purposes to be Progressive. Where a Labour Party existed, personal conflicts would often keep one or two trade unionists with the Progressives. Religious trade unionists, whether Catholic or Free Church, were also noticeable among them. In Bermondsey, for example, although the Catholics split with the Progressives in 1903-6, in other elections the Irish trade unionists preferred to work with the Progressives rather than with the chapel-inspired I.L.P.[3] But these trade unionist Progressives were a very small minority. In the whole of the East End, apart from a few Irish and Primitive Methodists in south Poplar, the only working class Council candidates were Labour men.[4] The same is true of west London, except for three or four candidates in Fulham, where Irish influence was again important. Perhaps the most remarkable case was Stepney, a working class borough in which for most of the period no co-ordinated Progressive Party existed, and local politics were wholly in Conservative control.[5]

A middle class Progressive party did not necessarily result in a conflict with the Labour Party and even in boroughs where there were three-cornered fights in some wards there were often arrangements with Labour candidates in others. In Lambeth, a borough stretching from working class riverside poverty to the prosperous suburban

---

[1] T. C. Waterland, treasurer of Battersea Liberal and Radical Association, to J. Burns, 10 February 1908, Burns Collection.

[2] Analysis of working class Liberals and Progressives in Council elections, Appendix D. 'Labour-Progressive' Parties were often little more than frauds: e.g. *Hackney & Kingsland Gazette*, 25 October 1909, 22 of the 24 Labour-Progressives opposing Labour were middle class men.

[3] *Southwark Recorder*, 24 October and 7 November 1903 (letter from M. J. Fitzgerald saying that the Progressives and Irish had worked together for 15 years), 3 and 10 November 1906, 11 October 1912; *South London Press*, 24 September 1909.

[4] Five of the Poplar councillors elected in 1906 and in 1909 were Primitive Methodists, although their chapel on the Isle of Dogs had only 320 members— *East London Observer*, 16 October 1909, 26 March 1910.

[5] *East London Observer*, August-November 1903, 1909, 1912. In most years there was complete chaos, with different policies in each ward. In 1909 only two Progressives stood (ibid., 6 November 1909).

southern heights, all the various strata of Liberalism could be found: at the wealthiest end, compromises with the Conservatives; a middle belt of Nonconformist influence; and in the working class wards, either arrangements or three-cornered fights with Labour.[1] But tactics of this variety prevented a coherent policy, and even if the labour vote was not lost through direct conflict it was as likely to be lost through apathy. In the same way the Progressive claims in some boroughs to have worked through Ratepayers' Associations or bodies such as the Stepney Council of Public Welfare confused their reputation in other boroughs. More directly damaging was the indecision of Progressive parties in strong Labour areas such as Woolwich, West Ham, Deptford and Poplar, dwindling middle class rumps which were sometimes absorbed by the Labour Party, sometimes threw in their lot with a Conservative Municipal Alliance, and sometimes split between the two.

Fundamental to the difficulties of the Progressive Parties was the role of Nonconformity. Because they were the backbone of middle class Liberalism, Nonconformist ministers and laymen, especially schoolteachers, provided a high proportion of the Progressive candidates. A Progressive canvasser in St. Pancras found the typical opinion that 'London artisans consider that we have heard too much of dissenting parsons in our public affairs of late', and advised them to confine their duties to their chapels.[2] This was an unlikely solution. Even where the Liberals had been absorbed into the Labour Party the Free Church ministers felt it part of their duty to speak for progress. But in supporting a Labour Party they became a less dominant and therefore more useful element securing some middle class votes without alienating the working class. On the other hand, in the Liberal ranks, particularly where co-operation with trade unions was poor, they too easily became the standard-bearers. This was particularly likely to happen where the Party was in opposition. Nonconformity alone could not win elections. If the alliance with Labour could lead to absorption, the reliance on Nonconformity was certain to lead to complete political collapse.

A good example of collapse occurred in Hammersmith. Here the hostility between the radical-labour and Nonconformist sections was especially acute. In 1900 the Liberal organisation was being run from the Hammersmith Club, and no Nonconformists were apparently attending. They refused 'to appear at meetings held in a building where an obsequious and white-aproned potman is in constant attendance on the "thoughtful" politician, and numbers of them object to association with club members whose views and ideas

[1] E.g. *Brixton Free Press*, 15 October–5 November 1909.
[2] *St. Pancras Chronicle*, 28 February 1907.

strangely contrast with their own.'[1] Consequently the Nonconformists decided to set up their own election organisation, a Progressive Association with a self-elected committee based on 'worth personally' rather than political opinion. The officers included 'a staunch Conservative' but 'no extremists'. The organisers believed that 'a labour candidate ruins the chances of his middle-class fellow-candidates' and that the weak state of Hammersmith Liberalism was due to a 'slavish regard for so-called "democratic principles" '.[2] They seem to have ignored the chronic debts of the old Liberal Association, which they could have easily paid off. Registration work had in fact ceased.

By 1903 some agreement had been reached between the two groups, and the Nonconformists came back into the Liberal Association. A long struggle then followed over the selection of a parliamentary candidate, ending in the secession of the best middle class Liberals to the Labour Party and a three-cornered fight. Hammersmith, which population movements had made by this date into a working class borough, should have been comfortably won in the 1906 General Election; in fact it was held by the Conservatives. The disappointed Liberals then dissolved their Progressive organisation for local elections and went into a non-political Ratepayers' Association which was supported by the Conservatives. The Progressive Association had already prepared the way for this transformation by arranging joint lists for the Guardians' elections with the Conservative Association. No moderation of Conservative policy seems to have been secured by the alliance.[3] Similarly, while it was in control of the Borough Council, although it included some 'rabid teetotallers', the Ratepayers' Association trimmed its policy to suit the local licensed trade. It cut the wages of Borough Council employees and refused to receive trade union deputations.[4] Even so the Conservative Association decided to oppose its candidates in 1909, and nearly every former Liberal was defeated. It is hardly surprising that, although there was no Labour candidate at the General Elections of 1910, the Liberal remnant could not win any trade union support. As a local political force, Hammersmith Liberalism was dead.

This decay was not a peculiar product of Metropolitan apathy. Similar signs could be found in the other great cities. In 1906 and 1910 the Liberals won no seats in Birmingham, and scarcely touched Sheffield or Liverpool. In all three the Conservatives and their allies

[1] *West London Advertiser*, 30 November 1900.

[2] Unidentified cutting of January 1901, Bull Collection.

[3] Joint letter from Conservative and Progressive secretaries, *West London Observer*, 15 March 1901; *Hammersmith Constitutional Year Book*, 1904.

[4] *West London Observer*, 17 September 1909, etc.; reports of Hammersmith and Shepherds Bush Ratepayers' Association, 1907 and 1914, Hammersmith public library.

had controlled the city council since the 1890s. In Leeds, while the constituencies were nearly all Liberal, on the council the Liberals only won an absolute majority in 1904; from 1907 Labour councillors held the balance with the Conservatives. In Manchester the Liberals shared the parliamentary seats with the Labour Party but Conservatives controlled the council, with a growing Labour element in opposition. Finally, in Glasgow only a minority of seats were Liberal, while the council was controlled by enterprising but anti-Labour independents; a Citizen's Union was formed to fight Labour as early as 1898, and by 1912 the election issue was 'socialism or no socialism'.[1] Perhaps in medium-sized towns the position was different, for in December 1910 the Liberals won over half the seats in towns with two to four M.P.s. But in the six great cities they won only 12 seats out of 40; and nowhere could they point to a successful council party working in harmony with Labour. If the pattern of the conurbations was to be that of the future, the prospects were bleak.

For the moment the parliamentary Liberal Party was a great power, held together by success. But like the local Progressive Parties it was in danger. The recovery of the 1900s gave a deceptive illusion of strength, for it was not based on the solution of the Liberal Party's real problems. It still lacked a firm working class basis, a secure financial backing and a coherent political standpoint. The test would come after defeat. London Liberalism did not appear well equipped to withstand a political setback.

[1] *Scotsman*, 2 November 1898, 6 November 1912.

IX

THE LEAN YEARS OF SOCIAL DEMOCRACY

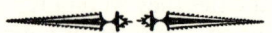

THE official history of the S.D.F. declares that the decision to withdraw from the newly founded Labour Representation Committee in August 1901 was 'a sad mistake'.[1] Certainly it proved a fatal handicap in London.

The decision was by no means inevitable. It was opposed by the principal Lancashire branches. In London the stronger branches owed their success to local Labour alliances. In fact the balance between the purists, who regarded such alliances as compromising, and the pragmatists, was held by the group around Hyndman and Quelch who controlled *Justice* and dominated the S.D.F. executive. When the T.U.C. had summoned the conference at which the L.R.C. was formed, Hyndman wrote in *Justice* that the S.D.F. must participate, without 'any attempt to dictate' to the other delegates. 'Of course, we cannot expect to convert the trade union delegates to our opinions all at once, but every time we meet them in conference we gain ground against the old school and hearten up the new.'[2]

Why was this attitude not maintained by the S.D.F. leadership? Firstly, because Hyndman chose this crucial moment to retire from political life. He was worried by his personal finances, depressed by the unpopularity of opposition to the Boer War and by the small results of twenty years propaganda, and finally irritated by the election to the S.D.F. executive of a rival Marxist theoretician, Theodore Rothstein.[3] Secondly, Hyndman had not wholly convinced Quelch, whose understanding of Marxist political theory was somewhat cruder, of the wisdom of the Labour alliance. Quelch must have seen the danger of a split in the party. Moreover, as editor of *Justice* he had become adept at expressions of intransigence, and

[1] Lee and Archbold, op. cit., p. 158.
[2] 16 September, 28 October 1899. [3] Tsuzuki, op. cit., Ch. VIII.

did not show any inclination to change his style. Instead of pointing out the slender socialist majority on the L.R.C. committee, or the chance of S.D.F. Members of Parliament, *Justice* attacked the L.R.C. for its theoretical shortcomings and the I.L.P. for conniving at them. Once Hyndman had retired there was therefore no strong voice against the proposal to disaffiliate, which was moved at the 1901 conference by Quelch.

The attempt to put the clock back did not in fact prevent a serious disruption of the S.D.F. At the 1901 conference contact was established between 'impossibilist' groups in London and Scotland which wanted a purer socialism and had been influenced by American Socialist Labour Party publications such as the *People*. The London nucleus was in the Finsbury Park S.D.F. A year later a quarrel developed between Quelch and this branch, resulting in its expulsion at the 1903 conference.[1] Some of its members joined the newly formed Socialist Labour Party, but, although two branches[2] followed them, the party failed to establish a hold on London.

Another group of London impossibilists had in fact anticipated this failure and advised the Finsbury Park branch against intransigence. Led by Jack Fitzgerald, a self-educated Irish bricklayer,[3] they were able to work up considerable support in London before Fitzgerald was in turn expelled by the 1904 S.D.F. conference. He used his 'economic classes' to preach impossibilism, and the rebels succeeded in attacking the S.D.F. executive through the delegate meetings of the London District Council, proving such a menace that the national organiser broke down under the strain. Even so at the 1904 conference a resolution condemning those who had campaigned with 'calumny and intrigue' against the executive was opposed by five London branches, and six others abstained, while fourteen supported it. Three entire branches and sections of three others followed Fitzgerald into exile.[4] In Peckham and Wood Green the S.D.F. was unable to re-establish branches for some years.

Fitzgerald's new party, the Socialist Party of Great Britain, showed considerable vigour and tenacity even if it acquired little influence. In London it had 15 branches in 1905, rising to 20 in 1910, and probably consisted of about 200 members. But these members included some of the most fervent younger S.D.Fers, such as T. A.

[1] W. S. Jerman, 'The London Impossibilist Movement', *Socialist*, December 1906, forms the basis of this account. See also comments in *Socialist Standard*, January 1907.
[2] Wimbledon and Bethnal Green.
[3] R. M. Fox, *Smoky Crusade*, London 1937, p. 43; T. A. Jackson, op. cit., p. 60.
[4] Battersea, Wood Green and Central West Ham, and part of Southwark, Kensal Town and Peckham.

Jackson. Nearly every branch ran weekly outdoor meetings in summer, and several devoted branch secretaries kept to their posts for more than five years.

The standpoint of the S.P.G.B. was simple. The education of the electorate for revolution was to be achieved through the election of socialist candidates. Trade unions were scorned, the Osborne Judgement even welcomed. In practice three-cornered election fights were also welcomed, since a straight fight 'between Capital and Labour' would mean that the 'solid revolutionary vote' could not be distinguished from mere anti-Conservatism. The same necessity for distinction meant that S.P.G.B. speakers spent more effort in exposing 'the fraudulent nature' of the I.L.P. and S.D.F. 'in sledge-hammer style' than in advancing the case for socialism.[1] Their leaders were obsessed by theory, intoxicated by speaking. Fitzgerald, inseparable from a bag full of books, was 'death on confused thinking', and in the excitement of debate 'owlish and grim, shot out his fists and nailed his points, with a deep throaty roar'.[2] Hans Neumann, who used to debate with Herbert Morrison at Kennington Triangle, would begin with the gravity appropriate to a translator of Karl Kautsky, 'but soon worked himself into red-faced incoherence'.[3] The S.P.G.B.'s most effective speaker was a housepainter, A. Anderson, a tireless talker with a huge voice crying woe and desolation at north London street corners, on weekdays almost alone, at weekends to large crowds. One of his admirers, convincingly assesses this type of socialist. 'It took me a long time to realise that Anderson and his colleagues were completely satisfied with preaching socialism. They had no real desire to accomplish any change, even though they thought they had. All they wanted was to gain artistic expression. For this they were prepared to endure hunger, to face hardship, provided always that they could interpose between themselves and that hardship a barrier of beautiful words. For a long time I found compensation in exactly the same way. Day dreams in the workshop and night dreams on the Socialist platform masked the uglier realities of life.'[4]

The S.D.F. was probably better off without its impossibilists, but the losses caused by its severance from the Labour Representation Committee were serious. Thorne and Lansbury, the two S.D.F. candidates supported by the L.R.C. at the 1900 General Election,

---

[1] *Socialist Standard*, April and January 1909.
[2] Fox, op. cit., pp. 84–86.
[3] Ibid., pp. 43, 86: H. Morrison, *Herbert Morrison: an Autobiography*, London 1960, p. 55.
[4] Guy Aldred, *No Traitors Gait!* Glasgow 1956–7, p. 260; Fox, op. cit., pp. 37–43.

were in a particularly difficult situation. Lansbury, with characteristic candour, decided not to stand for Bow again. 'I don't agree with the policy of fighting independently, but, had I time, and were I in good health, and my business not so exacting, I should have a real good try to get the S.D.F. round to my view.'[1] Only in 1907, when he was assured the local support of an I.L.P. branch and a Trades and Labour Representation Committee as well as the S.D.F., did he consent to become candidate again in Bow.[2] In January 1910 Lansbury beat the Liberal candidate into third place and in December 1910 he captured the seat. The backbone of his local electoral organisation was, as he admitted himself, the Bow S.D.F. and the Bromley Gas Workers.[3] Nevertheless he was now seen as the leading figure in the London I.L.P., and by his defection, following that of Hyndman, the London S.D.F. as a whole lost its two most influential leaders. (It was in Lancashire rather than London that Hyndman placed his political hopes after his return to politics on the Free Trade issue in 1903.)

Thorne, as a trade union leader, was able to ignore the decision. His Gas Workers Union remained affiliated to the L.R.C., and was in fact its strongest trade union support in London before 1903. The West Ham Trades Council affiliated in 1901 and sent Jack Jones of the S.D.F. to subsequent L.R.C. conferences. Like Lansbury, Thorne made unsuccessful attempts to persuade the L.R.C. to support him as a 'Labour and Socialist' rather than Labour candidate, and similarly gave way, although he described his platform in 1906 as 'Labour and Social Democracy'. He was elected, with the support of the local Free Church Council and United Irish League, by a comfortable majority of over 5,000 votes.[4]

Thorne remained a member of the S.D.F., boasting that he was the oldest surviving member of his branch, and declaring when his position was attacked that he had 'no intention of resigning from the party until I am expelled'.[5] The South West S.D.Fers as a whole remained loyal to him. There was some friction in 1901, when the I.L.P. adopted a rival candidate, but they withdrew when Thorne's determination became apparent, and a Social Democratic Council was formed in 1902 to reunite the movement.[6] On Thorne's electoral Committee formed in 1905, S.D.F., I.L.P. and Trades Council each

[1] G. Lansbury to H. W. Lee, 23 February 1902, printed in *Socialist*, May 1905.
[2] G. Lansbury to Frank Smith, 12 September 1907, Lansbury Collection.
[3] G. Lansbury to R. C. K. Ensor, 6 September 1909, Ensor Papers.
[4] *Stratford Express*, 6, 13, 20 January 1906.
[5] S.D.P. conference report, 1909.
[6] *Justice*, 29 June 1901, 5 April, 26 April, 31 May 1902; *Labour Leader*, 12 April 1902.

had six delegates.¹ Jack Jones was able to declare in 1906 that 'in all local and parliamentary elections the S.D.F. and I.L.P. had worked together successfully'.² Nevertheless the S.D.F. was severely hit by difficulties. In North West Ham, a lower middle class constituency in which the chief trade unionists were the strongly Liberal Railway Servants, the Stratford S.D.F. branch was captured by impossibilist sympathisers, and the Central West Ham branch seceded to the S.P.G.B. in 1904. After Thorne's election the North West Ham men became a serious nuisance, attacking his positions as 'illogical and harmful to the party'.³ The result of these dissensions was that the West Ham S.D.F., which had grown to five branches in 1900, was immediately reduced to three, and later to two. Thorne turned increasingly to the local I.L.P. for support, speaking at their meetings, and in spite of his nominal loyalty to the S.D.F. based his strength on trade unionism. His socialism fossilised in the face of criticism, and the S.D.F. were unable to use his victory to stimulate the movement.

The S.D.F. also lost a number of members to the National Democratic League. This organisation was called together in 1900 by the radical editor of *Reynold's Newspaper*, W. M. Thompson, who had long been dissatisfied by the Liberal leadership, but wanted an alliance wider both socially and politically than the newly-formed L.R.C. As a London man he recognised the influence of the S.D.F.; he had urged the election of 'a Burns, a Champion, a Hyndman', to Parliament as early as 1889, and 1892 expressed the opinion that the S.D.F. had 'permeated the working community with its doctrines'.⁴ *Reynold's* was fierce in tone, giving vigorous backing to strikers. It supported Labour representation, but had little faith in the I.L.P.⁵ The National Democratic League was intended to support a number of socialist candidates, as well as some thirty sitting radical M.P.s.⁶ At the founding convention, at least three London S.D.F. branches sent delegates, and others present included Thorne, James Macdonald the London Trades Council secretary, and Fred Knee representing the Workmen's Housing Council. Most other trade unionists present were advanced men, and Tom Mann became the League's national organiser.⁷ Probably even at the start recruits from socialism outnumbered the delegates from eight radical clubs and the Metropolitan Radical Federation.

¹ National Union of Gas Workers and General Labourers report, May 1912.
² S.D.F. conference report, 1906.   ³ S.D.P. conference report, 1909.
⁴ *Reynold's Newspaper*, 20 January 1889; 26 June 1892.
⁵ Ibid., 6 January 1889, 8 September 1889, &c.; 21 July 1895.
⁶ Ibid., 16 September, 23 September 1900. *Reynold's* contributed to Lansbury's and Burns' election funds.
⁷ Ibid., 28 October 1900.

As an attempt to revive radicalism in London the League proved a decisive failure. Over thirty branches had been formed by November 1901, but they proved shortlived, disintegrating after internal dissension in 1902.[1] The League in fact revealed the extent to which London radicalism had been supplanted by socialism, for in 1902 its London secretary was James Dobson of Camberwell and its national organiser Jim Connell of Deptford, author of *The Red Flag*, both formerly local S.D.F. leaders. For a while the S.D.F. also enjoyed the publicity of a regular column in *Reynold's*. At least some active workers seem to have been brought into the S.D.F. through the League.[2] On the other hand, the League was undoubtedly a diversion of energy, and few of its leaders returned to the socialist movement.

Because of these losses and its self-imposed isolation from the national Labour Party, the S.D.F. never fully renewed its growth during the 1900s. Its national and London membership patterns were similar, although its performance in London was exceptionally disappointing. In the years up to 1906, when radicalism and socialism were generally reviving, it remained virtually stagnant, with some 40 London branches and about 1,700 London members.[3] It had no more branches in 1905 than in 1895. Between 1905 and 1909 definite progress was made, and a total of 54 branches was reached, but this was nothing when compared with the spectacular growth of the London I.L.P. at the same time. Relatively the S.D.F. was losing influence. Its amalgamation into the British Socialist Party in 1911–12 resulted in a peak of 69 branches probably representing nearly 3,000 London members, more than the I.L.P., but this total was not held. The failure to publish branch lists after 1912 makes it difficult to estimate whether the decline was more serious than that suffered by the I.L.P. at the same time. But it is clear enough that, while the

[1] Ibid., November 1901; *Democrat*, June-November 1902.
[2] E.g. Victor Fisher and John Stokes: *Labour Record*, 1907; *London Trades Gazette*, May 1909.
[3] Numbers of branches mentioned in *Justice*. *London Trades Gazette*, August 1903, gives a figure of 1687 London members, an average of 39 members per branch. Since the number of members probably fluctuated more than the number of branches, it is likely that membership fell below 1300 in 1902, the worst year. The national average branch strength had risen to about 45 in 1908 (Tsuzuki, op. cit., p. 284), and in this year the London committee claimed an increase in membership of 75 per cent (S.D.P. conference report 1908). If the average branch membership in 1910–12 reached 50, which would have been below the national average, the peak membership in London would have been 3450. The rarity of branch membership figures makes it impossible to confirm this estimate, but five branches mention a membership exceeding 100. *Justice* gives no branch lists after 1911, and the B.S.P. issued a list only in 1912; the decline to 51 branches mentioned in *Justice* in 1914 is therefore exaggerated. There were still 53 branches in the London district in 1915 (*Socialist Record*. June 1915). See Appendix B.

S.D.F. was not protected by its aloof position from slumps in the socialist movement, it was quite unable to take the full benefit of prosperous years. It is particularly notable that in years of radical political excitement, such as 1905 and 1910, the S.D.F. actually lost branches, while the I.L.P. grew in strength.

In spite of the disaffiliation from the L.R.C., many S.D.F. branches continued to work in local labour alliances. This was made easier by the fact that the national L.R.C. had no official concern with local elections. Between 1903 and 1905 at least eleven branches were either working with or directly affiliated to some kind of local Labour Party. The policy favoured by Quelch of socialist rather than labour unity was not adopted by any branch at this time. With one exception, Edmonton, every branch which had any election success secured it through a labour alliance. The degree of involvement varied. In Battersea, the S.D.F. was given a free run in the poorest ward in return for support of the Labour-Progressive majority on the Borough Council.[1] In Hackney, the S.D.F. attended local L.R.C. conferences without affiliating, and secured support for its election candidates.[2] Other branches, notably Bow and Bromley and Hammersmith, were directly affiliated to and closely involved with local Labour Party organisation.[3] Nevertheless these electoral alliances did no more than protect the S.D.F. from electoral extinction. Where they were successful, as in Poplar and West Ham, the credit did not go to the S.D.F., and even here the number of its members elected declined over the years. More usually the alliance proved unstable. The general policy of criticism of the Labour Party received far more notice than that of local compromise, made the S.D.F. an unreliable ally peculiarly sensitive to questions of political principle, aggravated

[1] *Municipal Journal*, 4 January 1901; *Daily Herald*, 17 October 1912. In 1900 3 S.D.Fers were elected and Fred Knee made an alderman.

[2] Hackney S.D.F. minutes, 1903–6; the branch was even willing for arrangements with the Progressives, 18 September 1903. One S.D.Fer was elected in 1903.

[3] E.g. Erith: *Justice*, 14 April 1906; Bow and Bromley, and Poplar: Poplar Trades and L.R.C. annual reports, 1904–7, Ensor Collection; Westminster, where J. G. Butler organised both: *London Trades Gazette*, February 1903; Morrison, op. cit., p. 38; S.D.P. conference report, 1909; and South West London L.R.C. (from which Fulham and Hammersmith Labour Parties developed) whose secretary and candidate (George Belt) were both S.D.Fers: *Labour Leader*, 21 March 1903; *Clarion*, 7 and 30 October, 13 November 1903; S.D.F. conference report, 1903. Belt was not endorsed by the national Labour Party, to which the South West London L.R.C. and the South West London Trades Council were affiliated, but he stood with their support as a Labour candidate in 1906, and his poll of 885 votes prevented the Liberals from capturing the seat. He then became the S.D.F. Scottish organiser (*Justice*, September 1906). An unskilled labourer born in Hull, he also belonged to the I.L.P. (*Reformers Year Book* 1905.) The L.R.C. secretary was Tom Wall.

THE LEAN YEARS OF SOCIAL DEMOCRACY

the confusion of newspaper reporting, and made it especially difficult to establish a branch where the L.R.C. had been previously organised. The weakness of the S.D.F. in Woolwich and Deptford was significant.

At the same time there were other electoral handicaps. The replacement of vestries by Borough Councils reduced the number of candidates required and helped the Liberals to tighten their local election organisation. The new boroughs were given responsibilities towards the unemployed in 1904 which lessened the importance of the Boards of Guardians, where the S.D.F. had made some reputation. At the 1900 London School Board election the S.D.F., in spite of a swing to the Conservatives, polled over 10,000 votes in Chelsea and Tower Hamlets: but the London Education Act of 1903 abolished the Board, transferring its responsibilities to the L.C.C. While the Progressive Party remained in power the L.C.C. was electorally hopeless for the S.D.F. As a result, outside West Ham and Poplar the S.D.F. had little more than ten councillors and five Guardians in 1905, a miserable achievement.

Labour alliances of various kinds remained frequent after 1905. At least nine branches in 1906–9 and eleven in 1912–14 were involved in them.[1] But at the same time more was heard of fighting elections on a purely socialist basis. There were two conflicting reasons for this. On the one hand the success of the national Labour Party, resulting in a rapid growth of the I.L.P., made socialist unity more desirable and worthwhile. On the other hand the obvious dependence of the Labour Party on the Liberal government after 1906 produced a demand for independent socialist M.P.s, leading to the dramatic election of Victor Grayson for Colne Valley in June 1907.

In London the most significant indication of the growing political influence of socialism at this time was the sudden flowering of the Clarion movement. Hitherto it had been largely provincial. In 1906 the London Clarion Scouts were organised and Fred Hagger and Fred Bramley conducted the first London Clarion van tour. Districts were prepared by advance meetings of the Scouts, and by mass rallies of cyclists from the five London Clarion cycling clubs 'with

---

[1] In both periods, Poplar, Bow and Bromley, West Ham South, Shoreditch; in 1906–9, Hammersmith (Belt was still delegate at the 1908 Labour Party conference), Lambeth (Morrison, op. cit., p. 44), Islington (*Labour Leader*, 9 November 1906), Westminster, Erith (*Woolwich Pioneer*, 13 March 1908); in 1910 also Edmonton (*Justice*, 16 April 1910), Bermondsey (*Justice*, 1 October 1910), Woolwich (ibid.); in 1912–14 four St. Pancras branches (*Daily Citizen*, 25 October 1912, *Labour Leader*, 14 November 1912), North West Ham (*Daily Herald*, 24 February 1914), Acton (*Daily Herald*, 24 April 1912, 28 March 1914), Chiswick (*Daily Citizen*, 13 March 1913).

streamers flying, with bikes made bright with mottoes and texts'.[1] The tour was an undoubted success, bringing increased membership and new branches to both I.L.P. and S.D.F. It was repeated annually, with two separate vans from 1909 until 1914, and with it the number of cycling clubs went up to fifteen.

The Clarion van tours showed that in London a far wider sympathy with socialism existed than had been expected. The 1907 vanner 'failed to find the slightest justification for the now to me inexplicable pessimism' about London socialism. Meetings 'will bear comparison with the very best meetings held in any part of the provinces.'[2] In 1909 Fred Hagger reported that 'van meetings continue to attract large, generally attentive and enthusiastic meetings'. While opponents in early years had frequently broken up socialist meetings they now needed 'much coaxing and taunting' before they would voice their objections to socialism.[3] It was especially encouraging that the vans were most successful not in the poorest districts but in Labour Party strongholds such as Woolwich and in lower middle class suburbs like Streatham.[4]

At first S.D.F. efforts to profit from the socialist resurgence were unsuccessful. Socialist Councils formed in Camberwell and Bethnal Green in 1907–8 came to nothing.[5] A commoner result was in fact the formation of a united Socialist Society independent of both S.D.F. and I.L.P., depriving the S.D.F. of a branch.[6]

A more serious difficulty was that socialist unity frequently became the first step to extremism. In Battersea the S.D.F. alliance with the Progressives broke down in 1906 and the Battersea Trades Council was disaffiliated by the Labour Party because of its Liberal connections.[7] The S.D.F. was thus able to form a Socialist Council with the I.L.P. But none of the joint socialist candidates were elected, and when a new Battersea Labour Party was formed in 1908 the I.L.P. preferred to break off the alliance.[8] The Battersea delegates to S.D.F. conferences became increasingly bitter, calling for an alliance with the Socialist Labour Party and S.P.G.B., declaring they 'would sooner be related to the Cecil family than to the Labour Party', and finally even opposing a common socialist platform with the I.L.P. as compromising.[9]

While the I.L.P. remained wedded to the Labour Party a policy of socialist unity could only lead in this direction. Where the S.D.F.

[1] *Clarion*, 18 May 1906. [2] Ibid., 14 June 1907.
[3] Ibid., 15 October 1909. [4] E.g. ibid., 29 May, 25 September 1908.
[5] *Justice*, 9 February, 21 September 1907; *Labour Leader*, 25 September 1908.
[6] E.g. Ilford, New Southgate, Watford, Greenwich.
[7] *Justice*, 1 September 1906; Labour Party National Executive Committee minutes, 28 February 1906.
[8] *Justice*, 6 March 1909. [9] S.D.P. conference reports, 1908–10.

took part in a local Labour Party, even when it secured its own choice as candidate, its intransigence over formalities such as the title of 'Labour and Socialist' rather than 'Labour' only led to conflicts, and eventually either the local Party failed or the influence of the S.D.F. ceased to be important. Thus in Fulham, Hammersmith, Hackney and Erith the S.D.F. dropped out of the alliance, in Poplar and West Ham they found themselves in a minority and in Walthamstow and Westminster the Labour Party came to nothing. Socialist unity simply made these conflicts more certain.

Shoreditch, the best performance of socialist unity in London, illustrates the process. In 1909 and 1912 the S.D.F., I.L.P. and trade unions together succeeded in electing a number of councillors and Guardians in Whitmore ward, the poorest part of the borough.[1] The parliamentary constituency of Haggerston, which included Whitmore, was still represented in the 1900s by the veteran Liberal-Labour M.P. Randal Cremer, and there was thus a good chance that the seat would eventually fall to the Labour Party and that local influence would secure the nomination of a socialist candidate. The socialist unity policy prevented this. When Cremer died in 1908, and also at the General Election in January 1910, Herbert Burrows stood as a Socialist candidate. He was supported by East End figures as diverse as Stewart Headlam and George Lansbury; on both occasions, although in 1910 the Liberal candidate was a Fabian, Burrows was supported by many Fabians, and the local I.L.P. lent their rooms and worked hard for him.[2] But the national Labour Party was neutral, Burrows had no chance of a straight fight, and no strong local Labour Party had been built up. He failed to win most of Cremer's supporters and only polled 982 and 701 in an electorate of over 7,000.

Elsewhere the results of socialist unity were even worse. In Barking, Leyton and Leytonstone, where the policy was imposed on newly-formed local L.R.C.s, the result was simply to prevent further development.[3] In the General Election of January 1910 the result was two hopeless candidatures. Victor Grayson was clearly shaken by his own defeat in Kennington; he was 'not prepared for such a complete and overwhelming defeat'.[4] But the lesson was not taken. At Bethnal Green John Scurr polled only 134 votes at the bye-election of August 1911, in spite of the fact that the local radicals objected to

[1] *Justice*, 6 November 1909; *Daily Herald*, 17 September 1912.
[2] *Justice*, 1 August 1908, 15 January 1910; *Justice*, Hackney and Shoreditch edition, 19 February 1910; Fabian Society executive committee minutes, 13–14 January 1910.
[3] *Justice*, 2 September 1905; Labour Party National Executive Committee minutes, 28 February 1906; *Justice*, 24 April 1909.
[4] *Clarion*, 9 December 1910.

the choice of C. F. G. Masterman as candidate and seceded to form a Labour Association.[1] Nor were socialist candidatures at the L.C.C. elections much more convincing. The S.D.F. had wisely abstained in 1901 and 1904, and its independent candidates in 1907 only polled respectable votes in Fulham and Bow and Bromley where they were backed by local Labour Parties. No candidates were put up in 1910.

Even so the S.D.F. determined to throw its whole influence into the construction of an independent socialist party. It decided in August 1907 to alter its name to the Social Democratic Party, but the change had no discernible effect, and hence has been ignored here. But the next change of title, to British Socialist Party, was more important.

The British Socialist Party was intended to be an amalgamation of socialist forces rather than an extension of the S.D.F. The campaign for a new party was opened by Robert Blatchford in the *Clarion* in March 1910. 'I say without a spark of heat or a drop of bitterness, that I think the I.L.P. and the S.D.P. have failed.... The interests of socialism demand that you form a new party, and begin all over again.'[2] The S.D.F. conference in April 1911 passed a resolution supporting the 'United Socialist Party'. The idea had the backing of Victor Grayson and a considerable number of provincial I.L.P. branches. In August 1911 a circular invitation to a unity conference was issued by the S.D.F. executive and twelve provincial Socialist Societies, and Grayson opened the new party headquarters at the London *Clarion* office, asking subscribers to write in. But in fact the B.S.P. was formed through the adherence of existing organisations rather than individuals, and at the inaugural conference in September 1911 although the S.D.F. was outnumbered by Clarion Fellowships, I.L.P. branches and Socialist Societies, it was by far the largest single element in the amalgamation. By the end of 1911, to Grayson's distress, the S.D.F. central staff and premises had become the B.S.P. headquarters.[3]

Although the party's national strength was raised by half, in London the fusion resulted in a net increase of only about fifteen branches. Most of the new membership came from Clarion organisations; only one Socialist Society affiliated.[4] Recruits from the I.L.P., important in the provinces, produced three new branches, but were only really numerous in Woolwich.[5]

[1] Sir P. Harris, op. cit., p. 47; *Justice*, 29 July 1911; I.L.P. London District Council minutes, July 1911.
[2] *Clarion*, 25 March 1910.
[3] Tsuzuki, op. cit., pp. 173–5; *Clarion*, 5 January 1912.
[4] Ilford; *Clarion*, 5 January 1912.
[5] Balham, Stoke Newington and Streatham, I.L.P. London District Council minutes, 2 November 1911, 4 January 1912.

THE LEAN YEARS OF SOCIAL DEMOCRACY

The Woolwich I.L.P. had reached a peak of 500 members in 1909, easily the largest I.L.P. branch in London. It had given a tremendous reception to Grayson in 1908, and during 1909 went over to a policy of independent socialism, losing some members in the process. It started joint propaganda with the S.D.F., broke with the Labour Party in 1910, and in 1911 even opposed the Labour Party Secretary in a Council bye-election. Finally it seceded to the B.S.P., bringing with it the Plumstead Socialist Hall. By this time membership had fallen to 100, but it remained stronger than the new I.L.P. branch which was formed in its place.[1] Its whole story is suggestive of the extent to which S.D.F. difficulties in London were caused less by a lack of militant socialists than by its narrowminded attitude to the Labour Party. A fearless but realistic socialist policy in earlier years could have won more support than was later to be brought by disillusionment.

The majority of London B.S.P. branches were straightforward continuations of the S.D.F. branches, announcing the change of title in laconic notices to the effect that 'the local branch of the S.D.P. will in future be known' as the B.S.P. and that 'old members are turning up, signing on afresh'.[2] Not surprisingly there was little change in local electoral policy. In Shoreditch the socialist alliance continued, in West Ham, St. Pancras and Poplar the branches worked with the Labour Party. In Poplar the quarrel which developed between George Lansbury and the Labour Party National Executive resulted in the disaffiliation of the local Labour Party, so that the B.S.P. were able to run candidates with local Labour Party support at the 1913 L.C.C. election and the 1914 Poplar bye-election. Their failure in these Labour strongholds showed the impotence of independent socialism. The advent of the B.S.P. had done nothing to halt the steady decline in the electoral fortunes of Social Democracy.

The B.S.P., like the S.D.F. in the 1900s, failed to hold the younger revolutionaries. There was at first a syndicalist element in the B.S.P., centred on Birmingham but including conference delegates from London, but it proved shortlived.[3] Similarly the militant suffragettes did not find much sympathy in the B.S.P.[4] Consequently the defection of George Lansbury from the parliamentary Labour Party and the vigorous propaganda of the *Daily Herald* brought the B.S.P. little

[1] *Labour Leader*, 21 August 1913; *Woolwich Pioneer*, 30 April, 18 June 1909, 8 April, 15 April 1910, January 1911, &c.; *Socialist Standard*, August 1911; I.L.P. London District Council minutes, January-March 1912.
[2] *Clarion*, 12 and 26 January, 2 February 1912.
[3] From Woolwich, Bermondsey and Walthamstow: S.D.P. conference report, 1910, B.S.P. conference reports, 1912–13; Tsuzuki, op. cit., Ch. IX.
[4] Dora Montefiore resigned in 1912: D. B. Montefiore, *From a Victorian to a Modern*, London 1927, p. 154.

new support. The main effect of the *Daily Herald* was to give excessive publicity to extremist elements in the B.S.P.

The longer the S.D.F. and the B.S.P. kept out of the Labour Party the more dangerous it must have seemed to change the policy. Socialists who supported affiliation were unlikely to join, and the older members who from time to time attempted to reverse the situation, Hunter Watts in 1906, Fred Knee in 1908, Burrows in 1910, found themselves outnumbered. Conference blindly refused either to 'recognise that the Labour Party had the organised working class movement behind them' or that 'if the Labour Party had gone back since we left it, that was an excellent reason for our joining it again'.[1] But this blindness must have been a brittle facade, for in the end re-affiliation came very suddenly, following the death of Harry Quelch in September 1913.

Quelch had been the most convinced opponent of the Labour alliance. He was succeeded as editor of *Justice* by H. W. Lee, who as S.D.F. secretary since 1885 had shown little character, while Albert Inkpin, a member of the Hackney branch which believed in 'working amicably' with the Labour Party, became B.S.P. secretary.[2] *Justice* at once became less hostile to the Labour Party. At the 1914 B.S.P. conference Hyndman moved and succeeded in carrying a resolution in favour of re-affiliation, and this resolution was confirmed by a ballot of members in May.

The *volte-face* was not to be achieved without resistance. At the conference a number of London delegates spoke against the motion, and in July twelve branches from the greater London area met at North West Ham and decided to disaffiliate rather than join the Labour Party.[3] They included Bow and Bromley, North and South West Ham, Edmonton, Stepney and Kentish Town, all important branches. Yet of these all but Stepney had worked with their local Labour Party in the previous three years, and Stepney, where there was no Labour Party, had been represented at the 1914 conference by its secretary J. Fineberg, a strong believer in the Labour alliance. It would seem that this die-hard reaction was caused by inhibition rather than by conviction, for in the event none of these branches disaffiliated.

At the same time, again following the death of Quelch, the London Trades Council, with Fred Knee as secretary and John Stokes as chairman, called the conference at which the London Labour Party was founded, and at this conference Knee and John Stokes, the Glassblowers' President first secretary and chairman of the new Party. With two B.S.Pers holding the key offices the opportunity for

[1] S.D.P. conference reports, 1908 and 1910.
[2] *Daily Herald*, 14 August 1912.   [3] Ibid., 6 and 19 July 1914.

influence was unprecedented, and *Justice* published strong appeals to ensure that the chance was not thrown away.[1] At the 1914 B.S.P. conference Fineberg had predicted that 'if they decided to stop out, Social Democracy would be wiped out in London'. As a result a delegate meeting in August 1914 decided to affiliate,[2] and on the first London Labour Party executive elected in November the B.S.P. were able to secure five of eighteen seats. With the eight I.L.Pers elected the socialists were in a majority.

The change of B.S.P. policy in 1914 marked a turning point in the history of the London Labour movement, ending the long years of negative conflict. The B.S.P. was in fact given its second chance of influencing the Labour Party, although it was no longer the dominant representative of socialism as it had been in London in 1900. In fact the First World War was to transform the whole political situation, so that the chance was again lost. Nevertheless it is worth assessing the strength and character of the B.S.P. in 1914 and considering how strong an influence it could have been.

It was still the largest body of socialists in London, with about 55 branches and 2,500 members. Although these branches were widely spread their distribution indicates that the bulk of B.S.P. membership was working class. There were branches in some lower middle class suburbs but they tended to be weak. In wealthy districts there were usually no branches. There was, it is true, a centre of middle class intellectuals in the Central branch, which held monthly dinners, but its ranks had thinned over the years. In 1901 guests had still included the artist Walter Crane, the philosopher Belfort Bax, the suffragist Dora Montefiore, the historian Max Beer, the internationalist J. F. Green, and the old communard A. S. Headingley, industrial correspondent to *The Times*.[3] By 1914 only Headingley remained, together with Hyndman, to keep up the tradition. Bax had disapproved of disaffiliation from the Labour Party, Dora Montefiore and Green of Hyndman's militarism, and Max Beer of his anti-semitism.[4] In contrast to the intellectual socialists belonging to the S.D.F. in its early days, the B.S.P. appears sadly impoverished. Apart from refugees such as Theodore Rothstein and Zelda Kahan its thinkers, middle class or working class, were all of an older generation.

The B.S.P. was also very much a man's organisation. Its women's

---

[1] *Justice*, 23 July 1914.   [2] Ibid., 27 August 1914.
[3] Ibid., 9 November 1901.
[4] Bax: S. G. Hobson, *Pilgrim to the Left*, London 1938, p. 74; M. Beer, *Fifty Years of International Socialism*, London 1935, p. 165; Green: *Socialist Year Book and Labour Annual*, 1912, and Hobson, op. cit., p. 124.

central committee and branch Women's Socialist Circles never appear to have been very active and it had few influential women members. The B.S.P. never built up an army of women workers such as formed the electoral forces of the major parties. Thus its mainstay was the working man. There were very few working class districts without a branch. The only exceptions were due to the presence of an exceptionally strong I.L.P. branch. Its strongest districts remained West Ham and Poplar, and there were some twenty other good working class branches. In several of the poorest districts, however, the B.S.P. was still at great pains to establish a foothold, as in Stepney, 'most forlorn of London districts', where socialist propagandists tended to be West Ham men 'educating the natives'.[1] In Stepney the B.S.P. found the attachment of the Irish to the Liberal Party an added problem, although where there were strong Labour Parties, Irishmen were often prominent in the B.S.P.[2] The chief appeal of the B.S.P. was still to the politically conscious rather than the poverty-stricken working man.

Most of the active London leaders of the B.S.P. were trade unionists and the B.S.P. had some influence with a number of London trade unions. Although there was no union of importance in its control, several smaller unions had B.S.P. secretaries of presidents, and their support gave the B.S.P. its hold on the London Trades Council.[3] James Macdonald was Trades Council secretary until 1913, followed by Fred Knee, while Quelch was chairman in 1904–6 and 1910–13, followed by Stokes. Even so, this influence was limited. B.S.P. delegates were never in a majority on the Trades Council, and were able merely to keep the Council away from the Labour Party without committing it to independent socialism. They were only able to make a positive initiative in 1913 when they had changed their attitude to the Labour Party.

Of the major unions, B.S.P. influence was important with the compositors. Social Democrats were among their Trades Council and Labour Party conference delegates, including Fred Knee and A. E. Holmes, who became the union's organiser in 1903. Perhaps

[1] *Justice*, 25 March 1905, 17 July 1909.
[2] E.g. Jack Jones in West Ham, Moore Bell in Woolwich.
[3] J. G. Butler, Army Clothing Employees' secretary; E. Friend, Vellum Binders' secretary, *Labour Who's Who*, 1927; Stokes, Glass Blowers' President; F. A. Broad, Scientific Instrument Makers' President, *Labour Who's Who*, 1927, *Justice*, 16 October 1909 (Edmonton branch member, B.S.P. candidate 1919 General Election, M.P. 1922). Earlier, Richard Kendall, Stick and Umbrella Makers' secretary (*London Trades Gazette*, September 1901), J. G. Gordon, Tin Plate Workers and Sheet Metal Workers' secretary (*Labour Annual*, 1898), and W. T. Gooday, Upholsterers' secretary (*London Trades Gazette*, September 1901), were known to be S.D.Fers, but there is no evidence of their union's political position in 1914.

THE LEAN YEARS OF SOCIAL DEMOCRACY

the most remarkable measure of Social Democratic strength was the ballot for a parliamentary candidate in 1903, in which C. W. Bowerman, the union secretary, was selected against C. F. Davis of the S.D.F. by the narrow majority of 3,966 votes to 3,205.[1] Nevertheless this influence was restricted. There was rarely a Social Democrat on the executive. The Compositors remained firmly attached to the Labour Party, sympathetic to socialism but not to an independent socialist party.

The B.S.P. could claim several active members and until 1913 the secretary of the fast growing Shop Assistants Union,[2] but they had few other prominent men in national trade unions, with the exception of the Gas Workers, and one new convert as a result of syndicalism, Ben Tillett. But Tillett was too absorbed by industrial questions to be much of an asset to the B.S.P. The new trade union militancy only brought one other trade unionist of even local importance to the B.S.P., Fred Button of the Erith Engineers.

The position of the B.S.P. in their traditional London stronghold, the Gas Workers, had been seriously weakened. The Bromley and West Ham union branches were still the largest in London, and they supported Thorne and Lansbury as 'Labour' candidates, although not without efforts to change the title to 'Labour and Socialist'. But as the movement for independent socialism developed a split began. The Bromley branch supported Grayson's disruptive tactics in the House of Commons, which Thorne denounced as 'absurd'.[3] Eventually in 1913 the Bromley Gas Workers followed Lansbury into political isolation, and during 1913–14 the London District opposed the payment of Thorne's election agent, supported Jack Jones as B.S.P. candidate in the Poplar bye-election, and voted by a 'substantial majority' for disaffiliation from the Labour Party, at the very moment when the B.S.P. was deciding to re-affiliate.[4] It would seem that the influence of the Gas Workers in the B.S.P. branches in West Ham and Bow and Bromley, persuading them first to accept and then to reject the labour alliance, was more powerful than the influence of the B.S.P. on the Gas Workers' political policies.

Another very serious weakness of the B.S.P. was its electoral organisation. J. J. Terrett complained in 1905 that 'London Socialists have not yet learnt electioneering. . . . The proper making out of

[1] I. C. Cannan, 'The Social Situation of the Skilled Worker: a study of the compositor in London', London Ph.D. thesis, 1961, p. 94.
[2] James Macpherson, secretary; others, e.g. F. G. Jones, S.D.F. conference reports 1904–5, *Socialist*, November 1906, and G. Patterson, union President 1889, *Labour Who's Who*, 1927.
[3] National Union of Gas Workers and General Labourers minutes, delegate meeting, 17 October 1908.
[4] Ibid., August 1913, February 1914, November 1913.

canvass books, the economical use of volunteer help, the smart handling of the returns so as to put a strong broadside into the ranks of the doubtfuls—all these . . . are essentials which will have to be learnt if the working class is not always to be at the mercy of the professional election agents of Liberalism and Toryism.'[1] Yet even in 1912 A. A. Watts felt the need to argue the wisdom of canvassing, and registration work is scarcely mentioned in *Justice* before 1914.[2]

In other ways the London organisation had improved. Until 1906 the main effort of the London District Council, a delegate body, was to raise money to pay the national organiser for work in London. George Hewitt, who was organiser until 1903, exhausted himself in conflicts with the impossibilists, and Jack Jones, most of whose salary was provided by Lady Warwick, seems to have confined his London activity to West Ham.[3] The District Council continued to complain of 'want of cash'.[4] In 1907, however, a London organisation committee was formed which did much to improve the position.[5] E. C. Fairchild became London organiser for five years. In a little over a year £200 was raised by the branches, partly through the co-operative trading encouraged by the committee. Branches were asked to choose a 'reporter' to keep contact with the committee and to help avoid the 'blunders' in tactics.[6] A uniform method of branch bookkeeping was established 'whereby it was possible to ascertain the financial state of any branch'.[7] The committee ran unemployed meetings, supplied speakers, formed a cycling corps, a Students' Union, an orchestra and a Co-operative Clothing Company, distributed 100,000 tracts, supported a Socialist Van of the Clarion type, and in the autumn of 1908 began to publish a party members monthly, the *S.D.P. News*.[8] They were able to claim an increase of membership of 75 per cent in under a year. Not all this activity was maintained; there was not enough money in 1909 for a Socialist Van[9] or a massive tract distribution, and no more was heard of the Students Union. Nevertheless the committee were able to play an important part in unemployed agitation, and by the winter of 1910 Fairchild was being assisted by four unpaid assistant organisers.[10]

In 1912 the financial difficulties again became serious and Fairchild gave up organising work to concentrate on wholesale co-operative trading.[11] He was succeeded as organiser by Thomas

[1] *Justice*, 25 March 1905.
[2] Ibid., 19 August 1911, 14 September 1912, 21 May 1914.
[3] S.D.F. conference report, 1905. [4] *Justice*, 28 January 1905.
[5] S.D.P. conference report, 1908. [6] *Justice*, 15 June 1907.
[7] S.D.P. conference report, 1908.
[8] *Justice*, 28 March, 4 April, 9 May, 18 July, 7 November 1908.
[9] Ibid., 13 November 1909. [10] Ibid., 26 November 1910.
[11] *Socialist Record*, August 1912; Lee and Archbold, op. cit., p. 185.

Kennedy, an able Scotsman, even if his manner was 'something between a dominie and free kirk minister'.[1] When Kennedy was promoted to the post of national organiser in 1913 the work was taken over by J. G. Butler as half-time committee secretary, but by the autumn of 1914 it had been decided to appoint another full-time organiser.[2] Meanwhile London was organised into twelve groups of branches, each with a voluntary secretary and organiser.[3] The central committee continued *S.D.P. News*, started a *Socialist Workers' Circular*, organised winter demonstrations, and supplied speakers.[4] They could claim in 1914 that in spite of its problems the London B.S.P. had a lively organisation.

They could also claim that the lean years had failed to break the branches or blur their message. In the summer months the London branches organised more than 500 outdoor meetings a month. Until 1912, when the *Daily Herald* and *Daily Citizen* provided a socialist press with a large circulation, outdoor meetings were the mainstay of socialist propaganda. They were supplemented by the big demonstrations organised by the central committee, while mission weeks, Clarion van tours and cyclists' rallies helped to provide variety. Some branches published their own papers, such as the *Walthamstow Reformer* or the North West Ham *New World*. In the winter when trade was bad there would be unemployed work, and the social life of the branches would flourish in impressive variety—concerts and dramatic clubs, women's circles, bands and orchestras, lectures and economic classes.[5] For the young there were Socialist Sunday Schools and the Young Socialist League. In the stronger branches these winter activities would be focussed on a socialist hall, like William Morris Hall at Walthamstow built by the voluntary labour of the members.[6] The smaller branches, which met in private houses, were of course able to support a comparatively meagre fare, but there is little doubt that a major reason for the tenacity of the Social Democrats was the extent to which the movement provided a satisfying way of life.

[1] Lee and Archbold, op. cit., p. 250.
[2] Lee and Archbold, op. cit., p. 211; *Socialist Record*, July 1913, October 1914.
[3] *Justice*, 18 January 1913; *Socialist Record*, July 1913.
[4] *Justice*, 3 January 1912, 6 September 1913, 1 January 1914.
[5] Ibid., e.g. 15 and 22 February, 9 May, 18 July, 31 October 1908 for music and drama. During the winter of November 1909–April 1910 the London committee supplied 257 speakers for indoor lectures. For economic classes; Hackney S.D.F. minutes. During 1904–5 the branch had regular discussions on 'theoretical socialism', subjects including co-operation, science and religion, nationalism, the scientific method in social problems, temperance, and the materialistic conception of history; a Wednesday class studied 'Joynes Catechism', and the essays written were used to start discussion meetings.
[6] *Justice*, 25 September 1909.

It also provided for its members a vision of the future which helped them through the hard life of the present. Nor was this vision entirely utopian. The S.D.F. was still noted for its immediate policies for unemployment, education and housing. By 1914, however, its impact in these fields had weakened. The unemployed agitation had been vigorously backed by the I.L.P., the Labour Party and the trade unions, and although Fairchild was secretary of the London and District Right to Work Committee of 1909 the attempts of the S.D.F. to keep control of the unemployed movement caused resentment rather than gratitude.[1] There was, moreover, a certain ambivalance in the S.D.F. attitude to the unemployed. While Lansbury, whose defection deprived the S.D.F. of its most popular unemployed champion, was experimenting with farm colonies, Jack Jones was advising against submitting any scheme for the unemployed to 'a capitalistic Government. We knew that they would not accept it: they would be fools if they did.'[2] In fact both Conservative and Liberal governments made much greater efforts to assist the unemployed after 1903. Borough Councils were given powers to provide public relief works and start labour exchanges, and a Central London Body was set up. The Liberal government organised Labour exchanges nationally and started insurance for sickness and unemployment. These measures, together with a general improvement in the economic situation, took the wind out of the party's sails, and in 1912 the veteran S.D.F. unemployed organiser Jack Williams was pensioned off with a testimonial fund.[3]

In housing and education the Social Democrats could claim a more positive influence. Although the L.C.C. was building more and better housing after 1900, and other Councils had produced schemes, it was quite clear that this housing was not meeting the basic slum problem. There was not enough of it, and rents were too high. The Workmen's National Housing Council, with Fred Knee as secretary, continued to urge a more vigorous policy, and the S.D.F. candidates for the L.C.C. pointed out that at the present rate of clearance overcrowding would remain for 250 years.[4] The S.D.F., unlike the Fabians, refused to accept the principle that municipal housing must produce a profit.

Their attitude to education was also advanced. Unlike the I.L.P. and the Fabians, they argued that free school meals should be provided for all children who wanted them, not just those who were starving. They began an agitation for this in 1904, which drew in the T.U.C. and the London Trades Council. When the government had

[1] S.D.P. Conference report, 1909; *Justice*, 7 October 1905.
[2] S.D.F. Conference report, 1906.   [3] *Justice*, 24 February 1912.
[4] Ibid., 23 February 1907.

given Councils the power to provide free meals they played a leading role in exposing the inadequacy of charity organisations and so driving the L.C.C. to produce its own scheme.[1] This victory did not end their campaign. As John Stokes, as chairman of the 1914 conference, proclaimed, 'after bread, education'. They wanted 'a cultured and educated people to take full possession of the glorious future that awaits them'. The B.S.P. continued to fight for an educational system which was socially comprehensive, which provided free university education to all who deserved it, with a curriculum pruned of the humbug of religious compromise, teaching the economic facts of life and the social responsibility of the citizen and the fullness of culture. 'We want something better than a ladder, we want a broad and open road by which there shall be provided for all children all facilities and all means for a thorough education.'[2] If the Fabians had more opportunity for practical educational work, the B.S.P. could boast that their policy had been more percipient. A particularly striking vindication of their point of view was a lecture by J. A. Hobson republished by the Gas Workers Union in 1909. He warned that the government would protect vested interests by selecting 'certain particular boys out of the primary schools, and put them into schools which are suffused with a class spirit'. The school curriculum would be built upon 'a sociology in which the individual is understood to be dependent upon his *own* thrift, his *own* interest for his *own* success in life—a sociology under which property is sacred. ... Instead of organic remedies for social diseases, you would have charitable palliatives recommended.' So the class system, like the mediaeval Church, would perpetuate itself by taking working class children 'because they were intelligent and dangerous, away from their class'.[3]

Although in general the atmosphere of the movement had changed little over the years, in two ways the B.S.P. in 1914 differed from the early S.D.F. With age it was growing a little more conventional and institutional. Both the secularist and temperance beliefs which Social Democrats had inherited from the radical tradition had weakened. Militant atheism had become rare, even if attacks continued on the 'canting hypocrisy of the Nonconformist conscience'.[4] The 1906 S.D.F. conference resolved that religion was a private question, and Jack Jones, perhaps because he was an Irishman, asserted that 'the man in the street believed in religion, if he did not practise it'. There

[1] S.D.F. Conference reports, 1904, 1905, 1908; *Justice*, 11 January 1908.
[2] *Justice*, 1 March 1913.
[3] National Union of Gas Workers and General Labourers report, March 1909.
[4] S.D.F. conference report, 1907 (Jack Jones).

were even signs of the development of a religious atmosphere in the movement. During the 1900s two branches were meeting in churches, and the S.D.F. started a Labour Church in Edmonton.[1] Something of an ethical ritual was developing in the Socialist Sunday Schools, and the B.S.P. encouraged similar tendencies at branch meetings. Sunday meetings should be 'congregational rather than propagandist'. There should be 'a greater attention to display and decoration': portraits of great socialists of the past on the walls, illustrations from William Morris' poems, choirs and bands dressed up for the occasion, and plants to decorate the platform. Poems by Morris, Whitman and Carpenter should be set to music, and portraits shown on a lantern screen while a recorded speech by some prominent Internationalist was played on the gramophone. Outdoor meetings should also be conducted with more dignity, in quieter places, the platform supported by banners and a band.[2]

Similarly, many of the early S.D.Fers had been temperance men, but this was less so by 1914. Although the branches did not, like trade unions, meet in public houses, they associated temperance with Nonconformity and joined attacks on the strict licensing policy of the L.C.C. Nevertheless, as late as 1907 temperance was common enough for the South-East London Socialist Unity Club to be formed on this basis.[3]

In other ways, however, the message of the Social Democrats remained unchanged; essentially a message of hope, confident in the Marxist prediction of inevitable victory. Its authentic voice can be read in *Appeal to the Workers of Camberwell* of about 1910. 'You are slaves,' it declares. 'The wage given you by your masters is only a portion of the wealth you create.' The workers maintain society, yet they live in wretched houses in mean streets, their children grow up thin and weak, their daughters are driven to prostitution, their sons forced into the army. But if the workers were 'condemned to rot in the cavern of toil, to live lives of poverty, hunger and dirt', the socialists would awake them to 'realise what a grand thing life is . . . a dream of ease, of pleasure, of appreciation of the beauties of nature and the glories of art and the wonders of science'.[4] Beyond the bitterness of the class struggle lay the New Jerusalem.

The B.S.P. in 1914 had suffered seriously from inept leadership.

---

[1] In the Brotherhood Church, Islington, and the Iron Congregational Church, Lewisham. Edmonton: *Justice*, 13 February 1909.

[2] Special Propaganda Effort, August 1912, British Socialist Party, miscellaneous papers.

[3] *Justice*, 9 February 1907.

[4] Copy in the British Library of Political and Economic Science.

THE LEAN YEARS OF SOCIAL DEMOCRACY

Consequently it lacked political judgement and expertise. But it was still the largest socialist party in London, strongly rooted in the working class, with prescient practical policies, enthusiasm and idealism. It had an important contribution to make to the London Labour Party.

X
THE FABIANS AND THE INDEPENDENT LABOUR PARTY AFTER 1900

JUST as Fabian accounts of the early achievements of the Society have been misleading, so the nature of the 'second blooming' has never been very satisfactorily analysed. Because its influence is exaggerated and its political difficulties underrated, the internal conflicts of the Society have been treated as purely personal squabbles.[1]

It is generally agreed that during the first years of the Labour Party the Fabian Society failed to exert much influence on its development. The Fabian Society was probably in these years the least important of the three London socialist bodies. Its numbers were small, remaining below 400 until 1906. On the dominant political issues of the period its collective view clashed with the rest of the labour movement. The Society failed to declare against the Boer War, and issued a tract showing a distinct sympathy with imperialism. An unsuccessful revolt against this attitude was led by S. G. Hobson, an I.L.P. journalist from Ulster, supported by Crooks and Steadman, the most notable Fabians on the L.C.C. labour bench, and among those who resigned from the Society in protest were Ramsay MacDonald and Barnes the Engineers' secretary.[2] Conflict on the war issue probably accounts for the absence of the Fabians, formerly so anxious to permeate radicalism, from the convention of the National Democratic League.

---

[1] M. Cole, op. cit., Ch. XII, and Pease, op. cit., Ch. VIII–XI, are unsatisfactory for this reason. They fail to show the evolution in the political thinking of Shaw and the Webbs. The part of the Labour Party supporters in the Wells episode has been generally ignored. McBriar, op. cit., gives little attention to the internal conflicts and developments of Fabian tactics in this period.

[2] Fabian Society minutes, 20 April and 12 October 1900.

On the education issue the Fabians were again ranged against the radical and labour men. Webb, who regarded the Education Bills as a triumph of his own influence, (another instance of Fabian self-delusion), defeated the resistance within the Society, led by Wallas and Headlam in favour of secular education. As a result Webb found himself estranged from the predominantly Nonconformist Progressives and the L.C.C. labour bench. Ramsay MacDonald, who was elected to the L.C.C. opposed at a bye-election in November 1901, worked up feeling against Webb's administration of the L.L.C.'s Technical Education Board, secured the backing of the labour bench, and was even approached by the Progressives to oust Webb from its chairmanship.[1] When MacDonald, as L.R.C. secretary, sought Fabian support for a conference in 1901 to protest against the Education Bill, the Fabians sharply replied that the L.R.C.'s action was 'ultra vires, and ... likely to lead to the withdrawal of constituent bodies and the disruption of the Committee'.[2]

On the issue of Free Trade versus Tariff Reform the Fabians again found themselves at odds with radical tradition. *Fabianism and the Fiscal Question*, issued in 1903, treated Free Trade with as much scorn as Protection. Wallas, exasperated by the education dispute, resigned in protest against this further betrayal.

These policy differences account for much of the Fabian lack of enthusiasm for the Labour Party before 1906. Although Pease belonged to the L.R.C. National Executive, the only important Fabian contribution to the development of the new Party was the financial scheme for the support of Labour M.P.s, drafted by S. G. Hobson in 1900 and eventually adopted in 1902. Pease had described the Fabian attitude as one of 'benevolent passivity'.[3] In fact the Fabians had little confidence at this time in the idea of an independent party, and saw the L.R.C. as a kind of parliamentary labour bench. Hence they resisted the development of an L.R.C. policy on general political questions such as education. At the Barnard Castle election, a crucial stage in the development of independence, Pease hastened to assure the Liberal Whips that the Labour victor was 'a very good Liberal and fully recognises that there are only two lobbies in the House of Commons'.[4] It was only after 1906, when the Labour Party had triumphed at the General Election, that this apologetic indifference was forgotten, and Shaw audaciously claimed that the

---

[1] S. Webb to B. Webb, 19 July 1902, Passfield Collection; J. R. MacDonald to J. K. Hardie, 5 March 1903, Francis Johnson Collection.
[2] Fabian Society minutes, 17 May and 14 June 1901.
[3] Pease, op. cit., p. 151.
[4] E. Pease to J. Herbert, 12 December 1902, Herbert Gladstone Collection.

Labour Party was a Fabian proposal which had 'at last been acted on'.[1]

In spite of its political vagaries the Fabian Society was given a new lease of life by the Labour Party triumph of 1906. Its London membership suddenly expanded, rising to over 1,200 by 1909 and reaching a peak of 1,342 in 1911, thereafter remaining relatively steady until 1914. It is clear, however, that the new members joined the Society as the most obvious home for intellectual socialists and not, as has been recently suggested, because they thought they saw in it the best 'means of bringing into being a Socialist society in Britain'.[2] In the same way it was as a forum of political intellectuals rather than as a political power that the Fabian Society continued to attract Liberals, such as Arnold Bennett, who thought that 'socialism has become the most convenient and effective name for the left wing of the Liberal Party'.[3]

The interests of the new membership are demonstrated by the London Fabian Groups, which had disappeared after a brief revival in 1900. They sprang up once more in 1907, and until 1914 there were between 10 and 15 active Groups or local Societies in the London area. They did not usually enter directly into local political contests, although occasionally a Group can be found actively supporting a local Labour Party, and in 1913, with peculiarly Fabian ambivalence, the Deptford Group actually announced that it had put up two L.C.C. candidates with separate party committee rooms, one Labour and one Progressive.[4] More usually they saw their role as technical advisers, acting 'as an intelligence department for the socialist body generally in the district'.[5] The Golders Green Group, for example, formed a committee 'to deal with the public affairs of Hampstead Garden Suburb', created a resident's council, held a conference on school clinics and took a special interest in town planning.[6] All the Groups arranged lecture courses and discussion meetings. Unlike the Groups of the 1890s they were wholly middle class, flourishing in the outer suburbs.

On the other hand this middle class and intellectual character of the new membership did not prevent a series of conflicts within the Society about its purpose and political position. These conflicts have usually been described in personal terms. Certainly much of the friction and exasperation of the Fabian rebels was due to the desire of the more talented new members to share in the running of the Society, which was still largely in the control of the early Fabian leaders, Bland, Shaw and Webb. Some new faces had been added,

[1] *Clarion*, 2 February 1906. [2] M. Cole, op. cit., p. 116.
[3] *New Age*, 30 November 1907. [4] *Fabian News*, February 1913.
[5] Ibid., December 1908. [6] Fabian Society reports, 1911–13.

but they were obviously outnumbered. Thus a crucial victory for the reformers in 1907 was the increase of the executive from 15 to 21. Immediately, the novelist H. G. Wells, the barrister R. C. K. Ensor, F. W. Pethick-Lawrence and other reformers were elected to the committee.[1] But although in succeeding years other talented younger members joined or succeeded them, until Shaw, Bland and Stewart Headlam retired in 1911 the 'old gang' were able to block any fundamental change in the policy of the Society. Even after 1911 Sidney Webb remained on the committee, and was joined by Beatrice in 1912. There was thus a strong element of personal frustration in the various attempts to alter the Society.

Nevertheless the protagonists may be divided into three political groups. Firstly there were those who wished to see the Society continue open to both Liberal and Labour Party supporters. Secondly there were those who wished to form an independent middle class socialist party. Thirdly there were the advocates of clear commitment to the Labour Party.

On the essential issue the traditionalists won. The diversity of the Fabians continued. In the General Election of December 1910 two Fabians were elected as Labour M.P.s in London, two as Liberals, and one stood as an independent socialist.[2] In the 1913 L.C.C. election nine Fabians stood as Progressive candidates, four of them successfully, and eight as Labour candidates, only one being elected.[3] Prominent Progressives such as Headlam and Reginald Bray, Liberal M.P.s such as Percy Alden or Chiozza Money, author of the bestseller *Riches and Poverty*, were still on the executive as late as 1911. There was, however, a slight shift in attitude. Because of objections by members Pease decided not to join the Progressive L.C.C. election committee in December 1906.[4] There were strong protests when H. G. Chancellor was elected liberal M.P. for Haggerston against a socialist candidate in 1910 although chiefly because he had issued posters declaring that 'Socialism is a dream'.[5] In December 1912, after a clash in Bermondsey between a Fabian Progressive and a Labour candidate for the L.C.C., a strong warning to avoid this kind of contest was issued to members, and the committee decided to 'neglect no opportunity to prevent clashing'.[6] New difficulties arose

[1] Hobson (1900), Percy Alden (1903), Cecil Chesterton (1904); in 1907 Haden Guest and Aylmer Maude were also added.
[2] George Lansbury and Will Crooks as Labour M.P.s; Percy Alden and H. G. Chancellor as Liberals; C. N. L. Shaw as Socialist candidate at Battersea.
[3] Reginald Bray, Montague Shearman, Phillimore and Headlam elected as Progressives; Susan Lawrence as Labour.
[4] Fabian Society minutes, 28 December 1906.
[5] Ibid., 13–14 January 1910.
[6] Ibid., 21 November 1912, 6 February 1913; Fabian Society report 1913.

in 1914 with the formation of the London Labour Party. The Society sent delegates, but instructed them to say that it could not 'control the action of its members who may run as Progressives' and to vote against a proposed clause pledging affiliated societies 'not to allow any of their members to stand as candidates for any other party'.[1] Increasingly Fabian detachment was becoming an embarrassment, and by 1914 the chief champion of detachment, Sidney Webb, had in fact finally changed his mind. He had done so as the result of a prolonged evolution.

The education issue had broken Sidney Webb's influence with the Progressives, whose whip told him in December 1903, 'They say that you have hitherto led us by the nose Webb, now it is your turn to follow.'[2] But the Webbs had remained hopeful of influencing the Liberal Party. In the early months of the Liberal government Churchill, Lloyd George, and even John Burns, seemed eager to listen to their views. It had soon become clear, however, that the government's measures were not intended as steps to socialism, and with the decisive rejection of the Webbs' scheme for a National Minimum in the Minority Report of the Poor Law Commission they decided to rally all their potential supporters in an independent national campaign. Bishops, medical officers, education officers, Liberal social reformers, Fabians and Labour Party, were all to be united in a 'new Crusade' intended 'to reach the heart of every man and woman of good will'.[3]

It was a last great attempt to organise all the good feeling which the Webbs had always believed could be turned to socialism by the sheer force of disinterested reason. An office was set up with a paid staff of seven, Cecil Sharp became editor of a new periodical, *Crusade*, and by the end of 1909 16,000 members had been enrolled. Branches were formed, and public meetings held all over the country.

The campaign failed. In spite of undoubted support won in the country, the Liberal leaders remained unpersuaded. By the end of 1910 the Webbs were 'both feeling weary and somewhat dispirited'.[4] What support remained for the campaign outside the labour movement became negligible when the government produced its own

[1] Fabian Society minutes, 23 April and 2 July 1914.
[2] B. Webb, diary, 1 December 1903. Webb was 'turned off' the Progressive party committee in 1905, ibid., 10 July 1905. He did not stand for the L.C.C. in 1910, with the result that the two Deptford seats, held in 1907, were lost by the Progressives. Had these two seats been held the Progressives would have had a majority of the councillors. By pure chance his defection was thus more decisive for the Progressives than all his years of support.
[3] E.g. National Conference on the Prevention of Destitution, 11–14 June 1912, Passfield Collection.
[4] B. Webb, op. cit., p. 466.

answer to destitution in the 1911 insurance schemes. The Webbs set off on a world tour in 1911, leaving Cecil Sharp to organise resistance to the Insurance Bill; a resistance which was confined to a section of the socialist movement. As Beatrice Webb observed after defeat, 'the plain fact is that Lloyd George and the Radicals have out-trumped the Labour Party'.[1]

The question was how to use the embers of the campaign. The Webbs' first reactions were to return to earlier ways. 'In case we had to wind up the National Committee, I should throw the remnant and some of our energy into reviving the Fabian Society. Whether that would be possible with E. Pease as secretary, I do not know.'[2] Beatrice Webb's second thought was even to return to pre-Fabian methods. 'I have a great idea of making our National Council the real Charity Organisation Society—that is to say, getting all volunteers and voluntary institutions grouped under the public authorities concerned with neglected infancy, neglected childhood and adolescence, old age, feeble mindedness and unemployment.'[3]

Finally, however, the Webbs made the crucial decision to reject past tactics. The National Committee was wound up on their return in October 1912. The 'Fabian Research Department', a committee to study the control of industry, was set up at the suggestion of Beatrice Webb. It was to be the brain of the labour movement. 'There seems to be a clear call to leadership in the Labour and Socialist movement to which we feel we must respond.'[4] This new sense of purpose marked a decisive change in the life of the Webbs and consequently in the history of the Labour Party. For twenty years they had sought to show that socialism could come without the class struggle, and had helped to prevent the development of the Labour Party in London. Now they aligned themselves with the working class. As late as 1907 Sidney Webb had believed that 'more is done in England in politics whilst ignoring elections and parties, than by or with them'.[5] In 1913 and 1914 the Webbs attended the Labour Party conferences together as Fabian delegates. 'The Labour Party exists and we have to work with it. "A poor thing, but our own." '[6]

Although a dwindling force, the traditionalists in the Fabian Society were able to hold their own until after 1914, because the opposition to them was split. The most vociferous group were those who wished to transform the Fabian Society into a new middle class

---

[1] M. Cole (ed.), *Beatrice Webb's Diaries, 1912-24*, London 1952, p. 8.
[2] B. Webb, op. cit., p. 467.
[3] B. Webb to G. Meinertzhagen, March 1911, Passfield Collection.
[4] *Beatrice Webb's Diaries, 1912-24*, p. 6.
[5] S. Webb to H. G. Wells, 15 June 1907, Fabian Society archives.
[6] *Beatrice Webb's Diaries, 1912-24*, p. 10.

party. In the earlier coherent phase of his rebellion H. G. Wells led this group, demanding admission to membership without nomination, the change of title to British Socialist Party, a new doctrinal Basis, a re-organised administration and a new weekly paper. Some of these points were accepted. The executive was enlarged, committees on organising and propaganda were formed, an organiser appointed, and a new class of member not required to sign the Basis was devised.[1] With the formation of local Fabians Groups, the Fabian Nursery, and special Arts, Biology and Education Groups, the Fabian Society was certainly able to present a broader appeal to middle class socialists. But development further than this was prevented by both the traditionalists and the Labour Party supporters, allowing Shaw as executive spokesman easily to out-manoeuvre the rebels.

At heart, however, Shaw was with the rebels. He wrote to Webb in November 1906 that a change of approach was needed. 'I now see clearly that "das Lied ist aus". We cannot sit there any longer making a mere habit of the thing.' They must 'consummate the Fabian section of our lives by setting on foot a Fabian parliamentary party.' The Labour Party example would soon produce 'the beginnings of a big middle class demand for an educated middle class handling of the new problems in Parliament. . . . We must spend the next two years in educating these chaps in committee work and public life; then throw the whole thing into their hands as a Federation of Fabian Socialist Associations, formally wind up the old Fabian, and make our bow.'[2] Shaw continued to alternate between moments of hope that 'suspended Socialism was at last going to precipitate itself in a political party', and moments of despair that 'apart from pure routine there has been absolutely no *raison d'etre* for the Society'.[3] It was in this mood of despair that Shaw at last resigned from the Fabian executive in 1911, and in the final revolt of 1913–15 he sided with the rebels.

A leading part in the demand for an independent socialist party had been played by *New Age*, a paper taken over in 1907 by a Fabian schoolteacher from Leeds, A. B. Orage.[4] He made it one of the liveliest papers of the period, notable regular contributors including Cecil Chesterton, J. A. Hobson, Patrick Geddes, Wyndham Lewis, St. John Ervine and Walter Sickert. *New Age* was in fact a rather brighter focus of intellectual socialism in this period than the Fabian Society

[1] Fabian Society minutes, 12 October 1906, 12 July 1907.
[2] G. B. Shaw to S. Webb, 25 November 1906, Passfield Collection.
[3] G. B. Shaw to E. Pease, 5 July 1907, Shaw Collection; G. B. Shaw to S. and B. Webb, 22 March 1911, Passfield Collection.
[4] P. Mairet, *A. R. Orage*, London 1936.

itself. S. G. Hobson, who resigned from the Fabian Society in 1909 after failing to convert it to 'the upbuilding of a definite and avowed Socialist Party', was a regular political contributor.[1] Independent socialism, as we have seen, enjoyed only a short period of success, and *New Age* found a new hope in a modified version of the syndicalist movement, Guild Socialism, which was also to secure considerable support in the Fabian Society. It was a typically Fabian modification of syndicalism, preferring 'encroaching control' to revolutionary strike action. Industrial unionism was rephrased in the form of industrial Guilds. These ideas were first put forward by *New Age* in an editorial series, written by Hobson, which began late in 1912.

The Guild Socialist rebellion was more difficult to quell, not only because it had the sympathy of Shaw, but also because the leading rebels had been entrenched in the Fabian organisation by the Webbs themselves. The research groups suggested by Beatrice Webb in 1912 developed into a Fabian Research Committee with its own office. Its secretary was William Mellor and another leading member G. D. H. Cole, both young Oxford Fabians and both Guild Socialists. Together in April 1913 and March 1914 they led two attempts to disaffiliate the Fabian Society from the Labour Party. They failed, but when Cole resigned in 1915 he was able to take the Research Department with him, thus depriving the Fabian Society of its most talented younger members and resulting in its subsequent stagnation in the 1920s.

The third political group within the Fabian Society, the supporters of clear commitment to the Labour Party, made two serious attempts to change Fabian policy. The first was in conjunction with Wells in 1906–7. Haden Guest, a fiery young Welsh doctor, had spoken in support of Wells' proposed reforms, arguing the need 'to get at the middle classes and organise them to work in co-operation with the Labour Party'. Before the 1907 Fabian executive election a reform committee, including Wells, Guest and Ensor with Sydney Oliver in the chair, held meetings at the I.L.P. office.[2] The committee failed because the conflict between Wells and the others was never settled. Ensor found Wells 'absurd' and recorded repeated 'tedious discussion' and 'silly personal bickering'.[3] Consequently although nine of the fifteen reform candidates were elected they were unable to form a united group. As Wells wrote to Ensor afterwards, 'There ain't no

---

[1] S. G. Hobson, op. cit., p. 118.
[2] Documents on the Wells affair, Fabian Society archives; R. C. K. Ensor, diary, 1907, Ensor Collection.
[3] R. C. K. Ensor, diary, 18 January, 15 and 20 February 1907, Ensor Collection.

parties in the F.S. ... You and Guest broke any reform party there was in the month before the Executive election and we fought as a parcel of fragments.'[1] Even the I.L.P. men were divided; Ensor attempted to form a 'right little tight little party' in the first months of the new executive, but by January 1908 experience had so altered him that he was speaking against Guest's proposal that Fabians should support only Labour candidates at elections.[2] Guest had also changed his mind by October 1909.[3]

This failure to keep their convictions explains why the Labour Party supporters were not able to secure a majority within the next few years. After 1907 they produced most of the newcomers to the executive. Four were elected in 1908–11, and six more in 1912–13.[4] Yet although all were active in the I.L.P. only one more attempt was made to change the Society's policy. Shortly after the Webbs set off on their world tour in the autumn of 1911 a Fabian Reform Committee, with Clifford Allen the fervent general manager of the *Daily Citizen* as secretary, issued a manifesto attacking permeation as 'worse than useless', urging closer links with the I.L.P. and a membership limited to 'supporters of the Labour Party'. But even this manifesto showed a divided mind, for if the Fabians were to 'expose the hollowness of Liberal democracy', they were also to 'smash the idea of class in the labour movement'.[5] The committee were also hampered by including the ambitious and distrusted trade union barrister H. H. Schloesser. Its resolution to exclude Liberals from the executive in February 1912 was defeated at a members' meeting by 150 votes to 80.[6]

The Labour Party supporters had to content themselves with less decisive achievements. A Fabian parliamentary fund was started which helped to support Crooks at Woolwich. At the same time the Society strengthened its links with the I.L.P. Bitterness between the two bodies had died down in the 1900s, partly because of the extreme weakness of the I.L.P. and partly because Fabians came increasingly to be the backbone of the London I.L.P. In December 1910, after an unsuccessful unity conference with the S.D.F. and I.L.P., the Fabian executive agreed to set up a committee to co-ordinate with the I.L.P. The Society had long supplied I.L.P. branches with lecturers,

[1] H. G. Wells to R. C. K. Ensor, 20 April 1907, Ensor Collection.
[2] A. Maude to R. C. K. Ensor, 16 May 1907, W. Shore to R. C. K. Ensor, 8 July 1907, and R. C. K. Ensor, diary, 24 January 1908, Ensor Collection.
[3] *Clarion*, 15 October 1909.
[4] Rev. R. J. Campbell (1908), Dr Ethel Bentham (1909), H. H. Schloesser (1910), Emil Davies (1911); Clifford Allen, C. M. Lloyd, Harry Snell and Marion Phillips (1912); Susan Lawrence and St. John Ervine (1913).
[5] Fabian Reform Committee, manifesto, November 1911.
[6] C. Sharp to B. Webb, 24 February 1912, Passfield Collection.

and in 1912 it was running a London speakers' class.¹ The Fabian Local Government Bureau was reconstituted as a joint concern in the same year.

The strengthening of Fabian links with the I.L.P., together with the change in the Webbs' attitude to the Labour Party, marked a crucial turning point in the last years of this period for the Fabians as for the Social Democrats. Indeed the change in both was symbolised by the Fabian decision in March 1914 to support the B.S.P. in its application to affiliate to the Labour Party and also to support an amendment to the Labour Party constitution enabling candidates to stand as 'Labour and Socialist'.² Both of the main London socialist groups, by persisting in political aloofness after the formation of the Labour Party, had reduced their national influence on the Labour Party and hindered its local development in London. The Fabian Society and S.D.F. should have been the principal agents in the building of the Labour Party in London. The Social Democrats frustrated their own work while the Fabian Society neglected its task altogether. It could not claim to have played an important part in the development of any local Labour Party in London in the 1900s.

The result of the failure of both the Fabian Society and the Social Democrats was the revival of the London I.L.P., which was enabled by their abstention to a certain extent to usurp the place of both of them. It is to the I.L.P. that we must now turn.

The I.L.P. in London was a mere shadow until 1905, when for the first time since the 1890s it exceeded twenty branches. But for the efforts of national leaders and the money of a few wealthy supporters it would have probably flickered out. In May 1902 the I.L.P. National Council planned a campaign for its revival. Lecture tours were arranged for Philip Snowden and Bruce Glasier, and special assistance was given by Keir Hardie, Ramsay MacDonald, and other national leaders. Yet in spite of this heavy battery the number of branches remained only fifteen, their reports 'the reverse of encouraging',³ and the total membership of the London region only 415—less than a quarter of the size of the Social Democratic Federation. In the list of London lecturers published at this time the notable socialists were national figures such as those just mentioned; the prominent Londoners were socially-conscious Liberals such as C. F. G. Masterman and Percy Alden.⁴

In 1903 the Metropolitan District Council acquired a secretary and

¹ Fabian Society minutes, 10 October and 15 December 1910, 4 January 1912.
² Fabian Society minutes, 12 September 1912, 13 December 1913; B. Webb diary, 8 March 1914.
³ *Labour Leader*, 9 August 1902.   ⁴ Ibid., 18 October 1902.

organiser, paid £50 a year. The money came from private donations, mostly anonymous, but including two gifts of £15 from Dr. Stanton Coit and Mrs. Cobden-Sanderson.[1] These two and the secretary, William Sanders, were the characteristic figures of the London I.L.P. at this date. Coit, the leading Ethical preacher in West London, was on the Metropolitan District Council. Annie Cobden-Sanderson,[2] the Council's treasurer, a daughter of Richard Cobden, was a headstrong vivacious woman married to a humourless Arts and Crafts bookbinder and living in Hammersmith Terrace. In the 1890s she had 'a furious fad towards vegetarianism'.[3] By the early 1900s the I.L.P. was her enthusiasm; later she became a militant suffragette.

William Sanders[4] had been discovered by Coit, and sent to Germany for two years education. He had come from a poor family, worked as a builder's clerk, and joined the S.D.F. On his return from Germany he became a well-known Ethical preacher, and an expert on German militarism, earning his living in various paid jobs for the labour movement. In the 1890s he worked for John Burns in Battersea; later he became organiser of the Fabian local societies, and his wife worked for the suffragettes. Beatrice Webb thought him 'a sturdy and sterling fellow, somewhat thick in body and mind. . . . He has a bureaucratic and organising mind.' As an I.L.P. organiser he was not much of a success. Ramsay MacDonald found his ineptitude peculiarly irritating. In November 1905 he complained that Sanders had failed to organise the nominations to the London Central Unemployed Committee. 'So far as I can gather there are several nominations of our kind of people *few of whom know the others are up*. Now Sanders is paid to look after the interests of the I.L.P. in London and for his £50 he ought to put himself to the trouble of getting some unity imparted into our action. Instead of that things have been allowed to drift and once more the I.L.P. looks as if it were going to be out of it. . . . I am sick of London I.L.P. maudling and muddling by superior persons, and I am afraid I wrote a letter to Sanders which showed pepper. I can't help it. Fulham, the unemployed, the Labour group on the L.C.C.—it is all very sickening—especially when on top of it all is £50 and we know the self-sacrificing work done by our men in other places.'[5]

Fulham and the L.C.C. Labour group were part of the same problem, the problem of I.L.P. policy in local elections. In these

[1] I.L.P. Metropolitan Divisional Council report, 1903–4.
[2] Cobden-Sanderson, op. cit.   [3] Henderson, op. cit., p. 193.
[4] Sanders, op. cit.; *Reformers Year Book 1905*; *Labour Elector*, 28 December 1889; B. Webb, diary, August 1918; Pankhurst, op. cit., p. 224.
[5] J. R. MacDonald to J. K. Hardie, November 1905, Francis Johnson Collection.

years the London I.L.P. decided to adopt Fabian tactics. After two disastrous L.C.C. elections in 1895 and 1898 and the equally demoralising first London borough council election of 1900, at which not a single I.L.P. success could be claimed, it was not surprising that compromise was attempted. At the 1901 L.C.C. election Frank Smith and Robert Williams (a socialist architect) were elected as Progressives, and later in the year Ramsay MacDonald, who had already stood unsuccessfully as a Progressive at a bye-election in 1900, was returned unopposed when Frank Smith resigned to resume temporarily his Salvation Army work.[1] The *Labour Leader* in 1901 was enthusiastic in its support for the Progressives who it was considered had 'shown during the past three years an amount of zeal and ability in forwarding genuine measures of reform which it would be hard to equal in any part of the country'.[2] In 1904 negotiations between the Progressive whip and the I.L.P. were apparently repeated and two candidates given straight fights.[3] The Rev. Jenkins Jones, the Unitarian Labour Mayor of Woolwich, was elected, and William Sanders and Isaac Mitchell, secretary of the General Federation of Trade Unions, were chosen as Aldermen.

Inevitably this policy of compromise produced friction within the I.L.P. The Labour group on the L.C.C. made no pretence of independence, and was regularly used to support Liberal candidates in three-cornered fights against independent Labour. Will Crooks continued to do this even after his election as a Labour M.P.; Steadman was more straightforward, and declined to sign the L.R.C. constitution.[4] The Fulham bye-election to the L.C.C. was one of these occasions;

[1] Frank Smith had been elected for Central Finsbury, Robert Williams for North Lambeth. MacDonald had previously stood for Woolwich. He was unable to stand again in 1904, because he was omitted from the electoral register; Beatrice Webb welcomed this 'strange piece of luck', diary, 18 November 1903.

[2] *Labour Leader*, 2 March 1901.

[3] *Municipal Journal*, 8 March 1901, reported that 'another difficulty which the (Progressive) Whip got over was the intervention of third candidates running as quasi-independent or labour candidates'. In 1904 Jenkins Jones stood in Woolwich, Charles Duncan in Westminster; 'endeavours were made to secure the nomination of I.L.P. candidates' in Finsbury, Clapham and North Lambeth but without success, I.L.P. Metropolitan District Council report, 1903-4. The *Clarion*, 4 March 1904, urged electors to vote Progressive; the *Labour Leader* reported Labour-Progressive successes as 'Labour gains'. There cannot be much doubt that negotiations had taken place. The *Municipal Journal*, 29 June 1906, attacked the I.L.P. for its 1907 plans, and for rejecting 'all offers of conference from the Progressive side'.

[4] *London Trades Gazette*, March 1905. For complaints against Crooks, see e.g. I.L.P. conference report, 1913; Labour Party National Executive Committee minutes, 6 March 1913; J. Lane to J. R. MacDonald, December 1903, T. Hastie to J. R. MacDonald, 4 May 1904, &c., Labour Party Correspondence.

the local Labour Party and Progressives had fallen out, and Alderman Joseph Clarke, a Plasterer who had been given his dignity as part of a bargain to secure Progressive control of the Borough Council, was put up against Harold Spender. The result was a Moderate victory.[1]

Most of the small number of I.L.Pers elected to local bodies at this time were undoubtedly Progressives.[2] For those ambitious to become councillors, particularly middle class socialists who found it easy to work with Liberals, the minor successes achieved justified compromise. But on few Councils were there were more than three I.L.P. representatives, and on most only one. The two contrasting examples of real success were West Ham and Woolwich, where the I.L.P. was working within a united labour movement. The West Ham branches had six or more councillors and three Guardians, the Woolwich branch twelve councillors, a majority of the Labour Party which captured the borough council in 1903.[3] In spite of claims to the contrary, both of these labour movements had arisen essentially from

---

[1] *Fulham Observer*, 13 November 1903—the Progressives 'have descended to the low level of subsidising the labour vote by granting them two Aldermanic seats'. The result of the Borough Council election had been 16 Conservative, 18 Progressive, 2 Labour. But already at a bye-election in April there was a three-cornered fight, and at another in the autumn a Labour candidate was elected against both parties (*Fulham Observer*, 6 October 1905). The Labour Party were not invited to the Progressive selection conference. Steadman and G. N. Barnes both supported Spender against the Labour candidate. (*Fulham Observer*, 27 October 1905.)

[2] R. McKinley was elected a Fulham Guardian as a straight Progressive (*Fulham Observer*, 1 April 1904); H. W. Bingley was elected a Hackney councillor as a Labour-Progressive (*Labour Leader*, 14 November 1903); in Finsbury Borough Council elections were confused, but the Progressive-Labour alliance was cemented by Frank Smith and Ramsay MacDonald as county councillors; in St. Pancras the Progressives and Labour men were 'united in one solid phalanx' (*St. Pancras Chronicle*, 7 November 1903) and the three successful I.L.Pers were a Congregational minister (Harley), an insurance agent (Horne) and an electrical engineer (James); in Lewisham there was no I.L.P. branch and A. J. Thorogood, a company secretary, was elected as a Progressive (*Kentish Mercury*, 29 October and 3 November 1903); the Westminster Labour Representation was formed with a view to 'uniting the Progressive forces' (*London Trades Gazette*, February 1903), and was given a free run in St. Johns Ward, two I.L.Pers (Bannochie and Penfold) elected among six; W. J. Pincombe in Willesden, a schoolteacher, worked with Progressives and not Labour candidates (*Willesden and Kilburn Chronicle*, 8 March 1901); in Tottenham, although there had been some Labour activity, R. W. Broadbank, a designer, had become a Councillor and Guardian as a progressive independent (e.g. *Wood Green and Tottenham Weekly Herald*, 22 March 1901); in Walthamstow F. C. Krailing, a company manager, did not become a socialist or join the I.L.P. until after his election as a councillor (*Walthamstow and Leyton Guardian*, 10 April 1903, 6 April 1906).

[3] I.L.P. Conference Reports, 1903 &c.

political forces other than the I.L.P., and their essential character remained independent of it. Nevertheless it was clear that once a strong labour movement had developed the I.L.P., unlike the S.D.F., would secure a large share in its victories.

Thus the strong growth of the London I.L.P. between 1905 and 1910 was caused not by any internal effort but by the new national prestige of the Labour Party. By 1908 the Annual Conference report boasted that 'London, which up to a short time ago had been looked upon as a hopeless place for the Party, has made considerable progress'.[1] Some of the increases of membership were startling. South London, for example, had 180 members in 1907, 1,500 in 1908.[2] The total membership of the London region reached a peak of about 2,500 in 1910 in 59 branches.[3] With this expanding membership some improvement in organisation became possible. By 1908 the whole area was arranged into four Councils, each with a paid organiser subsidised by the head office, and all 'tackling the huge problem before them with spirit'.[4] In 1906–7 and 1910 the London I.L.P. Council felt strong enough to attempt to organise the labour movement for the L.C.C. elections, and at the end of 1907 it even proposed to start a fund for L.C.C. and London parliamentary elections.[5] These gestures were not, however, very successful, and criticism of organisation continued to be more frequent than approval. London had its own Metropolitan District Council, but its area and duties were ill-defined. It was meant to cover Middlesex and any other 'strictly suburban area'. With the growing number of branches and the local federations it became 'cumbrous and unsatisfactory', and the National Council decided to replace it by a small executive committee and twice-yearly conference for the whole South Eastern Division.[6] Consequently the committee found itself organising rural propaganda, and the pleasant distractions of strawberry teas, while purely metropolitan districts like Lewisham found themselves separated from the London federations and linked with the Kent country

[1] I.L.P. Conference Report, 1908.
[2] *Labour Leader*, 3 September 1909.
[3] I.L.P. Conference Reports, branch reports in *Labour Leader*, minutes of London Divisional Council, &c. for number of branches in existence. The membership is an estimate; the Divisional Council Documents (File IV C, Herbert Bryan Collection) give total membership in March 1910 as 3537 for 97 branches, including 38 outside the London area. But with some 500 members at Woolwich, 200 at Clapham, and probably more at East Ham, it is likely that about 2500 were London members.
[4] I.L.P. Metropolitan District Council report, 1906–7; I.L.P. conference report, 1908.
[5] I.L.P. Metropolitan District Council minutes, 24 November and 15 December 1906, 9 December 1907.
[6] Ibid., 13 July 1908, 21 May 1909.

branches.¹ In spite of strong pressure the National Council refused to set up a special London office to co-ordinate the movement.²

The weakness of the organisation was shown clearly by its failure to arrest the decline in membership which set in after 1910. Fundamentally the cause of the decline, as of the earlier increase, was the national reputation of the Labour Party. Dissatisfaction with its treatment of Victor Grayson, the independent socialist M.P., its lack of sympathy with syndicalism and militant suffragism, and its support for the Insurance Bill carried many of the rank and file to the B.S.P., the suffragettes or the Daily Herald League. The defection of the Woolwich branch and of George Lansbury were the worst blows. The membership remained above 2,000 and the branches over 50 in 1914, but most of the earlier enthusiasm had disappeared.³ 'I am going out', the Divisional organiser announced in a typical mood before the 1913 L.C.C. election, 'to find that elusive body called "The Movement" '.⁴

Certainly, judged as an independent electoral organisation, the I.L.P. had little to boast of by 1913. It could get an occasional member elected to the L.C.C. (one in 1907, three in 1910, one in 1913), but only with Progressive support, and all efforts to win over the Progressive Labour bench had failed. Displays of electoral independence were unsuccessful. For the 1907 election the Metropolitan District Council rejected Progressive overtures.⁵ Ten candidates stood on a slightly more advanced programme, repeating the old Progressive demands for control of the port, electricity, police, markets and hospitals, and adding municipal milk and coal, an extended county boundary, and slum clearance at the cost of slum landlords. Six of the candidates were directly opposed by Progressives, and only polled between 295 and 897 votes; one, who gave both Progressive and independent Socialist 'cold shoulder' but secured a free run, secured 3,139 votes, a good performance although far short

---

¹ I.L.P. London Divisional Council report, 12 March 1910; *Labour Leader*, 5 July 1913.

² I.L.P. London Divisional Conference report, 12 March 1910; I.L.P. conference report, 1910.

³ Exact figures are impossible. From the *Labour Leader*, Divisional Council documents, etc., 43 branches in the London area can be proved to have existed, and 9 others probably survived. The total Divisional membership in June 1914 was 2976, but it is not clear how many branches there were in the whole Division. Of the unusually large London branches, only Clapham remained. London membership was probably below 2200.

⁴ *Labour Leader*, 6 March 1913.

⁵ I.L.P. Metropolitan District Council minutes, 15 December 1906; *Municipal Journal*, 29 June 1906. At a later stage the Labour Party leaders attempted to negotiate, but the Progressives then in turn refused, J. K. Hardie to G. Lansbury, 7 March 1907, Lansbury Collection.

of victory; three received Progressive support, two narrowly failing, and one only, Frank Smith in North Lambeth, being elected.[1] Although the *Labour Leader* could hardly find much comfort in a victory where there was not even a local I.L.P. branch supporting the candidate, it had 'no tears to shed over the defeat of the Progressives. Rent by internal dissension, contemptuous of the claims of labour to a larger representation on the Council, and only half-hearted in its labour policy, the Progressive party openly invited defeat.'[2]

In 1910 the Progressive whip again attempted to avoid three-cornered fights, and of the nine I.L.Pers standing only three stood against both parties.[3] Their performance was again far short of those who were given straight fights, but better than in 1907; in Bermondsey Dr. Salter polled 1,876. In Woolwich and North Kensington I.L.Pers with Progressive support came closer to success, in North Lambeth Frank Smith was re-elected, in Bow and Bromley George Lansbury captured a seat held until 1907 by the Liberal-Labour Ben Cooper who had then been ousted through S.D.F. opposition, and in Poplar R. C. K. Ensor succeeded to Will Crooks' seat. Ensor, Lansbury and Frank Smith tried to form an L.C.C. Labour Party, but since Ensor's election manifesto had openly advised the electorate to give their second vote to the Progressive ship-owner Sir John McDougall, and Frank Smith had sat for many years as a Progressive councillor, only Lansbury could claim much real independence.

[1] The candidates opposed by the Progressives were W. H. Humphreys, Battersea, 489; George Horne, East St. Pancras, 295; Rev. J. H. Harley, South-West Bethnal Green, 512; W. T. Kelly, Peckham, 499; Dr W. T. Davidson and J. T. Westcott, Hammersmith, 897 and 737. For J. J. Stephenson in Fulham, *Fulham Observer*, 22 February 1907. The three supported by the Progressives were Frank Smith, and Rev. Jenkins Jones and George Lansbury in Woolwich, who polled 7880 and 7661 against 8904 and 8677.

[2] 8 March 1907.

[3] In Kennington Gilbert Dale was offered a straight fight as a Progressive, but refused (*Daily News*, 24 February 1910). He polled 980. In Bermondsey Dr Salter had come over to the I.L.P. after his election as a Progressive County Councillor in 1907, and the I.L.P. hoped that he would be given a straight fight (*Southwark Recorder*, 10 September, 17 September 1909). The I.L.P. had opposed the Progressives in the Borough Council elections, and Salter had stood as Labour candidate in a three-cornered bye-election in November 1909, resulting in a Conservative gain. Although he stood down in January 1910 the bitterness of the local Liberals was such that they insisted, in spite of pressure from their local leaders, in opposing Salter (*Southwark Recorder*, 11 February 1910). In Greenwich there was no strong I.L.P., but Gilbert, London district secretary of the Engineering & Shipbuilding Trades' Federation, benefitted from the adjacent Labour strength of Deptford, and polled 1161. The candidates supported by the Progressives were Rev. Jenkins Jones and Margaret Bondfield in Woolwich, Dr Ethel Bentham in North Kensington, Frank Smith in North Lambeth, George Lansbury in Bow and Bromley and R. C. K. Ensor in Poplar.

The 1913 election was worse. Both Lansbury and Ensor were disillusioned and did not stand again. S.D.F. candidates stood for Bow and Bromley, and lost in a three-cornered fight; Susan Lawrence of the I.L.P. was given a straight fight in Poplar, and held the seat. All the other candidates were defeated, including Frank Smith at North Lambeth, two candidates at Woolwich and one at Deptford, all of whom were given straight fights. Nearly all these opposed by Progressives fared worse than in 1910.[1]

The record for the London Borough Councils was equally disheartening. In each of the triennial elections of 1906, 1909 and 1912 the I.L.P. claimed some responsibility for about eighty of the candidates standing, although over 1,200 seats were vacant.[2] In nearly every borough except Woolwich these candidates were opposing all parties, and in a number of cases they ran as socialists jointly with the S.D.F. (or B.S.P.). Except for Islington, conflict with S.D.F. candidates was always avoided. Wherever a local Labour Party existed the I.L.P. worked with it. On each occasion about twenty candidates were successful. Nearly all of them were elected in Poplar, Shoreditch, Woolwich and Kensington; no other borough had more than two I.L.P. victories. Of these four boroughs, only Kensington could claim a strongly-rooted I.L.P. movement. In Shoreditch the S.D.F. was the dominant influence in a socialist rather than Labour Party alliance. In Woolwich the I.L.P. had developed as a propagandist ally of the Labour Party, and at one time had nearly 500 members including more than half the Labour borough councillors. In spite of this it was overshadowed in every way by the Labour Representative Association, which had a larger membership, committees in every ward, a more active social life, an outstandingly successful local weekly newspaper, and complete control of the labour movement in the borough. When the branch came under the control of local extremists, and eventually in 1911 seceded to the B.S.P., the Woolwich labour movement was not significantly disturbed.

In Poplar the I.L.P. blossomed and withered into equal sudden-

[1] The candidates supported by the Progressives were Susan Lawrence in Poplar, Frank Smith in North Lambeth, William Sanders and Margaret Bondfield in Woolwich, and C. M. Lloyd in Deptford. Those opposed were Gilbert Dale in Kennington, Dr Salter and Charles Ammon in Bermondsey, and Dr Ethel Bentham and W. J. Jarrett in North Kensington. They polled 1121, 1632, 1374, 1099 and 998 respectively.

[2] Analysis from local newspapers, the *Labour Leader, Justice, Clarion,* September-November 1906, 1909 and 1912; and *Daily Herald* and *Daily Citizen,* September-October 1912. In a number of cases it is not possible to distinguish I.L.P. candidates from others running as Labour or Socialist, so that the number of candidates cannot be exact. Until 1909 lists of elected I.L.P. councillors were published in I.L.P. conference reports.

ness. The Poplar Labour Party had been built up by the Bow and Bromley S.D.F., and the Bow and Bromley I.L.P. only came into being in 1906 because George Lansbury and his friends were unable to accept the S.D.F. hostility to the Labour Party. Within four years Poplar had three I.L.P. branches with six members on the borough council, six Guardians, two London County Councillors, and Lansbury as Member of Parliament.

In George Lansbury the London I.L.P. at last acquired a champion of the kind it needed; a man who somehow contrived to be both a local employer and a man of the people, reconverted to Anglicanism yet a convinced revolutionary, a militant suffragist, a syndicalist and a democrat; a man whose transparent honesty and flair for publicity built up an exceptional personal following. Lansbury's election propaganda already mixed religious and socialist phrases in a strange and scarcely logical manner: 'the flag we march under is the flag which means that we are all members one of another, that the highest thing in life is giving and not receiving, and that human life and human happiness is of more importance than money'.[1] But even if offensive to the purist, it was certainly effective. The same can be said of his behaviour in Parliament. However much Ramsay MacDonald scorned 'the Lansbury antics', they displayed a genuine conviction and strength of feeling that was shown by too few Labour M.P.s.[2]

At the same time Lansbury's reputation was heightened by his appointment to the Royal Commission on the Poor Law, by the attacks of John Burns the humane policy of the Poplar Guardians, by the issue of the Commission's Minority report in which he gave his assistance to Beatrice Webb, and finally by the launching, in the spring of 1912, of the *Daily Herald*. As editor of the *Herald* he gave it all his wide sympathy and zest; the paper was exciting to read, its cartoons memorable, its leaders aggressive without being bitter, its news open to all sections of the labour movement.

The *Daily Herald* was not, however, to the liking of the parliamentary leaders of the I.L.P., and in October 1912 the *Daily Citizen* was brought out as a rival. It was pompous and monotonous, weak in its news coverage, roused little support in London, and to Lansbury must have seemed a calculated insult. Shortly afterwards, equally provoked by the failure of the parliamentary Labour Party to give sufficient support to women's suffrage, Lansbury made his extraordinary decision to resign from Parliament and fight a bye-election

[1] G. Lansbury, manifesto, Borough Council election 1906, Poplar public library.
[2] J. R. MacDonald to J. B. Glasier, 11 November 1911; Lord Elton, *The Life of James Ramsay MacDonald*, p. 162.

as an independent socialist on the issue of votes for women. Bewildered by his behaviour, by the influx of suffragette canvassers and by the indifference of the national Labour Party, the loyalty of Lansbury's supporters proved insufficient to hold the seat. The only I.L.P. constituency in London was thus thrown away. The Bow and Bromley I.L.P. disintegrated, and the energy of the Poplar socialists was henceforward expressed through the B.S.P. and the suffragette movement. In the rest of London the Daily Herald League formed a kind of personal Lansbury party. The loss of Poplar was a bitter blow to the London I.L.P., revealing its lack of strong local roots. In vain Lansbury was asked to 'come back into the movement, come back with your old fire and enthusiasm, resume your place at the head of the London movement'.[1]

There was one other field of I.L.P. success outside the county, West Ham, where the I.L.P. had six or more of the Labour councillors. West Ham suggests another characteristic of the London I.L.P. Here again there was an old Labour Party, taking its tone from the trade unions and the S.D.F., but in this case there had been a less dramatic shift to the I.L.P. after 1900. It was notable that the I.L.P. councillors included only one trade unionist. Of nine others who were at some time councillors, two were teachers, one in social work, two in business and two lawyers.[2] The social contrast with the S.D.F. is clear.

Certainly the rank and file of the East End I.L.P. branches in these years was largely working class. R. C. K. Ensor warned potential middle class recruits from the Fabian Society that they would find 'men and women of every grade; . . . perhaps a Gasworker in the chair, and a clerk or railway servant reading the minutes; their dialect, their modes of thought, their lack of education which he has, their knowledge of things about which he is entirely ignorant, all bewilder and repel him. He needs something of a "conversion" to find his feet.'[3] Even so there were more middle class men than trade unionists among the leaders of the London I.L.P.

Certainly a number of important trade unionists belonged to the I.L.P., among them the Secretaries of the Furniture Trades Association, the Bakers' London district, and the Compositors. The Engineers were strong in prominent I.L.Pers, and so were the women trade unionists. But very few of these were active supporters. Tom Naylor of the Compositors, a colourless person, was not strong enough to

---

[1] I.L.P. conference report, 1913.
[2] Professions of election candidates from *Stratford Express, West Ham Guardian* and *West Ham and South Essex Mail*.
[3] R. C. K. Ensor, memorandum on the I.L.P., September 1907, Fabian Society archives.

maintain the union's parliamentary levy after the Osborne Judgement or to impose any unity on the labour movement in Islington. Alex Gossip of the Furniture Trades Association gave most of his energy to the Socialist Sunday Schools. Only Charles Ammon of the Fawcett Association and R. M. Gentry of the Bakers were active members of decent local I.L.P. branches, and Ammon's union disaffiliated from the Labour Party in 1908.[1] No London trade unions were spheres of I.L.P. influence, and on the London Trades Council the I.L.P. was damagingly weak. Apart from Woolwich and Poplar, none of the stronger branches had any firm local trade union backing. In North Kensington the trade unions were unimportant, while in Bermondsey and Finsbury they were closer to the Liberal Party.

The geographical distribution of the London I.L.P. branches emphasises this weakness. There were a number of notably weak working class districts.[2] On the other hand in the 'better class districts' of 'black-coated proletarians',[3] there was a good spread of branches. Two of the best branches, at one time each with over 200 members, were significantly in Clapham and East Ham.[4]

It would appear that the I.L.P. was fulfilling a dual role. In some districts it was taking the place of the S.D.F. as the socialist element in the Labour Party. In others it was developing into the middle class socialist party which had been the ambition of some of the Fabian rebels. In contrast to the scarcity of trade union leaders, it was easy to find schoolmasters and clergy, rich City men, stockbrokers and company secretaries, in the I.L.P. ranks. Ensor knew of 'no branch

---

[1] Ammon was a leader of the Bermondsey I.L.P., L.C.C. candidate in 1913, and editor of his union's journal. Gentry was a Fulham I.L.P. Borough Council candidate in 1909 and 1912, and later branch secretary (*Fulham Observer*, November 1909 and 1912, *Labour Who's Who*, 1927). Of the Engineers, Barnes the secretary belonged to the City I.L.P.; J. J. Stephenson was prominent in the Lewisham Labour Party, but not in the weak I.L.P. branch, which did not claim him as a member; Isaac Mitchell was a nominal member of Clapham I.L.P., an L.C.C. Progressive alderman until he resigned in 1907 to join the Board of Trade (I.L.P. Metropolitan District Council report, 1903–4; *Fabian News*, December 1907). In addition, William Devenay, the Dockers' London organiser, appears in I.L.P. conference reports as a West Ham I.L.P. councillor, and A. G. Cameron, the Carpenters' London organiser, was on the London I.L.P. speakers list, 1910 (Herbert Bryan Collection).

[2] E.g. Southwark, Deptford, North Camberwell, North Lambeth, Battersea, Bethnal Green, Stepney.

[3] Ensor, op. cit., memorandum on the I.L.P., and memorandum on 'the position of East London', 1907, to the I.L.P. National Council, Ensor Collection.

[4] Clapham, *Labour Leader*, 30 April 1909; East Ham branch revived 1906, within a year average branch attendance 85 (G. Dean to R. C. K. Ensor, 26 November 1907, Ensor Collection), membership reached 300 (*Labour Leader* 6 March 1908), but after 1910 few signs of existence.

which would not welcome a middle class candidate for membership; and so far from suspecting him, the danger usually is that the less educated members will defer to him for more than he is worth. . . . Few branches do not contain some, many contain many, and some contain a majority.'[1]

As a result in working class districts the I.L.P. was often like a missionary organisation, revolving round a middle class leader. C. M. Lloyd ran the Bethnal Green branch from Toynbee Hall, Clement Attlee the Limehouse branch from Haileybury House.[2] Ben Keeling decided after Cambridge to 'select a working class borough and settle down there next October or September, do everything I can in the way of local politics and administration, possibly try my hand at some writing, anyhow finish off my Bar exams, and look out for the secretaryship of any public or semi-public committee which is going.'[3] He chose Walworth, but was not very successful. R. C. K. Ensor went down from Oxford to Poplar in the same spirit. In two districts, Bermondsey and Hammersmith, local doctors formed the branch nucleus.[4] Characteristically the Bermondsey branch ran a poor man's lawyer service and took over a bakery to produce unadulterated bread on co-operative lines. In West Islington Dora Goddard concentrated her effort on a factory girls club, arranging country holidays for girls, raising funds through evening school teaching. She thought it 'the only way of forming a women's movement in this slum'.[5] Margaret McMillan opened a clinic in Bow in 1908, and settled in Deptford in 1910.[6] In the opinion of the *Daily Citizen* the Margaret MacDonald infant clinic in Kensington did 'more for the labour cause in that borough than a thousand bitter and angry speeches'.[7] The branch leaders here were a doctor, and a sociologist.[8] The secretary, G. E. O'Dell, was a clerk and a 'highly respected lecturer in the Ethical church', author of *The Problem of the*

---

[1] Ensor, op. cit., memorandum on the I.L.P.
[2] Both were branch secretaries; letters in Ensor Collection.
[3] E. Townsend (ed.), *Keeling Letters and Re-collections*, London 1918, p. 30.
[4] In Bermondsey Dr Salter and his partners Dr Lowe and Dr Stratton (Brockway, *Bermondsey Story*, London 1949, p. 33), in Hammersmith, Dr Davidson, chairman of the Liberal Association, resigned to support the Labour candidate in a three-cornered fight after failing to secure a compromise because of the obstinacy of 'the Whigs' (*West London Advertiser*, 16 September 1904); an I.L.P. branch was then formed, he was its best candidate in the borough council elections of 1906–9 and superintendent of the Socialist Sunday School (*Young Socialist*, September 1906).
[5] D. Goddard to H. Bryan, 29 April 1914, General Correspondence, Herbert Bryan Collection.
[6] D'Arcy Cresswell, *Margaret McMillan; a Memoir*, London 1948.
[7] 4 November 1912.
[8] Dr Ethel Bentham and Marion Phillips.

Disappointed Soul.[1] He was quite ready to admit that the locals were 'not our best members. North Kensington is such a dead place that nearly all our really smart members come in from surrounding districts.'[2]

The two aspects of the I.L.P. could sometimes produce serious friction. Middle class men too easily tended to treat their poorer comrades as pupils rather than equals, and when a clash of policy came this could be awkward. Ensor himself in Poplar had to be frequently reminded by Lansbury that the Labour Party had been built before he came. When at the 1910 L.C.C. election the Poplar Labour Party refused to accept Ensor's determination to ask voters to support the Progressive as well as himself, he was enraged at their ingratitude. 'I have a fairly wide and deep knowledge of the middle class men in our movement and I honestly do not know a single man who has sacrificed to it nearly what I have. I have sacrificed, not great wealth but what is much harder, the practically certain prospects of it. I have sacrificed not merely leisure, pleasure and comfort but personal distinction, social esteem, friendships and family ties.'[3] Lansbury replied with commendable restraint that 'the discussion was an impersonal one so far as you were concerned. We all may be born fools but we certainly did discuss the matter without any personal heat.'[4]

Equally, these recruits could bring the I.L.P. great distinction. The City branch far outshone its Social Democratic equivalents. There were two City branches in this period. The first, which broke up in about 1906, published as series of tracts, including *Beginnings of Education* by Margaret McMillan, *Socialism for Children* by Katherine Glasier, and *William Morris* by his biographer Mackail. The second branch, founded in 1908, ran midday meetings for business men and specialised on industrial and financial problems. Among its members were Ensor, Haden Guest, Clifford Allen, Emil Davies and H. H. Schloesser, all talented Fabians. Meetings were addressed by Norman Angell, Beatrice Webb, Edward Carpenter, Patrick Geddes and Josiah Wedgewood. Destined to become an outstanding centre of anti-war propaganda after 1914, it showed its awareness (rare among English socialists) of international problems by setting up a special committee on foreign affairs.[5]

The City branch was an extreme example of the I.L.P. playing a

---

[1] Fred Hughes, *By Hand and Brain: The Story of the Clerical and Administrative Workers' Union*, London 1953, p. 18.
[2] G. O'Dell to J. R. MacDonald, 23 July 1906, Labour Party correspondence.
[3] R. C. K. Ensor to G. Lansbury, 4 February 1910, Lansbury Collection.
[4] G. Lansbury to R. C. K. Ensor, 4 February 1910, Ensor Collection.
[5] I.L.P. City branch minutes and correspondence, Herbert Bryan Collection.

Fabian role. The life of the typical I.L.P. branch was much closer to that of the S.D.F. Although individual house to house canvassing was already a feature of the I.L.P. in south-east London, for most branches the summer was devoted to outdoor propaganda. Any competent socialist speaker was in great demand. Ensor received a 'call from Tottenham' in typical style. 'I might say we intend to give the working people of our district an opportunity this summer of knowing what socialism is. We must strain every effort for such an inspiring object and I feel certain if you can you will give us a helping hand to do so. We must leave no stone unturned in spreading the good news.'[1] There was more concentration in the I.L.P. on special national campaigns, such as for school meals, and on local weeks 'missions', but in general the work was very similar to that of the S.D.F. Similarly in the winter there would be lectures and socialist songs, often in somewhat discouraging premises. The Finsbury branch met in a basement with no furniture but a few chairs, a dresser for the branch library, a floorcloth, and a table covered with green baize. On the walls three Walter Crane cartoons, and portraits of Morris, Hyndman and Hardie, helped to conceal the damp patches. Sometimes in their cellars, the I.L.P. showed some of the fervour of a religious sect. The Finsbury branch indeed included the most fashionable Congregational preacher in London, the Rev. R. J. Campbell.[2] The Bermondsey branch included an Anglican clergyman, two Nonconformist ministers, and five Methodist lay preachers; 'the early supporters were in fact drawn largely from the chapels and missions of Bermondsey'.[3] There was a definite difference here from the Social Democrats, who would not often have a member described as 'a "revolutionist" and a Christian';[4] but the spirit could easily be paralleled, and in the Socialist Sunday Schools the two traditions were intertwined.

The fact that the I.L.P. contained more professing Christians and more middle class men than the S.D.F. did not necessarily mean that its political standpoint was more cautious. The *Labour Leader* in 1907 had declared that London needed less of the S.D.F. and 'more of the I.L.P. and its saner methods of propaganda'.[5] Yet the London branches, to Ramsay MacDonald's irritation, welcomed Grayson with widespread enthusiasm, and eventually at least two of the

[1] G. E. Miller to R. C. K. Ensor, 1908 n.d., Ensor Collection.
[2] Finsbury I.L.P. branch minute book, 1900–2 Francis Johnson Collection; F. Brockway, *Inside the Left, Thirty Years of Platform, Press, Prison and Parliament*, London 1942, pp. 21–23.
[3] F. Brockway, *Bermondsey Story*, p. 33.
[4] Hope Johnson of Clapham, described by H. M., *Labour Leader*, 18 September 1913.
[5] 8 March 1907.

largest branches followed Grayson into the B.S.P.[1] Another of the largest branches, Clapham, refused to accept official suggestions that Thomas Jackson, late of the revolutionary S.P.G.B., was an unsuitable recruit.[2] The London District Council is to be found on more than one occasion planning joint demonstrations with the B.S.P. It declared that membership of the National Liberal Club was inconsistent with membership of the I.L.P.; it condemned the failure to contest the second seat at Leicester in 1913; it passed a resolution at its conference in February 1912 calling for more independence from the parliamentary Labour Party.[3] Clearly, even if the growth of the I.L.P. had been due to the political failure of the S.D.F., the new recruits were easily influenced by the atmosphere of London socialism.

In its political role, substituting the S.D.F. as the socialist element in the Labour Party, the I.L.P. had met with a few successes and a good many failures. Its unsuccessful efforts to found a London Labour Party are described in a subsequent Chapter. But what of its impact on this atmosphere of London socialism? How far had its 'thoroughly English' version of socialism replaced the S.D.F.'s 'sour creed, imported from abroad'? Can it in fact be claimed that the prevailing theoretical atmosphere in 1914 was derived either from the Social Democrats, the Fabians or the I.L.P.?

Certainly there is little evidence that in London the influence of either Fabians or I.L.P. had succeeded in 'putting paid to Marxism'.[4] Where Marx was mentioned in the 1900s (outside the inner circles of the Fabian Society) it was not to abuse him. In a characteristic exchange between an S.D.Fer and an I.L.Per on political tactics the

[1] E.g. J. R. MacDonald to C. Hill, secretary North Islington I.L.P., 20 October 1908; 'I have no intention, nor have any of my colleagues in the House, of repeating the silly theatricalities of Mr. Grayson. ... Any fool can get suspended, but it requires push and consistent work to get something done'; Hill replied that the branch considered this letter a 'deliberate insult'; Labour Party correspondence. The demand for Grayson as a speaker is shown by numerous letters in the Ensor Collection. East Ham branch, the second largest in London at the time, demanded a ballot on whether the I.L.P. should remain affiliated to the Labour Party (I.L.P. National Council minutes, 4 October 1907). Stoke Newington, the second largest north London branch, and Woolwich, the largest branch, seceded.
[2] It was claimed that 'letters exist which state his intention of joining the I.L.P. to "bleed the swine"'; W. G. Gilbert, South London Federation secretary, and Arthur Peters, national Labour party agent, made Jackson's admission a personal question, and resigned when defeated (H. Dubery to R. C. K. Ensor, 1909 n.d., Ensor Collection).
[3] I.L.P. Metropolitan District Council minutes, 14 January 1907; I.L.P. London Divisional Council minutes, February 1912 and January 1913.
[4] See Introduction; M. Cole, op. cit., p. 328.

latter protested 'it is as devout admirer of Karl Marx that I support the L.R.C. movement'.[1] Although the Engineers' leaders at this time were I.L.Pers, the union's *Journal* can be found publishing articles describing Marx as 'a profound thinker' who 'put socialism on a scientific basis', a man of 'great and generous' character who gave forty-four years 'service to humanity'.[2] In 1905 the Labour Mayor of Woolwich, a Unitarian minister, the Rev. Jenkins Jones, a man throughout his career associated with the most moderate wing of the labour movement, can be discovered advancing the Marxist theory of history. He declared Marx to be 'one of the greatest, if not the greatest writer of the 19th century on economic questions'. He expounded the theory of historical change based upon productive methods, and argued that 'religion was an effect rather than a cause'. Jenkins Jones concluded that he would like his audience to 'take their share in the revolution which was coming; it might be a bloodless one, or a bloody one, but it was coming. They could not stop it— Marx had pointed that out to them absolutely. He urged them all to be prepared to take their part in the upheaval and transformation of social life, which must be the climax and purpose of our existence in this world.'[3]

His audience, a branch of the Engineers, greeted his conclusion with applause. But what is equally revealing is that they were not so much Marxists and anti-Marxists; they were largely unaware of his theory. Jenkins Jones expected that he had chosen 'a subject which was perhaps a little strange to them. . . . He did not think that Marx was as widely known in England as he ought to be.' Some years later, in 1917, when a newly-convinced pacifist joined the Bermondsey I.L.P., he took out the volumes of *Capital* in the Bermondsey public library. The librarian, who had been in charge since the I.L.P. branch had been founded in 1908, told him that he was the first person that he could remember borrowing the book.[4]

There were no S.D.F. branches in Bermondsey and Woolwich, but these two incidents do suggest that the real situation was not one of strong pro-Marxism or anti-Marxism so much as theoretical vacuum. There were two reasons for this. Firstly, although the early Fabians had succeeded in discrediting Marx with many intellectual socialists, they had soon lost interest in their alternative Jevonsian theories, and after the death of William Morris few of the best writers among socialist intellectuals showed much interest in socialist theory. In fact the most videly read socialist theorist was almost certainly still John

[1] *Woolwich Pioneer*, 21 July 1905.
[2] *Amalgamated Engineers Journal*, April-June 1907.
[3] *Woolwich Pioneer*, 14 April 1905.
[4] Jimmy Jacques; interview, 1 April 1963.

Ruskin.[1] The Fabians failure to produce a widely held revisionist doctrine meant that their theoretical influence was largely negative. Secondly, although London with its lack of working class Nonconformity and its secularist traditions offered no strong resistance to Marxist theory, its widespread religious indifference resulted in an indifference to political doctrine. It was significant that many of the best known London Marxists came from exceptional religious minorities such as the Jews and the Irish. Consequently the Social Democrats were able to preach Marxist socialism without encountering much hostility, but it cannot be said that their ideas were ever widely held. An instinctive acceptance of certain Marxist concepts, such as the class struggle, became a characteristic of the Labour Party, but its implications were not worked out.

It has frequently been argued that this Fabian abdication of theoretical leadership was compensated by a concentration on practical problems. But Dr. McBriar has shown that in fields such as education and municipal socialism the original Fabian contribution was small.[2] In this period, while there were plenty of Fabian tracts on questions such as school nurseries and health committees, the real problems ahead, such as the control of finance and banking or the nationalisation of the major industries had been largely forgotten. As Bland wrote to Shaw in 1910, 'we have published a tract upon Railway Nationalisation, but we did not do even that until another Society had been formed for the same end and had also published tracts. The socialism of the Basis, the transfer of industries, has been entirely sidetracked by the Society. We never even mention it. ... If everything that we have been proposing were carried out tomorrow we should be no nearer or very little nearer to Socialism or to anything worth fighting for than we are today. The working people's children would be cleaner, and have better teeth; most of them would be wearing spectacles, and the wives of them would have comfortable lyings-in; but the capitalist would still be ramping over them as he is today and making even more profit out of them than he makes today. ... Look at our lectures for the coming season! Socialism and the Subject Races, Socialism and Crime! But what on earth is the use of our talking about socialism and anything when we do nothing whatever to advocate socialism? Consider all this ferment

[1] An analysis of reading in London libraries, *London*, 19 April 1894, showed the great popularity of Ruskin, especially *Unto This Last*. In Whitechapel Marx and Thorold Rogers were read extensively. George Lansbury read William Morris, *News From Nowhere*, Hyndman's *England for All*, Bellamy's *Looking Backward*, and 'with much mental strain', *Capital*, but the 'Fabians were much too clever and superior for ordinary persons like myself'. (*Labour Leader*, 17 May 1912.)
[2] McBriar, op. cit., pp. 193, 209, 215, &c.

and unrest in the labour world just now. The Society does not ever think about it, much less say anything about it. It is deaf and dumb, our lecturers go forth and lecture on the care of the aged, on the endowment of maternity, etc., etc., but they never so much as mention a proposal that would put a half-penny into the workman's pocket. . . . We know all about the paupers and invalids but nothing at all about the people who do the work.[1]

This is a harsh assessment, but it is difficult to contradict. The most important practical socialist policies in housing, education and economic policy came from the S.D.F., and the S.D.F. with the I.L.P. campaigned for them in London. In practical policies, just as in political theory and in political tactics, Fabian influence had been seriously over-estimated. The London socialist movement in 1914, in spite of the growth of the I.L.P., still owed more of its character and achievement to the much abused S.D.F.

[1] H. Bland to G. B. Shaw, 13 October 1910, Shaw Collection.

XI

LOCAL LABOUR PARTIES

BEFORE discussing the growth of the Labour Party as a whole in London, and the events which led to the founding of the London Labour Party, it will be best to consider the separate development of local Labour Parties in the London boroughs. They were the political basis upon which the London Labour Party was built, and their history illuminates its character, the difficult processes by which it was formed, and the prospects which faced it in 1914.

By 1914 most London districts were covered by a local Labour Party or by a Trades Council serving the same purpose. Some covered more than one constituency and several were irregular in their affiliation to the national Labour Party. Thus in 1911 there were 15 affiliated local Labour Parties within the county and 6 others out of the county. By 1914 the number of affiliated parties had fallen to 10 within and 5 out of the county. In contrast, at the London Labour Party conference in May 1914 23 local Labour Parties were represented from the county alone.

There were six boroughs in which there was no Labour Party. Three, Chelsea, Stoke Newington and the City, were wealthy districts, politically hopeless for Labour. But the other three, Bethnal Green, Stepney and Camberwell, were working class boroughs, and the failure of the Labour Party to establish a foothold in them is interesting. In all three the most serious difficulty was probably the chronic poverty typical of the inner working class districts, breeding a political apathy which made a labour or socialist movement peculiarly hard to establish. In Bethnal Green the small scale industry and stable population of the borough assisted the survival of an old-fashioned passive radicalism which has been described in Chapter Eight. In 1914, with the Liberal loss of one constituency in a bye-election and the election of the first Labour councillor, there were signs of impending change. In Stepney and Camberwell there were no such successful local Progressive Parties and the Borough Councils were controlled by the Conservatives, but the local importance in Camberwell of H. R. Taylor and in Stepney of W. C. Steadman and then Harry Gosling acted as a similar obstacle to a new alignment. Steadman was a Liberal-Labour M.P. and all three were L.C.C. labour bench Progressives who depended upon local Liberal Party support. Finally, in Stepney and Camberwell the Irish colonies with their attachment to Liberalism proved an added obstacle.

In six predominantly middle class boroughs, Hampstead, St. Marylebone, Westminster, Wandsworth, Greenwich and Lewisham, Labour Parties were founded but predictably failed to make any headway. In the last three boroughs although there were considerable working class districts the middle class population had still been growing rapidly in the 1900s, and the stage of social decline, which would bring them to the Labour Party within a generation, had not yet set in.

There are thus twenty remaining Labour Parties to be considered. They fall into four political groups. Firstly, eleven were based on local socialist movements. Secondly, four were of a Liberal-Labour character. Thirdly, four districts were hopelessly divided between these two approaches. Finally, one borough, Woolwich, had a Labour Party which had brought the two wings together and which showed the potential strength and quality of such an alliance.

The eleven socialist-led Labour Parties illustrate the effects of the policies and characteristics of the Social Democrats and the I.L.P. described in Chapters Nine and Ten.

By far the strongest were the two old parties which had developed in West Ham and Poplar before 1900. Both were strongly backed by local trade unionism, particularly by the Gas Workers' branches. Whether known as trade unionists or as socialists, most of their leaders were in fact declared socialists, and before the disaffiliation of the S.D.F. from the Labour Party most of them were Social Democrats.

In West Ham the Party organisation was rudimentary. The Trades Council was affiliated to the national Labour Party from 1901 until 1905, when it disaffiliated on the ground that the fees for Trades Councils were too high.[1] It was an active body, forming ward committees, publishing a monthly paper the *West Ham Tribune*, and conducting registration work.[2] For elections it formed a joint committee with the I.L.P. and the S.D.F. In 1906 the Trades Council formed a local L.R.C. which affiliated to the Labour Party, but it was apparently shortlived, and the joint election committee arrangement was probably revived in 1907. It is unlikely that any ward committees

[1] J. Gilbey to J. R. MacDonald, 21 July 1905, Labour Party correspondence.
[2] *West Ham Tribune*, January and August 1903.

LOCAL LABOUR PARTIES

survived. But although its organisation remained elementary, the West Ham Labour Party was undoubtedly vigorous, securing a clean sweep of the fifteen seats in the southern half of the borough in most local elections and a comfortable majority for Will Thorne in Parliament, and maintaining through its socialist branches a constant propaganda.

In Poplar similarly a constant minority of ten Labour members of the Borough Council was secured and a vigorous socialist propaganda was maintained. The party organisation, however, was much more elaborate. Until 1904 it was somewhat confused, the S.D.F. dominant in Bow, the Gas Workers and the Trades Council in Bromley, and the Poplar Labour League in south Poplar. In 1904 the whole borough was organised into a Trades and Labour Representation Committee, to which socialist and trade union branches and the Labour League affiliated.[1] Within a year 28 trade union branches were affiliated, providing a total income of £158, not a large enough sum for effective work.[2] In 1908 the party therefore decided to develop individual membership 'Woolwich pattern'.[3] Membership could be either through affiliated societies, or, for residents, by paying 1/– a year. Members were formed into ward committees, and the party governed by a general committee of one delegate from each ward and one for every 100 members from affiliated societies. The party's executive was composed of nine members elected by affiliated societies and three elected by the ward committees.[4] This constitution proved very successful. In 1909 the ward committees claimed 1,500 supporters.[5] By 1914 43 trade unions were affiliated, with an affiliated membership of more than 15,000.[6] Registration work was conducted with energy, and the party published a periodical, the *Bow and Bromley Worker*, from 1909 until 1912.

Although in 1914 its local strength was undiminished, the Poplar Labour Party had been disaffiliated by the national Labour Party for its support for George Lansbury as an independent socialist. The process, described in Chapters Nine and Ten, by which Lansbury as a Social Democrat was Labour Party candidate for Bow and Bromley in 1900, left the S.D.F. when it disaffiliated from the Labour Party

---

[1] Poplar Trades and L.R.C. report, December 1904.
[2] Poplar Trades and L.R.C. report, 1905.
[3] R. C. K. Ensor, diary, 4 July 1907, Ensor Collection.
[4] Poplar Labour and Socialist Representation Committee rules, 1908, copy in Ensor Collection.
[5] *Bow and Bromley Worker*, December 1909.
[6] They included 6 branches of Gas Workers, 4 of Railwaymen, 2 of Engineers and 3 of Dockers—Poplar L.R.C. circular, March 1914, copy in Poplar Library; cf. *Bow and Bromley Worker*, November 1911, which reported that 40 trade union branches were affiliated with 10,000 members.

and did not stand again until 1910, captured the seat and finally threw it away in protest against the parliamentary Labour Party's subservience to the Liberals, shows both on the one hand the self-inflicted loss brought to the S.D.F. by its isolation from the Labour Party and equally on the other hand the Labour Party's need to pursue a vigorous independent policy if it was to hold a constituency with a socialist-led Labour Party.

The effect of S.D.F. disaffiliation is equally evident in the nine other socialist-led Labour Parties. Hackney and Walthamstow, which had begun with S.D.F. backing, failed to take root. In Shoreditch S.D.F. influence resulted in the fruitless tactics described in Chapter Nine. Hammersmith and Fulham, in which the S.D.F. had also been the leading element, became I.L.P. parties, dogged but not very successful. Subsequently the I.L.P. led the formation of Labour Parties in Wood Green and Willesden, and with increasing assistance from the Social Democrats these achieved good local election performances. The I.L.P. also established a strong party in North Kensington, with a foothold on the Borough Council, and in Bermondsey the outstanding I.L.P. branch was by 1914 beginning to win over the local trade unionists to the Labour Party which it had formed. Some of these parties undertook registration work, but none had a significant organisation outside their affiliated trade unions and socialist branches.[1] Their elementary state of development clearly reflects both the failure of S.D.F. support and the weakness of the London I.L.P. with the trade unions.

There were four local parties of a Liberal-Labour character. Of these four, by 1914 the party in Finsbury was moribund. The borough was an old working class area, the traditional centre of London secularism and militant radicalism, but it was suffering from the same kind of political apathy as Bethnal Green and Stepney, and Conservative control of its politics was made easier by the encroachment of City warehouses and offices on its southern fringe. In the early 1900s a Borough Council labour group was formed with Edward Garrity, assistant secretary of the Railway Servants and President of East Finsbury Liberal and Radical Club, as its chairman,[2] and W. C. Steadman was selected as a Labour Party candidate. He refused, however, to sign the Labour Party constitution, and thus sat

---

[1] Registration work was reported by the Hackney Trades Council (Hackney S.D.F. branch minutes, 12 August 1904), Hammersmith L.R.C. (A. Batstone to J. R. MacDonald, 15 October 1905, Labour Party correspondence, and *West London Observer*, 24 September 1907) and Wood Green Labour League (H. Tudor Rhys to J. R. MacDonald, 18 June 1907, Labour Party correspondence).

[2] *Holborn and Finsbury Guardian*, 27 October 1906; see also Appendix D.

from 1906 until his defeat in 1910 as a Liberal-Labour M.P. The socialists, who had earlier co-operated, were alienated and the labour movement split. Although *Justice* was produced in Clerkenwell and the I.L.P. head office which was nearby helped to run a vigorous I.L.P. branch, the socialists failed to make much local impact, securing only one councillor in 1912. The radical tradition was upheld with little more success by Garrity, who from 1909 was the only Liberal-Labour member of the Borough Council. His radicalism was clearly ageing, for in 1912 he accepted the chairmanship of the Conservative-controlled Holborn Board of Guardians.[1]

In contrast to Finsbury, the Liberal-Labour parties in Southwark and Battersea were very much alive. They have been described in detail in Chapter Eight as the principal examples of successful Progressive Parties based on trade union support. In both boroughs there were also well established socialist movements exerting a pressure against their Liberal allegiance. In Southwark it was clear that the Trades Council, which was affiliated to the Labour Party but maintained its Liberal connections, would soon be forced to commit itself more explicitly to either the Liberal or the Labour Party. In Battersea, where the Progressive Party was controlled by a working class majority, the ambiguous Liberal-Labour position was only maintained through the local influence of John Burns. Thus although there was as yet no more than a nominal affiliated Labour Party in either borough, the situation in both was unstable and there was a prospect in the not so distant future of their coming over to the Labour Party.

The fourth party in this group, Deptford, was rather different. It illustrates how a non-socialist Labour Party could succeed where the Liberal Party had failed, and then fall back into dependence on Liberalism.

Although the S.D.F. and the I.L.P. had originally prospered in Deptford, and a strong S.D.F. branch was to be revived after 1907, in the early 1900s the only socialist influence was that of the Fabians, Sidney Webb and R. C. Phillimore, who represented Deptford on the L.C.C. Consequently the initiative for independent labour representation came from the Deptford and Greenwich Trades Council. Working with the Liberals in 1900 and 1903 it secured the election of a minority of Labour borough councillors. The candidate at the 1900 General Election had been the Liberal-Labour Co-operator, Benjamin Jones, and although the Trades Council insisted that the candidate at the next General Election should be a Labour candidate endorsed by the national L.R.C. it was not expected that there would be difficulty in again securing the support of the Liberals.

[1] *Daily Herald*, 18 April 1912.

The Liberals, however, refused to co-operate. The difficulty began with the adoption of W. E. Clery, secretary of the Fawcett Association. Although talented, Clery was unreliable, frequently in debt through personal extravagance, and unwilling to accept the methods of the L.R.C.[1] Both Liberals and Trades Council agreed in repudiating his candidature in 1903.[2] The Labour men then adopted Bowerman, but although they made every effort to win over the Liberal Association they were forced into a three-cornered fight.[3] Bowerman's easy victory demonstrated the superior strength of the Labour Party.

The Liberals also forced a three-cornered fight in the 1906 Borough Council elections. The chairman of the Deptford Labour Association, B. T. Hall, secretary of the Working Men's Clubs and Institute Union and an old Fabian friend of Sidney Webb, managed to persuade the Association to send ten members to a confidential meeting with 'leading residents in the Borough . . . who prominently supported Mr. Bowerman M.P. at the General Election and whose sympathies and support are known to be with the labour cause'.[4] After this meeting, however, it was reported that 'no arrangement had been arrived at with the leading Liberals who supported Mr. Bowerman M.P. owing to the fact that the Liberal Association claimed all the seats in each ward contested'.[5]

The result of the 1906 Borough Council election was a disaster for both parties, and henceforward the Liberals favoured co-operation. The Deptford Labour Association endorsed the two Fabian Progressives at the 1907 L.C.C. election, allowed them to use the office as a committee room, and held a meeting in their support. Later in 1907 they decided to allow the Deptford Women's Liberal Association to meet in the Labour Association's office.[6] Then in the summer of 1908 they accepted 'overtures' by the Deptford Liberal, Radical and Progressive Association for 'joint action for registration purposes only'. A joint registration committee was set up, most of the funds coming from the Liberal side.[7] The arrangement was in fact vital to

[1] F. W. Galton, manuscript autobiography; L.R.C. conference report, 1903.
[2] J. Park to J. R. MacDonald, 7 July 1903, Labour Party correspondence.
[3] G. Vernall to J. R. MacDonald, 14 December 1903, ibid., states that Bowerman's committee 'attended' at the Liberal Association; see also Chapter 8.
[4] Deptford Labour Association. General Council minutes, 29 August 1906.
[5] Deptford Labour Association executive committee minutes, 16 September 1906.
[6] Deptford Labour Association General Council minutes, 5 December 1906 and 6 February 1907; 12 November 1908.
[7] Deptford Labour Association annual report, 1908; in the first year the joint committee's income was £105, including £5 from the Compositors and £25 from the Labour Association.

the Labour Association, for Bowerman's sponsors, the Compositors, refused to pay for registration work. It was negotiated by B. T. Hall, after he had had 'a friendly chat at the House of Commons' with Bowerman.[1] Although the Labour Association's General Council was not asked to ratify the decision until after the work had been finished, at its meeting in November 1908 the delegate who 'in strong terms denounced any arrangement with the Liberal Party' found only one supporter.[2] Encouraged by the Compositors and condoned by the national Labour Party, the joint registration committee continued annually until 1914.

It opened the way to further arrangements. Early in 1909, with Hall as intermediary, negotiations were opened for the next Borough Council and L.C.C. elections. It was decided to run three candidates for the six seats in each Borough Council ward 'as Labour candidates only and the Secretary was instructed to inform the Liberal Association accordingly'. There were also negotiations with the United Irish League for 'candidates running in conjunction with the Labour Party'.[3] All this was agreed without opposition by the Association's General Council, which accepted Hall's proposal for a 'Round Table Conference ... of all progressive forces'. The Council also agreed 'after a brief discussion' to sanction a joint candidature for the L.C.C. of Campion Watson the Tramworkers' secretary and Pethybridge 'a subscriber to this Association and the nominee of the Liberal Association ... as a safer means of securing success.[4] In fact, although Webb and Phillimore had held Deptford in the Progressive year of disaster in 1907, Deptford was lost to the Progressives in 1910.

By 1910 the Deptford Labour Association was beginning to worry the national Party. In reply to inquiries, the Association claimed that the joint registration committee was 'non-party', and refused to disaffiliate the Deptford Liberal Club as this had 'been connected with their organisation since its inception'.[5] Under the threat of disaffiliation they did agree to delete from their constitution a clause which allowed support not just for Labour candidates but for 'such other candidates as secure the endorsement of the Association'.[6]

[1] Deptford Labour Association executive committee minutes, 1 June 1908.
[2] Deptford Labour Association General Council minutes, 9 November 1908.
[3] Deptford Labour Association executive committee minutes, 8 February and 22 April, 3 and 23 September 1909.
[4] Deptford Labour Association General Council minutes, 2 July 1909, 18 February 1910.
[5] Deptford Labour Association executive committee minutes, 19 July 1910, and Labour Party National Executive Committee minutes, 30 January 1911.
[6] J. Middleton to J. Reid, 20 December 1911, and Reid to Middleton, 27 January 1912, Labour Party correspondence.

Nevertheless it was agreed in 1912 to support the candidates of the Women's Liberal Association for the Borough Council, and Hall again 'met three representatives of the Liberal Association' and agreed to concentrate on different wards.[1] At the same time a joint mass meeting 'with the local Progressive Associations' was held in support of the Home Rule Bill. In the 1913 L.C.C. election Phillimore decided to stand again, and the Labour Association ran only one candidate, C. M. Lloyd of Toynbee Hall, organised on an 'entirely independent basis', but making it clear that the Association 'were also wishful to see Mr. R. C. Phillimore elected'.[2]

There were two reasons for these compromising arrangements with the Liberals. The first was a cynicism due to success. In its early days the Association had been prepared to take a stand on the principal of independence. Bowerman's first agent even complained with most bitterness in 1903 about Labour men such as Crooks who supported Liberals. 'At Deptford, up till now we have been consistent, although we have had offers to trim that most of these men would have jumped at and considered quite orthodox. We intend to continue to be consistent if possible.'[3] Later, however, when Bowerman was secure, principle seemed less important, and the Labour Association was willing to co-operate with the Liberals in any way which would not lead to open repudiation by the national Labour Party.

The second reason was financial. The constitution of the Deptford Labour Association provided for individual members 'grouped into Ward Committees' as well as affiliated organisations.[4] Individual members and affiliated organisations each paid the same small sum, 1/- a year. In fact the individual membership remained low because the Association totally failed to draw in local socialist enthusiasts. It had no sympathy with the local S.D.F., and although when an I.L.P. branch was founded it agreed that it might affiliate, it refused to provide a meeting room at the office.[5] In spite of efforts in 1910 and 1913 to revive them, most of the Association's ward committees never met.[6] Thus, although the affiliated organisations included working men's clubs and the Deptford Fabian Group, it was in effect

[1] Deptford Labour Association executive committee minutes, 5 January 1912 and 11 October 1912.
[2] Deptford Labour Association annual report, 1912.
[3] G. Vernall to J. R. MacDonald, October 1903, Labour Party correspondence.
[4] Constitution, printed with Deptford Labour Association annual reports.
[5] Deptford Labour Association executive committee minutes, 7 February and 4 April 1911.
[6] Deptford Labour Association report of sub-committee, 25 May 1910, advising a 'special effort be made at once to re-organise the ward committees', and executive committee minutes, 11 October 1913.

a trade union party. But because the affiliation fee was only 1/– the income from the impressive list of affiliated trade unions was pathetically small, no more than £5 in most years, and the Association was forced to rely on donations and subscriptions. Some of these came from local trade unions and sympathisers, but in most years Bowerman and the Compositors between them provided nine tenths of the money.[1] Even so, it was not enough; the Association was driven to reduce the secretary's salary in May 1907, to fall back on the Liberals for registration funds, and eventually in 1910 to dismiss the secretary and replace him by voluntary helpers.[2]

The Deptford Labour Association in this period was an interesting local reflection of the national Labour Party in its close dependence on the Liberal Party. It showed that a local Labour Party of this type could win a constituency which the Liberal Party had found impossible. Equally, its failure in local elections and its financial weakness suggested that this kind of Labour Party could never become a formidable political organisation. In addition, it depended for its stability on a lack of serious friction with either Liberals and socialists, so that its future could never be very secure.

In fact in the last months of this period there were signs of change in the Deptford Labour Association. The formation of a Labour Choir in November 1913 and a Ladies Committee to assist on social occasions in January 1914 suggested that the Association was more genuinely eager to build up rank and file activity.[3] A scheme was drawn up for affiliation fees proportionate to membership, and submitted to trade union branches.[4] Delegates were sent to the London Labour Party Conference. Finally, encouraged by an offer of financial help from the Labour Party and by a surprise revival of friction over registration with the Liberal Association secretary, the Association decided to re-appoint its own paid agent and to face the task of finding the money for his salary.[5] The logical completion of these moves in the direction of political and financial independence would be to make use of the help of the local socialists.

The four hopelessly divided areas, Erith, Islington, Lambeth and St. Pancras, display in miniature the factors which hindered the unification of the London labour movement as a whole before 1914. It will be sufficient to take one example.

[1] E.g. 1912, when the income recorded in the annual report was £111, and the ledgers show donations from the Compositors totalling £100.
[2] Deptford Labour Association General Council minutes, 12 May 1907 and 2 June 1910.
[3] Ibid., 19 November 1913, and executive committee minutes, 6 January 1914.
[4] Deptford Labour Association executive committee minutes, 12 May 1914.
[5] Ibid., 23 June and 21 July 1914, and annual report, 1914.

Erith was a small Thameside industrial settlement just downstream from Woolwich, and like Woolwich dominated by the local Engineers, who controlled its Trades Council.[1] The S.D.F. had a branch of fluctuating strength, but there was never a successful I.L.P. branch. Throughout the period the theme was the alternating co-operation and hostility between the Trades Council and the Social Democrats.

The Trades Council secured its first important success at the District Council of 1904, when it put up eight candidates, including one Social Democrat, for the eight seats, and five were elected.[2] Unfortunately the Labour councillors did not work together well, so in 1905 it was decided to impose 'better discipline' on the candidates by running them on a detailed programme. Seven Labour candidates ran, supported by one independent socialist, Will Hampton, but none were elected. One Engineer who refused to accept the Labour programme was elected as a Progressive.[3] This precipitated the triple split of 1906, when Hampton and another socialist attacked the Labour candidates for no longer insisting on secular education, two former Labour councillors were re-elected as independents, and the Trades Council ran six Labour candidates of whom one was successful.[4]

In 1907 unity was recovered. Six Labour candidates, including a Social Democrat, were elected. In the Guardians election Hampton, who had supported the Labour candidates, narrowly missed election and in the Kent County Council election the Labour candidate, W. Ling of the Carpenters, was elected.[5] No doubt impressed by this success, the S.D.F. worked with the Labour Party until 1911. In fact the Labour candidates failed to repeat the success of 1907, largely because a frightened Ratepayer's Association redoubled its electoral efforts, easily outpacing the Labour canvassing, election motor cars and general organisation.[6] A united Labour Party might possibly have met this challenge, but the Social Democrats foolishly pushed their influence too far. Consequently in 1910 the candidates of the Labour Representation Association stood as 'Socialists' while Ling, the retiring Labour County Councillor, refused to run again 'under

[1] The Engineers' three branches had 600 members, the Trades Council 1000 members: Amalgamated Society of Engineers, quarterly reports; A. Scarlett to J. R. MacDonald, 7 February 1908, Labour Party correspondence.

[2] Labour election manifesto, including A. Scarlett, 28 March 1904, Labour Party correspondence; *Erith Times*, 5 February, 4 March, 1 April 1904.

[3] *Woolwich Pioneer*, 17 February, 18 August 1905; *Erith Times*, 17 March and 7 April 1905.

[4] *Erith Times*, 6 April 1906; W. Ling to J. R. MacDonald, 15 March 1906, Labour Party correspondence.

[5] *Woolwich Pioneer*, 29 March 1907; *Erith Times*, 22 March 1907 and 29 March 1907.

[6] *Woolwich Pioneer*, 13 March 1908.

the dictatorship of the S.D.P.' and was re-elected to the District Council as an independent.[1]

By 1911 the Social Democrats had again left the Labour Party.[2] In 1912 there were three-cornered fights between the socialists and the remaining Labour men, who had formed a United Workers' Association. Ling ran with this organisation in 1913, and was the only successful candidate, and at the same time his wife was elected a Guardian in a three-cornered fight in which Hampton, once so nearly successful, polled a miserable 193 votes.

The final twist to the story came in 1914, when socialists and Trades Council arranged to put up only seven candidates. One I.L.Per only was elected, although a socialist was able to win a straight fight for the Guardians election. Hampton, disgusted by this compromise (although he had accepted earlier arrangements of the same kind), decided to resign from the B.S.P., protesting that he had spent his 'whole life trying to build up a party of independent real Socialists and now just as it was becoming possible to force the issue with the vacillators the whole thing blows up'.[3]

Hampton and Ling spent most of these years working against each other, or at best in distrustful alliance. While together they could have made a powerful Labour stronghold of Erith, as rivals both were doomed to perpetual opposition. Yet although they represented the two wings of the Labour movement they had much in common. Ling, a carpenter, had first 'joined the Labour Party' in Australia in 1889. He was first elected to the School Board and the District Council as a labour representative in 1893-4, and remained a strong believer in the principle of independence. He refused to stand for re-election to the Kent County Council with Liberal financial assistance in 1910. He was convinced that capitalism could only produce waste and anarchy and that the future should be 'universal brotherhood'. He was a man of great personal integrity, noted for his 'courteous advocacy' and a 'popular favourite in the district'.[4]

Hampton was not a craftsman, and had none of Ling's moderate manner. He was a rough-looking man with keen eyes and strong features, a witty but somewhat 'rugged, uncouth' speaker with a talent for sledgehammer argument. But like Ling he was a man of great determination who had fought for his cause since the 1890s, a man who really believed in the brotherhood of man and was prepared to spend his life working for it. He was a total abstainer. Although

[1] *Erith Times*, 18 February and 18 March 1910.
[2] *Bexley Heath and Bexley Observer*, 31 March 1911.
[3] *Erith Times*, 14 March 1913; 20 and 27 March 1914.
[4] *Woolwich Pioneer*, 17 February 1905; cutting, 7 November 1911, scrapbook, Dartford public library; *Erith Times*, 8 and 22 March 1907, 18 February 1910.

largely self-educated he ran the Erith Socialist Sunday School, and was co-opted to the local Education Committee, seizing the opportunity to start free school meals. He lived for an ideal. 'I have nothing to recommend me,' he said, 'But my earnest desire to be of some service to the class to which I belong.'[1] It was a pathetic fate that, chiefly because of the misguided leadership of Hampton's party, these two idealists, in spite of all they had in common, were to spend their lives in fruitless antagonism.

The Woolwich Labour Party presents a happier contrast. It is the only example in London before 1914 of a Labour Party which absorbed both the Liberal-Labour and the socialist wings of the labour movement and showed the impressive force which could result from such a combination. The Woolwich Labour Party was more than a federation or an alliance. It was a new and powerful kind of political organisation with a character of its own.

The success of Labour in Woolwich was no doubt assisted by the character of the borough. Until the later 19th century Woolwich had been a small town, dependent on the dockyard, Arsenal and military barracks and so upon the politics of the capital, but still something of a market town with surrounding countryside and villages. There was no adequate tramway connection with London, and since the Thames passenger steamboats had ceased the only communication was by railway. Even when the houses of Greenwich gradually reached eastwards to link the town with the London built-up area, something of its independence remained. Woolwich was peculiar too in being a working-class community dependent on a single industry. In 1901, when the whole population including soldiers in the barracks was 118,000, the number of men employed in the Arsenal was 20,000.[2] A large proportion of these men were skilled artisans, and the Engineers alone had eight Woolwich branches with 2,000 members. Other nearby branches looked to Woolwich, and at the impressive Engineers' Club sixteen branches of the union held their meetings.[3] These skilled artisans, with their relatively stable employment, no doubt explain the success of the Royal Arsenal Co-operative Society. Although in West Ham and the north-east London suburbs Co-operative Societies were well established, Woolwich supported by far the largest, already covering the whole south-east London area from Greenwich and Lewisham to Erith. Besides being a commercial success, the Royal Arsenal Co-operative Society helped to develop the social and political consciousness of the

[1] *Erith Times*, 22 March 1907; Fox, op. cit., p. 119.
[2] *Woolwich Pioneer*, 19 April 1907.
[3] *Woolwich Labour Journal*, January 1902.

borough. Already in the 1890s it was sponsoring candidates in local elections, and in the general elections of 1892 and 1895 Ben Jones the Co-operator stood as a Liberal-Labour candidate. Through its Education Committee and its Womens Co-operative Guilds it fostered a spirit of self-improvement, which was practically encouraged by the model housing schemes which it built at Abbey Wood.[1] The same spirit was no doubt a factor in the strong working men's clubs of Woolwich. In addition to the Engineers' Club, there was the Woolwich Radical Club founded in 1880, the Plumstead Radical Club which split off in 1887, the Woolwich Labour Club formed in 1898, and the Dockyard Labour Club and the Abbey Wood Club formed in the 1900s. Of these seven clubs, the first five all built impressive premises and took an active interest in local politics.

Many of the Arsenal artisans were north-country and Scottish immigrants, and Woolwich was one of the few parts of London in which the Nonconformists found encouragement. There was also a Catholic following among the soldiers and riverside workers. But in spite of this hopeful basis, Liberalism failed to capture Woolwich. The Arsenal workmen were well aware that Conservative governments were more likely to bring them prosperity. Woolwich in the 1890s was a rare example of 'Tory Democracy'. Conservative working men candidates in local elections were common, and the Conservative M.P. Colonel Hughes, a talented organiser, was solicitor to the Royal Arsenal Co-operative Society, and claimed that 'on all matters tending to improve the social condition of the people, I have voted independently of party; and for that reason consider myself a true representative of LABOUR'.[2] Certainly it could not be said of Woolwich, as of inner working class districts, that Conservatism was simply a result of political apathy, for the election polls in Woolwich were always exceptionally high.

The labour movement, without the disadvantage of an anti-imperialist reputation, could hope to succeed in Woolwich where the Liberals had failed. The stability of population, the manifold voluntary activity, the sense of local community, the relative absence of commuters and also of desperate poverty provided a combination of advantages rare in London.

The origins of the Woolwich Labour Party go back to the 1880s. Because the leading local socialist, Robert Banner the Scots bookbinder, had been among those who seceded from the S.D.F. in 1884, the S.D.F. was always weak in Woolwich until 1910, while Banner remained the backbone of the local Socialist League and in the 1890s

[1] W. T. Davis and W. B. Neville, *History of the R.A.C.S.*, London 1918.
[2] *Handbook of 28th Co-operative Conference*, London 1896; election manifesto, 1892, Woolwich public library.

of the I.L.P. By 1891 a Woolwich Labour Representation League had been formed,[1] a labour candidate was put up for the L.C.C. and subsequently made an alderman, and although a Liberal candidate was already in the field the League was considering adopting a parliamentary Labour candidate. Eventually the Liberal retired and in March 1892 Ben Jones was adopted as 'a good Labour man' to 'unite the Progressive forces'. He was supported by the Co-operative Society, the local clubs, the Labour Representation League, the Engineers, the Gas Workers, and a number of local clergy.[2]

Although this first organisation failed, it led to the founding of the Woolwich Trades Council in 1893. The Trades Council had 3,000 affiliated members, including two of the radical clubs, within a year.[3] By 1896 it was putting up Labour candidates for the Woolwich Local Board and the Plumstead Vestry. Other Labour candidates, who included shopkeepers and clergy,[4] were put up by the Co-operative Society, the Woolwich Labour League and the Plumstead Labour Propagandist Society, but without proper co-ordination, so that although there were not many candidates standing as Progressives there was frequent confusion and conflict.

In 1898, in an attempt to sort this out and also to replace the defunct Woolwich Liberal Association, a Progressive Association with ward committees and a delegate council was formed.[5] The initiative came from a radical clergyman, but the Progressive Association did not remain long under Liberal influence, for Banner became its secretary in 1899.[6] At the same time the I.L.P. started to publish monthly *Woolwich Labour Notes*, of which 3,000 copies were distributed gratis. Its policy was tolerant; readers were advised to take *Justice* as well as the *Labour Leader*, and quotations from Ruskin and articles on Christian socialism were mixed with extracts from Engels introduced by Banner. The future Woolwich Labour Party secretary, William Barefoot, wrote of the need for 'an alliance between Co-operators, Trade Unionists and Socialists' and Keir Hardie pointed to the example of West Ham.[7]

For the 1899 local elections a joint committee of the Trades Council, the I.L.P. and the Co-operators was in fact formed and was

[1] S. D. Shallard to J. Burns, 18 April 1891, Burns Collection.
[2] *The Next Parliamentary Election: A Labour Representative for Woolwich*, a report of a meeting of 25 March 1892 with a foreword by T. White, secretary of the Woolwich Labour Representation League, published by the Co-operative Printing Society, copy in Woolwich public library.
[3] *Workman's Times*, 2 September 1893; *London*, 12 and 26 April 1894.
[4] Professions from nominations in *Kentish Independent*, 8 December 1894.
[5] *London*, 14 April 1898.
[6] *Woolwich and District Labour Notes*, November 1899.
[7] Ibid., November 1898, May and July 1899; February 1899.

supported by the Woolwich Temperance Council. The candidates were not very successful, and in February 1900 when Ramsay MacDonald was sponsored by the Trades Council for an L.C.C. bye-election there was again a Labour defeat. But these election disappointments at the height of the Boer War fever were not surprising, and *Labour Notes* already give the impression that the Woolwich movement was one of unusual vitality. In 1899, for example, the Trades Council can be found arranging a picture exhibition to provide 'Art for the Workers', advised by Val Prinsep and Hamo Thornycroft, and organising a conference on housing with the clubs and the Temperance Council. At the end of the year the Trades Council also decided to share the responsibility for *Labour Notes* with the I.L.P.[1]

Woolwich was the first of the London Trades Councils to affiliate to the national Labour Party. The decision was made in principle in March 1900, and confirmed by a subsequent reference to affiliated bodies.[2] It allowed the Progressive Association to organise the 1900 Borough Council elections, at which only ten Progressives were elected out of thirty-six, although five of these were working men. In the General Election the Conservative Member was returned unopposed. In the following year, however, the question of a parliamentary candidate was again discussed, and at a trade union and temperance conference in October, at the suggestion of the National Democratic League, F. H. O'Donnell was adopted.[3] In the same month the Trades Council started to issue a new monthly *Woolwich Labour Journal*. Edited from the Engineers' Club to 'voice the wishes and aspirations of the workmen', it supported the national Labour Party from the beginning. Moreover it soon backed this support with aggressive argument. After the Borough Council had abandoned a promised housing scheme in April 1902 it declared that 'all political philosophy teaches one clear, simple, indisputable principle . . . if you are to be represented on these governing bodies, you MUST be represented by men like yourselves, by men of your own class, and not by your betters, your masters, your landlords. . . . These people live by you and on you; you work for them, pay their incomes, keep them in comfort, and often luxury; and the better their condition, the worse yours; the worse theirs, the better yours.'[4]

In this spirit when O'Donnell refused to pledge himself to join the independent Labour members in Parliament the Trades Council

---

[1] Ibid., May-September 1899.
[2] W. Barefoot to J. R. MacDonald, 4 March, 13 June and 28 November 1900, Labour Party correspondence.
[3] *Woolwich Labour Journal*, March 1902.
[4] Ibid., October and November 1901; April 1902.

repudiated him, and the bye-election when Hughes finally retired in May 1902 was not contested. This event was significant, for it makes clear the fact that the Trades Council was now the decisive political body in Woolwich. In July 1901 it had sponsored a radical shopkeeper, E. T. Fennell, as a Labour candidate in a Borough Council bye-election against Colonel Hughes himself, who had no doubt expected a walk-over. Fennell's astonishing victory was the first of a series of Labour triumphs, including the election of the Rev. Jenkins Jones at another bye-election in 1902. But these victories could equally be claimed by the radicals, and the influential Plumstead Radical Club had declared its ambition to 'send a Democrat to Parliament'. The Trades Council had now shown that the Club was impotent in isolation, and that a democrat alone was insufficient. At the same time the Trades Council took the crucial step of setting up a committee 'to secure the registration of every eligible trade unionist in the district'. This developed into a joint committee with representatives of the Progressive Association, the National Democratic League and the I.L.P., although the I.L.P. branch in Woolwich had disappeared earlier in the year.[1] Meanwhile the search for a Labour parliamentary candidate continued and eventually, against the feeling of the national I.L.P., Will Crooks was chosen in November 1902.[2] A central committee room was opened, and in response to appeals 500 volunteers came forward, financial support was promised by trade union branches, and the radical clubs voted £105. 'Given the man, and Woolwich can be won for labour. . . . He has come forward . . . a champion of justice and right, a hater of oppression and wrong. . . . The game of political shuttlecock the workers have decreed must cease. . . . To work! To work! The fiat has gone forth! Woolwich will be contested at the next parliamentary election, whenever that may be.'[3]

By an astonishing coincidence it was within a few weeks. Hughes' successor, Lord Charles Beresford, resigned in February 1903 to take up a naval appointment, and Crooks went to the poll as Labour candidate on 11 March. For once Labour election organisation was as good as the Conservatives, and the number of volunteers on the election day was 'fully 3,000'.[4] There was considerable local disillusionment with the Conservative government, which had allowed the number employed at the Arsenal to drop by 4,000 since 1901, and the two Borough Council bye-elections had suggested that Woolwich

[1] *Woolwich Labour Journal*, March, May and July 1902.
[2] Ibid., December 1902; I.L.P. National Council minutes, 28 July and 1 December 1902.
[3] *Woolwich Labour Journal*, December 1902 and January 1903.
[4] Ibid., March 1903.

might no longer be a Conservative stronghold. Even so the comfortable Labour majority of 3,229 was totally unexpected, and received with wild enthusiasm. There was no doubt that a Liberal could not have won over so much of the Conservative working class vote, and that this was not just another Liberal-Labour victory.

Nevertheless the personality of Crooks, who as a member of the L.C.C. labour bench and as a Poplar councillor and Guardian was always a straight Progressive, to some extent confused the significance of the result. The *Daily News* had raised election funds, although those raised locally would have been sufficient. The Social Democrats declared scornfully that 'the Liberals have succeeded in smuggling in a man of their own under the Labour flag', and their view found ample support in the jubilation of the Liberal press.[1] The Woolwich organisers had to assure an anxious Ramsay MacDonald that Crooks was 'wholly free from Liberal influences. We have unhesitatingly from the outset refused all help of both money and personal service unless it has come to us unconditionally.'[2] But their replies could not completely conceal anxiety for Crooks' consistency. 'I think there is little fear that Crooks will support ordinary or special Liberals. . . . We have done all that we possibly can this end, to make it definite that Crooks was a Labour candidate and is a Labour member. But unfortunately our own people play into the hands of the enemy and make our paths difficult. *There is no fear however that Woolwich will depart from strict Labour lines.*'[3] Without doubt in the long run Crooks, although always a conscientious M.P. and a popular personality, was an inadequate representative of Woolwich. He did not share the conviction of his sponsors in independent Labour as an ideal. He had joined the Fabian Society in the 1890s, but he was no longer more than a nominal socialist, and he was not a working class intellectual like many of the London Labour pioneers, so that he failed to express the remarkable ferment of progressive ideas which was a feature of the Woolwich Labour movement. He was no longer young, and ill-health was to limit his activity. In January 1910 the general election caught him abroad, convalescing, and by a narrow margin he lost the seat. He was lucky to be able to recapture it in December 1910. Crooks had only been chosen after prolonged consideration in 1902, and as it happened he proved an ideal candidate for the sudden by-election. Later, as a prematurely decrepit father figure, he was hardly the statesman that Woolwich deserved.

Immediately after the election the Labour Representation

[1] *Justice*, 21 March 1903.
[2] C. H. Grinling to J. R. MacDonald, 3 March 1903, Labour Party correspondence.
[3] W. Barefoot to J. R. MacDonald, 17 March 1903, ibid.

Association was formed. From the beginning it was organised in what was eventually to become the universal pattern for constituency Labour Parties. The Association consisted of affiliated trade unions, working men's clubs and socialist societies, which sent delegates to a General Council, and 'associated members' paying individual subscriptions grouped in ward committees which also sent delegates to the General Council. All matters of principle were decided by the General Council, which elected the executive committee.[1] Woolwich is generally regarded as the first constituency Labour Party to have organised individual membership. The ward committees were an immediate success, meeting monthly for lectures 'on various subjects of social reform', and providing a firm basis for registration and election canvassing. There were nearly 2,000 individual members in 1904, rising to 3,000 in 1909.[2] In only one ward, St. George's, which was the barracks area, were there no individual members, but it is noticeable that the strongest wards were the old town centre and the southern and eastern parts of Plumstead, the districts of Woolwich in which Booth had recorded over 40 per cent of the population living in poverty.[3] Thus it does not seem that the majority of individual members were the more prosperous artisans, as might perhaps have been expected. These subscriptions were collected by regular weekly collectors, and brought in about £200 annually. This compared with a similar sum from the working men's clubs, principally the Plumstead Radical Club, Woolwich Radical Club and the Engineers' Club, and a little over £100 from the Trades Council and trade union branches, chiefly the Engineers, Labour Protection League and Woolwich Workers Union. There was only a very small income from the I.L.P. branch and Clarion Club. In all there were twenty affiliated bodies in 1904, with a membership of 5,000.[4] In addition to this annual income special funds were raised to fight general elections, on which £1,000 was usually spent in Woolwich. These special funds drew on outside sympathisers, some of whom were wealthy Liberals. Sydney Buxton was a generous contributor, no doubt out of gratitude for Crooks' support in his own constituency of Poplar.[5] For its regular income, however, the Woolwich Labour Representation Association relied on its own local efforts, and it showed that a vigorous Labour Party could raise as much money as the Woolwich Conservative Association.

[1] *Woolwich Labour Journal*, May 1903.
[2] Woolwich Labour Representation Association annual reports, 1904, 1905 and 1909–10. The reports list all affiliated bodies, subscriptions received through ward committees, and all other subscriptions.
[3] Booth, op. cit., II.
[4] *Woolwich Labour Journal*, May 1904.
[5] Subscription lists are printed at election times in the *Woolwich Pioneer*.

It was probably C. H. Grinling who conceived the scheme for the Labour Representation Association. Something of his earlier work in Woolwich for social reform has been described in Chapter Four. In the 1900s he threw his energy, his private income and his wide imagination wholly into the Labour movement. It was Grinling who in 1902 first called for a united Labour Party with individual members in ward committees.[1] As leader of the Progressives on the Borough Council his influence was crucial in persuading the Progressive Association to dissolve itself and advise its members to join the new party. Grinling became first chairman of the Labour Representation Association, which he asserted stood for 'a new conception of organisation, in which the individual is the unit'.[2] In William Barefoot, secretary of the Trades Council from 1899 and editor of the *Woolwich Labour Journal*, an engineer, who became the secretary of the new party and held the post for the next thirty-eight years, Grinling found an ideal counter-part, a man whose exceptional administrative ability was essential to the smooth functioning of a political party of 'ultra-democratic character'.[3]

The most obvious advantage of this democratic character was that the Association could accept support from sources that would have compromised the independence of a weaker body. Besides the support of the radical clubs and individual election subscriptions from Liberals, regular contributions were received from the United Irish League and the Eltham Liberal Association. But even in a middle class ward like Eltham the individual members subscriptions rapidly became more important than these donations. All the sources of income were unashamedly printed in the Association's annual reports. Ramsay MacDonald protested that the affiliation of the clubs could cause 'no end of trouble' and was 'highly improper and simply enabling the enemy to once more quote Woolwich where things are done reasonably'.[4] Barefoot, knowing the local situation, found MacDonald's attitude perplexing. 'Why so much anxiety about Woolwich? Surely we have given an object lesson of how it can be done! Our position is so clear, at any rate to Woolwich folk, that I confess I fail to grasp your point of view.'[5] Much of this misunderstanding was in fact due more to the personal position of Crooks than to the success of the Woolwich party in securing a broad political basis. Certainly at a later date, when a Liberal and Radical Association

[1] *Woolwich Labour Journal*, July 1902.
[2] Ibid., May 1903, June 1904.
[3] Ibid., 2 November 1903 (quotation); R. B. Stucke (ed.), *Fifty Years History of the Woolwich Labour Party, 1903–53*, London 1953.
[4] J. R. MacDonald to W. Barefoot, 13 October 1905, Labour Party correspondence.
[5] W. Barefoot to J. R. MacDonald, 7 July 1903, ibid.

LOCAL LABOUR PARTIES

had been refounded in Woolwich, the Labour Party flatly refused even to consider its offers of an electoral arrangement.[1]

The democratic character of the Association was clearly shown at the Borough Council elections of 1903. There was no abrupt break with the Progressives of 1900. The new Labour Programme was drafted with the 1900 programme as 'a basis for discussion', and at a later date when the party procedure of the new Labour group required definition it was decided 'that the practice of the old Progressive Party be reduced to writing and brought up at a special meeting of the Party'.[2] The Labour policy was in fact a typical model Progressive programme (of a kind rarely fulfilled) for trade union wages and conditions, housing schemes and health administration. There was, however, a difference. 'During this campaign the people have been told that they should have such control over the Labour councillors as they never had over any councillors in the past. This is something more than mere electioneering bombasting.'[3] There was justification in the claim. In the first place, Labour councillors were selected democratically through the wards. Ward committees could send in any number of nominations, and those suggested were questioned by the executive committee, which would submit its recommendations to the wards. The ward committee would then make the selection. Cases of conflict were referred for decision to the General Council. Labour councillors found it wise to attend the monthly ward meetings, and the ward committees even sent delegates to listen to council proceedings.[4] There had never been any such contact between the Progressive councillors and their constituents. Secondly, the Labour programme had been drafted and adopted by the executive committee and all candidates were pledged to support it.[5] Thirdly, once elected, although the Labour councillors held 'party meetings' to discuss regular council proceedings, major matters of policy such as the choice of Aldermen, the provision of road work for the unemployed, and the decision to start at once with the building of the Plumstead Baths rather than to wait until the Council was in a position to build it by direct labour, were decided at joint meetings of the councillors and the Association's executive committee.[6] It was agreed that questions of particular difficulty should be decided by a joint meeting of councillors and the Association's General Council, so that a clear majority of the General Council

[1] Woolwich Labour Representation Association minutes, 3 January 1912.
[2] Ibid., 31 July 1903 and 2 May 1904.
[3] *Woolwich Labour Journal*, 2 November 1903.
[4] Ibid., December 1903 and May 1904; Woolwich Labour Representation Association minutes, 16 April 1907.
[5] Woolwich Labour Representation Association minutes, 31 July 1903.
[6] Ibid., 4 and 14 November, 18 and 30 December 1903.

would be in a position to impose its view on the Labour councillors.[1] Councillors were expected to attend party meetings 'when possible' and 'understood to accept the decision of the majority and to be prepared to vote in accordance with that decision, unless they state that they are unable conscientiously to do so'.[2] Members of the Association's executive committee who were not councillors were provided with copies of the borough council minutes and agendas.[3]

This was certainly a more clearly defined system of democratic political responsibility than had ever been seen in any Progressive Party. It appears to have worked without difficulty. The Labour councillors were elected with a clear majority of fourteen in 1903, and during the first few weeks consultation between the councillors and executive committee was frequent. Once the major administrative decisions had been taken it became less regular. The Labour group, with C. H. Grinling as its first whip, strictly adhered to its programme, and accepted the resignation from the Labour Party of two ex-Progressives who refused to accept its policy decisions.[4] While in control of the council, Labour introduced evening meetings so that working men could attend, tightened up the labour clauses in contracts, negotiated tramway extensions with the L.C.C., eliminated the contractors in dust collection, introduced a 30/- minimum wage for council employees, engaged more sanitary inspectors, set up a works department, built the Plumstead Baths and Plumstead library, started a brickmaking plant and an electricity scheme, and provided a large amount of winter work for the unemployed. In addition, the housing scheme proposed under the previous council was continued, and work was begun on a library and baths in Eltham.[5]

In spite of its record, the Labour Party was dislodged in 1906, sharing the fate of the Progressives throughout London. Immediately the new situation was discussed by a special meeting of elected councillors, defeated candidates, ward secretaries and the executive committee. The councillors decided after this discussion not to accept the chairmanship or vice-chairmanship of any committee, and to refuse any membership of the Distress Committee.[6]

[1] Ibid., 30 January 1904.
[2] Ibid., 18 July 1904.
[3] Ibid., 21 March 1904.
[4] Ibid., 16 May 1904 and 15 May 1905; Councillor Fennell resigned because the Plumstead Baths were not built by direct labour, Councillor Widger because he opposed the electricity scheme. Fennell was a tradesman, Widger a schoolmaster.
[5] *Woolwich Labour Journal*, December 1903, January, April, July and August 1904; *Woolwich Pioneer*, 14 October and 23 December 1904; hostile series of articles in the *Standard*, 23–28 May 1906, 'How and Why the Rates go Up'.
[6] Woolwich Labour Representation Association minutes, 5 and 12 November 1906.

After 1906 there were a number of significant changes in the Association's constitution. In order to stimulate ward organisation it was decided that instead of electing their secretaries independently ward committees should send nominations to the executive committee for comment, and then elect their secretary in the light of the executive's recommendations. In the case of weaker wards prominent Labour men were induced to take on the secretaryship for short periods.[1] In 1910 part-time paid collectors were employed for the first time, and in 1912 a full-time canvasser was engaged for some months.[2] Seen in isolation these steps appear to tend towards a concentration of power in the party's leadership. But Woolwich had always been a strongly-led party, and the real purpose of these changes was to create a more active rank and file. The ward parties now took on more responsibility for outdoor meetings. Canvassing for registration and party membership was developed into a continuous activity with a 'system of organised street captains'.[3] Regular meetings of canvassers were held to discuss local affairs 'and other matters of current interest'. Similarly the Association encouraged 'occasional meetings of members of all wards to consider the fundamental principles of the Labour movement and their application to current affairs and problems'.[4] Winter lectures were a regular feature of the monthly ward meetings. In addition there was a Sociological Group, a cricket section, a choir and a band, and frequent bazaars and tea meetings. A strong effort was made to draw women into the organisation, not only for the 'tea and social committee', but also for discussion meetings.[5]

It was probably a sign of the success of all this activity that at the beginning of 1909 the constitution was again altered. The General Council became a fortnightly body of delegates, two from each ward and each affiliated organisation, and the executive committee handed over responsibility to it. The party office could be relied on to administer normal business, advised in urgency by an elected Emergency Committee.[6] A special committee was elected to deal with finance. On questions of political importance power now lay directly with the General Council, and it at once took the opportunity to remind Labour councillors of the need to attend party meetings. The Borough Council group was asked 'to concentrate at each meeting

[1] Ibid., 16 April and 20 August 1907.
[2] Woolwich Labour Representation Association, Pioneer and Finance committee minutes, 25 January 1910 and 20 February 1912.
[3] Woolwich Labour Representation Association minutes, 20 August 1907, 24 March 1908.
[4] Ibid., 29 April and 17 March 1908.
[5] Ibid., 16 April and 27 August 1907, 17 and 24 March 1908, &c.
[6] Ibid., 5 January 1909.

of the Council on some salient point involving an important Labour principle, and so enable the Labour policy to be made as widely known as possible.'[1] Shortly afterwards it was agreed that Labour councillors should be ex officio members of the General Council, and that members of the General Council should attend meetings of the councillors, although they should not vote on questions of party procedure.[2] This constitution remained unaltered until 1914.

It might be argued that the real power lay not with the General Council but with the affiliated trade unions and socialist societies. Certainly with a weaker party this would have been so. But the Woolwich I.L.P., although it reached the unusually large membership of 500, was never more than a subsidiary of the Labour Representation Association, organising propaganda meetings. When it was captured by a militant wing, at first its new leaders were given their share of work in the Association, and no political discrimination against them can be traced.[3] Later the I.L.P. branch seceded to join the B.S.P. and for a period openly opposed the Labour Representation Association. Its hostility appears to have little influence on events. Similarly the Trades Council, the originator of the Association, was soon by comparison numerically and financially weak. It never challenged any of the choices for Labour candidates. Except for a break of two years, Barefoot was in any case secretary of both organisations, and no doubt helped to prevent interference. Certainly the Trades Council was never a conservative influence on the Association. It fully responded to the local enthusiasm for Grayson, and later to Tom Mann's industrial unionism.[4] In one of the few declarations which defined its political standpoint it resolved to 'endeavour to obtain for the workers the full results of their labour by the overthrow of the present competitive system of capitalism, and the institution of a system of public ownership of all the means of production and distribution of wealth.'[5] The Trades Council was in one sense the official Woolwich Labour Party, for the Council and not the Association was affiliated to the national Labour Party. But in every other way it was primarily an industrial body, and content to trust the Association.

Perhaps the most remarkable feature of the Woolwich Labour

[1] Ibid., 16 February 1909.
[2] Ibid., 16 March 1909.
[3] E.g. ibid., 8 September and 1 December 1908, Moore Bell and William Clarke the leaders of the militants are still being selected as candidates and elected to the Association's executive committee. The decision to amend the constitution in January 1909 may well have been intended to give the rebels more responsibility.
[4] Woolwich Trades Council minutes, 22 October 1908, 16 May 1912, &c.
[5] Ibid., 31 January 1907.

Party was its newspaper. In 1904 the monthly *Labour Journal* was transformed into the weekly *Woolwich Pioneer*, and in spite of all odds it continued publication as a weekly newspaper until 1922. Barefoot was editor, and Grinling spent nearly all his personal capital on its promotion.[1] It had to face a hostility among local tradesmen which reduced the number of advertisements, and the disadvantage as a political paper in a circulation which was a 'barometer' of party enthusiasm.[2] By refusing to print news of police court proceedings when these would jeopardise the future of those involved, or when drunkenness or 'immorality' were involved, the *Pioneer* gave an invaluable advantage to its more salacious rival the *Plumstead News*.[3] It was only kept alive by annual subsidies from rich sympathisers such as Joseph Fels, and after 1909 by assistance from the funds of the Labour Representation Association.[4] But if it was never a commercial success, the *Pioneer* was an invaluable cohesive influence in the Labour movement. After 1909 canvassing for party members and *Pioneer* readers proceeded together.[5] Through its weekly news party members could receive regular and reliable political news, and were thus protected from the false rumours and unnecessary suspicions which are inevitable in an organisation only reported in a hostile press. The existence of the *Pioneer* must have been an important reason for the rarity of futile bickering in the Woolwich Labour Party. It was also an essential part of the internal party education which was characteristic of Woolwich. It was full of discussions of political ideas and policies, of an impressive variety. The theories of Marx and Lassalle, of William Morris and Ruskin, and by 1908 of the French syndicalists, were all discussed.[6] Among the specialists reviewed were Patrick Geddes the town planner and Tawney the historian on 'The Agrarian Problem in the 16th Century'.[7]

The Woolwich Labour Party has been described at length because it illustrates the potential quality of a Labour Party based on a mass membership and on broad socialist convictions. By this means it was

[1] *Labour Who's Who*, 1927; Karl Walter to Paul Thompson, 20 April 1960.
[2] Woolwich Labour Representation Association, Pioneer and Finance Committee, 17 June 1912; Woolwich Trades Council minutes, 9 May 1907.
[3] Woolwich Labour Representation Association, Pioneer and Finance Committee, 20 April 1915.
[4] Karl Walter to Paul Thompson, 26 April 1960 (Fels gave £1000 a year); Woolwich Labour Representation Association minutes, 3 November 1909.
[5] Woolwich Labour Representation Association, Pioneer and Finance committee minutes, 21 December 1909, &c.
[6] *Woolwich Pioneer*, 14 April and 8 September 1905 (Marx), 9 June 1905 (Lassalle), 8 December 1905 and 18 October 1907 (Morris), 10 March 1905 and 26 July 1907 (Ruskin), 27 January 1908 (syndicalism).
[7] Ibid., 27 January 1905 and 11 April 1913.

able to provide a financial and electoral organisation which made a political party based on working class support viable. In effect it extended the party organisation until it became an educational and social movement as well as a political machine. It was a movement essentially based on the recognition that Liberalism was an outdated philosophy of 'old, exploded fallacies' and that the Labour Party must put forward a new concept of society. 'In the name of Justice it claims for all who toil, not only increased leisure, but fuller means to life; it claims free play for every human faculty no less urgently than it demands for the disinherited their due share in the world's wealth, in books and art, in the beauty and music of life. In the name of Justice the *Woolwich Pioneer* will make a constant protest against the vain and idle existence of all who live on the toil of the workers.'[1] In short, the Labour Party must be a socialist party.

Socialism was not only necessary if the party organisation was to be extended as at Woolwich into a wider social and educational movement. To many trade unionists the Labour Party was nothing more than an extension of industrial bargaining into politics, and some of them resented the part which socialists and middle class men were able to play in it.[2] There was only one local Labour Party in London, Deptford, in which this attitude was predominant, and its obvious result was political stagnation. In all the other parties the socialists were an essential element, and middle class socialists were welcome as supporters and as candidates. If the Labour Party was to be based upon extensive individual membership and was to secure some measure of middle class support, it must be not merely on a common class interest but also on a common political standpoint.

These twenty local Labour Parties were the foundation upon which the London Labour Party was to rise to power. Although in their development of organisation and registration work they were a big advance on the socialist bodies of the 1890s, they still did not look a formidable force. They were scarcely represented on the L.C.C. There were little more than seventy Labour councillors in the whole area. But the failure of the Labour Party to make more rapid progress can be explained by special factors, by the indifference or hostility of the Social Democrats and the Fabians, by the relative weakness of the I.L.P. and the trade unions, and in some districts by the survival of Liberal-Labourism. While the fundamental problems which had undermined the local Progressive Parties seemed no nearer to solution in 1914 the principal Labour Party handicaps had disappeared. The attitude of the Social Democrats and the Fabians was

[1] Ibid., 14 October and 4 November 1904.
[2] E.g. G. Vernall to J. R. MacDonald, October 1903, Labour Party correspondence.

changing, trade unionism was expanding, and Liberal-Labourism was in decline. In 1918 the Labour Party was to adopt a socialist constitution and individual as well as affiliated membership. Its prospects in London are best judged by the success of those local Labour Parties which were already moving in this direction.

XII

THE FOUNDING OF THE LONDON LABOUR PARTY

THE London Labour Party is an organisation of a special nature. London is the only county in which a fully developed and separate party organisation exists in addition to constituency and borough parties. It was, however, a development anticipated well before its foundation in 1914. In the 1900s all the main parties except Labour had special London organisations. The London Liberal Federation, the Metropolitan Radical Federation, and the London Reform Union (for local elections) managed London for the Liberal Party; the Metropolitan Division of the National Union and the London Municipal Society (for local elections) for the Conservatives. The Fabian Society was essentially a London organisation in itself; the I.L.P. had its Metropolitan District Council and later its London Divisional Council; the S.D.F. and B.S.P. their London District Council. It is more remarkable that until 1914 the Labour movement in London remained a diverse collection of separate borough movements than that a special party was eventually formed to unite it.

This was of course but one aspect of the failure of Labour in London. One should have expected a great city with one fifth of the country's population to provide at least a similar share of Labour Party strength. Yet while the party's affiliated membership grew to a million by 1907, probably only one in ten of these were Londoners (Figure 2). Likewise of the 30 Labour M.P.s elected in 1906 and the 40 elected in 1910, London contributed only 3 and 4 respectively.

The principal reasons for this failure are simple. Firstly there was the weakness of the I.L.P. In the experience of the Labour Party organisers one of the 'essentials to the success of a L.R.C. is that the I.L.P. should have a strong hold in the constituency; otherwise you are in great danger of suffering from the dominance of the Liberal-Labour section.'[1] This opinion was not due to any pro-I.L.P. bias; indeed Ramsay MacDonald, although a leader of the I.L.P., already felt its initiatives 'impertinent', and only inescapable need made him willing 'to grin and bear the patronising helping hand'.[2] In fact, in spite of its rapid growth between 1905 and 1910, the I.L.P. was never the leading element in any London Labour stronghold.

This would not have been a disadvantage had the S.D.F. continued to support the Labour Party. The effect of its disaffiliation was to stunt the growth of both the S.D.F. and the Labour Party in London. While in old Labour strongholds the Social Democrats continued in general to work for the Labour Party, and no fatal damage resulted, the development of newer parties was made much more difficult. Similarly, with trade unions, although no important union was persuaded to disaffiliate from the Labour Party, the affiliation of some other unions was held up when the Social Democrats used their influence to support the resistance of Liberal and Conservative members.[3] The most serious result of this new combination was in the London Trades Council. Most of its delegates were either Liberal-Labour or Social Democrats, and as a result, although nominally supporting the Labour Party, the Trades Council remained one of the most serious obstacles to progress in London until 1914.

Throughout this period the London Trades Council insisted on promoting its own invariably inadequate schemes for Labour electoral unity in London rather than supporting the Labour Party's efforts in the same direction. As the *Labour Leader* aptly remarked, 'the leaders of the London Trades Council snarl at the L.R.C., but have nothing to offer as a substitute'; and although vehemently denying an 'alliance on the London Trades Council or anywhere else between S.D.F. men and Liberal Labour men', they could hardly claim that such an alliance would have produced much practical change in the Council's policy.[4] From the Labour Party point of view one of the most irritating results of this situation was the trickery of the Trades Council in organising demonstrations and campaigns. In December 1904, for example, Ramsay MacDonald discovered that 'the S.D.F. working the London Trades Council' had organised a National Conference on the feeding of school-children. 'The object of the conference is to take the wind out of our sails and is part of

---

[1] J. R. MacDonald to P. H. Noden, secretary of Brixton I.L.P., 23 November 1905, Labour Party correspondence.

[2] J. R. MacDonald to Francis Johnson, 24 June 1905, ibid.

[3] E.g. Printing Machine Managers, T. Oldham to J. R. MacDonald, 5 April, 23 June and 3 November 1903, ibid.

[4] 19 May and 23 June 1905.

the declared policy of the London Trades Council and the S.D.F. to temporarily capture the Political Committee (of the T.U.C.) to our damage. Opponents of the (Labour Representation) Committee are doing all they can to get the Political Committee to associate itself with matters which come within our range, but from the treatment of which we are excluded. We had never heard of this conference till we got circulars and we have had no invitation to be present. The I.L.P. is in a similar position. We are promoting a conference of our own.'[1] The following autumn the Trades Council called a conference on unemployment, inviting the S.D.F. and all its branches, the I.L.P. Metropolitan District Council but not its branches, and not inviting the L.R.C. at all. Previously the Trades Council had issued a circular saying that it was co-operating with the L.R.C. on this issue. MacDonald urged the I.L.P. to boycott the conference. 'I think, of course, it would be a great pity to do anything to spoil any good work (if any) that may result from the conference, but unless the L.R.C. and I.L.P. in London put their foot down and refuse to be cheated as they are undoubtedly being cheated in this instance, London will remain in the Slough of Despond into which the S.D.F. and Liberal-Labour gang have dragged it.'[2]

The national organisers could only protest with equal impotence at the effects of a similar combination of influences in the constituencies. In West Ham and Poplar, where the S.D.F. already had a secure position within a successful Labour Party, to leave the Labour Party was clearly to go into the wilderness, and in these boroughs the Social Democrats continued to be essential supporters. But in other boroughs, where a new Labour Party could hardly expect immediate triumphs, their assistance was always erratic. Even when the S.D.F. did work with the local Labour Party, the disagreements on whether candidates should be 'Labour' or 'Labour and Socialist', the difficulties on agreeing local election programmes, the different points of view argued at political meetings, the frequent S.D.F. attempts to secure recognition of the class war and the need for nationalisation, the personal friction caused by all this, and above all the unreliability of the S.D.F. as supporters, made local alliances unstable and essentially unfruitful. Yet because the national Labour Party did not interfere in local elections even so far as to prevent Labour Party candidates running as 'Labour-Progressives' or as 'Labour and Socialist',[3] the national organisers were obliged to watch helplessly

[1] J. R. MacDonald to J. Sexton, 6 December 1904, Labour Party correspondence.
[2] J. R. MacDonald to W. Sanders, 25 September 1905, ibid.
[3] E.g. J. R. MacDonald to E. W. Cox, secretary of Tottenham, Edmonton and Wood Green Trades and Labour Council, 2 March 1905, ibid.

when, as one pioneer complained, S.D.F. 'bully, bluff and bluster' destroyed 'the persistent work quietly which I have been doing in Lambeth for years'.[1] Ramsay MacDonald could only 'make it perfectly clear to local Trade Unions and Trades Councils that they are not in any way bound to invite the S.D.F. to join with them in Conferences called for the purpose of nominating Labour candidates and also to warn them that where the S.D.F. had been asked to co-operate only unfortunate results have taken place.'[2]

In London, because of the weakness of the I.L.P., this advice would only throw the Labour Party into the equally undesirable arms of the Liberal-Labour men. After January 1910 John Burns was the only remaining Liberal-Labour M.P. in London; the veteran Randal Cremer died in 1908, while Steadman lost his seat in 1910. In 1906 there had been three Labour Party M.P.s and only one Liberal-Labour M.P. But in local elections, and especially on the London County Council, which would clearly take a central place in any scheme for London Labour organisation, the Liberal-Labour men were certainly not yet extinct. While the L.C.C. Labour Party comprised three members in 1910 and one only in 1913, the Labour bench remained a steady four. They were respectable figures. H. R. Taylor of the Bricklayers, who sat for North Camberwell, had been made Mayor of Camberwell by the Progressives, and used his influence to prevent the development of any local Labour Party.[3] George Dew of the Carpenters, a councillor for South Islington, was well known as the founder and secretary of the Workmen's Cheap Trains Association. Charles Jesson of the Musicians' Union, a councillor for Walworth, was for a time secretary of the London Trades Council's Political Committee. Harry Gosling, who sat for St. George's in the East, was the Watermen's secretary, on the T.U.C. Parliamentary Committee, a union representative on the Port of London Authority, and from 1911 President of the National Transport Workers Federation, a quiet but formidable person. Both Jesson and Gosling were national supporters of the Labour Party. In addition to these four, Ben Cooper, secretary of the Cigar Makers', a regular delegate to Labour Party conferences, stood unsuccessfully as a Progressive at each L.C.C. election after 1904, twice against candidates supported by local Labour Parties, and Will Crooks, who resigned from the Council in 1910, continued to speak for the Progressives. There is no reason to doubt the *Daily Herald*'s assertion that the stultification of Labour on the L.C.C., weaker in 1913 than in 1892, was due to the

---

[1] G. T. Cox to J. R. MacDonald, 26 January 1904, ibid.
[2] J. R. MacDonald to S. Lewin, 22 February 1907, ibid.
[3] E.g. G. F. Woodward, secretary of Camberwell L.R.C., to J. R. MacDonald, 16 June 1904, ibid.

failure of the Labour bench to recognise the need for formal independence, and the consequent 'two voices' of Labour at elections.[1]

The influence of these Liberal-Labour men could no more be ignored in London than that of the Social Democrats. The successful Labour Parties in London depended on very wide political support, including Nonconformists and Radicals. In some cases radical clubs even took the initiative in forming local L.R.C.s, and Temperance Societies were invited to the initial conferences.[2] Provided that the principle of independence was clearly accepted, and that a socialist element was firmly established in the local party, there was everything to be gained from drawing in formerly Liberal supporters.

The Liberal-Labour problem was also exacerbated by the ambivalence of the Fabians. In 1913 there were still more Fabians standing with the Progressive Party than with Labour in the L.C.C. election, and four were elected. When Pease complained that a Labour Party scheme for London organisations in 1907 omitted the Fabians, who were 'more successfully concerned with London than any other Socialist body', Ramsay MacDonald observed it was 'quite true that you have got seven members on the L.C.C. and two in Parliament, but I am rather afraid that your successes have been owing not to work upon the lines of the Labour Party but upon lines which the Labour Party do not approve'.[3]

The final difficulty faced by the Labour Party in these years was the weakness of its position in the trade unions. This weakness was not merely a reflection of the general weakness of London trade unionism. It was due to a variety of reasons. Some unions were kept from the Labour Party by their sense of social status. The skilled Watermen had a traditionally Conservative membership, and only affiliated in 1913 as a result of the new wave of militancy following the 1911–12 dock strikes. Other important London unions such as the Clerks, the Railway Clerks and the Teachers, were middle class.

The Clerks did not affiliate until 1909, the Railway Clerks until 1911. In 1910 the Clerks were still very defensive about their politics, arguing that the union was 'absolutely independent of party politics. Its aim is to better the condition of clerks. . . . The Labour Party is in

[1] *Daily Herald*, 17 March 1913 and 18 April 1914.
[2] Rushton, political secretary of the Marylebone Liberal and Radical Club, to J. R. MacDonald, 18 October 1903; W. J. Lewis, secretary of the Boro' of Bethnal Green Radical Club, to J. R. MacDonald, 24 July 1907; C. Horner, secretary of Hackney Labour Council, to J. R. MacDonald, 9 November 1902; and J. Stanley, secretary Paddington L.R.C., to J. R. MacDonald, 10 January 1903, Labour Party correspondence.
[3] Pease to MacDonald, 16 March 1907, and MacDonald to Pease, 19 March 1907, ibid.

Parliament working for exactly the same ends.'[1] Surprisingly enough the union's rapid growth after 1910 brought in many socialists of the *Daily Herald* type. By 1913 the Clerks were calling for industrial unionism, social ownership of the means of production, and 'a more militant attitude on the part of the parliamentary party'.[2]

Several major London unions did not join or disaffiliated from the Labour Party under the influence of Liberal-Labour sympathisers, sometimes probably supported by S.D.Fers. The Coal Porters' secretary Harry Brill was an S.D.Fer and a member of the National Democratic League; the Navvies' secretary John Ward was a leader of the National Democratic League; the Labour Protection League was a loose federation of dockers with a large Irish membership, many of whom were unwilling to be bound to the Labour Party; the London Carmen's Trade Union branches seem usually to have supported Progressives, although their secretary Sam March was a Poplar Labour councillor. The Carmen never affiliated to the Labour Party, and the other unions had disaffiliated by 1904. Later the small Bargebuilders Union disaffiliated when their secretary Steadman decided not to sign the Labour Party constitution, and the strong Fawcett Association, whose two leaders, W. E. Clery and W. B. Cheesman, were both Liberal-Labour men, followed in 1908. The Osborne judgement of 1909 put a new test on the loyalty of trade union membership, and the number of trade unions with some London strength affiliated to the Labour Party, which had been about seventy since 1904, dropped to fifty by 1913. Nearly all the unions lost were small, but a major blow was the inability of the Compositors' leaders to maintain more than a Voluntary Political Association in support of Labour Party funds. Although the 1913 Act made a compulsory political levy possible, the Compositors only resumed it by a narrow majority in 1916, and in the first year a fifth of their members contracted out.[3]

The unions in the building industry, an important group in London, were a special difficulty. These unions were going through a bad period of industrial depression in the 1900s and losing numbers heavily. Their annual reports often urged members to concentrate on the industrial battle. 'Do not pin too much faith in what politics will do for us as workers,' warned the Masons' secretary in 1907. The secretaries of some unions, such as the Navvies and the Bricklayers, were only willing to support a Liberal-Labour party, and disaffiliated for this reason. The General Amalgamated Union of Labourers, which like many building unions had a strong Irish element, disaffili-

[1] *Clerk*, January, 1910.
[2] *Clerk*, report of branch referenda, September 1913.
[3] PP 1914–16 LIX, pp. 424–5.

ated in 1907, and in 1909–10 following the Osborne decision the Masons, Plumbers, Builders' Labourers and Plasterers did likewise. Only the two Carpenters unions remained with the Labour Party and resistance to the political levy in their membership was very strong.[1] No doubt the difficulties of the building unions were aggravated by the fact that they had been pioneers in local elections, due to their special interest in securing fair labour policies in municipal building work, and as pioneers they had a long tradition of co-operation with the Liberal Party. The Bricklayers, for example, supported a number of members on London borough councils through a Municipal Representation Levy. Of those who can be identified, two were socialists, two Labour, three Labour-Progressive, and four straight Progressive.[2] The same diversity can be found among the Carpenters. Perhaps most telling of all was the example of Michael Deller, the Plasterers' secretary, whose annual reports from 1899 urged the need for labour representation both locally and nationally, 'a good strong and pure Labour Party' which was the tool of neither party; 'Liberalism and Toryism, so far as we are concerned, are, or should be, things of the past. The fight now is Capital and Labour.'[3] Yet Deller stood for the Lewisham Borough Council in 1903 as a Progressive, and his successor as secretary, T. Otley, stood as a Progressive in St. Pancras in 1906.

Of the ten unions with a London strength of 7,000 during part of these years, the Carmen had never affiliated, the Amalgamated General Labourers had been lost, and the Amalgamated Carpenters and Compositors were ambivalent. So were the Railway Servants, with their Liberal district council and Osborne himself who had invalidated political levies, branch secretary at Walthamstow. The Engineers, although moving into a more aggressive phase after 1910, were still conservative in temperament in the early 1900s and their secretary would have supported looser Labour Party rules.[4] The Postmen's Federation, although staying with the Labour Party, likewise wanted their candidate free of 'useless red-tape restrictions' and 'so long as he had a free hand on postal and general Labour questions he was allowed to act on other political questions with whatever party his view accorded'.[5]

Only three of the ten, influenced by their socialist traditions, were secure in their Labour allegiance. The Shop Assistants were a

[1] Ibid.
[2] Operative Bricklayers' Society annual report, 1906. Six others are unidentified, and may have only been candidates.
[3] National Association of Operative Plasterers annual report, 1901 and 1902.
[4] G. H. Barnes to J. R. MacDonald, 31 August 1903, Labour Party correspondence.
[5] A. MacLaren to J. R. MacDonald, 26 January 1903, ibid.

growing union with an attachment to political methods secured by the Shop Acts of 1886 and 1904. The Dockers and Gas Workers, however, were both going through difficult periods in London, the Dockers remaining below 1,000 until 1910 and the Gas Workers falling to a nadir of 3,000 in 1909. Their support was therefore less helpful than at any other period. The immediate results of their recovery after 1910 was also discouraging, for the new industrial militancy accorded ill with a Labour Party which was 'a mere appendage of the Liberal Party'.[1] The Gas Workers London District voted for disaffiliation in 1913, and supported Jack Jones of the B.S.P. in the Poplar bye-election of February 1914.[2] One Poplar Gas Worker, probably representative, told Lansbury he was 'sure nothing really important will be done until the Labour members forget their "gentility" and the compliments of the Liberal press'.[3] Similarly in the Dockers' annual reports, Tillett, who had welcomed the Labour Party's 'promise for magnificent victories' in 1905, was by 1912 complaining of a 'dumb and acquiescent Labour Party, impotent where not indifferent'.[4]

The influence of the *Daily Herald*, due to its outspoken support of strikers, was clearly important in forming these attitudes of the Dockers. The Compositors, who had in fact brought out the original *Herald* as a strike organ in January 1911, also supported it in preference to the rival moderate *Daily Citizen*.[5] At the same time the new militancy was transforming the spirit of the engineers and building workers. It could not have caused more than a temporary weakening of Labour Party support. In fact in some cases it appears that syndicalism was drawing former Liberals directly to the Labour Party. In North West Ham, for example, the Labour Party had failed to make any progress owing to the Liberal-Labour sympathies of the Stratford Railway Servants. A principal member of this branch, C. Dear, who took a prominent part in the all grades movement on the Great Eastern Railway, and was elected a West Ham councillor as a Progressive, came over to the Labour Party and joined the S.D.F. at the end of 1911. His attacks on the settlement of the railway strike suggest that his political conversion followed a growing industrial militancy.[6] In 1913 the corresponding secretary of the West Ham

[1] National Union of Gas Workers and General Labourers report, May 1912: London district resolution, defeated by the union.
[2] National Union of Gas Workers and General Labourers executive minutes, November 1913 and February 1914.
[3] W. Andrade to G. Lansbury, 26 June 1912, Lansbury Collection.
[4] Dock, Wharf and Riverside Labourers' Union annual reports, 1905 and 1912.   [5] *London Typographical Journal*, December 1911.
[6] *Stratford Express*, 29 October 1910: *West Ham and South Essex Mail*, 13 October 1911; *New World*, January 1912.

Railway Servants was a prominent syndicalist speaker at a Transport workers meeting in Stratford Town Hall, and by 1914 the general Labour Party prospects had improved sufficiently for the West Ham Trades Council to form a Trade Union and Socialist Electoral Committee for North West Ham.[1] In the long run these new trade unions attitudes, which were affecting all the larger unions with Liberal-Labour traditions, were far more likely to undermine the Liberal Party.

After 1910, therefore, although the Osborne judgement was still reducing the actual numbers of affiliated trade unions, the Labour Party's prospects in London were good. Union strength was advancing fast and with it Labour Party affiliated membership, which had fallen from its peak of 1904, was again rapidly increasing. It was about 99,000 in 1910, over 160,000 in 1914. London, which had not shared the steady increase in national membership after 1904, was fast recovering. This improvement in the trade union situation, together with the reaffiliation to the Labour Party of the B.S.P., was to remove the fundamental obstructions which until 1914 prevented the formation of a London Labour Party.

These obstructions are clearly revealed in the ten or more serious attempts to organise London which failed before 1914.

Until 1905 the only efforts to unite the London Labour political movement came from the London Trades Council. The Trades Council had sent no delegates to the initial conference of the L.R.C., although most of its leading members had been present as delegates of their unions. It passed a resolution in May 1900 in favour of 'direct representation upon public bodies ... independently of any political party', but in the General Election and borough elections of that year took no unusual action. A Labour programme was drawn up for the Borough Councils and Burns, Steadman, Thorne and Lansbury were supported at the General Election.[2]

No further steps were taken until October 1901, when a sub-committee of diverse political complexion was appointed 'to report on the utility of appointing a permanent committee' in order to promote and financially to support candidates.[3] James Macdonald, the Council's secretary, thought it essential for such candidates to 'take up a class position against those who own and control the implements of industry'.[4] Steadman, the Council's treasurer, favoured a more flexible and modest scheme of a 'private list of three trade

---

[1] *Syndicalist*, January 1913; *Daily Herald*, 24 February 1914.
[2] London Trades Council minutes, 10 May, August and 26 September 1900.
[3] Ibid., 10 October 1901.
[4] *London Trades and Labour Gazette*, November 1901.

unionists in each constituency' to act as 'confidential correspondents' supplying information to the Council.[1] Eventually a combined scheme was agreed; there was to be a 'private directory' of correspondents, trade unions were to be circularised for funds to support candidates, and a political committee composed of district delegates was to mediate in disputes 'to prevent the waste of the trade union vote'. The idea of a London Labour Party was rejected, on the ground that there were too many parties already 'and it did not appear possible to unite the workers under any'. The scheme 'made it possible for all Trade Unionists to support Trade Unionist candidates, and the political ideas which were held by the different sections would ultimately work themselves out by a kind of survival of the fittest'.[2] This first scheme was in fact little improvement on open anarchy, and made no progress.

Early in 1903, after some discussion, the Trades Council resolved to affiliate to the Labour Party and to support only 'labour candidates who have the financial and moral support of their trade unions'. At this stage the only opposition to support for the Labour Party came from the Printing Machine Managers, who argued that 'the Liberal Party had done its work in the past, and had thousands of members who would make good Labour representatives'. At the same time, although 'the knotty question of finance has yet to be worked out', a new effort was made to form trade unionist political committees in the constituencies.[3] Local committees were reported from Battersea and Edmonton, a local L.R.C. was formed in Westminster, a trade unionist group in Stepney secured the election of Dan Haggerty of the Builders Labourers to the Borough Council, and a trade unionist conference in Walthamstow adopted A. E. Holmes, the Compositors organiser as parliamentary Labour candidate.[4] The Trades Council called a conference with suburban Trades Councils in June 1903, and this conference decided on a new scheme for local elections, a delegate political committee to provide financial assistance and help to avoid friction, but leaving initiative to the local bodies.[5] This delegate political committee was to be called the London Trades and Labour Council. There is no evidence that it was ever formed, or if it was that it had any effect on the 1903 Borough Council elections. Two further conferences convened by the Trades Council were held in July and October to discuss parliamentary

[1] London Trades Council minutes, 12 December 1901.
[2] Ibid., 9 January 1902; *London Trades and Labour Gazette*, February 1902.
[3] London Trades Council minutes, 8 January and 12 February 1903; *London Trades and Labour Gazette*, January and February 1903.
[4] Ibid., February and March 1903.
[5] Ibid., June 1903.

elections. Delegates were invited from trade unions, local Trades Councils, the Fabians Society, the I.L.P. and the S.D.F., but the eighteen delegates sent by the S.D.F. withdrew from the first conference 'amidst the ironical cheers of those remaining' after failing to carry an amendment pledging candidates to the class war.[1] At the second conference, which according to the *Labour Leader* 'showed an earnest spirit, and . . . augured well for a really strong and permanent movement in London', a political committee of fifteen, including Ramsay MacDonald, was set up.[2] It was decided to endorse Burns, Bowerman, Crooks and Steadman provided that they signed the L.R.C. constitution, and candidates were to be considered for seven other constituencies. Once again these moves came to nothing. Now that the S.D.F. had disaffiliated from the L.R.C. the difficulty, as Jesson, the political committee's secretary, explained to Ramsay MacDonald, was that 'there is practically no organisation outside the Trade Union movement . . . I may also say that we do not want to set up a lot of rival organisations to the London Trades Council.' He also mentioned the lack of funds, and that in local elections 'we always advocate that they should co-operate with any other progressive, local, organisation that is prepared to accept our views and the programme of the London Trades Council'.[3]

The political committee in fact was not genuinely interested in independent Labour representation. It merely wanted trade unionists elected to local councils and Parliament and did not mind which party supported them. Two of the four candidates which it endorsed did not in fact sign the L.R.C. constitution. Of the six members of the committee who were politically active at this time, four were Progressives rather than Labour men.[4] No serious effort was made to find funds to support Holmes as a Labour Party candidate at Walthamstow, so that eventually he was forced to withdraw.[5] In April 1904 the committee ceased regular meetings,[6] and later in the year the Trades Council's true political feelings were clearly shown in its protests at the refusal of the Labour Party to endorse Quelch as Labour and Socialist candidate for Dewsbury. In moving the Council resolution which demanded an alteration of L.R.C. rules, a delegate

[1] Ibid., August 1903.   [2] 24 October 1903.
[3] C. Jesson to J. R. MacDonald, 14 January 1904, Labour Party correspondence.
[4] Jesson, Stevenson, Hennessey, Cheesman; against J. R. MacDonald and J. G. Butler.
[5] J. R. MacDonald to James MacDonald, 26 June and 20 September 1905, to A. E. Holmes 7 November and 16 December 1905, and James MacDonald to J. R. MacDonald 13 July and 6 November 1905, Labour Party correspondence.
[6] London Trades Council minutes, 5 April 1904.

of the Labour Protection League said that the 'L.R.C. was departing from every principle which it was understood by most people to support', and the seconder from the Cab Drivers thought 'the committee was running amok, and working the whole thing into the hands of a clique'. Steadman declared his admiration of Quelch, and conviction 'that if the Labour Party in this country was to make headway and succeed, a policy of give and take was indispensable'. Ben Cooper also stated he 'disliked the constitution of the L.R.C.'. Balancing these Liberal-Labour views with a Social Democratic contribution, Fred Knee declared that 'the L.R.C. had developed into a political party without principles and without a programme, possessing only one thing—a title, and that unsatisfactory and indefinite . . . Steadman and Quelch, stalwarts, had been barred, while men weak on vital points are favoured . . . Get a proper Labour man, whose proper credential is his past, a man of the stamp of those he had mentioned, and let no cast iron or wooden regulation of the L.R.C. or any other body stand between him and the electorate.'[1]

Hostility to the restrictiveness of the Labour Party constitution was the one feeling in which both Social Democrats and Liberal-Labour men could find agreement. At the General Election of 1906, for example, unendorsed socialists were supported along with Liberal-Labour and official Labour candidates.[2]

Because of this support of Liberal-Labour men the Council was able to persuade wealthy Liberals to subsidise its journal, the *London Trades and Labour Gazette*.[3] But there were frequent disputes between the two sides; the Trades Council insisted on supporting the S.D.F. candidate in a bye-election for the L.C.C. in spite of the protests of Steadman and Cooper, while on the other hand Quelch was unable to prevent a congratulatory message when John Burns was made a Cabinet minister.[4] Voting figures suggest that both sides could rely on 35–40 votes, and the balance was held by about 30 delegates with no particular political alignment. It was the fact that the Trades Council was 'so sharply divided politically', rather than, as the *Labour Leader* believed, that it was 'bossed and dominated by a small clique' which was 'a combination of the Liberal-Labour with the S.D.F. element', which prevented it from making further efforts to unite the Labour Party in London.[5]

Undeterred by the failure of the London Trades Council, in

[1] *London Trades and Labour Gazette*, August 1904.
[2] London Trades Council minutes, 11 January 1906.
[3] J. R. MacDonald to F. Knee, 6 December 1905, Labour Party correspondence.   [4] *London Trades and Labour Gazette*, April 1905 and April 1906.
[5] Ibid., June 1905; *Labour Leader*, 19 May and 16 June 1905.

1905–6, two rival groups of local Trades Councils made fresh attempts to organise London. The first group, the Federation of Trades and Labour Councils of the South and East of England, had been formed in 1900, and was supported by Woolwich, Deptford and Greenwich, and Croydon Trades Councils. The twelve councils represented at the original conference had also included West Ham, Poplar, South Western London, and the London Trades Council itself.[1] The Federation's secretary, Arthur Field, a voluble speaker who described himself as a 'stout gas-pipe', had been an S.D.Fer in the 1880s, and then settled in Maidstone organising I.L.P. branches all over Kent.[2] His Federation believed in independent Labour representation and wanted to build up a strong section in London. The second group was started in 1905 by the chairman of the Islington Trades Council, A. T. Gould, recently affiliated to the Labour Party, with the support of Hackney, Brixton and Southwark Trades Councils, and called itself the Federation of Metropolitan Trades and Labour Councils.[3] Ramsay MacDonald was inclined to support Gould, although his Federation had no backing in strong Labour constituencies. MacDonald failed to mediate between the two groups. Field abandoned his efforts, and shortly afterwards decided to rejoin the S.D.F. Gould's group convened a delegate meeting in July 1905, and decided to call another conference in 1906 for the dual purpose of developing the London trade union movement and securing independent Labour representation. The London Trades Council opposed the formation of a Metropolitan Federation. The conference, held in Islington Town Hall in July 1906, proved a disaster. Only 11 of the 23 Trades Councils invited sent delegates, and of these Woolwich and Lambeth left after being refused permission to move an amendment which would have restricted the Federation to trade union matters and recommended the formation of a separate London municipal Labour Party. There was a strong feeling that any conference for political purposes should have included representatives from the I.L.P. and S.D.F. and the chairman appears to have lost control. The meeting was reported as 'one of the most disorderly ever held in connection with the Labour Movement in London'.[4]

A week later another conference was held in which the socialists

[1] A. G. Field to J. R. MacDonald, 2 June and 7 July 1905.
[2] A. G. Field to J. Burns, 14 February 1900, Burns Collection; A. G. Field to H. Bryan, 27 February 1915; I.L.P. City branch correspondence, Herbert Bryan Collection.
[3] A. G. Field to J. R. MacDonald, 29 June and 7 July 1905 and A. T. Gould, to J. R. MacDonald, 26 July 1905, Labour Party correspondence.
[4] E. H. Jarvis to J. R. MacDonald, 21 April, 10 May and 18 June 1905, and MacDonald to Jarvis, 13 June 1905, Labour Party correspondence; *Daily News*, 23 July 1907.

were in turn dominant, at the S.D.F. headquarters Chandos Hall, with William Sanders the London I.L.P. secretary in the chair. This conference decided to set up an advisory committee to prevent friction in the 1907 L.C.C. elections, and resolved that since 'the Progressives have apparently exhausted their mission' there was a need for 'representation on the L.C.C. independent alike of Progressive and Moderate parties, and pledged to a definite and united working class policy'.[1] The new advisory committee did not secure any general support outside the socialist parties; only the Hammersmith and Poplar Labour Parties and the Deptford and Greenwich Trades Council, all of which were running candidates against the Progressives, affiliated to it. The Labour bench and the candidates supported by Progressives were able to rally much more impressive support at the election, including the Woolwich and Southwark Labour Parties, Steadman, Crooks, John Burns, Arthur Henderson and Bowerman.[2] In fact, although the I.L.P. Metropolitan District Council rejected the suggestion of an arrangement with the Progressive Party whips, the Labour Party leaders later made private but unsuccessful efforts to secure four or five straight fights for independent candidates.[3] Not surprisingly Frank Smith, the one I.L.P. candidate who was elected with Progressive support failed to convince the rest of the labour bench of the need to form 'a distinct group on the Council'.[4] He told George Lansbury 'a more hopeless broken-minded jelly fist crew [than the] "Labour men" on the Council I never met, not one I can rely on. If you were there we could worry them.'[5]

The continuing failure in London was by now making the Labour Party National Executive Committee consider some direct intervention. After a discussion in March 1906 it decided to encourage the formation of local Labour Parties, in the hope that these would prove more sympathetic than Trades Councils.[6] A scheme was drawn up in the summer of 1906 for a London Labour Party, with carefully balanced representation from the London Trades Council, local Trades Councils or Labour Parties, the I.L.P., the S.D.F., and trade union district committees. Because of the confusion of the situation it was decided to postpone action until after the L.C.C. election in

---

[1] *Justice*, 4 August 1906.
[2] E.g. Progressive election leaflet 20, 1907, Ensor Collection.
[3] J. K. Hardie to G. Lansbury, 7 March 1907, Lansbury Collection.
[4] As Hardie suggested, ibid.
[5] F. Smith to G. Lansbury, 28 March 1907, ibid.
[6] Labour Party national executive minutes, 15 March 1906. After this letters were sent out by the Labour Party saying 'we strongly recommend that local organisations should be created in our boroughs on the model of the provincial L.R.C.s'; e.g. J. R. MacDonald to F. Carter, 5 May 1906, Labour Party correspondence.

March 1907. It was then proposed to call an informal meeting of the Trades Council and I.L.P. at the House of Commons and present to them a scheme for a formal conference, to which local Trades Councils and Labour Parties, trade union district committees, I.L.P. branches and Fabian Groups, but not S.D.F. branches were to be invited. At this second conference a committee modelled on the Labour Party National Executive would be elected.[1] Ramsay MacDonald thought 'the important thing will be to get a firm Chairman, together with a good secretary, both of whom are in favour of our policy. The S.D.F. will try to capture the machinery, but if the Chairman and secretary are sound and determined to carry things with a high hand, the S.D.F. will probably find a difficulty in working their way. I would suggest that we should try to put one of our M.P.s in the chair for the first year.'[2] But these men were not easy to find. By August 1907 MacDonald was 'inclined to let it drift' and the Executive decided in October to take no action. In reply to complaints at the Labour Party's inactivity, MacDonald said that they were 'carefully watching' but intended no move unless conditions altered.[3]

The next moves were in fact made by the London Trades Council, due to the initiative of William Johnson, the Theatrical Employees' secretary. A sub-committee of four was appointed, comprising one Woolwich I.L.Per (the veteran Robert Banner), two Labour Party supporters who were Progressives (Gosling and Cooper) and one Labour Party supporter from the S.D.F. (Fred Knee).[4] This sub-committee met the Labour Party National Executive in March 1908, and were told that no London organisation on irregular lines would be recognised.[5] Nevertheless the Trades Council scheme adopted in April was certainly irregular. Local Trades Councils and trade unions affiliated to the London Trades Council were to subscribe to a political fund on the basis of their affiliated membership. Socialist organisations were to have no regular place in the scheme, but were to be invited to election conferences 'when deemed necessary' by the London Trades Council. These conferences would adopt a programme and endorse 'Labour and Socialist' candidates.[6] The scheme was another failure. Twelve local Trades Councils sent delegates to

[1] Labour Party national executive minutes, 2 August, 23 October 1906, 22 March 1907.
[2] Ibid., memorandum on London organisation by J. R. MacDonald.
[3] J. R. MacDonald to A. Batstone, 19 October 1907, Labour Party correspondence.
[4] London Trades Council minutes, 6 February 1908.
[5] Labour Party national executive minutes, 11 March 1908.
[6] London Trades Council minutes, 30 April and 27 August 1908; *London Trades and Labour Gazette*, May 1908.

the first meeting to discuss the scheme in June 1908, but in August when the scheme was formally adopted only four, none important were represented.[1]

The approach of the 1910 L.C.C. election stimulated a new effort by the Labour Party National Executive. The National Agent called a meeting in the summer of 1909 and a London for Labour Committee was set up.[2] It seems to have relied on the I.L.P. for support, but the intention was to draw together the various local Labour parties in the hope 'that a successful L.C.C. election fought well in the limelight would give this litter of bodies some common inspiration and coherence'. A vague but ambitious scheme was produced for a body to which 'every society or organisation in London which supports the general policy of the Labour movement and within whose power it is to adopt candidates' could affiliate; it was to issue an election news sheet, organise concentration on election weak-points, and issue extensive literature to 'make clear the conception of a united and closely inter-related London'. It was a badly drafted scheme; as Ensor commented, it was 'merely pious wishes. Every wise Labour man wants such a body to come into existence, but you don't get it simply by saying so. You require a strong desire for and belief in the possibility of such a central body on the part of London Labour organisations; a satisfactory basis of representation; a man of great practical ability and high trade union standing to devote himself to this as his principal job.' As far as the basis of representation was concerned the scheme was 'no proposal at all'; no secretary of the required character had been found; and the intervention of the parliamentary election in January 1910 'makes the limelight and perhaps the success largely out of the question'.[3] In the event the Labour candidates for the L.C.C. once again fought in two separate camps.

Nevertheless three candidates pledged to form an independent Labour Party were elected to the L.C.C., Ensor, Lansbury and Frank Smith. They rejected Gosling's invitation to join the Labour bench, formed a party of three, Lansbury acting as chairman, Ensor as treasurer and Frank Smith as secretary and whip, secured places on the Housing, Establishment, Supplies and Parliamentary Committees, made their headquarters Frank Smith's office at Clifford's Inn, and issued writing paper boldly headed 'L.C.C. Labour Party'.[4] They

[1] London Trades Council minutes, 18 June and 27 August 1908.
[2] Labour Party national executive minutes, 7 July 1909.
[3] London for Labour Committee, report of campaign sub-committee, with comments by R. C. K. Ensor, December 1909, Ensor Collection.
[4] H. Gosling to R. C. K. Ensor, 9 March 1910, F. Smith to R. C. K. Ensor, 20 March 1910, Ensor Collection.

do not appear to have had any regular party meetings, although at first they kept in touch through frequent informal contact.[1] Ensor was a zealous member throughout (and much disliked by the Progressive Party organisers),[2] but Lansbury had more important work in the House of Commons after December 1910 and the three members became largely independent of each other in 1911. Frank Smith had a variety of other responsibilities, and Ensor, who had fallen out with the Bow and Bromley socialists, had probably decided relatively early not to risk more controversy by seeking re-election. By 1911 it must have been clear that the L.C.C. Labour Party had none of the personal stability of the Progressive Labour bench. But it was a start, and was used as the basis for another attempt at London Labour unity.

This time the initiative was taken by the I.L.P. London Divisional Council. Delegates from local Trades Councils and Labour Parties, I.L.P. branches and the Fabian Society were invited to a conference at which the three Labour members described their work on the L.C.C.[3] In this encouraging atmosphere a second conference was arranged a month later, in March 1911, to discuss various schemes for unity. It was decided not to invite the S.D.F. to affiliate; local parties or trades councils with a 'prospective candidate in view' were to be allowed one delegate, the Fabian Society two, and the I.L.P. Divisional Council four. These delegates were to form a London Labour Electoral Committee, which would report to quarterly conferences.[4] At the initial conference in April, attended by thirty-six delegates, the organisers made it clear that they had little idea of how the committee would function in practice. William Sanders thought 'the first thing to do was to get the Committee established. He had had twenty-four years of experience trying to do London Electoral organising work, and every attempt that had been made had failed owing to the policy of trying to organise from the centre. The best way was to get the committee established, give it instructions to call quarterly meetings, and then the quarterly meetings from time to time could revise the work of the committee. If they started discussing policy now they would never get any candidates for the next L.C.C.

[1] R. C. K. Ensor, diaries, 1910–13, and correspondence, Ensor Collection.

[2] In 1912, F. W. Galton, London Reform Union secretary, was reported to be looking for potential L.C.C. candidates. 'He told me the other day that the Progressives would be quite glad to let us have labour candidates in many places—but "none of your young Fabians thanks!" He wants good, stodgy, harmless Trade Union officials; but he doesn't like Ensors.' C. M. Lloyd to Beatrice Webb, 10 April 1912, Passfield Collection.

[3] Report of conference, 4 February 1911, North London Federation correspondence, Herbert Bryan collection.

[4] I.L.P. London Divisional Council minutes, 9 March 1911.

election.' Harry Dubery, the I.L.P. Divisional Council secretary, said the committee 'would leave it to the affiliated bodies to develop themselves and find out their own policy. It was not suggested that this body should be an autocratic body. The best method would be to allow its powers to develop, and his own idea was that it should be more of a consultative body, not one that would thrust candidates and policies upon particular areas.'[1]

By not inviting the S.D.F. or the London Trades Council, and not imposing any electoral tactic on affiliated bodies, the London Labour Electoral Committee continued in existence longer than any of its predecessors. It became in practice the L.C.C. election committee for the I.L.P., whose candidates ran in its name in 1913. Once again the Progressive Labour bench candidates ran separately, and this time there were also B.S.P. candidates running with the support of local Labour Parties but not endorsed by the London Labour Electoral Committee. After the failure of its candidates, of whom only Susan Lawrence was elected, the Committee does not seem to have dissolved, but its meetings were no longer reported.

The I.L.P. must have been disillusioned by its disappointments, for it did not support the penultimate scheme for London unity. The London Labour Electoral Committee had ignored the trade unions. By 1913 the industrial unrest had eroded the former Liberal-Labour strongholds and the outlook appeared far more promising to the Labour Party. In October 1913 a large private meeting of 500 London trade union delegates was attended by Ramsay MacDonald, Bowerman and Arthur Henderson, and 'laid down the lines of advance'; the *Daily Citizen* reported that 'the feet of the organised workers of London, as revealed by the Memorial Hall conference, are set not in quagmire but on the rock of combined industrial and political progress'.[2] But the I.L.P. Divisional Council decided against the 'joint labour organisation for London' proposed, and it was taken no further.[3] The reason for this was almost certainly the fact that the London Trades Council was now again ready to take the initiative, this time along lines sympathetic to the Labour Party. Its action was in fact to result in the foundation, after so many failures, of a successful London Labour Party.

Its change of policy was simultaneous with the change of attitude in the B.S.P., and in the same way directly followed the death of Harry

[1] Report of conference, 29 April 1911, I.L.P. North London Federation correspondence, Herbert Bryan collection.
[2] 25 August 1913.
[3] I.L.P. London Divisional Council minutes, 2 October and 4 December 1913.

THE FOUNDING OF THE LONDON LABOUR PARTY

Quelch in September 1913. The official hostility of the B.S.P. to the Labour Party then almost immediately disappeared, and the decision to re-affiliate was taken in 1914. Quelch had been chairman of the London Trades Council since 1910, and James Macdonald, its secretary, shared his political standpoint. Macdonald, perhaps sensing the changing atmosphere, had retired earlier in the year, and his successor Fred Knee was a Social Democrat who had persistently urged re-affiliation to the Labour Party. John Stokes, also a Social Democrat, secretary of the London Glassblowers (a small union not affiliated to the Labour Party), became the new chairman. In March 1914 Stokes' proposal that the London Trades Council should call a conference of those 'eligible for affiliation to the national Labour Party, for the purpose of establishing a united working class party on the L.C.C. at the 1916 election', was carried with one dissentient.[1]

The inaugural conference of the London Labour Party was held on 23 May 1914. In many ways it no more appeared to be a vital turning point in London politics than had the first conference of the Labour Representation Committee in national politics in 1900. It did not receive any prominent attention in the press. Moreover, by preserving the London Trades Council's traditional belief in political tolerance, it seemed very like many of the well-meaning loosely conceived efforts which had failed in the past. The invitation was to a 'friendly conference of all sections of the working class movement . . . to devise some means of uniting upon essentials while differing with freedom on details'.[2] At the conference Knee argued strongly for tolerance, appealing to the delegates 'to sink all differences and let the aim of working class unity stand before them as one to be gloried in, aimed at, and achieved . . . They had before them a difficult task. The work was only beginning. London was divided, and up to the present the working class movement was divided . . . It was the object of the conference to unite them. What they would have to do was to form what was called on the Continent a "Bloc" party, in which nobody should be top dog and no one bottom dog.' He wanted to see 'a party formed on easy going lines at first'.[3] There is no doubt that the London Labour Party was formed in this spirit. In describing it a year later, Herbert Morrison, by then secretary, called it 'essentially the product of a long evolutionary process, in which the Trades

[1] London Trades Council minutes, 12 March 1914.
[2] London Trades Council circular, 14 April 1914, copy in I.L.P. London Divisional correspondence, Herbert Bryan Collection.
[3] There are various versions of this speech. The agenda of the conference, I.L.P. City branch correspondence, Herbert Bryan collection, is annotated in shorthand by Bryan, and much of this can be decyphered. Bryan published a report in *Christian Commonwealth*, 27 May 1914. Another good report was in the *Morning Post*, 25 May 1914.

Councils and local Labour Parties of the various London districts have played an important part. From the locality to the centre had been the principle of development which has created the London Labour Party. The Party will not determine the character of the local efforts; its work will be one of helpfulness, co-ordination and expression chiefly concerned with the organisation of a Labour Party on the London County Council.'[1]

In the past such efforts had failed. Why should the foundation of the London Labour Party be regarded as a turning point?

There were two reasons. The first was purely mechanical. The London Labour Party conference was not presented with mere vague wishes. Its constitution had been drafted with great skill.[2] It was closely modelled on the national Labour Party. The object was to promote candidates pledged 'to sit and act on the Council as a Party strictly independent of all other parties'. The Party was to be a federation of trade unions, trade union branches, trade union district committees, Trades Councils, local Labour Parties, branches and London District Councils of socialist societies and women's organisations and co-operative societies in the county of London. Where a Labour Party and a Trades Council existed in the same constituency the executive committee could decide to affiliate one, both or neither of them. Voting at the annual conference was to be by card on demand. The conference was to elect the executive committee and chairman, treasurer and secretary; the committee was to be separately elected by the various sections, six members to represent the trade unions, two the London Trades Council, one local Trades Councils, one local Labour Parties, one the B.S.P., one the I.L.P., one the Fabian Society and one the women's organisations. A fifteenth seat was to be available if any co-operative society affiliated. Candidates for the L.C.C. must be promoted and financially supported by an affiliated society, selected at a properly convened local conference of bodies in the constituency affiliated to the Labour Party, and endorsed by the executive committee of the London Labour Party, and they must run under the official title of 'candidate of the London Labour Party'.

This constitution was passed at a second conference in July 1914 with only two alterations. The trade union representation on the executive was increased to seven, and the candidate's title, which the B.S.P. wanted to be 'Labour and Socialist', was altered to 'Labour candidate only'. The carefully judged balance on the executive was shown at the first annual conference in November 1914, when of

[1] *Daily Citizen*, 19 May 1915.
[2] Conference agenda 23 May 1914, I.L.P. City branch correspondence, Herbert Bryan collection.

the eighteen officers and executive committee elected, five belonged to the B.S.P. and eight to the I.L.P. This balance of power on the executive, combined with an equally careful balance between central authority and local autonomy, was an important contribution to the success of the London Labour Party.

The second reason for regarding the founding of the London Labour Party as a turning point was the immediate and comprehensive support which it secured from the different sections of the London labour movement. At the conference in May there were over 420 delegates, 18 from local Labour Parties, 29 from Trades Councils, 11 from the Women's Labour League, 39 from the I.L.P., 39 from the B.S.P., and, best of all, 292 from the trade unions. The local Labour Parties and Trades Councils included those with a straight Labour policy like Woolwich, socialist-led parties like Poplar, and those which supported Progressives such as Southwark and Deptford. On the one hand the Social Democrats were able to decide to affiliate to the new Party after a delegate meeting in August. On the other hand, equally important and hopeful as a turning point, Knee was able to say at the conference that the existing Progressive L.C.C. labour bench was likely to come into line with an independent party.

The impression that most of the hitherto conflicting elements of the London labour movement were fully behind the new Party was confirmed by the figure of 134,000 affiliated members reported by November 1914.[1] The total strength of trade union and socialist membership in London nationally affiliated to the Labour Party was probably about 170,000. To have reached a comparable figure from the voluntary affiliation of branches and district councils was highly encouraging. With such support its success seemed assured.

[1] Report of executive committee, London Labour Party annual conference 1916, London Labour Party archives.

EPILOGUE

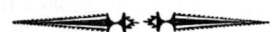

By November 1914 the process of selecting candidates, securing funds and drafting an election programme had begun. But already the First World War had intervened, so that the L.C.C. election of 1916 never took place. The first local elections fought by the London Labour Party were in 1919, and they took place in a transformed political situation. On the one hand the Liberal Party had split, one half following Lloyd George into coalition with the Conservatives, the other half remaining with Asquith. On the other hand Labour had taken part in the wartime government, and trade unionism had been immensely strengthened by official recognition and secure employment during the war. In the next two decades the Labour Party, whose affiliated membership had trebled since before the war to reach over four million, ousted the Liberals as the chief party of the left and formed the first two Labour governments.

Even in this national context, the advance of Labour in London was spectacular. In the 1919 local elections Labour gains in London outnumbered those in the whole of the rest of the country. Labour secured control of half the 28 Metropolitan Borough Councils, and of 4 Boards of Guardians, while 15 Labour members were elected to the L.C.C. By 1925 the Progressive Party had been reduced to a rump and Labour had replaced it as the L.C.C. opposition. Finally in 1934 Labour captured the L.C.C., and held it at every successive election until the L.C.C. was merged into the Greater London Council in 1965. Moreover, although the relative weakness of metropolitan trades unionism meant that the affiliated membership of the London Labour Party was less than a tenth of the national figure, after 1923 London contributed one fifth of Labour's Members of Parliament. London had formerly been the 'Sphinx of Labour'. Why this dramatic change?

Politicians in a capital city can be expected to respond quickly to a changing political situation, being close to the centre of events; and the relative weakness of local allegiances in London must have eased a transfer from the Liberal Party as soon as Labour offered better

EPILOGUE

political chances. Thus of the survivors of the L.C.C. Progressive labour bench, Harry Gosling accepted the leadership of the council's Labour Party in 1919, while even Ben Cooper had joined the new Stepney Labour Party before his death in 1920.[1] John Burns, the last Liberal-Labour M.P. in London, could have been an official Labour Party candidate in Battersea (finding his own election funds) as before, but he refused to sign the party constitution and so was not nominated. He decided not to fight for his constituency 'at the cost of much estrangement and bitterness as my regard for Labour and love of Battersea forbids', and retired from political life.[2] In Deptford Bowerman's Labour Party, which had like Battersea been ambivalent in its relations with the Liberals before 1914, also came into line with national policy, and by 1925 had become a model party of the Woolwich type with 1,000 individual members, regular ward meetings, youth and women's sections, a tennis club and a Labour Choir.[3] In Greenwich when a new party was formed in 1918 it had from the outset 'an astonishingly mature air; its proceedings were brisk, businesslike and informed with a sense of political realities. Nor is this surprising, since most of its new officials had long been active in local politics in other capacities, and three of them until recently had held office in the Liberal Party. It adopted a parliamentary candidate within a few days of its formation—no "wild man", but a trade union secretary carefully chosen for his blameless Liberal past.' The Greenwich Liberal Association, unable to decide on its attitude to this candidate, split, never to recover its former strength.[4] All over London rapid realignments of this kind were occurring.

Behind the shifting political scene, other slower changes were also favouring Labour. When Charles Booth's survey was revised in the *New Survey of London Life and Labour* of 1929, it was apparent that the segregation of the working and middle classes into different residential districts had proceeded still further. While the proportion of middle class inhabitants in the fashionable west London boroughs had risen steeply to a level of about 40 per cent, thus strengthening the Conservative hold on Westminster, Holborn, Hampstead and similar constituencies, in the old inner south and east districts the middle class population had been halved, and was now generally below 5 per cent, making it extremely difficult to maintain a local Liberal Association of the old type. Formerly mixed districts, like Islington, some of which had once been Liberal strongholds, were

[1] *London Labour Chronicle*, February 1920.
[2] Ibid., January 1919; Kent, op. cit., pp. 256-7.
[3] Deptford Labour Party annual reports, 1924-5.
[4] Mark Benney, A. P. Gray and R. H. Pear, *How People Vote*, London 1956, p. 41.

moving in the same direction; Camberwell, Hammersmith and Fulham were changing particularly rapidly.[1] These changes were gradually increasing the number of potential Labour seats.

Working class districts were consolidating in other ways. Migrants to London were now settling either in the outer suburbs or in the middle class West End. While only Bethnal Green had less than a fifth of its population born out of London in 1881, there were eight such boroughs in 1931, all working class. At the same time, there seems to have been a decline in working class migration within the conurbation. Hours of work had fallen by more than 10 per cent since 1914, while real wages had risen, thus encouraging a wider working class use of public transport to get to work.[2] It was no longer necessary to change house with every change of job.[3] A stronger sense of local community, fewer removals on the register and more men with time at home in the evenings would clearly help Labour.

There was also much less of the abject poverty and ignorance which bred political apathy, and had helped to explain the Conservative hold on some of the poorest riverside constituencies. In 1890 only half of the parents of London children had themselves been at school; by 1930 the proportion was nineteen out of twenty. In the same period there had been a fall in the birth rate by almost half; and with smaller families, there were fewer overcrowded houses, fewer verminous children, and far fewer families in chronic poverty. Even in the East End, the proportion in poverty had fallen from a third to one tenth.[4]

The Conservatives had also been favoured by the small craft shops characteristic of the London service industries and also by the fact that most migrants to London came from the agricultural south. There was a marked increase of factory work in the service trades after 1920. Tailor's shops, for example, were giving way to clothing factories, while there was a rapid growth of the motor car and electrical industries in outer London. This industrial expansion at a time when the older manufacturing regions of the country were stagnant attracted industrial workers from the provinces to settle in London. Hitherto—except in Woolwich, a happy omen for Labour—this kind of migrant had been unusual. Their influx, together with industrial change, assisted trade union organisation in London, so that while in most of the country trade union membership in 1930

[1] H. Llewelyn Smith (ed.), *New Survey of London Life and Labour*, London 1930-5, III, p. 151; VI, p. 133.
[2] Ibid., I, pp. 117, 130, 190; VI, p. 262.
[3] *London Statistics* 1914–15, p. 158, 22 per cent of L.C.C. tenants moved during the previous year; 1915–20, p. 130, 7 per cent moved during the previous two years. Unfortunately the series does not continue.
[4] Smith, op. cit., I, pp. 51, 155, 211; VI, p. 3.

was little above that of 1914, there is evidence of notable advances of London strength. The dockers, railwaymen and builders, for example, had together almost trebled their membership.[1]

Contemporaries were less aware of these long term changes, and thus much of the credit for the Labour advance went to the unusual organising abilities of the London Labour Party's secretary, Herbert Morrison, who had taken over when Fred Knee died in 1915. Morrison himself rose to power with his party, and he symbolised many of the changes which came over it during that process. Unlike most of the earlier leaders of the labour movement, his strength was not his oratory, or his conscience, but his genius for administration. A policeman's son, born in 1888, he was not physically strong, and had almost lost the use of one eye; as a young man he worked as a shop assistant and as a switchboard operator. Although for two years he was active in the S.D.F., by 1910 he concluded that 'the fight for socialism depended less on street-corner rabble-rousing (though that had its use) and dramatic isolated action than on the slow but steady construction of an organisation devoted to running a planned programme of propaganda, social work and organization. The work might not be spectacular but I found it deeply satisfying. I invested 30/– in an ancient Yöst typewriter and managed to get hold of a jettisoned duplicator which I got into some semblance of working order. From my bed-sitting-room I wrote letters booking halls for meetings, duplicated tickets, and typed agenda papers.'[2] Thus he began to make a name for himself in the south London I.L.P.

The outbreak of war brought new alignments on the pacifist issue. The B.S.P. split, most of its older members supporting the war, and so allowed the I.L.P. to supplant it as the principal socialist body in London. Morrison was thus elected in Fred Knee's place as a left-winger; and in 1916 John Stokes was ousted from the chairmanship by Fred Bramley of the I.L.P. for the same reason. The shift of power to the I.L.P. did not represent any deep change in the London socialist movement but it was nevertheless a turning point.

For his first three years as secretary Morrison, who had been sent to a farm at Letchworth as a conscientious objector, worked part time for the party. He only became a full-time organiser at the end of the war. Nevertheless there can be little doubt that Labour went into the 1919 local elections better prepared than the other parties. The London Municipal Society admitted to 'special difficulties' in finding candidates and funds, and came to an electoral arrangement with the Progressives; at the polls it found its supporters apathetic. Labour, in contrast, put up more impressive lists of candidates than ever before

[1] Ibid., II, V, VIII; cf. Table 8.
[2] Lord Morrison of Lambeth, *Herbert Morrison*, London 1960, p. 53.

and 'polled its full strength'.[1] Leading opponents conceded that Labour organisation 'deserved credit'; as the *Morning Post* observed after the borough polls, 'No great interest was taken in the election by anybody except the enthusiasts of the Labour Party'.[2] Morrison did not create the tide of Labour enthusiasm, which was felt all over the country, but he helped to make its impact more spectacular in London than elsewhere. The results made his reputation. He was chosen Mayor of Hackney in 1920, elected to the Labour Party National Executive in 1920, and to Parliament in 1923; in 1925 he became Labour leader on the L.C.C., and in 1929 a Cabinet Minister.

By this date the revolutionary ardour which had once drawn him to the S.D.F. had cooled. It is true that during the 1920 'Hands off Russia' crisis he admitted to 'visions of organising a London Soviet as part of a temporary national mechanism whereby the constitutional liberties of the masses might be secured'; but he did his best to make sure no such opportunities recurred. Socialism increasingly came to mean for him administrative efficiency, which should appeal to any social class. 'Can Labour win London without the support of the "Middle Classes"?', he asked in 1923; and by 1929 he was assuring 'every business man and every business manager' that he wanted to 'treat him as a man and a brother, and help to make his commercial or industrial enterprise more successful than it has been in the past'. This approach, reinforced by the taste for the type of party member who 'prefers electoral organisation to talk', made Morrison a leader of the campaign to expel the Communists from the Labour ranks. 'The bores must be cleared out. Herbert cleared them out. . . . He saw to it that branches had work to do.' By 1927 he had achieved his aim, even at the cost of disaffiliating twelve local Labour Parties in two years.[3]

London as a bastion of the Labour Party's right wing was a far cry from its left wing notoriety in pre-war days. How had this happened? It would be easily explained if the Labour Party was in fact drawing on the middle class support for which Morrison appealed: if he was indeed building the party on new foundations. Yet an analysis of the labour vote by constituencies grouped on a social basis does not suggest any shift to middle class support,[4] while the

[1] London Municipal Society annual reports, 1919–19 and 1919–20; circular appeal for funds, 30 July 1919.
[2] *Daily Telegraph*, 4 November 1919; *Morning Post*, 3 November 1919.
[3] *London Labour Chronicle*, August 1920, October 1923; *Daily Herald*, 30 June 1929; *London News*, March 1926; Mary Hamilton, *Remembering My Good Friends*, London 1944, p. 167; London Labour Party annual reports, 1926–7.
[4] J. Bonham, *The Middle Class Vote*, London 1954, pp. 153–4. If the continuing geographical penetration of the working class is remembered, the slight

EPILOGUE

Labour seats of this period (Map 30) very clearly reflect the pre-war pattern. The safe seats were all part of, or adjacent to the pre-war Labour seats of Bow and Bromley, Deptford, West Ham and Woolwich; while new advances were confined to overwhelmingly working class constituencies, almost always pioneered before 1914, and in most cases pioneered by the Social Democrats. In contrast, Morrison's own pre-war efforts in suburban south London had brought no visible fruits.

A closer look reveals, however, a persistence of the old patterns beneath the new political alignments. The Social Democratic tradition was not forgotten, but rather too exactly followed. The B.S.P. had split twice since 1914; first it lost its older members, and with them the control of West Ham, when it resolved to oppose the war; and then it lost further members through its decision to merge in the new Communist Party, which had been formed as a result of the Russian Revolution. The new party was not affiliated to the Labour Party, so that those who joined it found themselves once more in the political wilderness. Once again its prominent members were faced with a choice between the party and their own success; and of the two parliamentary candidates of 1918 and three London County councillors elected in 1919, four refused to join the Communist Party, and three subsequently became Labour M.P.s.[1] When Will Thorne and Jack Jones in West Ham, and George Lansbury in Bow, are added to the list, the losses of the Social Democrats are manifest.

In spite of their independence of the Labour Party, and generally bitter hostility to it, the Communists at first made considerable headway in London, notably in Bethnal Green and Battersea. But as with the Social Democrats, these successes were based on local alliances with Labour; and eventually they were destroyed by the national conflict between the parties. The Communists also continued the S.D.F. tradition through their influence on the London Trades Council, and through Wal Hannington's work in organising the unemployed. One failing of the Communist Party, however, was

[1] In 1918 F. A. Broad stood in Tottenham and V. McEntee in Walthamstow; both were subsequently successful. A. A. Watts, J. G. Butler and W. S. Cluse were elected to the L.C.C. F. A. Broad told the last B.S.P. conference that 'in Edmonton they had a small branch of about 60 members affiliated to a local Labour Party of about 6000 members, and the policy and programme of that Labour Party were dictated by a few representatives of the B.S.P. On the District Council out of the 15 seats held by the Labour Party 8 were held by members of the B.S.P. This was not done by working in hostility to the rest of the Labour movement, but by working hand in hand with it.'

---

swing to Labour in 'middle class' seats can be explained without any change in middle class opinion.

entirely its own: an exaggerated emphasis on continual reorganisation. Again and again elaborate systems of factory groups, street nuclei, locals and districts were broken up and reformed, so that far too much energy was spent in ineffective administration and the continuity of the old branches was lost. As E. W. Cant complained, 'The truth is we have become so involved in organisational machinery that the essential spirit and life of the Party is being sapped. Initiative is at a discount, and members are regarding themselves as mere Robots. . . . "Down with the Old Time Branch" was the slogan of communism'. It shows the persistence of London's social democratic tradition that in 1939 two fifths of the Communist Party's 18,000 members were Londoners.[1] The tenacity of their tradition was also revealed in the long and difficult struggle which Morrison had to fight to overcome them.

The Fabian Society was equally ineffective in its response to the post-war political situation; indeed during the 1920s, in spite of the new eminence of the Webbs in the Labour Party, it was little more than a historic relic, with the indolent former Progressive, F. W. Galton, as secretary, and London membership slumping to less than half its 1914 level. The I.L.P., on the other hand, once again prospered with Labour success, so that by 1925 its London membership had doubled, to reach 5,000. With Morrison as Divisional Chairman, the *New Leader* now edited from London, and Clifford Allen, a Londoner, as national chairman, the focus of the party appeared to have shifted to the south. The impression was only momentary. London branches, especially in working class districts, continued to be small, and 'flickered in and out of existence'. The only exception was Bermondsey, where Alfred Salter had created a devoted following. The other large branch was more characteristic, the City branch, a forum of intellectual discontent, which had especially flourished through its vigorous support of pacifism during the war. The tendency of the London I.L.P. to a middle class missionary atmosphere thus persisted, and once the I.L.P. leadership came into conflict with the Labour Party its London support melted away. Even Bermondsey refused to disaffiliate from the Labour Party in 1932.[2]

The political suicide of the I.L.P., following that of the Social Democrats, deprived the left of its last organised influence within the London Labour Party. The chances of building *A Commune for*

---

[1] *Imprecorr*, 1926, 17,558: 5 out of 12 executive members of the London Trades Council are Communists; E. W. Cant, *Communist Review*, March 1924; H. Pelling, *The British Communist Party*, London 1958, pp. 39, 104.

[2] A. Marwick, 'The Independent Labour Party, 1918–32', Oxford B.Litt. thesis, 1962.

EPILOGUE

London were finally thrown away in the 1920s. Some of the ideas of the Social Democrats, such as comprehensive education, have shown a continuing vitality; while at a local level, and in a number of trade unions, the old militancy has remained endemic. The fruits of victory, however, fell into other hands; into those of the Fabians, whose history now paid handsome personal dividends; and to the former Progressives, equally late to join the fold, whose policies were the foundation of Labour's political programmes, and whose elder statesmen now gave a new tone to the London labour movement. A Conservative spectator at the Labour Victory Demonstration after the 1923 election thought it 'a very tame show. It struck no note of revolution but rather of respectable middle class nonconformity. They sang hymns between the speeches, which were all about God.'[1] Political obstinacy had, in turn, extinguished London secularism, radicalism, Liberalism and Social Democracy; but one can hardly suggest that, had they all acted with uncharacteristic political adroitness since the 1880s, the result would have looked very different.

[1] Duff Cooper, *Old Men Forget*, London 1953, p. 122.

CONCLUSION

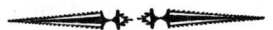

THE best conclusion to this study of London working class politics would be a detailed comparison with other parts of Britain. But no similar political studies of other urban regions in this period exist, and it would be rash to make serious comparisons of the present basis of knowledge. Several commonly accepted features of London political history have been proved to be mistaken. How sound are the present broad outlines of other regions? Without being more certain it is unfortunately impossible to say whether or not the more interesting aspects of London politics were exceptional.

Even so, London politics in this period have an important bearing on national history. If an exception, London was not an exception to be ignored. It was a large enough region to be a political weight of its own in British politics. It was the capital city, with the interest and influence of the political focus of the country. In addition, as the first conurbation, with its social segregation, its commuters and office workers, its relative lack of heavy industry, its religious indifference and its lack of strong local community feeling, it provided a glimpse into the political future.

The first fact which requires comment is the extent to which the years between 1885 and 1894 mark a real political watershed in London. In tracing the origins in Birmingham of the political caucus, historians have perhaps failed to point out why a system which was still exceptional in the early 1880s so rapidly became the rule in both the major parties after 1885. In London the change from small political oligarchies to democratic local parties based on armies of voluntary election workers was especially sudden. It was caused by the coincidence of the redistribution of 1885 with the effective ending of corruption and unlimited election expenses by the Corrupt Practices Act of 1883.

These years also saw the local elections brought within the normal sphere of activity of the political parties. This change was partly a reflection of improved local party organisation, but it was also a response to the democratic reform of local government by the creation of elected County Councils and the extension of the electoral qualifications and franchise in 1894. From this date local elections play an important part in political development. They have been too generally ignored by historians. The common impression that the major political parties were not closely involved in London local politics in this period is mistaken.

This was also the point at which the Conservative Party became the dominant political power in London. This change can again be linked to the new character of the political system. With each extension of the franchise the division of the parties on class lines rather than by sectional interests became more significant. It can be clearly shown that voting in London was principally decided by class divisions after 1885. The electoral system was not, however, by any means fully democratic. If was still weighted in favour of the wealthier classes. The quality of the electoral register still depended on the efforts of the local parties. In this situation a successful political party had to be at the same time a cause and an interest. It must be a cause, it must have a coherent standpoint and appealing principles, in order to keep up the enthusiasm of its voluntary election workers. Equally, it must be an interest if it was to find sufficient money. Politics in this period were not cheap.

In this situation the Conservative Party had an obvious advantage. It represented the interests of the wealthier classes and so was financially secure. Its policies and principles were able to rouse the active support of the middle classes and the passive sympathy of a sufficient minority of the working classes. In the widespread political apathy fostered by the impersonal conurbation this was a sound basis. The Liberal Party, in contrast, was based on a working class majority and a middle class religious minority interest. Its difficulty was to rouse the enthusiasm of the one without alienating the funds of the latter. This conflict was exacerbated by the class segregation, religious indifference and community weakness of London, and it explains the ignominious Liberal failure in the General Elections of 1885–1900.

There has been a recent tendency to think of the Liberal revival in the 1900s as a genuine recovery which was only interrupted by the First World War and the personal split between Lloyd George and Asquith. This view is not supported by the situation in London. The Liberal recovery was not based on a solution of its problems, but on the temporary revival of Nonconformist and trade union support and of old radical political issues. Contrary to current impressions, the electoral arrangement between the Liberal Party and the Labour Representation Committee brought more advantage to the Liberals than to Labour in London. The Liberal Party in the 1900s still lacked a coherent political standpoint, a firm electoral basis in

CONCLUSION

working class enthusiasm, and a secure financial backing. Its disastrous decay in local politics anticipated its national eclipse after 1918. It is especially striking that this was so in London, where the Labour Party was late to emerge as an obvious rival.

The Labour Party, supported by trade union funds and by working class voters, had the necessary coherence of cause and interest. Why was it so slow to develop in London? Undoubtedly the structure of London industry, the prevalence of small-scale trades and office work, and the extent of commuting and social segregation even among the working class, did not provide the kind of close working class community in which either trade unionism or socialism could make easy progress. Although histories of the early years of the labour and socialist movement frequently imply that either the trade unions or the socialists played the major part in its formation, in London both were equally vital. The first independent labour candidates were the immediate consequence of the great trade union expansion of 1889-91, and it was only with the equally important expansion after 1910 that London trade unionism could provide the Labour Party with a formidable foundation. Equally, it must be remembered that the men who led the trade unionists into independent labour politics in 1889 were socialists, and that the failure of the Labour Party to make much progress in London in the 1900s was principally due to the indifference or hostility of the largest socialist groups, the Social Democrats and the Fabians. This was why the London Labour Party was not founded earlier, and why their change in attitude was immediately followed by its formation in 1914. The same vital need for a combination of socialist and trade union backing can be found in the differing fortunes of the various local Labour Parties in London.

London socialism has more frequently received the comments of historians than other aspects of its politics, and it is thus perhaps not surprising that a closer study reveals the most marked misapprehensions in this field.

Firstly, the achievements of the Fabian Society have been grossly exaggerated. Dr. McBriar has shown how limited was the influence of the Fabians on the political policies of the Liberal Party, the Progressive Party and the Labour Party, but the implications of his work have been widely ignored. A close examination of London politics shows the failure of Fabian practical tactics and the false basis of Fabian claims to have imposed their ideas through the permeation of the Liberal Associations and the exploitation of newspapers such as the *Star*. The legendary accounts of Fabian victories at L.C.C. elections are false. The Fabian Society was not responsible for the formation of the Progressive Party in 1889, for its programme, for the idea of municipal socialism, or for the election of the first L.C.C. labour bench in 1892. Nor, on the other hand, was the Fabian Society ever a help in the development of local Labour Parties in London either in the 1890s or the 1900s. Its influence was obstructive.

The misleading account of Fabian political tactics given by most historians of Fabianism has meant that the reasons for them have not been explained. An attempt has therefore been made here to understand why the Fabians took to permeation and how they came to believe in its success, and to trace the gradual disillusionment of the Webbs in the 1900s and the conflicts which the policy then produced within the Society.

Secondly, a misleading picture has been painted of the Social Democrats as a bitter, dogmatic and impractical sect inherently unsuitable to English politics. It is easy enough to discover their idealism. Their practical policies for education, for housing, for unemployment, even for municipal socialism, have proved quite as percipient as those of the Fabians. It can be shown that in London they were quite capable of political success, and that their electoral failure after 1900 was due to inept leadership and their rejection of the labour alliance rather than to any inherent characteristic. Where the Social Democrats worked within the Labour Party they were clearly successful. Their more common lack of confidence in the labour alliance, a feeling which they shared with the Fabians, was due rather to their failure to appreciate Marxist doctrine than to their excessive insistence upon it. There is no evidence that their Marxist theory impeded the spread of socialism in London. The real situation was rather one of indifference to political doctrine, reflecting the indifference to religion. Although the early Social Democrats inherited some of the attitudes of the London secularists, by the end of the period there were signs of the development of a vague religious tone, reflecting the replacement of secularism by the ethical movement. In 1914 the Social Democrats were still the largest and most influential element in the London socialist movement. Their characteristics, their inconsistencies, were thoroughly English, produced by London and successful because they met its needs.

On the other hand, the failure of the I.L.P. in London until 1905, and the fact that its development after that represented a curious blend of Fabian and Social Democratic characteristics, suggests that it was not, as is frequently suggested, the only natural form of English socialism. Here for once its Nonconformist vocabulary proved a handicap. It only came to power in London after 1914, when the issues of the First World War and the Russian Revolution broke up the Social Democrats.

Thus on a number of particular issues a closer understanding of

CONCLUSION

London politics can contribute to a more accurate account of English political history. It can also provide a useful opportunity for examining in detail the forces at work in history. It is possible to see the political geography which is the framework behind political change, the geography of industry, or work and home, of class, race and religion. Equally fundamental in the scale of time are the economic cycles of boom and depression, prosperity and unemployment. Closely related to these, yet with their own independent and sometimes contrary influence, are the development and effects of religious and political creeds, Nonconformity and secularism, radicalism and socialism. Finally, twisting the pattern in unexpected ways, are political leaders and innumerable local personalities. Local history is a microcosm, and that ultimately, must be its justification.

APPENDIX A

ELECTIONS: GENERAL ELECTIONS 1885–1900

The constituencies are divided into groups based primarily on the social survey in Charles Booth, *Life and Labour of the People in London*, 1892–7, Volume II. The intention is to distinguish the proportion of middle class electors in each constituency. Booth's was based on the reports of School Board visitors in 1889, and is presented by small street blocks, with the numbers of middle class, working class in steady earnings, and working class in poverty, in each block. It is possible to apportion these numbers to constituencies, and although in some cases exactness is not possible the general character of each constituency can be established. The figures were compared with the census returns for 1891. It was assumed that the number of resident middle class electors would not exceed one fifth of the middle class population. The number of non-resident voters in most London constituencies is given in PP 1888 LXXIX, and in the three constituencies for which no figure is given can be estimated from the registers in the Record Room, County Hall. All non-resident electors were counted as middle class. As a check on these figures, a rough estimate of working class electors was made: one sixth of the working class population in steady earnings, and one twelfth of the working class in poverty. The resulting total numbers of electors corresponded closely to the actual numbers on the registers, and the figure for the working class in poverty to the number of lodger electors. Finally, in order to distinguish the wealthy from the lower middle classes, comparison was made with the proportion of domestic servants to families given by registration districts in Booth, op. cit., *Religious Influences*, 3, Appendix.

Group A. Ten constituencies in which middle class electors were less than 10 per cent of the electorate. Average 7·5 per cent. Bermondsey, Bethnal Green North East, Bethnal Green South West, Finsbury Central, Hoxton, Lambeth North, Mile End, Poplar, St. George's in the East, Walworth.

Group B. Twelve constituencies in which middle class electors were between 10 per cent and 16·6 per cent of the electorate. Average 14·2 per cent. Battersea, Bow and Bromley, Camberwell North, Finsbury East, Hackney South, Haggerston, Islington South, Newington West, Rotherhithe, Southwark West, Stepney, Woolwich.

APPENDIX A

Group C. Twelve constituencies in which middle class electors were between 16·6 per cent and 40 per cent of the electorate. Average 25·5 per cent. Less than 0·25 domestic servants per family, and thus without a strong upper class element. Clapham, Deptford, Hackney Central, Kennington, Islington West, Limehouse, Peckham, St. Pancras East, St. Pancras North, St. Pancras South, St. Pancras West, Whitechapel.

Group D. Four constituencies in which middle class electors were 33–40 per cent of the electorate, with a strong upper class element. Over 0·25 servants per family. Chelsea, Holborn, Kensington North, Paddington North.

Group E. Nineteen constituencies in which middle class electors were over 40 per cent of the electorate. Average 52·5 per cent. Over 0·25 domestic servants per family. Brixton, Dulwich, Fulham, Hackney North, Greenwich, Hammersmith, Hampstead, Islington East, Islington North, Kensington South, Lewisham, Marylebone East, Marylebone West, Norwood, Paddington South, St. George's Hanover Square, Strand, Wandsworth, Westminster.

Group F. Two odd constituencies, in which middle class electors were over 60 per cent, the City of London, a two-member constituency, and the University of London. They are omitted from percentage tables.

Group H. Twelve constituencies beyond the administrative boundary of London and excluded from Booth's survey. Brentford, Dartford, Ealing, Enfield, Harrow, Hornsey, Romford, Tottenham, Walthamstow, West Ham North, West Ham South, Wimbledon. Owing to the number of unopposed contests these are also omitted from percentage tables.

TABLE 1. PERCENTAGE OF ELECTORS VOTING

An allowance is made for unopposed seats. Note the increasing tendency to low polls in the Conservative safe seats in Group E.

Group	A	B	C	D	E
1885	67·6	72·4	75·9	74·6	76·3
1886	58·0	65·0	66·8	70·7	65·6
1892	72·3	73·2	74·6	70·8	71·1
1895	70·6	71·9	70·0	66·0	65·7
1900	68·4	70·4	66·7	59·9	58·3

APPENDIX A

TABLE 2. SEATS WON BY LIBERALS

The Labour seats are counted with the Liberals.

Group	A	B	C	D	E	F	G	Total
Seats in group	10	12	12	4	19	3	12	72
1885	6	8	7	1	1	1	4	28
1886	3	5	2	0	0	0	0	10
1892	9	8	4	1	0	0	2	24
1895	3	3	2	0	0	0	0	8
1900	1	5	2	0	0	0	0	8
	22	29	17	2	1	1	6	78

TABLE 3. LIBERAL SHARE OF VOTE

Percentage of Liberal votes in total vote in group. Method as Table 1; Liberal votes do not include Liberal, Liberal Unionist or Labour candidates who opposed the principal Liberal standing, but includes votes for Labour candidates not opposed by official Liberal candidates.

Group	A	B	C	D	E
1885	53·0	51·2	50·7	44·6	39·3
1886	50·0	46·3	44·4	44·3	32·5
1892	55·3	52·0	49·5	44·5	40·0
1895	48·4	45·0	45·5	37·3	34·2
1900	45·6	42·6	38·3	36·0	28·6

TABLE 4. PERCENTAGE OF ELECTORATE IN GROUP VOTING LIBERAL

Method as Table 3.

Group	A	B	C	D	E
1885	35·8	37·1	38·5	33·4	30·0
1886	29·4	30·1	29·7	31·2	21·3
1892	40·0	38·2	37·0	31·5	28·5
1895	34·2	32·3	31·8	24·6	22·5
1900	31·3	29·9	25·6	21·5	16·8

GENERAL ELECTIONS 1900–1910

The grouping of constituencies has been revised, especially with reference to the changes recorded in Charles Booth, *Life and Labour of the People in London*, revised edition 1902, third series, *Religious Influences*. In certain constituencies the increasing number of non-resident electors also affects the grouping. The new groups are:

Group A. Fifteen constituencies in which working class electors were more than 90 per cent of the electorate: Battersea, Bermondsey, Bethnal

APPENDIX A

Green North East, Bow and Bromley, Camberwell North, Hackney South, Haggerston, Islington South, Mile End, Newington West, Poplar, St. George's in the East, Stepney, Walworth, Woolwich.

Group B. Twelve constituencies with 80–90 per cent working class electors: Bethnal Green South West, Finsbury Central, Hoxton, Islington West, Kennington, Lambeth North, Limehouse, Peckham, Rotherhithe, St. Pancras East, Southwark West, Whitechapel.

Group C. Twelve constituencies with 60–80 per cent working class electors: Clapham, Deptford, Finsbury East, Fulham, Hackney Central, Hammersmith, Islington North, Kensington North, Paddington North, St. Pancras North, St. Pancras South, St. Pancras West.

Group D. Eighteen constituencies with less than 60 per cent working class electors: Brixton, Chelsea, Dulwich, Greenwich, Hackney North, Hampstead, Holborn, Islington East, Kensington South, Lewisham, Marylebone East, Marylebone West, Norwood, Paddington South, St. George's Hanover Square, Strand, Wandsworth, Westminster.

Group E. City of London and London University.

Group F. Three county constituencies in which the working class was a high proportion of the electorate: Tottenham, Walthamstow, West Ham South.

Group G. Nine other county constituencies: Brentford, Dartford, Ealing, Enfield, Harrow, Hornsey, Romford, West Ham North, Wimbledon.

TABLE 5. PERCENTAGE OF ELECTORS VOTING

Groups E and G omitted. Method as in Table 1.

Group	A	B	C	D	F
1900	70	66	64	57	59
1906	81	77	78	67	71
1910 January	85	82	85	79	80
1910 December	76	73	76	71	71

APPENDIX A

TABLE 6. SEATS WON BY LIBERALS

Labour seats are also indicated.

Group Seats in group	A 15	B 12	C 12	D 18	E 3	F 3	G 9	Total 72
1900	5	3	0	0	0	0	0	8
1906	13 & 1 Lab.	11	9 & 1 Lab.	5	0	2 & 1 Lab.	6	49
1910 January	11	8	5 & 1 Lab.	1	0	2 & 1 Lab.	2	31
1910 December	12 & 2 Lab.	10	3 & 1 Lab.	1	0	2 & 1 Lab.	3	35
	44	32	20	7	0	9	11	123

TABLE 7. LIBERAL SHARE OF VOTE

Method as Table 3, except that the three Labour constituencies of Bow and Bromley, Deptford and Woolwich are given separately.

Group	A	B	C	D	F
1900	48·1	44·0	35·7	28·1	41·8
1906	60·4	57·4	53·6	45·5	60·2
1910 January	55·1	52·0	48·1	41·3	54·8
1910 December	54·2	52·7	47·2	37·2	57·0

	Bow and Bromley	Deptford	Woolwich
1900	Lab. 36·7	Lib.-Lab. 38·0	unopposed Cons.
1906	Lib. 53·5	Lab. 52·2; Lib. 6·1	56·6
1910 January	Lab. 33·2; Lib. 24·4	Lab. 52·0	49·1
1910 December	Lab. 55·6	Lab. 51·2	50·7

TABLE 8. PERCENTAGE OF ELECTORS IN GROUP VOTING LIBERAL

Method as Table 3, but Bow and Bromley, Deptford and Woolwich are omitted.

Group	A	B	C	D	F
1900	33·6	29·1	22·8	16·2	24·9
1906	47·8	44·6	41·3	30·5	43·1
1910 January	45·7	43·0	41·1	32·9	43·9
1910 December	38·1	39·0	35·7	26·6	40·7

APPENDIX A

LONDON COUNTY COUNCIL ELECTIONS

All constituencies elected two members, except for the City, which returned four. London University was unrepresented. The same two groupings of seats are used.

TABLE 9. SEATS WON BY PROGRESSIVES 1889–98

Group	A	B	C	D	E	F	Total
Seats in group	20	24	24	8	38	4	118
1889	16	20	14	6	13	2	71
1892	20	23	21	4	15	0	83
1895	16	20	16	1	6	0	59
1898	18	22	21	2	7	0	70
	70	85	72	13	41	2	283

TABLE 10. SEATS WON BY PROGRESSIVES 1901–13

Group	A	B	C	D	E	Total
Seats in group	30	24	24	36	4	118
1901	25	24	19	16	0	84
1904	29	21	16	17	0	83
1907	22	16	4	0	0	42
1910	24	21	8	2	0	55 & 3 Lab. (2 A, 1 B)
1913	22	20	6	2	0	50 & 1 Lab. (A)
	122	122	53	38	0	314

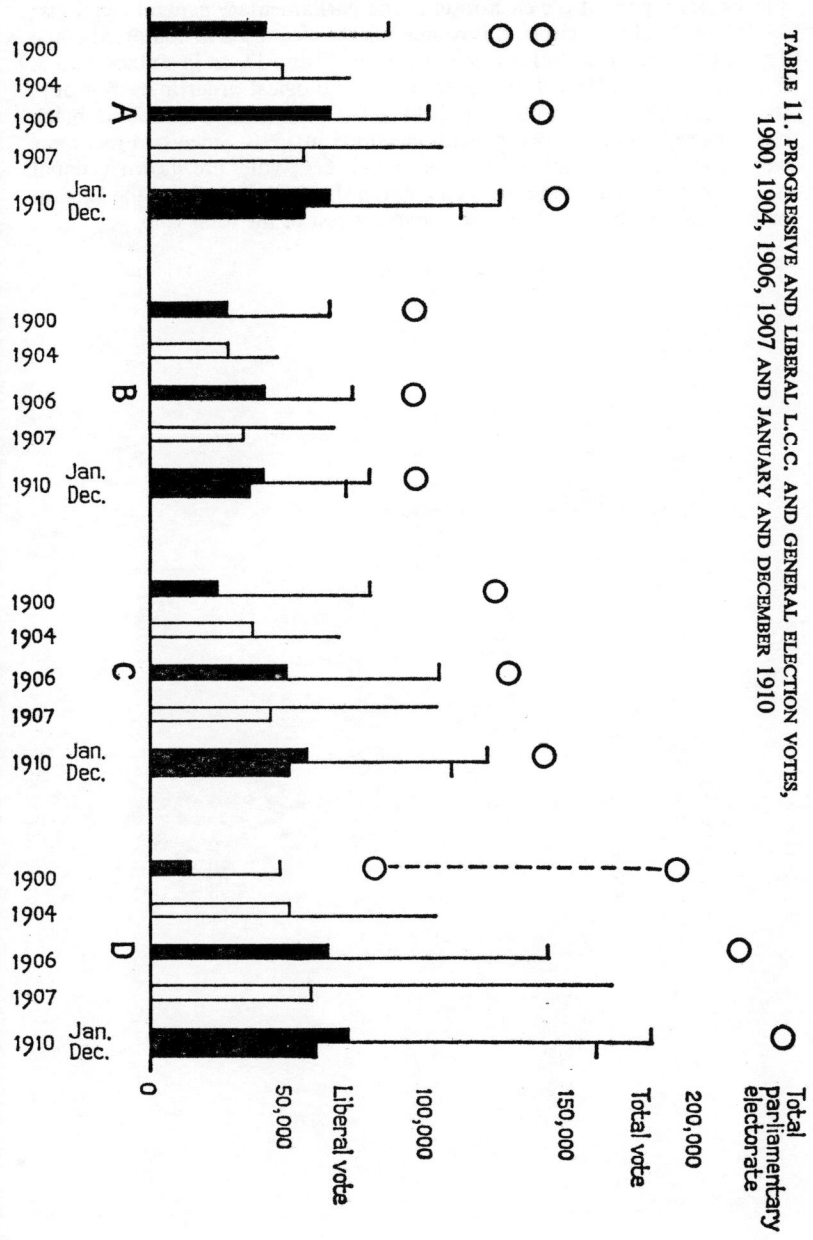

TABLE 11. PROGRESSIVE AND LIBERAL L.C.C. AND GENERAL ELECTION VOTES, 1900, 1904, 1906, 1907 AND JANUARY AND DECEMBER 1910

APPENDIX A

The circles represent the electorate in the parliamentary general elections; where this is a lower circle, this represents the electorate in contested seats. The results are given in four groups, A, B, C and D, as in Tables 5 to 8, from left to right. The elections are in chronological order in each group, the general elections in black and the L.C.C. in white. The double black columns represent the two general elections in 1910. Since two members were elected for each L.C.C. division, two L.C.C. votes are shown as equal to one parliamentary vote. In each column the thick line shows the Liberal or Progressive vote, the thin line above the rest of the total vote.

APPENDIX B

STRENGTH OF SOCIAL DEMOCRATIC FEDERATION (& S.D.P. & B.S.P.), FABIAN SOCIETY, SOCIALIST LEAGUE AND INDEPENDENT LABOUR PARTY IN LONDON

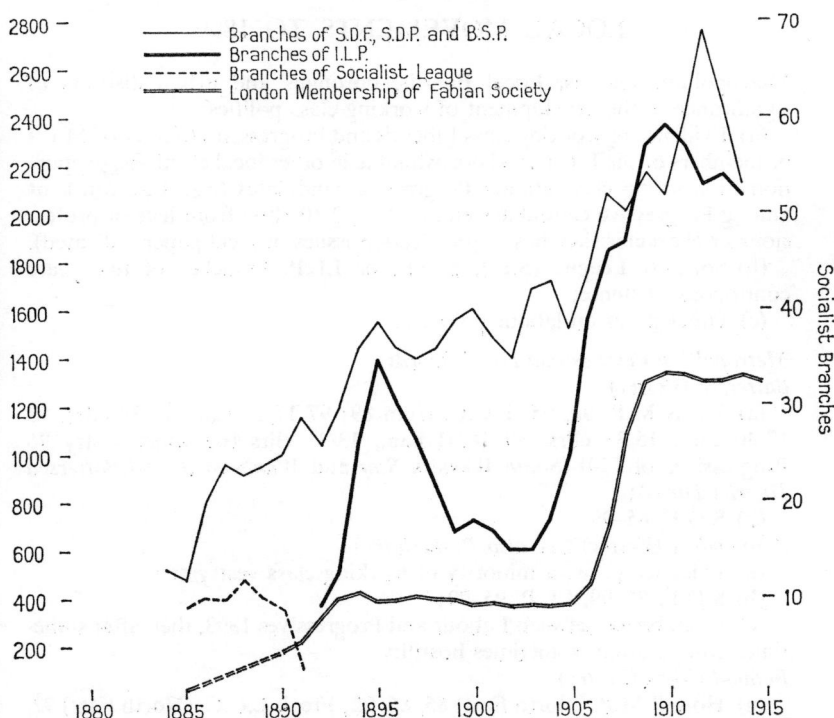

The Fabian Society London membership is given from annual reports; for the other organisations membership figures for London are unobtainable, but the numbers of branches gives an indication of strength. Membership fluctuated more than this. Such evidence as exists (Chap. 9, no. 29, Chap. 10, nos. 72 and 79) suggests that an average branch in the 1900s had at least 40 members, and the graph is drawn to this scale. The number of branches is taken from conference reports, *Justice*, *Labour Leader*, *Commonweal*, local newspapers, etc. The evidence for 1913–14 is less good than for previous years, and the fall in B.S.P. strength is probably exaggerated.

APPENDIX C

LOCAL MOVEMENTS TO 1899

Metropolitan vestries, Local Boards, boroughs and urban districts of significance in the development of working class politics:

(a) Evidence of working class Liberals and Progressives (names of M.P.s or members of the L.C.C.; where available in other local elections, proportion of working class among Progressive candidates (e.g. 4/32 can.), or among Progressive candidates elected (e.g. 2/10 cllrs) from lists of professions or character sketches in pre-election issues of local paper indicated).

(b) Socialist League (S.L.), S.D.F. or I.L.P. branches of five years continuous existence.

(c) Other notes on labour politics.

Metropolitan Vestries and Local Boards
Battersea (Vestry)
   (a) Burns M.P. 92, 95, L.C.C. from 89; 97 17/39 can., 16/32 cllrs, 98 17/40 can., 15/33 cllrs, 99 14/41 can., 13/31 cllrs (by when vestry 96 Progressives of 120) (*South Western Star* and *Wandsworth and Battersea District Times*);
   (b) S.D.F. 85–99.
Bermondsey (Vestry) (see also Rotherhithe)
   (a) Evidence poor; a minority of working class vestrymen;
   (b) S.D.F. 86–99, I.L.P. 95–99;
   (c) Open break between Labour and Progressives 1893, thereafter sometimes co-operation, sometimes hostility.
Bethnal Green (Vestry)
   (a) Howell M.P. (North East) 85, 86, 92; Freak L.C.C. (North East) 92, 95, 98; few working class on vestry;
   (b) S.D.F. 88–99.
Camberwell (Vestry)
   (a) Taylor L.C.C. 98; 98 3/26 cllrs, 99 1/31 cllrs (*South London Press*);
   (b) S.D.F. one 86–93, two 94–99, I.L.P. 94–99;
   (c) Labour and socialist candidates from 1891 commonly co-operating with Progressives.
Clerkenwell (Vestry)
   (a) Very little;
   (b) S.D.F. 84–99, S.L. 86–90, I.L.P. 95–99;
   (c) Labour and socialist candidates from 1893.

APPENDIX C

(*Deptford see Greenwich*)
(*Finsbury see Clerkenwell and St. Luke*)
Fulham (Vestry)
   (a) 99 3/18 cllrs (*Fulham Observer*);
   (b) None;
   (c) Labour candidates from 1893. Progressives sometimes co-operating, sometimes hostile.
Greenwich (Local Board):
Deptford St. Paul (Vestry)
   (a) No good evidence, but at least 94 3/20 cllrs, 97 2/8 cllrs, 98 2/30 cllrs, 99 1/23 cllrs (*Kentish Mercury*);
   (b) S.D.F. 86–99, I.L.P. 92–98;
   (c) Labour candidates, including socialists, usual from 1893, working with Progressives; in 1893 a Labour Guardians Election Committee, secretary B. T. Hall, including S.D.F., Liberal and trade union delegates, put up 15 candidates, of whom Hall stated 'only three of the candidates are getting their living by manual labour': *Kentish Mercury*, 7 April 1893, and *London*, 9 February 1893.
Greenwich (Vestry)
   (a) No good evidence;
   (b) I.L.P. 94–99;
   (c) Labour candidates from 1894.
Hackney (Vestry)
   (a) Humphrey L.C.C. 95, not readopted as not a sound Progressive; 97 2/22 cllrs, 98 3/31 cllrs (*Hackney and Kingland Gazette*); S.D.F., two, 94–99, S.L. 86–90, I.L.P. 94–98;
   (c) Labour candidates from 1893.
Hammersmith (Vestry)
   (a) Little or none;
   (b) S.L. 84–90, I.L.P. 94–98;
   (c) Labour candidates from 1891.
Hampstead (Vestry)
   (a) None;
   (b) I.L.P. 92–97;
   (c) Labour candidates from 1894.
Islington (Vestry)
   (a) 96 5/46 can., 4/21 cllrs, 97 8/40 can., 5/16 cllrs (*Islington Gazette*);
   (b) S.D.F. one 87–88, 99, two 89–98, I.L.P. 94–99;
   (c) Vestry labour group of eleven elected 1894, apparently not as a party, but holding together; by 1897 Labour and Progressives clashed in some wards, by 1899 complete split.
Kensington (Vestry)
   (a) Baum L.C.C. (North) 92; few or none on vestry;
   (b) S.D.F. one 86–90, 96–99, two 91–95, I.L.P. 94–99;
   (c) Labour candidates in North Kensington supported by Fawcett Club from 1889.
Lambeth (Vestry)
   (a) Frank Smith L.C.C. (North) 92, 98; vestry varied from north, where

APPENDIX C

usually some working class Progressives but also many conflicts, to middle class south; by 1899 about 6/70 cllrs (*South London Press*);

(b) S.D.F. one 88–92, two 93, 99, three 94–98;

(c) Some labour candidates, including socialists, elected in northern wards from 1894; always confused.

Limehouse (Local Board)

(a) Very little;

(b) S.D.F. 85–90, I.L.P. 92–96;

(c) Trade unions and Liberals co-operated in 1894, but probably only O'Connor of Coal Porters successful; Conservatives secured control of Local Board, and from 1896 occasional independent labour candidates due to Liberal-Conservative election compromises; political apathy.

Mile End Old Town (Vestry)

(a) Steadman M.P. (Stepney) 98, L.C.C. (Stepney) 92, 95, 98; Labour men the backbone of vestry Progressives from 1894, but no exact figures;

(b) S.D.F. 88–99;

(c) Steadman and his Stepney Labour League put up successful candidates, chiefly in East Centre Ward, from 1890, and, after early hostility, became the dominant element in the local Liberals; in other wards apathy enabled Conservatives to control the vestry, except 1894–5.

Newington (Vestry)

(a) 96 4/27 can., 99 7/20 cllrs (*South London Press*);

(b) S.D.F. one 89–94, two 95–99;

(c) Labour candidates from 1891, successful from 1892; Progressive vestry.

Paddington (Vestry)

(a) No evidence obtained;

(b) I.L.P. 94–98.

(*Plumstead (Vestry) see Woolwich*)

Poplar (Local Board)

(a) Cooper L.C.C. (Bow and Bromley) 92, 95, 98, Crooks L.C.C. (Poplar) 92, 95, 98; many working class Progressives on the three vestries, especially Poplar, but no exact figures;

(b) S.D.F. 91–99;

(c) See Chap. 5, 6, 7.

Rotherhithe (Vestry)

(a) Some trade union progressive candidates from 1892, no exact figures;

(b) None.

St. George's in the East (Vestry)

(a) Mercer L.C.C. 92; Ballard of Carmen and Haggerty of Builders' Labourers among vestrymen;

(b) None;

(c) Conservative vestry; socialist labour candidates opposed Progressives; frequent Liberal overtures for election agreement with Conservatives.

St. Luke (Vestry)

(a) Rowlands M.P. (East Finsbury) 86, 92; vestry very little;

(b) None.

APPENDIX C

St. Pancras (Vestry)
   (a) 94 2/37 cllrs, 96 1/14 cllrs (*St. Pancras Guardian*);
   (b) S.D.F. two 90–95, one 96–99, S.L. 85–91, I.L.P. 92–99;
   (c) From 1897 Labour and Progressives split.

Shoreditch (Vestry)
   (a) Cremer M.P. (Haggerston) 85, 86, 92; 97 7/34 cllrs, professions of 10 others could be artisan or small manufacturer, 98 6/36 cllrs, 3 others doubtful (*Hackney and Kingsland Gazette*);
   (b) S.D.F. 91–99, S.L. 85–89.

(*Southwark see also Newington*)

Southwark St. George (Vestry)
   (a) Vestry chairman, 1897, Thomas Haynes, a working man, the first working man J.P. in London (*London*, 9 September 1897); no other evidence;
   (b) None.

Southwark St. Olave (Local Board)
   (a) Horselydown vestry, 99 3/8 cllrs (*South London Press*);
   (b) None.

Southwark St. Saviour (Local Board)
   (a) Christchurch vestry, 94 13/23 can., 99 3 to 5/10 cllrs (*South London Press*);
   (b) S.D.F. 86–94.

(*Stepney see Limehouse, Mile End Old Town, St. George's in the East, Whitechapel*)

Wandsworth (Local Board)
   (a) Henderson L.C.C. (Clapham) 92; no exact details for vestries, some working class Progressives in Wandsworth;
   (b) S.D.F. 85–95.

Whitechapel (Local Board)
   (a) Very little;
   (b) S.D.F. 94–99.

Woolwich (Local Board) and Plumstead (Vestry)
   (a) See Chap. 11;
   (b) S.D.F. 95–99, I.L.P. 95–99;
   (c) See Chap. 11.

Suburban Districts

Barking
   (a) 94 4/8 cllrs, etc. (*Barking Advertiser*);
   (b) None;
   (c) First Labour School Board members elected 1889, first Labour District Board member 1890; candidates not successful 1891–2, and thereafter Labour and Liberal alliance, controlling the District Council from 1894; early impetus thus lost; the first independent Labour candidates had been put up by the Gas Workers' branch, which was then very large, covering East Ham as well as Barking, and in the first enthusiasm at the start of the union; later it was divided and less vigorous.

APPENDIX C

East Ham
 (a) Trade unions worked with Progressives, elected several members to District Council;
 (b) None;
 (c) Two Gas Workers elected to School Board as Labour candidates 1891; joint committee with Progressives from 1894 for Urban District Elections.

Edmonton
 (a) District Council, 94 4/5 cllrs, 97 5/6 cllrs (*Tottenham and Edmonton Weekly Herald*);
 (b) S.D.F. 90–99;
 (c) Two Labour candidates elected to School Board 1892, defeated 1895; first Labour candidates for Local Board 1892; 1894–7 successful Labour-Progressive co-operation in District Council elections, but by 1899 Socialist and Labour combined against Progressives, and 1898 two Socialist School Board members elected.

Erith
 (a) None;
 (b) None;
 (c) First Labour candidate elected to School Board 1892; first Labour candidate for Local Board 1892; 1894 well organised Labour Party for District Council elections, Ling elected, and 1898 three Labour elected; see also Chap. 11.

Tottenham
 (a) Labour-Progressive candidates for District Council 1894, but usually non-political;
 (b) S.D.F. 84–96, I.L.P. 95–99;
 (c) Lead taken by socialists, who secured one School Board member 1888, re-elected 1891, defeated 1894; a Labour member elected 1891, re-elected 1894; also socialist local candidates, but labour candidates only 1893–4.

Walthamstow
 (a) Woods M.P. 97; 94 4/15 can., 97 4/12 cllrs (*Walthamstow and Leyton Guardian*);
 (b) S.D.F. 93–99;
 (c) In addition to working class Progressives, also independent Labour candidates from 1894.

West Ham
 (a) See Chap. 6;
 (b) S.D.F. one 86–93, two 94–99, I.L.P. one 93–94, two 95–99;
 (c) See Chap. 6.

Willesden
 (a) Very little;
 (b) None;
 (c) Labour candidates from 1894.

Wood Green
 (a) 4 working class Progressive candidates defeated 1894, little else;
 (b) S.D.F. 87–99.

APPENDIX D

LOCAL MOVEMENTS 1900–1914

Boroughs and urban districts of significance in the development of working class politics:

(a) Political control of the council (P = Progressive; L = Labour; M = Moderate, Municipal or Conservative; where no majority party, number of councillors indicated);

(b) Evidence of working class Liberals and Progressives (names of M.P.s or members of L.C.C.; borough or urban district elections, proportion of working class among Progressive candidates (e.g. 4/32 can.) or among Progressive candidates elected (e.g. 2/10 cllrs) from lists of professions or character sketches in pre-election issues of local paper indicated);

(c) S.D.F., S.D.P., B.S.P. or I.L.P. branches of five years continuous existence (S.D. signifies S.D.F., S.D.P. or B.S.P.);

(d) Affiliated local Labour Party;

(e) Other notes on labour politics.

Metropolitan Boroughs
Battersea

(a) P 00 03 06 12; M 09;

(b) Burns M.P. throughout, and L.C.C. until 1910; 00 20/37 cllrs (*South Western Star*), 03 22/38 cllrs (*Battersea Mercury*), 06 16/29 cllrs (*South Western Star*), and many old names reappear 12;

(c) S.D. 00–14, I.L.P. 05–14;

(d) Battersea Trades Council 02–06, Battersea Labour Party 08–12;

(e) See Chap. 8.

Bermondsey

(a) M 00 03 06 12; 09 27 P, 1 L, 26 M;

(b) 06 16/53 can., 4/22 cllrs, some standing as Labour-Progressive; also 7/11 independent Roman Catholic candidates (*Southwark Recorder*); 09 6/27 cllrs (*Southwark Recorder*); 00, 03, 12 similar names reappear;

(c) S.D. 01–14, I.L.P. 09–14;

(d) Bermondsey Labour Representation Committee 12–14;

(e) Labour Party led by I.L.P.; difficulties with Irish, and local trade unions weak until 1911, but L.R.C. had 3,490 affiliated members 1913.

Bethnal Green

(a) PP 00 03 06 09 12;

(b) Branch L.C.C. 01; borough council information only 09, working class insignificant (*East London Observer*);

(c) S.D. 00–14, I.L.P. 06–14;

(d) Bethnal Green Labour Representation Committee 10–13;

(e) See Chap. 8: the local L.R.C. was nominal.

APPENDIX D

Camberwell
  (a) P 00 03; M 06 09 12;
  (b) Taylor L.C.C. throughout; 09 4/47 can., 3/27 cllrs (*South London Press*); other years similar names;
  (c) S.D. two branches 00–04 and 11–14, one 05–11, I.L.P. one branch 03–07, two 07–14.
  (e) See Chap. 11: shortlived unaffiliated local L.R.C. 1904.

Deptford
  (a) M 00 06 09 12; P 03;
  (b) Progressives insignificant after 03, but names later Labour suggest 00 4/16 cllrs, 03 7/18 cllrs;
  (c) S.D. 04–14, I.L.P. 04–14;
  (d) Deptford Labour Representation Association 06 and 11–14;
  (e) See Chap. 11: 9 Labour cllrs 1909, 11 1912.

Finsbury
  (a) M 00 06 09 12; P 03;
  (b) Steadman M.P. 06, Smith L.C.C. 01; confused party situation, but 00 approx. 3/10 cllrs (*Holborn and Finsbury Guardian*), more elected in bye-elections, forming a council labour party, chairman Garrity (*Labour Leader* 19 July 1902, and J. M. Gallington of Gasworkers to J. R. MacDonald, 4 September 1902, Labour Party correspondence); 03 perhaps 4/32 cllrs (*Holborn and Finsbury Guardian*); 06 3/14, 09 2/8 cllrs, 12 1/5 cllrs (*Islington Gazette*);
  (c) S.D. 00–14, two 08–10; I.L.P. 00–05, 09–14;
  (e) See Chap. 11.

Fulham
  (a) P 00; 03 18 P, 2 L, 16 M; M 06 09 12;
  (b) 00 4/21 cllrs, 03 3/18 cllrs, 06 4/30 can., 09 2/30 can., 12 5/30 can. (*Fulham Observer*);
  (c) S.D. 00–12, I.L.P. 00–13;
  (d) Fulham Labour Party 09;
  (e) Labour Party survived withdrawal of S.D.F., but made little progres s.

Greenwich
  (a) M 00 03 06 09 12;
  (b) No information, except that borough council labour candidates worked with Progressives 06 (*Daily Chronicle*, 26 October 06);
  (d) Greenwich Labour Representation Committee 05–06;
  (e) Greenwich Labour Representation Association failed to secure a labour candidate in 1904 after the Liberals had refused co-operation, although its secretary claimed to 'have nearly 200 trade unionist votes in the Borough that have nearly all voted Tory before who would support us and work for us' (J. Emerson to J. R. MacDonald, 22 June 1904, 9 May 1905, Labour Party correspondence). Independent Labour candidates stood for the council in 1909 and 1912, one elected in 1909, and Gilbert, secretary of the Combined Smiths, for the L.C.C. in 1910.

Hackney
  (a) M 00 06 12; P 03 09;
  (b) Watson stood for Hackney South, L.C.C. 13; 00 3/50 can., but 7

APPENDIX D

candidates no information (*Hackney and Kingland Gazette*), 09 Progressives opposed Labour until title 'Labour-Progressive' but only 2/24 candidates (*Hackney and Kingland Gazette*); no information 03 06 12;

(c) S.D. one 00–07, two 07–14, I.L.P. 08–14;

(d) Hackney Labour Representation Committee 06, Hackney Trades Council 08–14;

(e) Stevenson, secretary Builders' Labourers, was selected in 1903 as Labour candidate for Hackney South, and both Nonconformists and S.D.F. were co-operating with the Trades Council; the candidature was very promising, and registration work done, but Labour prospects were ruined when Stevenson was removed from his trade union post for fraud. Labour and Socialist council candidates separate but not conflicting 1909 and 1912.

Hammersmith

(a) M 00 03 09 12; Ratepayers' Association 06;

(b) Cooper stood for L.C.C. 1910; no others;

(c) S.D. 07–14, I.L.P. 05–14;

(d) South Western Trades Council 04–07, Hammersmith Labour Representation Committee 07–14;

(e) See Chaps. 8, 9; Labour Party initially in strong position due to split, but discouraged by national party and losing S.D.F. support made little progress.

Hampstead

(a) M 00 06 09 12; 'Non-Political Progressives' 03;

(b) Working class 'non-political Progressives', 03 2/25 cllrs, 06 3/13 cllrs, 09 0/6 cllrs, 12 0/6 cllrs (now sponsored by Hampstead Citizens' Union) (*Hampstead and Highgate Express*);

(c) S.D. 08–14, I.L.P. 08–14;

(d) Hampstead Trades Council 09–14;

(e) Although the Trades Council secretary complained that the non-political Progressives refused to support nearly all its proposed borough council candidates in 1903 (cuttings book, Hampstead library), and *Hampstead and Highgate Express*, 27 October and 3 November 1903), the first independent Labour candidates were not put up by the Trades Council until 1912—without success.

Islington

(a) M 00 06 09 12; P 03;

(b) Dew L.C.C. Islington South from 04; 00 0/10 cllrs, 3/45 can., 03 9/36 cllrs, 06 2/42 can., 09 2/42 can., 12 5/42 can, (*Islington Gazette*);

(c) S.D. one 00–02, two 03–14, I.L.P. one 05–08, 11–14, two 09–10;

(d) Islington Trades Council 05–08, 10–11, Islington Labour Party 11–14;

(e) Extreme example of confused development. At the 1900 council election some trade unionists stood as Progressives, others including Parker of the Compositors as independents against them, and two Social Democrats and Cole the Plasterers' London secretary, stood as candidates of the Islington Socialist and Labour Council, whose treasurer was Naylor, future Compositors' secretary. None were elected. In 1903 the newly-

APPENDIX D

formed Islington Trades Council ran 18 candidates, working with both socialists and Progressives, including Parker, Cole, Copeland (another Compositor), Gould (an I.L.P. brassworker), and the 9 elected formed a separate group on the Council. In 1905 Gould, as chairman, secured the Trade Council's affiliation to the Labour Party. Meanwhile, owing to the opposition of some Progressives to a 30/– minimum wage for council employees, the Labour councillors split with the Progressives. Chaos followed. Parker, who belonged to the I.L.P., tried to secure his own adoption as an independent Labour candidate. In the 1906 borough council elections two Nonconformist working men stood as Progressives, others including Copeland and Watson, the Tramwaymen's secretary, as Labour candidates, and yet others including Gould as socialists, all conflicting, and all disastrously defeated. Parker now led the Trades Council in a Liberal direction, acting as George Dew's L.C.C. agent and securing his own re-election as a Guardian in 1907, while opposing 'bogus labour' socialists. As a result he was ousted from influence by moderate socialists, who formed the Islington Labour Party with Trades Council backing. Gould meanwhile in turn had become Progressive, so that in 1909 there was again conflict and confusion, the largest group including Parker, Naylor and Copeland standing as Labour Party candidates, but some as Progressives, some with the support of Gould's largely middle class Progressive Labour Party, and the Social Democrats as candidates of the Socialist Election Committee. Following this Parker, who was re-elected a Guardian in 1910, appears to have reasserted his influence, so that the Trades Council (allegedly because of the Osborne judgement) disbanded the Islington Labour Party, and in the general elections issued pro-Liberal manifestoes, one supporting Horatio Bottomley. For this it was disaffiliated by the national Labour Party, and the Islington Labour Representation Committee, formed by left-wing I.L.Pers as a rival body, was affiliated in its place. After protests by moderate I.L.Pers the national party imposed negotiations, Parker was again ousted, and a joint Islington Labour Party was formed with Naylor as chairman. The 14 Labour candidates in 1912 included Parker, a number of left-wing I.L.Pers, and Copeland, who was elected. Most of these Labour candidates appear to have secured a working arrangement with the Progressives. Watson now stood as a Progressive, while 18 Social Democrats stood independently, usually against Labour candidates. These continual conflicts made progress impossible.

Kensington
   (a) M 00 03 06 09 12;
   (b) 00 1/10 cllrs, and this councillor a Labour candidate 1903 (*Kensington News* and *West London Times*);
   (c) S.D. 00–08, I.L.P. 04–14;
   (d) Paddington and Kensington Trades Council 1907;
   (e) In North Kensington Labour was independent from 1903, consistently opposed by the Progressives, but nevertheless securing six councillors in 1906, two in 1909 and four in 1912; strong I.L.P. working with good Trades Council.

APPENDIX D

Lambeth
 (a) M 00 03 06 09 12;
 (b) North Lambeth, Gosling stood December 10, Frank Smith L.C.C. 07, then became independent Labour; borough council complex situation, southern wards all middle class, northern working class wards always some three-cornered fights between Labour and Progressive and some electoral arrangements; 06 2/50, 09 1/50, 12 5/50 (*Brixton Free Press* and *South London Press*);
 (c) S.D. two 00–03, 10–14, one 04–09, I.L.P. two 05–14;
 (d) Lambeth Trades Council 03–06, 09, Lambeth Labour Representation Committee 10–13;
 (e) Good I.L.P. and S.D.F. as well as some radical support for independent Labour, but lack of unity between districts, lack of consistency, and lack of strong local leadership prevented much success; one Labour borough councillor elected 1906, two 1909, Frank Smith L.C.C. 1910.

Lewisham
 (a) M 00 06 09 12; P 03;
 (b) 00 1/32 can., 03 0/34 cllrs, 06 0/29 can., 09 0/26, 12 2/22 (*Lewisham Borough News*);
 (c) S.D. 07–12, I.L.P. 06–10;
 (d) Lewisham Labour Representation Association 04–06;
 (e) Little working class electoral strength except in Sydenham; Labour Party formed by trade unionists in 1904, put up 7 Guardians candidates, won several bye-elections, forming a council Labour group including Deller, the Plasterers' secretary, and Stephenson of the Engineers, but in 1906 both Labour and Progressives were eliminated in a three-cornered fight and the Labour Party organisation disappeared. Although Progressives and Labour co-operated in 1909 and 1912 none were elected.

Paddington
 (a) M 00 03 06 09 12;
 (b) Probably none after 1900;
 (c) S.D. 08–14, I.L.P. 07–14;
 (d) See Kensington;
 (e) From 1903 independent Labour candidates run by the Trades Council with Kensington, opposed by the Progressives, and unsuccessful.

Poplar
 (a) M 00 06 09 12; 03 18 P, 17 M, 7 L;
 (b) Crooks L.C.C. 01 04 07, Cooper L.C.C. 01 04 (defeated 07 13); 00 in Poplar Labour-Progressives run by Labour League, 4 elected, elsewhere friction; 03 friction in Bow, not in Bromley or Poplar, 4 Labour-Progressives elected; 06 four Progressives work with Labour, 5 with Municipal Alliance; 09 friction only in one ward, but parties clearly separate, Progressives now entirely middle class; 12 similar, by now only 2 Progressives elected (*East London Observer* and *East London Advertiser*);
 (c) S.D. two 00–14, I.L.P. two 06–13, one 14;
 (d) Poplar Labour Representation Committee 06–13, Poplar Labour Party 14;
 (e) See Chaps 9, 10, 11; Lansbury M.P. December 1910, Ensor and

APPENDIX D

Lansbury L.C.C. 1910, Susan Lawrence L.C.C. 1913; 11 councillors 1903, 9 1906, 11 1909, 9 1912.

St. Pancras
  (a) M 00 06 09 12; P 03;
  (b) Hennessey L.C.C. candidate 03; 00 2/21 cllrs, 6/50 can., 03 worked with Labour but no details, 06 8/50 can., 12 6/50 can. (*St. Pancras Chronicle* and *St. Pancras Guardian*);
  (c) S.D. 00–14, I.L.P. 00–14;
  (d) St. Pancras Labour Representation Committee 05–06;
  (e) In 1900 and 1903 Socialists and Labour ran as Progressives, those elected including Hennessey of the Plasterers and G. B. Shaw; in 1906 three-cornered fights in many wards, but Otley the Plasterers' secretary elected as a Progressive; 1909 Labour Party ran with Progressives against S.D.F.; 1912 S.D.F. and most I.L.P. run as Socialists against Labour-Progressives; little Labour progress.

Shoreditch
  (a) P 00; M 03 06 09 12;
  (b) No details, but Progressives opposing Labour at least from 1906;
  (c) S.D. one 00–08, two 09–14, I.L.P. 06–11;
  (d) Shoreditch Labour Party 08–09, Shoreditch Labour Representation Committee 10, Shoreditch Trades and Labour Council 11;
  (e) See Chap. 9.

Southwark
  (a) P 00 03 09 12; M 06;
  (b) Jesson L.C.C. from 07; 00 9/43 cllrs (*South London Mail*), 03 not enough detail, 06 3/27 cllrs, 8/46 can., 09 6/37 cllrs, 15/60 can. (*Southwark Recorder*), 12 2/30 cllrs (*South London Press*);
  (c) S.D. one 00–08, 14, two 09–13;
  (d) Southwark Trades Council 06–14;
  (e) See Chap. 8.

Stepney
  (a) M 00 03 06 09 12;
  (b) Steadman L.C.C. 01 04, Gosling L.C.C. from 04; none except 12 2/22 cllrs (*East London Advertiser*);
  (c) S.D. one 00, two 01–05, 12–14, three 06–11, I.L.P. 06–14;
  (e) In early 1900s no Liberal Association in Stepney, and Stepney Labour League ran candidates; 1903 a Parliamentary and Municipal Council formed, Haggerty of Builders' Labourers elected; Stepney Labour League shared rooms with the I.L.P. after 1906, but local apathy, differences between districts, frustrated efforts to form a proper Labour Party.

Wandsworth
  (a) M 00 03 06 09 12;
  (b) 00 Progressives opposed Labour candidates, 06 1/50 can. (*South Western Star*);
  (c) S.D. 03–13, I.L.P. one 00–04, two 05, three 06–14;
  (d) Wandsworth Trades Council 06–11;
  (e) Little working class electoral strength; I.L.P. backbone of Labour Party election work in Clapham and Tooting.

APPENDIX D

Woolwich
   (a) M 00 06 09 12; L 03;
   (b) 00 5/10 cllrs, 16/40 can.; from 1903 Labour only;
   (c) S.D. 03–07, 09–14, I.L.P. 03–14;
   (d) Woolwich Trades Council 01–14, Woolwich Labour Representation Association 05–06;
   (e) See Chap. 11; Crooks M.P. from 1903, except January-December 1910; 25 councillors 1903, 13 1906, 10 1909, 15 1912.

Suburban Districts

Acton
   (a) Non-political;
   (b) Insignificant (*Acton Gazette*);
   (c) S.D. 05–13 or 14, I.L.P. 06–14;
   (e) Working class district, but inactive before first independent Labour candidates in 1906; S.D.F. and I.L.P. work together, two Labour councillors elected 1907, re-elected 1910, but not 1913.

Barking
   (a) M 00–14;
   (b) No Progressives (*Barking Advertiser*);
   (c) S.D. 03–14, I.L.P. 09–14;
   (e) Labour and Socialist candidates against (Conservative) Ratepayers' Association, one Labour councillor elected 1900, one 1904, two 1908, two 1910, one 1911, one 1912, one 1914; apart from a joint I.L.P.-S.D.F.-Gas Workers' committee 1909, no Labour Party organisation.

Brentford
   (a) M 00–14;
   (b) None (*Middlesex County Times*);
   (e) Little sign of working class activity until an Irishman stands as a Labour candidate in 1914.

Chiswick
   (a) M 00–14;
   (b) None (*Acton Gazette*);
   (c) I.L.P. 06–12;
   (e) Little working class activity, although two Labour councillors elected c. 1906, and again candidates 1913–14.

Ealing
   (a) M 00–14;
   (b) Insignificant (*Middlesex County Times*);
   (c) I.L.P. 04–14;
   (d) Ealing Labour Representation Committee 06–07, 12–14;
   (e) Wealthy suburb, but considerable independent Labour activity 1904–7 and from 1910.

East Ham
   (a) No consistent parties;
   (b) One or two working class Progressives, most Labour or Socialist; (*Barking Advertiser*, *East Ham Echo*, *Stratford Express*, and *West Ham and South Essex Mail*);
   (c) I.L.P. 00–04, 06–14;

APPENDIX D

(d) East Ham Labour Representation Committee 08–14;

(e) Socialist and Trade Union Committee, then 1903 Labour Representation Committee formed, secretary Pope, a Socialist schoolmaster, 1,200 affiliated members 1913; also a Labour League which supported Socialists; Hutchins the Gas Workers' President, elected a Labour councillor 1904, 1905, 1908; another Labour man 1905; Dean, a Socialist commercial traveller, from 1908; Howlett, a Labour civil servant, from 1909; and Ford, a Labour insurance agent, from 1911; and a trade unionist in 1912; so that by 1914 four Labour councillors of 18.

Edmonton

(a) M 00–14;

(b) Throughout 2 or 3/7 or 10 cllrs (*Wood Green and Tottenham Weekly Herald*);

(c) S.D. 00–14;

(e) Socialists first elected with Progressive support, then from 1902 rapid rise of the independent socialist party (S.D.F.) with Trades Council support, 7 councillors 1906; but fail to work with I.L.P., no councillors remain by 1913.

Erith

(a) M 00–14;

(b) Very little;

(c) S.D. 06–14;

(d) Erith Trades Council 03–04, Erith Labour Representation Association or Committee 08–11;

(e) See Chap. 11.

Tottenham

(a) Party lines not consistent;

(b) Dobson, organising secretary of the Railway Servants, district councillor and county councillor, and two carpenters, district councillors, one by 1914 becoming a builder (*Wood Green and Tottenham Weekly Herald*);

(c) S.D. 00–14, I.L.P. 00–14;

(d) Tottenham Trades Council 03–09, Tottenham Labour Party 10;

(e) Labour Party effectively organised, some stand as Labour, some as Socialist; three independent Labour councillors elected 1905, one re-elected 1907, another 1908 and 1911.

Walthamstow

(a) P 00–12; M 13–14;

(b) 06 4/21 cllrs, falling to 14 1/12 cllrs (*Walthamstow Guardian*);

(c) S.D. one 00–08, two 09–14, I.L.P. 04–14;

(d) Walthamstow Trades Council 08–11;

(e) See Chap. 8, n. 22; the failure of the Labour candidate selected in 1903 to secure financial backing and the lack of S.D.F. support prevented development.

West Ham

(a) L 00; M 01–08; 09 16 M, 17 L, 3 P; 10 16 M, 16 L, 4 P; 11 17 M, 16 L, 3 P; M 12–14;

(b) None;

(c) S.D. two 00–02 and 08–14, three 03–07, I.L.P. two 00–14;

APPENDIX D

(d) West Ham Trades Council 01–05, West Ham Labour Representation Committee 06;
(e) see Chaps 9, 11.

Willesden
  (a) M 01 04 07 10; 13 11 M, 8 L, 5 P;
  (b) 04 1/10 cllrs; 07 2/20 can. (*Willesden and Kilburn Chronicle*); no others;
  (c) S.D. 06–14, I.L.P. 01–11;
  (d) Willesden Labour Party 08–14.
  (e) Vigorous I.L.P.-led Labour Party, 5 Guardians 1905–8, 5 councillors 1910, 8 councillors 1913; Grimwood, headmaster, parliamentary candidate 1911.

Wood Green
  (a) Parties not clear, probably P 00–10; 11 9 M, 7 P, 2 L; M 14;
  (b) Gibson, a compositor, a Progressive councillor from 1904; little else (*Wood Green and Tottenham Weekly Herald*);
  (c) S.D. 00–04, I.L.P. 07–11;
  (d) Wood Green Labour Representation Committee 06–07.
  (e) Some Labour successes 1905–7.

SELECT BIBLIOGRAPHY

1. UNPUBLISHED SOURCES

(A) OFFICIAL RECORDS

At Transport House;
Minutes of the National Executive Committee of the Labour Representation Committee and the Labour Party, and correspondence, 1900–14.

At Herbert Morrison House;
Minutes of the London Labour Party, from 1919.

At the Fabian Society;
Fabian Society meetings minutes 1883–5, executive committee minutes 1885–1914, correspondence, miscellaneous records, and East London (Poplar and Hackney) Fabian Groups minute book 1890–3.

At the British Library of Political and Economic Science;
Labour Representation Committee, minutes and papers collected by Edward Pease 1900–12; Independent Labour Party, Herbert Bryan Collection, London District Council minutes and correspondence 1909–16, North London Federation minutes and correspondence 1910–12, general correspondence 1910–19, City branch minutes and correspondence 1907–22, and Watford branch minutes and correspondence 1904–10; British Socialist Party, miscellaneous papers, 1911–12.

In the possession of Francis Johnson;
Independent Labour Party, National Administrative Council minutes, 1893–1918, London District Council minutes 1892–8, Metropolitan District Council minutes 1906–9, L.C.C. Election Committee minutes 1898 and Finsbury branch minutes 1900.

At the British Museum;
Hammersmith branch, Social Democratic Federation and Socialist League, and Hammersmith Socialist Society, minutes 1884–96.

At Marx Memorial Library;
Social Democratic Federation, Hackney branch minutes 1903–6; British Socialist Party, West Ham branch minutes 1917–19.

In the possession of Julius Jacobs;
London Trades Council, Executive Committee minutes, 1883–1914.

At the Guildhall;
London Municipal Society, Guard Book, 1900–1.

SELECT BIBLIOGRAPHY

At the Conservative Research Department;
London Unionist Members Committee minutes, 1906–19.

At Thorne House;
Municipal Employees Association, Executive Committee minutes, 1900–1914.

At Deptford Labour Party Office;
Deptford Labour Association, Executive Committee and General Council minutes, 1906–14.

At Hammersmith Public Library;
Hammersmith Conservative Association, minutes and cash book, 1886–1915.

At Islington Public Library;
North London Socialist Club minutes, 1896–9; Brotherhood Church minutes, 1926–33, and miscellaneous papers.

At Kensington Public Library;
South Kensington Conservative Association, The Boltons and Radcliffe Ward minutes, 1882–1929.

At South Kensington Conservative Association Office;
South Kensington Conservative Association Executive Committee, General Council and Annual Meetings minutes, 1885–1911.

At St. Pancras Reform Club;
St. Pancras Reform Club minutes 1908–12.

At Woolwich Labour Party Office;
Woolwich Labour Party minutes, 1903–14, correspondence 1903, and Finance and Pioneer Committee, 1909–21; Woolwich Trades Council minutes, 1903–17.

At the Boro' of East Ham Club;
East Ham Progressive Club minutes, 1903–9.

In the possession of Tom Braddock;
Wimbledon Socialist Society, minutes, 1907–8, and other papers.

(B) PRIVATE PAPERS

At the British Museum;
Burns Collection, diaries of and correspondence of John Burns, 46284–46344, and correspondence of Joseph Lane, 46345; Herbert Gladstone Collection, correspondence and whip's papers, 45985–46118; William Morris Collection, diaries and correspondence, 45298–45335; Avebury Collection, correspondence of Sir John Lubbock, 1888–92, 49648–49653; T. J. Cobden-Sanderson, Time Book, 49061; Dilke Collection, diaries and correspondence of Sir Charles Dilke, 43885–43941; Shaw Collection, correspondence and papers of George Bernard Shaw, 46507 and 50508–50730; Balfour Collection, correspondence of A. J. Balfour and J. Sandars, 49760–49768.

SELECT BIBLIOGRAPHY

At the British Library of Political and Economic Science;
Passfield Collection, diaries and correspondence of Sidney and Beatrice Webb; Graham Wallas Collection, correspondence; George Lansbury Collection, papers and correspondence; Courtney Collection, diary of Kate Courtney 1888–92; MacDonald Collection, some papers and correspondence of Margaret and Ramsay MacDonald; F. W. Galton, manuscript autobiography; H. M. Hyndman, letter to Robert Banner.

At Corpus Christi College, Oxford;
Ensor Collection, papers, diaries and correspondence of R. C. K. Ensor.

At Norwich City Library;
Fred Henderson, papers and correspondence.

At Kent Record Office;
Akers-Douglas Collection, papers and correspondence of 1st Viscount Chilston.

In the possession of Henry Pelling;
Copies of correspondence of J. R. MacDonald with J. Keir Hardie and J. Bruce Glasier (originals in the possession of Mr. Francis Johnson) and of H. M. Hyndman to Morris Hillquit (originals at Wisconsin State Historical Society).

In the possession of Karl Walter;
Manuscript autobiography.

In the possession of Ken Weller;
Notes on the working class movement in North London.

(C) THESES

I. C. CANNAN, "The Social Situation of the Skilled Worker: a study of the compositor in London", London Ph.D. thesis, 1961.

J. CHILD, "A History of Industrial Relations in the British Printing Industry", Oxford D.Phil. thesis, 1955.

L. A. CLARK, "The Liberal Party and Collectivism, 1886–1906", Cambridge M.Litt. thesis, 1957.

D. W. CROWLEY, "Origins of the Revolt of the British Labour Movement from Liberalism, 1875–1906", London Ph.D. thesis, 1952.

A. E. P. DUFFY, "The Growth of Trade Unions in England, 1867–1906", London Ph.D. thesis, 1956.

H. J. DYOS, "Suburban Development of Greater London South of the Thames, 1836–1914", London Ph.D. thesis, 1952.

P. S. GUPTA, "History of the Amalgamated Society of Railway Servants, 1871–1913", Oxford D.Phil. thesis, 1960.

R. J. HARTRIDGE, "The Development of Industries in London South of the Thames, 1750–1850", London M.Sc. thesis, 1955.

E. J. HOBSBAWM, "Fabianism and the Fabians, 1884–1914", Cambridge Ph.D. thesis, 1949.

K. S. INGLIS, "English Churches and the Working Class, 1880–1900", Oxford D.Phil. thesis, 1956.

SELECT BIBLIOGRAPHY

J. A. JACKSON, "The Irish in London", London M.A. thesis, 1958.
S. LERNER, "The History of the United Clothing Workers Union", London Ph.D. thesis, 1956.
A. MARWICK, "The Independent Labour Party, 1918–1932", Oxford B.Litt. thesis, 1962.
M. MOORE, "A Century's Extension of Passenger Transport Facilities (1830–1930) within the London Transport Board's Area, and its Relation to Population Spread", London Ph.D. thesis, 1948.
R. W. MORRIS, "Geographical and Historical Aspects of the Public Water Supply of London, 1852–1902", London Ph.D. thesis, 1941.
H. M. PELLING, "Origins and Early History of the Independent Labour Party, 1880–1900", Cambridge Ph.D. thesis, 1950.
B. PRIBICEVIC, "Demand for Workers' Control in the Railway, Mining and Engineering Industries, 1910–1922", Oxford D.Phil. thesis, 1957.
H. REES, "The North Eastern Expansion of London since 1770", London M.Sc. thesis, 1946.
N. ROBERTSON, "A Study of the Development of Labour Relations in the British Furniture Trade", Oxford B.Litt. thesis, 1955.
H. A. SHEARRING, "London, 1800–1830", Oxford D.Phil. thesis, 1955.
C. T. SOLBERG, "The Independent Labour Party, 1893 to 1918", Oxford B.Litt. thesis, 1939.
C. TSUZUKI, "H. M. Hyndman and British Socialism, 1881–1921", Oxford D.Phil. thesis, 1959.
C. L. WHEBLE, "The London Lighterage Trade: Its History, Organisation and Economics", London M.Sc. thesis, 1939.
M. S. WILKINS, "The Influence of Socialist Ideas on English Prose Writing and Political Thinking, 1880–1895", Cambridge Ph.D. thesis, 1957.
E. P. M. WOLLASTON, "The Irish Nationalist Movement in Great Britain, 1880–1908", London M.A. thesis, 1958.

2. NEWSPAPERS AND PERIODICALS

These are indicated in footnotes, but the following local Socialist or Labour papers may be mentioned:

Bow and Bromley Socialist, 1897–8.
Bow and Bromley Worker, 1909–12.
Chelsea Pick and Shovel, 1900–1.
Finsbury, 1900.
Hammersmith Searchlight, 1900.
Hammersmith Socialist Record, 1891–3.
New World, 1908–13 (West Ham).
Walthamstow Socialist Critic, 1900–1.
West Ham Citizen, 1899–1900.
West Ham Tribune, 1901–3.
Willesden Labour Monthly, 1896.
Woolwich and District Labour Notes, 1898–9.
Woolwich Labour Journal, 1901–4.
Woolwich Pioneer, 104–14.

SELECT BIBLIOGRAPHY

3. OFFICIAL REPORTS, MANIFESTOES, COLLECTIONS OF CUTTINGS AND MISCELLANEOUS PRINTED MATERIAL

(A) PARLIAMENTARY PAPERS

PP 1883 LXXVIII–LXXX, *General Report and Returns of the Census of England and Wales* (1881).
PP 1884–5 XXX, *First Report of the Royal Commission on Housing of the Working Classes.*
PP 1887 LXXIX, etc., *Annual Reports by the Chief Labour Correspondent of the Board of Trade on Trade Unions.*
PP 1888 XX–XXI, 1889 XIII–XIV, 1890 XVII, *Report of Select Committee on Sweating.*
PP 1892 XXXIV–VI, 1893–4 XXXII–IV, XXXIX, 1894 XXXV, *Reports of the Royal Commission on Labour.*
PP 1893–4 CIV–CVI, *General Report and Returns of the Census of England and Wales* (1891).
PP 1894 XVII–XVIII, *Report of the Royal Commission on Amalgamation of the City and County of London.*
PP 1902 CXX, 1903 LXXXIV, 1904 CVII, *General Report and Returns of the Census of England and Wales* (1901).
PP 1904 XXXII, *Report of the Inter-Departmental Committee on Physical Deterioration.*
PP 1905 XXX, *Report of the Royal Commission on the Means of Locomotion and Transport in London.*
PP 1905 LXXXIV, *Memoranda, Statistical Tables and Charts prepared in the Board of Trade ... Changes in the Cost of Living of the Working Classes in Large Towns.*
PP 1909 XXXVII, *Report of the Royal Commission on the Poor Law.*
PP 1909 CIII, *Statistical Memoranda and Charts prepared in the Local Government Board relating to Public Health and Social Conditions.*
PP 1912–13 CXI–CXIII, 1913 LXXVII–LXXX, *General Report and Returns of the Census of England and Wales* (1911).
PP 1914–16 LIX, *Report of the Chief Registrar of Friendly Societies.*

(B) OTHER STATISTICS AND ALMANACS

Dod's Parliamentary Companion.
Labour Annual 1895–9.
Labour Who's Who, 1927.
Electoral registers (copies on Record Room, County Hall).
London and Suburban Trade Union Guide, 1891 (copy at British Library of Political and Economic Science).
London Statistics, 1890–1916.
Reformers Year Book, 1900–9.
Socialist Year Book and Labour Annual, 1911–12.

SELECT BIBLIOGRAPHY

(C) ANNUAL AND CONFERENCE REPORTS OF POLITICAL ORGANISATIONS

Chelsea: Combined Political Committee of the Four Radical Clubs, 1885 (copy at National Liberal Club).
Christian Social Union, 1895–1918.
Christian Social Union London branch, 1893–1914.
Dartford Liberal Association, 1902–8 (copies at Dartford public library).
Deptford Labour Association, 1906–19 (copies at Deptford Labour Party).
English Land Restoration League, 1891–7.
Fabian Society, 1888–1918.
Fulham Liberal Association, 1912–16 (copies at Fulham public library).
Fulham Liberal Unionist Association, 1901 (copy at Fulham public library).
Hammersmith and Shepherd's Bush Ratepayers' Association, 1907 and 1914 (copies in Bull Collection, Hammersmith public library).
Hammersmith Conservative Constitutional Association, 1899–1900 (copy in Bull Collection, Hammersmith public library).
Independent Labour Party, 1893–1918.
Labour Representation Committee and Labour Party, 1900–18.
Land Nationalisation Society, 1883–1910.
London and Counties Liberal Union, 1882 (copy at National Liberal Club).
London Labour Party, 1916–30 (copies at Herbert Morrison House).
London Liberal and Radical Union, 1889–1901 (copies at British Library of Political and Economic Science) (gaps).
London Municipal Society, 1896–1914 (copies at Guildhall).
London Reform Union, 1892–1918 (copies at British Library of Political and Economic Science).
National Committee of Organised Labour, 1899–1909 (copies at Southwark public library).
Social Democratic Federation, Social Democratic Party and British Socialist Party, 1894–1918 (copies at British Library of Political and Economic Science and at Marx Memorial House, with a few gaps).
South Kensington Conservative Association, 1885–1914 (copies at South Kensington Conservative Association).
Woolwich Labour Party, 1903–18 (copies at Woolwich Labour Party).

(D) TRADE UNION REPORTS

Note: Those seen at the British Library of Political and Economic Science are marked (a); at the Trades Union Congress library (b).
Operative Bricklayers' Society (at Amalgamated Union of Building Trade Workers).
London Society of Compositors (a).
Dock, Wharf and Riverside Labourers' Union (a and b).
National Union of Gas Workers and General Labourers (at Thorne House).
London Building Trades Committee and Federation (a).
London Trades Council (a).
Municipal Employees' Association (at Thorne House).

SELECT BIBLIOGRAPHY

National Union of Railwaymen (at Unity House).
National Association of Operative Plasterers (at N.A.O.P.).
Operative Stonemasons' Union (at Amalgamated Union of Building Trade Workers).

(E) FABIAN SOCIETY TRACTS

6. *The True Radical Programme*, 1887.
8. *Facts for Londoners*, 1889.
9. *An Eight Hours Bill*, 1889.
10. *Figures for Londoners*, 1889.
11. *The Workers' Political Programme*, 1890.
20. *Questions for Poor Law Guardians*, 1890.
21. *Questions for London Vestrymen*, 1890.
25. *Questions for School Board Candidates*, 1891.
26. *Questions for London County Councillors*, 1891.
40. *Fabian Election Manifesto*, 1892.
41. G. B. Shaw, *The Fabian Society: What it has done and How it has done it*, 1892.
49. *A Plan of Campaign for Labour*, 1894.

(F) OTHER PAMPHLETS, COLLECTIONS OF MANIFESTOES AND CUTTINGS

At the British Library of Political and Economic Science;
J. L. Mahon, *A Labour Programme*, 1888.
Social Democratic Federation, *To the Electors of Deptford*, 1898.
Social Democratic Federation, *Herbert Burrows*, Haggerston, 1908.
Sidney Webb and R. C. Phillimore, *Fifteen years' work on the London County Council*, Deptford, 1907.

At the Guildhall;
Large collection of cuttings, manifestoes and posters.

At the National Liberal Club;
Large collection of manifestoes, and some printed documents of Libera Central Association, etc.

In the possession of Henry Pelling;
Bloomsbury Socialist Society, manifesto, 1890 (copy).
Labour Union, manifesto, c. 1890 (copy).
Kyd Collection, cuttings relating to the political career of David Hope Kyd.

At Dartford public library;
Local cuttings collection.

At Finsbury public library;
Local cuttings collection, 1894–1909, the volume 1894–9 containing printed instructions issued by the Conservative Vestry Whip.

At Greenwich public library;
Greenwich Advanced Liberal Association notices, 1869–72.

SELECT BIBLIOGRAPHY

At Hackney public library;
Local manifestoes collection.

At Hammersmith public library;
Bull Collection, 33 volumes of cuttings and miscellaneous notices, etc. relating to the career of Sir William Bull and the Conservative party in Hammersmith, 1890–1931; including printed notices, etc. relating to some other Conservative parties, e.g. Bethnal Green, Fulham and Lewisham.

At Hampstead public library;
Cuttings collection relating to Hampstead Non-Political Progressive Association and to Hampstead Citizens' Union.

At Poplar public library;
Local manifestoes and cuttings collection, 1870–1915, seven volumes.

At St. Pancras public library;
Local manifestoes collection.

At Shoreditch public library;
Local cuttings collection, 1885–1914, five volumes.

At Stepney public library;
Local manifestoes collection, 1830–90.

At West Ham public library;
E. Gawthorn, *Fetters or Freedom*, c. 1905 (anti-socialist).
Saunders Jacobs, *A Warning*, 1900.
J. J. Terrett, *Municipal Socialism in West Ham; a Reply to the Times*, c. 1903.

At Willesden public library;
F. A. Wood, *History of the Willesden Local Board*, c. 1900.
F. E. Chennell, *History of the Willesden District Council*, 1913.

At Woolwich public library;
Local manifestoes and cuttings collection.

4. PRINCIPAL SECONDARY WORKS

ALDRED, GUY, *No Traitor's Gait*, Glasgow 1956–7.
ANON., *Browning Hall and Settlement*, London 1913.
ANON., *How I Became a Socialist*, London 1896.
ANON., *Twenty-One Years at Mansfield House*, London 1911.
ATTLEE, C. R., *As It Happened*, London 1954.
BAGWELL, P., *The Railwaymen*, London 1963.
BARNETT, HENRIETTA, *Canon Barnett*, London 1918.
BAX, E. B., *Reminiscences and Reflections of a Mid and Late Victorian*, London 1918.
BEALEY, F. and PELLING, H. M., *Labour and Politics 1900–1906*, London 1958.

SELECT BIBLIOGRAPHY

BENNEY, M., GRAY, A. P. and PEAR, R. H., *How People Vote, a Study of Electoral Behaviour in Greenwich*, London 1956.
BETTANY, F. G., *Stewart Headlam*, London 1926.
BILLOWS, F. H., "Socialism in West Ham", *Economic Review*, Vol. X, 1900.
BOOTH, CHARLES, *Life and Labour of the People in London*, London 1892–1897, and revised edition, London 1902.
BOSANQUET, HELEN, *Social Work in London, 1869–1912; a History of the Charity Organisation Society*, London 1914.
BRIGGS, ASA, *Victorian Cities*, London 1963.
BRIGGS, ASA and SAVILLE, JOHN, *Essays in Labour History*, London 1960.
BROCKWAY, FENNER, *Bermondsey Story*, London 1949.
BROCKWAY, FENNER, *Inside the Left*, London 1942.
BROWN, W. H., *A Century of London Co-operation*, London 1928.
CHAMPION, H. H., *The Great Dock Strike*, London 1890.
CHAMPNESS, E. A., *Frank Smith, M.P.*, London 1943.
CHESTERTON, G. K., *Napoleon of Notting Hill*, London 1904.
CLEGG, H. A., FOX, ALAN and THOMPSON, A. F., *A History of British Trade Unions since 1889*, Vol. 1, Oxford 1964.
COLE, MARGARET (ed.), *The Webbs and their Work*, London 1949.
COLE, MARGARET (ed.), *Beatrice Webb's Diaries 1912–24*, London 1952.
COLE, MARGARET, *The Story of Fabian Socialism*, London 1961.
CRESSWELL, D'ARCY, *Margaret McMillan*, London 1948.
DAVIES, C. M., *Heterodox London*, London 1874.
DAVIES, C. M., *Unorthodox London*, London 1873–5.
DAVIS, W. T. and NEVILLE, W. B., *History of the Royal Arsenal Co-operative Society*, London 1918.
DEARLE, N. B., *Problems of Unemployment in the London Building Trades*, London 1908.
DUFF, U. G. (ed.), *The Lifework of Lord Avebury*, London 1924.
EASTWOOD, C. G., *George Isaacs*, London 1952.
EDELMAN, MAURICE, *Herbert Morrison*, London 1948.
ENGELS, FRIEDRICH and LAFARGUE, LAURA, *Correspondance*, Paris 1956.
ENSOR, R. C. K., *England 1870–1914*, Oxford 1936.
EVANS, HOWARD, *Sir Randal Cremer*, London 1909.
FELS, MARY, *Joseph Fels*, London 1920.
FIRTH, J. F. B., *Municipal London*, London 1876.
FOX, R. M., *Drifting Men*, London 1930.
FOX, R. M., *Smoky Crusade*, London 1937.
GARDINER, A. G., *John Benn and the Progressive Movement*, London 1925.
GEDULD, H. M., "Bernard Shaw, Vestryman and Borough Councillor", *Californian Shavian*, 1962.
GIBBON, G. and BELL, R. W., *History of the London County Council 1889–1939*, London 1939.
GOSLING, H. *Up and Down Stream*, London 1927.
GOULD, F. J., *The Life Story of a Humanist*, London 1923.
GRANT, BETTY, *J. J. Vaughan*, London n.d.

SELECT BIBLIOGRAPHY

HALL, B. T., *Our Fifty Years: the Story of the Working Men's Club and Institute Union*, London 1912.
HALL, P. G., *The Industries of London since 1861*, London 1962.
HANHAM, H. J., *Elections and Party Management*, London 1959.
HARRIS, SIR PERCY, *Forty Years in and out of Parliament*, London 1947.
HARRISON, S., *Alex Gossip*, London 1962.
HAW, G., *From Workhouse to Westminster: the Life Story of Will Crooks, M.P.*, London 1907.
HENDERSON, P. (ed.), *The Letters of William Morris to his Family and Friends*, London 1950.
HENDERSON, ARCHIBALD, *Bernard Shaw*, New York 1932.
HOBSBAWM, E. J., "General Labour Unions in Britain, 1889–1914", *Economic History Review*, 2nd series, Vol. 1, 1949.
HOBSON, S. G., *Pilgrim to the Left*, London 1938.
HOFFMAN, P. C., *They Also Serve: the Story of the Shop Worker*, London 1949.
HOWARTH, E. G. and WILSON, M., *West Ham*, London 1907.
HOWE, E. and CHILD, J., *The Society of London Bookbinders*, London 1952.
HOWE, E. and WAITE, H. E., *The London Society of Compositors*, London 1948.
HYNDMAN, H. M., *The Record of an Adventurous Life*, London 1911.
INGLIS, K. S., *Churches and the Working Classes in Victorian England*, London 1963.
JACKSON, T. A., *Solo Trumpet*, London 1953.
JEFFERYS, J. B., *The Story of the Engineers*, London 1946.
JEPHSON, H., *The Sanitary Evolution of London*, London 1907.
JOAD, C. E. M., *Shaw and Society*, London 1953.
JONES, JACK, *My Lively Life*, London 1928.
JONES, R. B., "Balfour's Reform of Party Organisation", *Bulletin of the Institute of Historical Research*, Vol. XXXVIII, 1965.
KENT, W., *John Burns*, London 1950.
LANSBURY, GEORGE, *My Life*, London 1928.
LANSBURY, GEORGE, *Looking Backwards—and Forwards*, London 1935.
LEE, H. W. and ARCHBOLD, E., *Social Democracy in Britain*, London 1935.
LEGGE, H., "Socialism in West Ham", *Economic Review*, Vol. 9, 1899.
LLOYD, JOHN, *London Municipal Government: History of a Great Reform, 1880–8*, London 1910.
LOW, S. J., "The Rise of the Suburbs", *Contemporary Review*, Vol. 60, 1891.
MACCOBY, S., *English Radicalism, 1886–1914*, London 1953.
MANN, TOM, *Memoirs*, London 1923.
MCBRIAR, A. M., *Fabian Socialism and English Politics 1884–1918*, Cambridge 1962.
MASTERMAN, C. F. G. (ed.), *The Heart of the Empire*, London 1901.
MASTERMAN, C. F. G., *The Condition of England*, London 1909.
MASTERMAN, L., *C. F. G. Masterman*, London 1939.

SELECT BIBLIOGRAPHY

MONTAGU, L., *Samuel Montagu*, London 1913.
MONTEFIORE, D. B., *From a Victorian to a Modern*, London 1927.
MORRISON OF LAMBETH, LORD, *Herbert Morrison*, London 1960.
MUDIE-SMITH, R. (ed.), *The Religious Life of London*, London 1904.
NETHERCOT, A. H., *The First Five Lives of Annie Besant*, London 1961.
O'CONNOR, T. P., *Memoirs of an Old Parliamentarian*, London 1929.
O'CONNOR, T. P., "Men, Women and Memories", *Sunday Times*, 6 May 1928.
OLDERSHAW, L. F. (ed.), *The English City*, London 1904.
PANKHURST, E. S., *The Suffragette Movement*, London 1931.
PEASE, E., *The History of the Fabian Society*, London 1916.
PELLING, H. M., "H. H. Champion", *Cambridge Journal*, Vol. 6, 1953.
PELLING, H. M., *The Origins of the Labour Party, 1880–1900*, London 1954.
PHELPS-BROWN, E. H. P., *The Growth of British Industrial Relations*, London 1959.
POLLARD, S., "The Decline of Shipbuilding on the Thames", *Economic History Review*, Vol. 3, 1950.
POPE, W. and others, *The Story of the Star, 1888–1938*, London 1938.
POSTGATE, D., "A Child in George Lansbury's House", *Fortnightly*, Vol. CLXIV, 1948.
POSTGATE, R., *The Builder's History*, London 1923.
POSTGATE, R., *The Life of George Lansbury*, London 1951.
PRIBICEVIC, B., *The Shop Stewards Movement and Workers' Control*, Oxford 1959.
RACKHAM, CLARA, "Susan Lawrence", *Fabian Quarterly*, 57, 1948.
REASON, W., *University and Social Settlements*, London 1898.
ROBSON, W. A., *The Government and Misgovernment of London*, London 1939.
ROCKER, RUDOLF, tr. LEFTWICH, J., *The London Years*, London 1956.
SANDERS, W. S., *Early Socialist Days*, London 1927.
SAUL, S. B., "House Building in England, 1890–1914", *Economic History Review*, Vol. 15, 1962.
SHEPPARD, F. H. W., *Local Government in St. Marylebone, 1688–1835*, London 1958.
SIMS, G. R., *Living London*, London 1902–3.
SLESSER, H. H., *Judgement Reserved: Reminiscences*, London 1941.
SMITH, H. L. (ed.), *New Survey of London Life and Labour*, London 1930–5.
SMITH, H. L. and NASH, V., *The Story of the Dockers' Strike*, London 1890.
SNELL, LORD, *Men, Movements and Myself*, London 1936.
SOUTTER, F. W., *Fights for Freedom*, London 1925.
SOUTTER, F. W., *Recollections of a Labour Pioneer*, London 1923.
SPILLER, G., *The Ethical Movement in Great Britain*, London 1934.
STERN, W. M., *The Porters of London*, London 1960.
STUCKE, R. B. (ed.), *Fifty Years History of the Woolwich Labour Party*, London 1953.
SYMONS, J., *Horatio Bottomley*, London 1955.

SELECT BIBLIOGRAPHY

TATE, G., *London Trades Council, 1860–1950*, London 1950.
THOMPSON, E. P., *William Morris: Romantic to Revolutionary*, London 1955.
THORNE, W., *My Life's Battles*, London 1925.
THURTLE, ERNEST, *Time's Winged Chariot*, London 1945.
TILLETT, BEN, *Memories and Reflections*, London 1931.
TILLETT, BEN, *A Brief History of the Dockers' Union*, London 1910.
TILLETT, BEN, *History of the London Transport Workers' Strike, 1911*, London 1911.
TORR, D., *Tom Mann and his Times*, London 1956.
TOWNSEND, EMILY (ed.), *Keeling Letters and Recollections*, London 1918.
TSUZUKI, C., *H. M. Hyndman and British Socialism*, Oxford 1961.
TUCKWELL, G., *The Life of Sir Charles Dilke*, London 1917.
WEBB, B., *My Apprenticeship*, London 1926.
WEBB, B., *Our Partnership*, London 1948.
WEBB, S. and B., *The History of Trade Unionism, 1666–1920*, London 1920.
WELLS, H. G., *The New Machiavelli*, London 1913.
WILLIS, FREDERICK, *101 Jubilee Street*, London 1948.

MAPS

Note: the outline in maps 1, 2, 4, 5, 6, 7, 8, 9, 10, 12, 15, 19, 20 and 27 is borough and urban district boundaries (*key map* 27). For maps 4, 5, 6, 7, and 8 no figures were available for Erith and Bexley.

The outline in maps 3, 13, 16, 17, 21, 22, 23, 28 and 29 is constituency boundaries (*key map* 22).

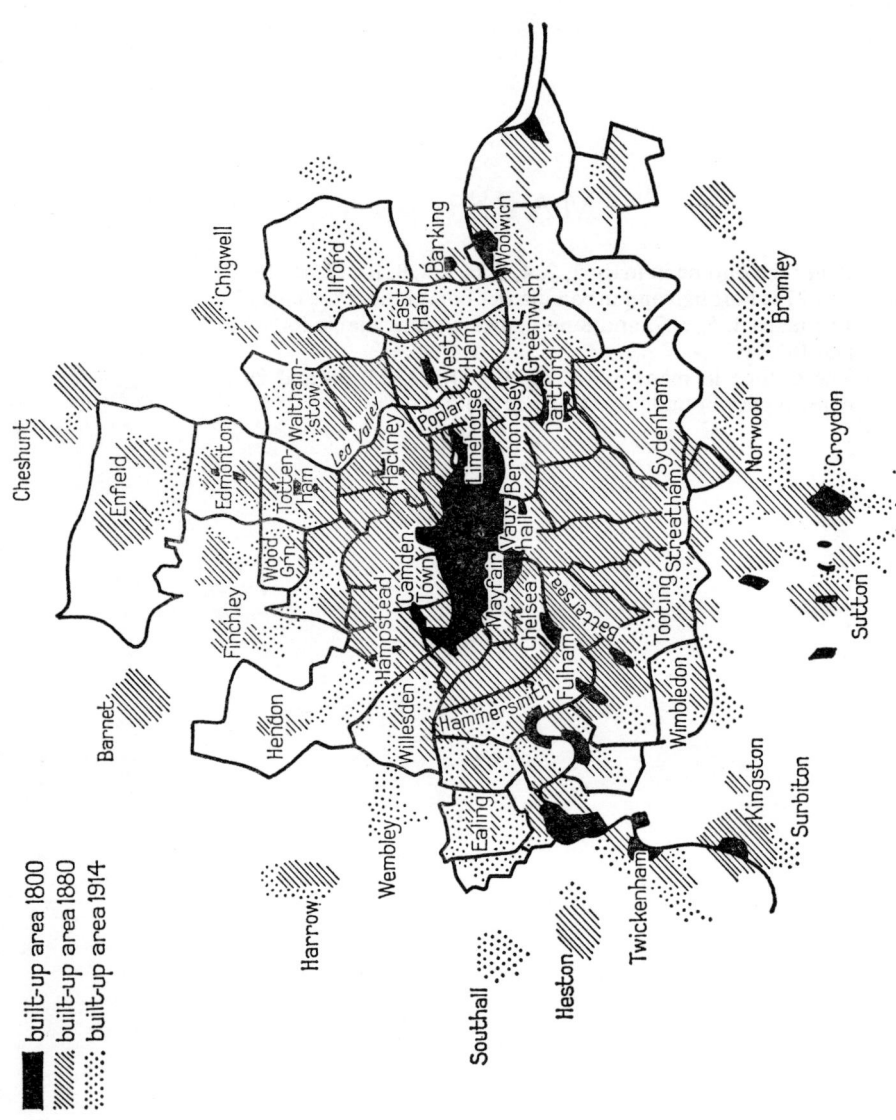

2. EDGE OF LONDON.

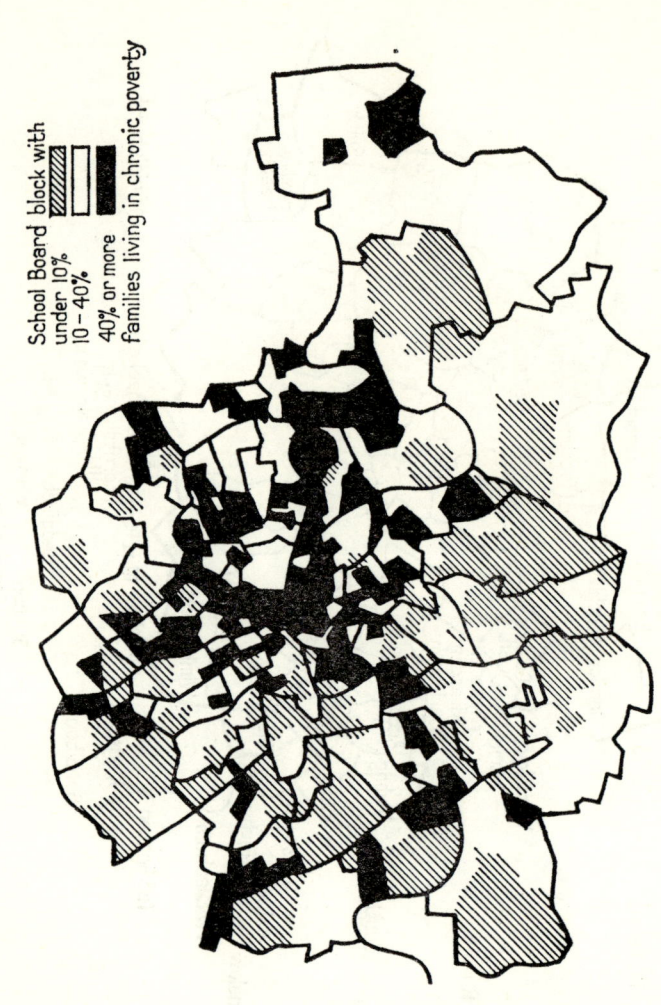

3. MIDDLE CLASS DISTRICTS AND POVERTY.
Booth, op. cit., II.

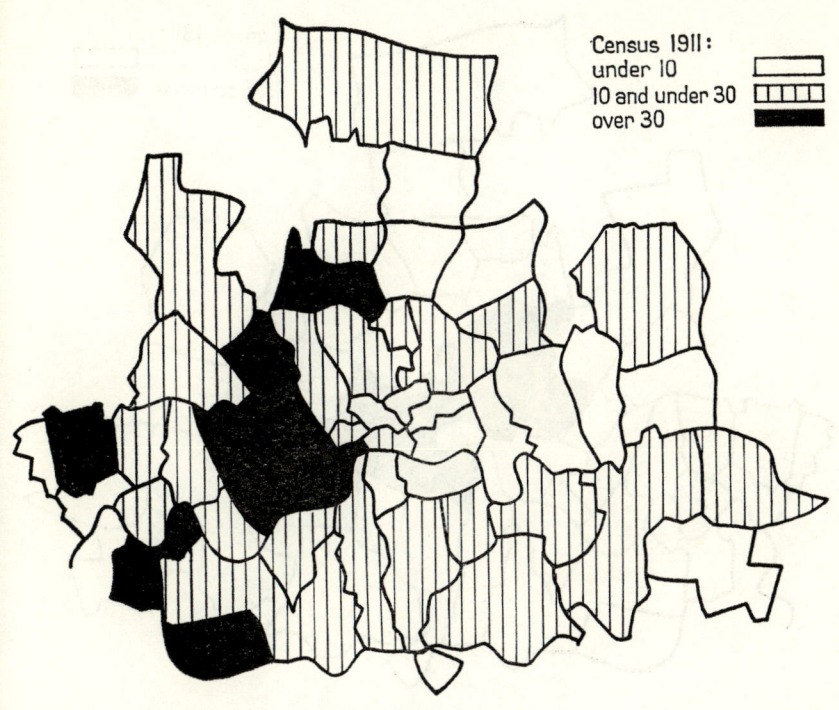

4. DOMESTIC SERVANTS. Female domestic indoor servants (other than in hotels, lodging houses or eating houses) per 100 resident families or separate occupiers: *London Statistics*, 1914–15, p 48.

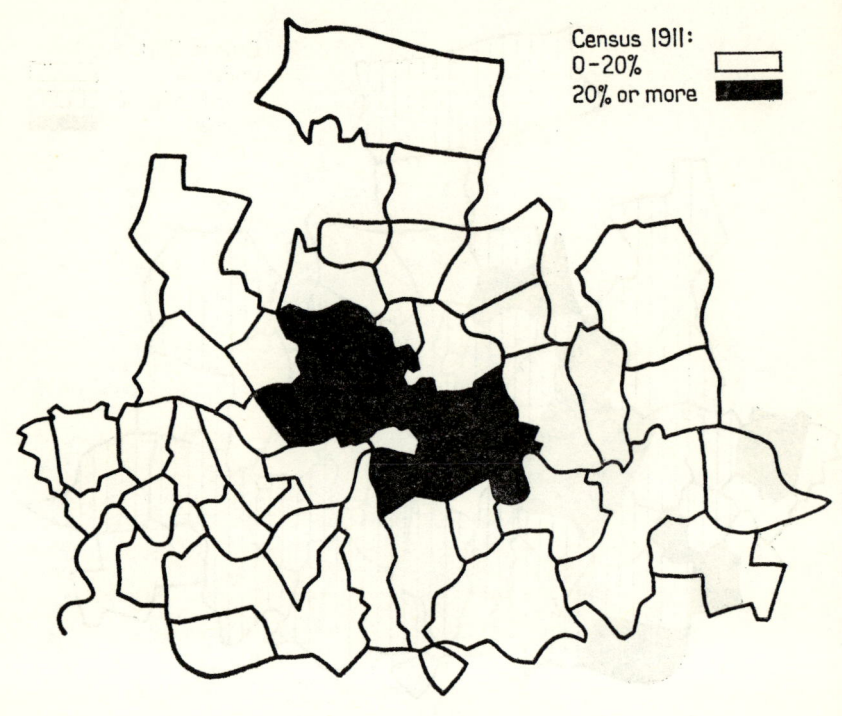

5. OVERCROWDING. 20 per cent or more of the resident population in the black area were overcrowded (more than 2 persons per room): *London Statistics*, 1914–15, p 48.

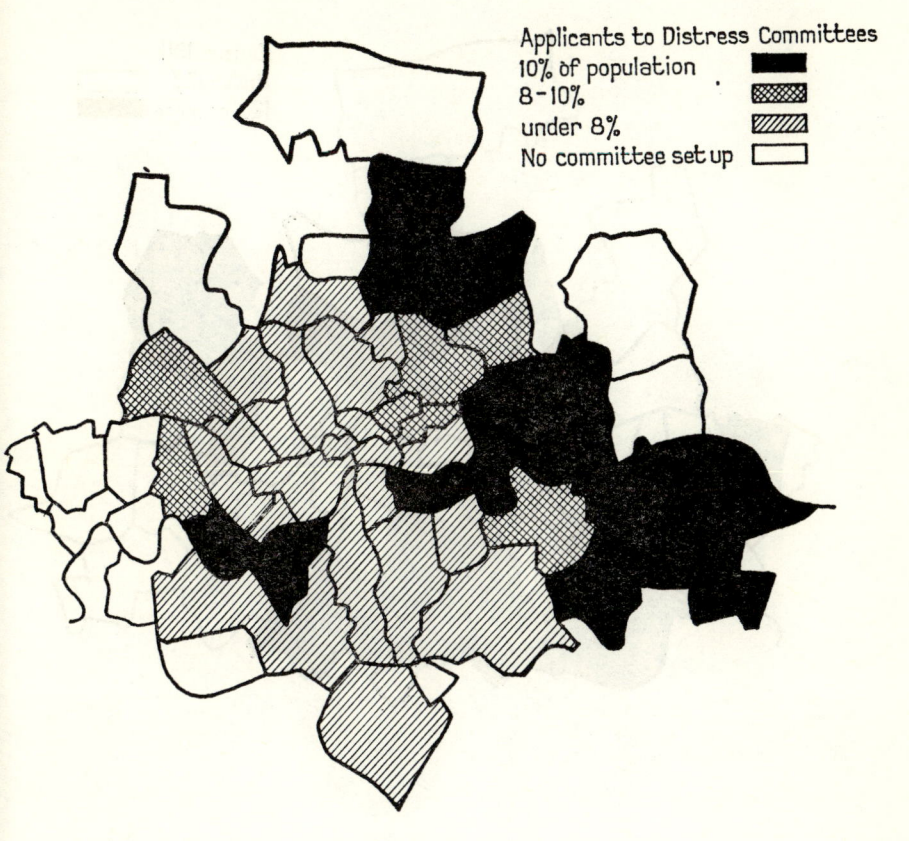

6. APPLICANTS TO DISTRESS COMMITTEES 1905–8:
PP 1909 CIII, p 765. The population of the county in 1901 was
4.15 times the number of families or separate occupiers (PP 1902
CXX, p 172).

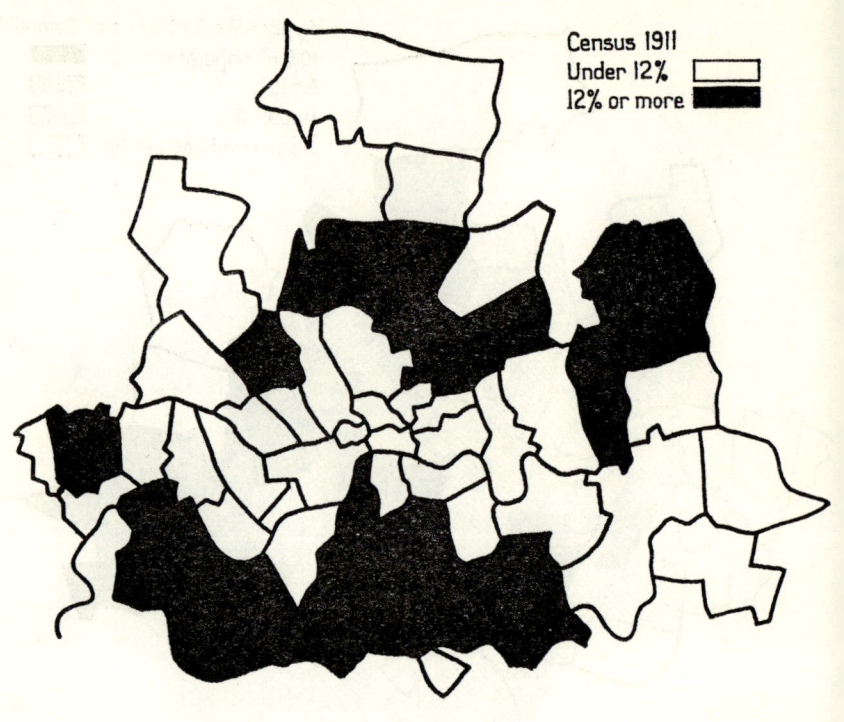

7. COMMERCIAL OCCUPATIONS. Resident occupied males engaged in commercial occupations (merchants, agents, accountants, bankers and clerks but not shopkeepers: and N.B. night population): *London Statistics*, 1914–15, p 48.

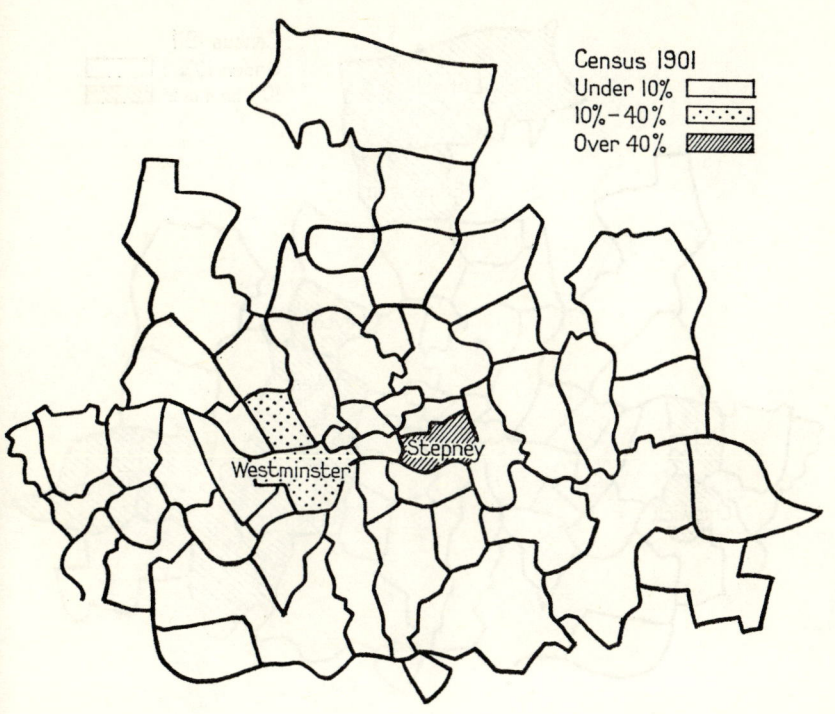

8. TAILORS. Resident occupied males engaged in the tailoring trade: *London Statistics*, 1902–3, p 336.

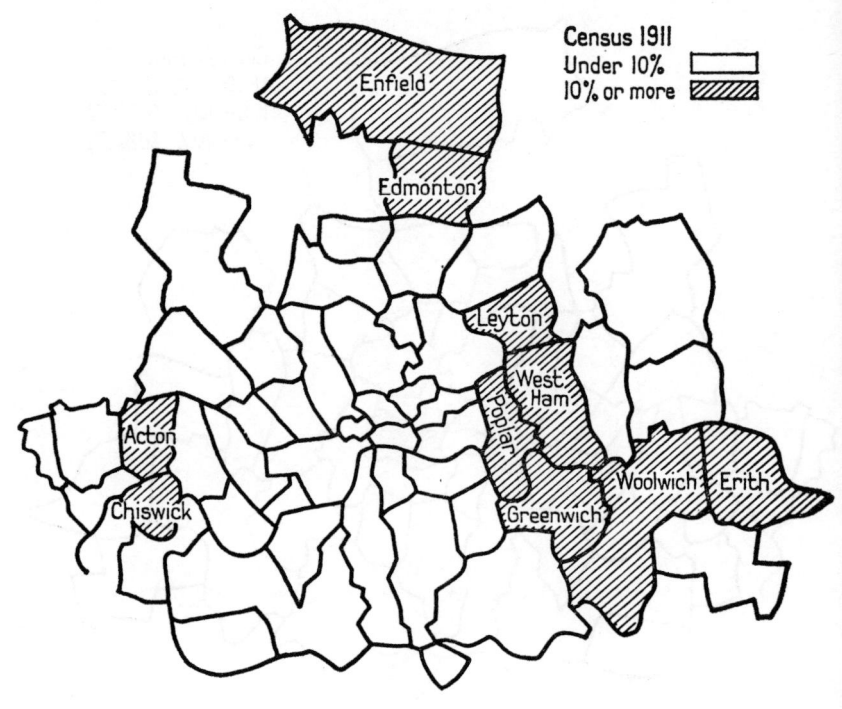

9. ENGINEERING AND METAL WORKERS. Resident occupied males engaged in the manufacture of metals, machines, implements and conveyance: *London Statistics*, 1914–15, p 48.

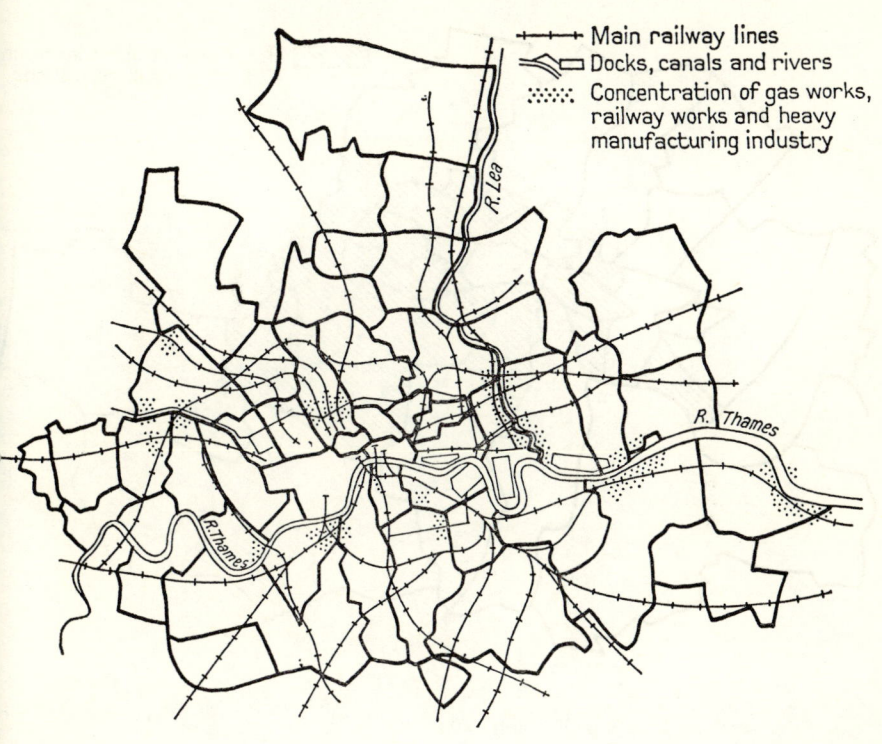

10. RAILWAYS, PORT AND HEAVY INDUSTRY.

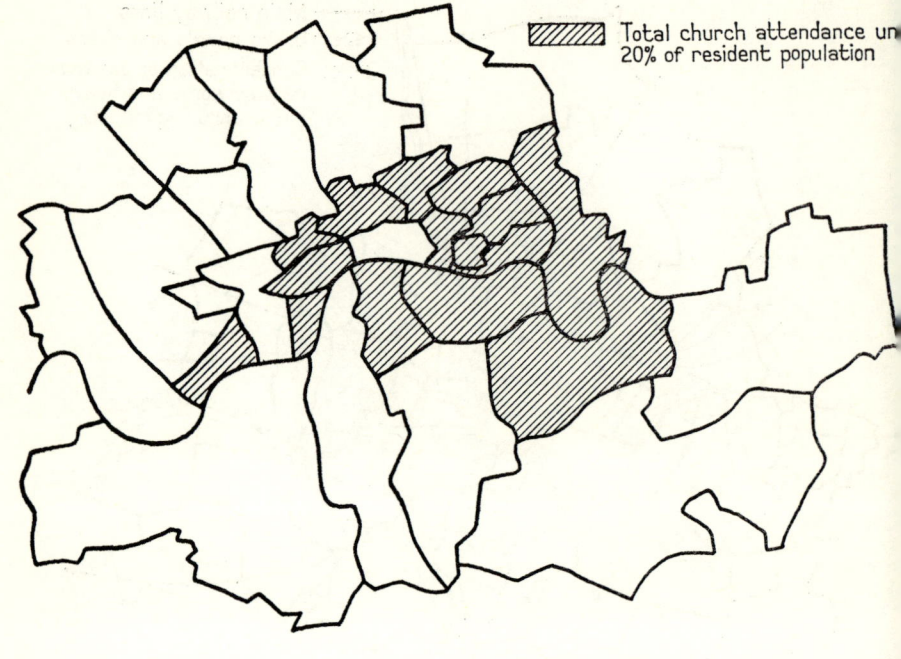

11. 1886: ATTENDANCE UNDER 20 PER CENT OF RESIDENT POPULATION. *British Weekly*, November–December 1886.

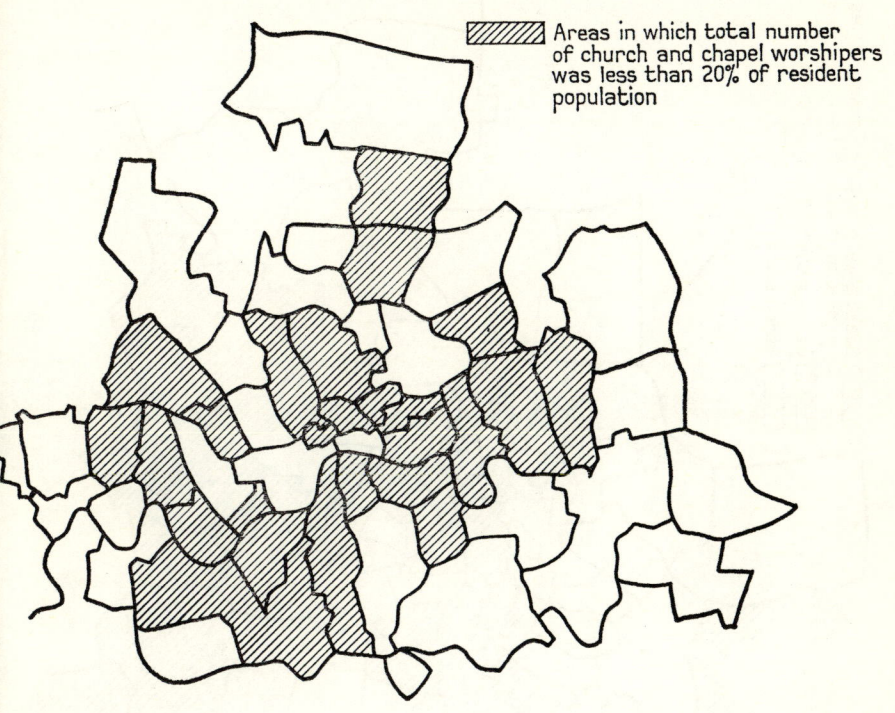

12. 1903: WORSHIPPERS UNDER 20 PER CENT OF RESIDENT POPULATION. Mudie-Smith, op. cit.

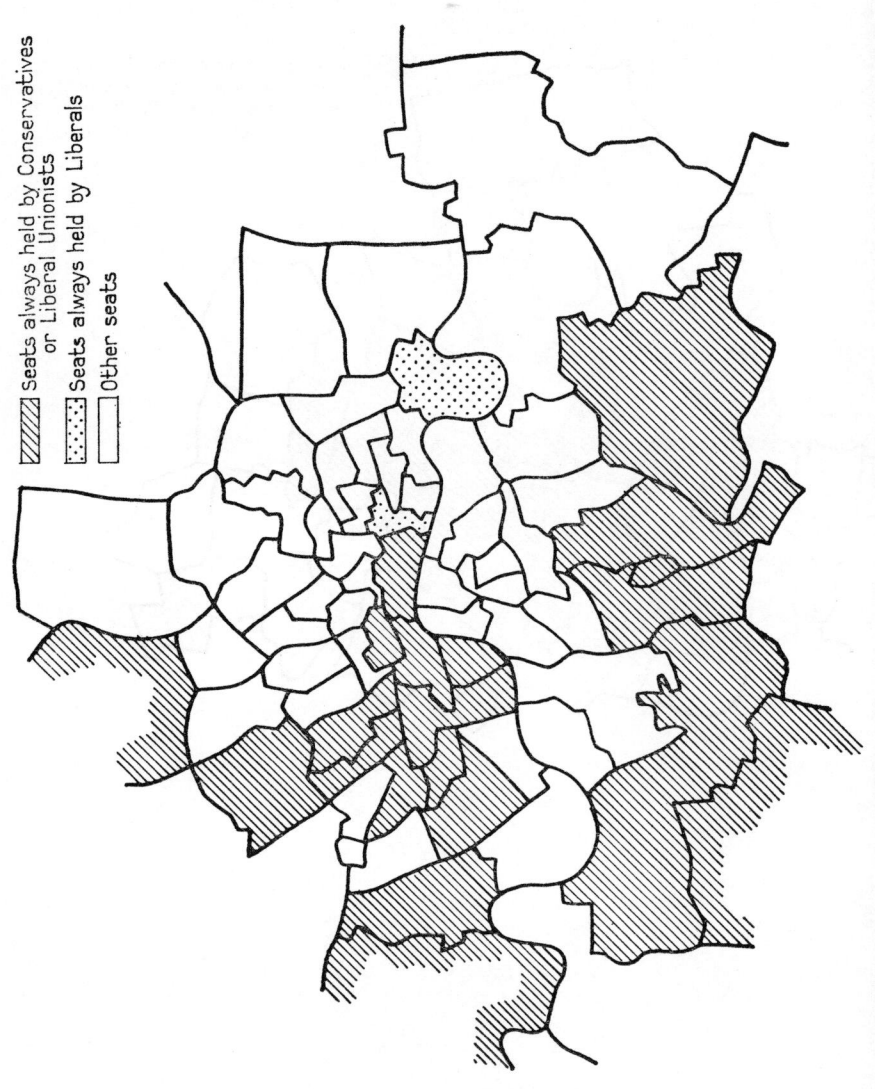

13. CONSTITUENCIES: CONSERVATIVE AND LIBERAL SAFE

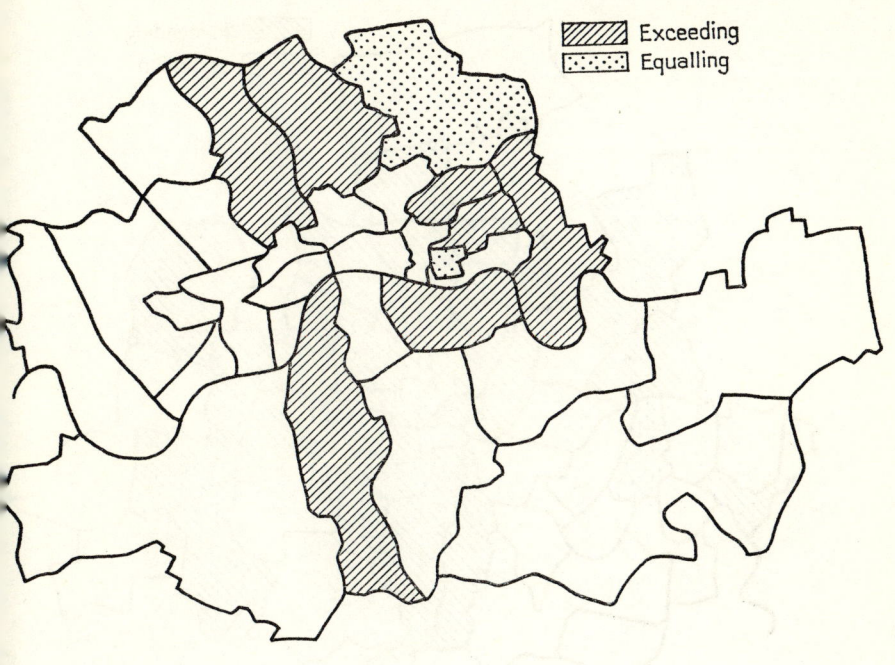

14. 1886: NONCONFORMISTS EXCEEDING ANGLICANS.
Protestant Nonconformist worshippers exceeding/equalling
Anglicans: *British Weekly*, November–December 1886.

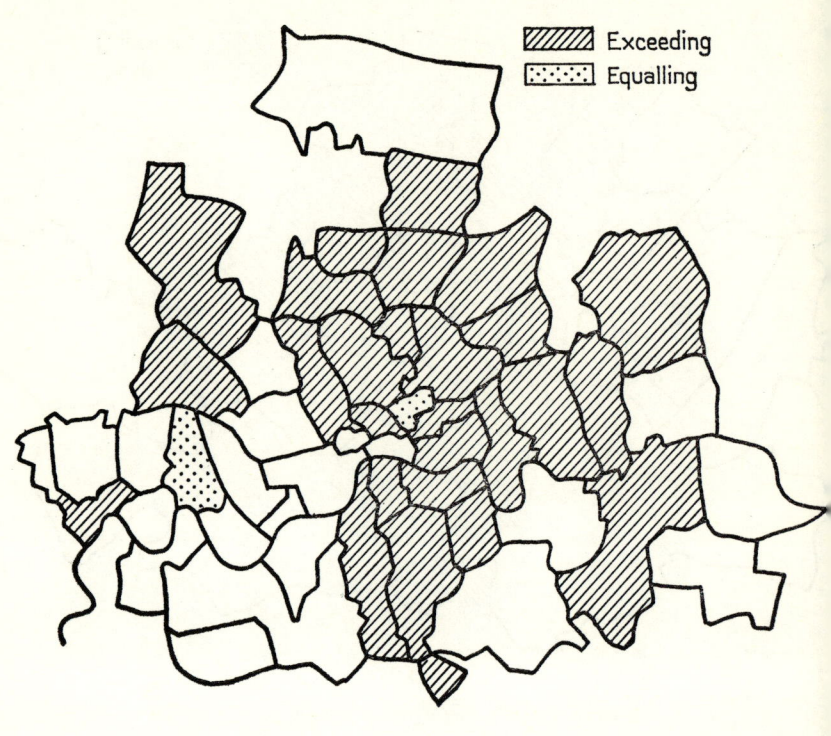

15. 1903: NONCONFORMISTS EXCEEDING ANGLICANS.
Protestant Nonconformist worshippers exceeding/equalling
Anglican: Mudie-Smith, op. cit.

16. CONSTITUENCIES: LIBERAL SEATS 1885.

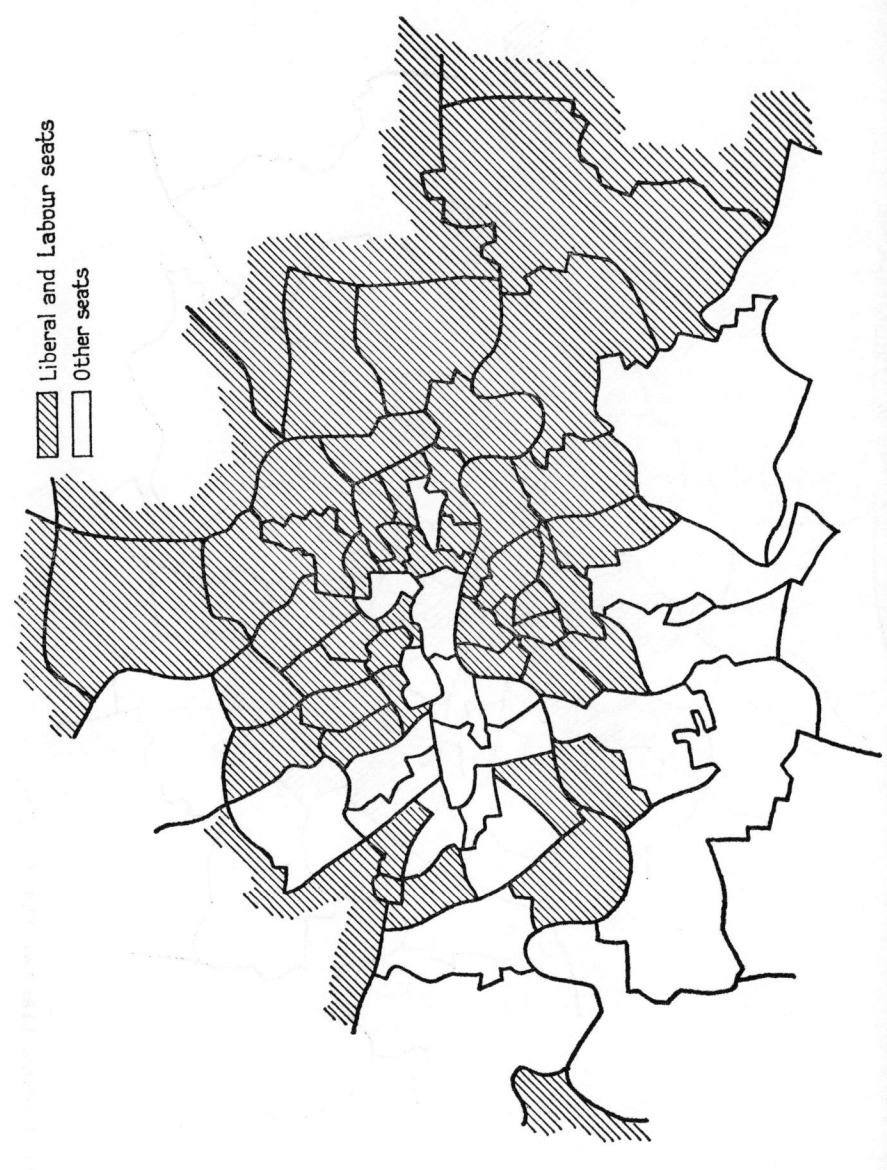

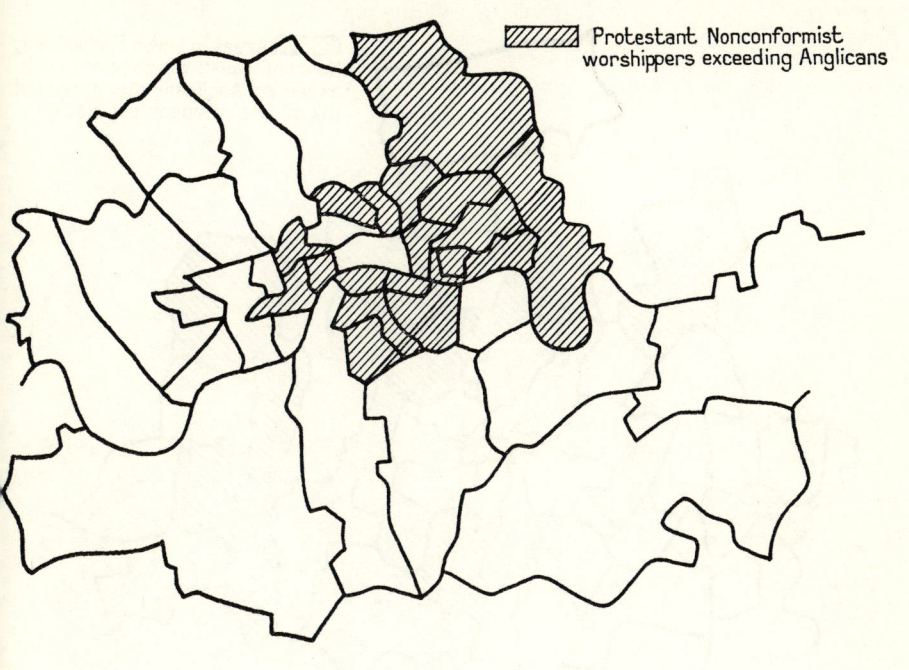

18. 1851: NONCONFORMISTS EXCEEDING ANGLICANS.
PP. 1852–3 LXXXIX.

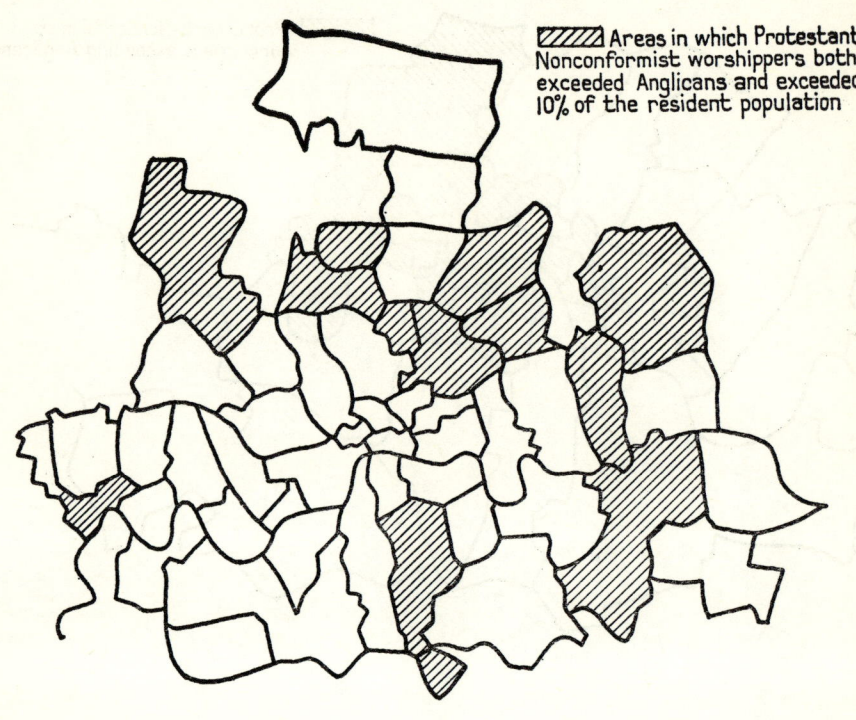

19. 1903: NONCONFORMISTS EXCEEDING ANGLICANS AND
10 PER CENT OF RESIDENT POPULATION. Mudie-Smith, op. cit.

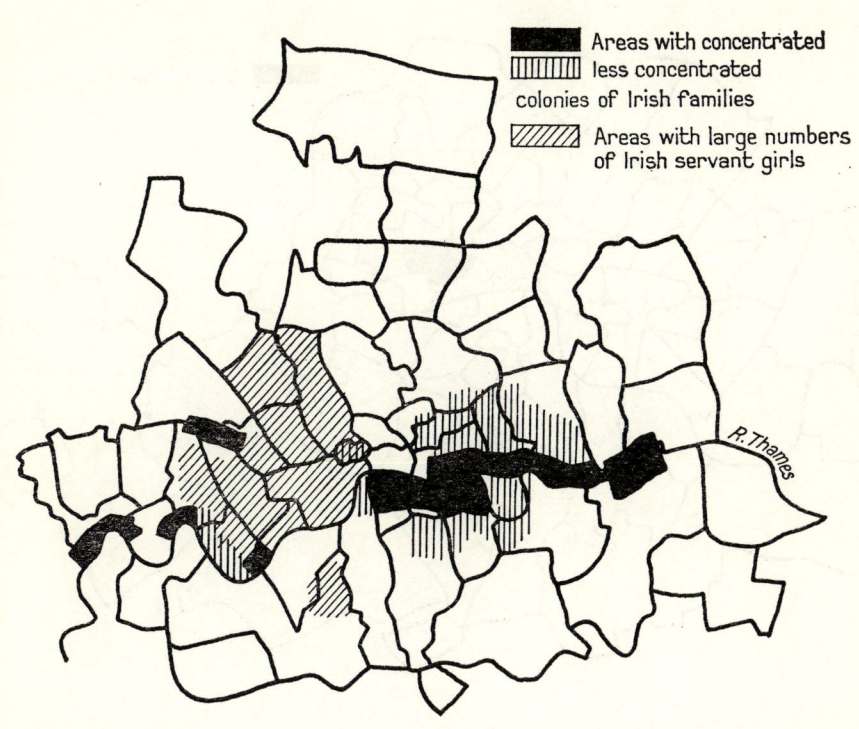

20. IRISH COLONIES. An impression of Irish distribution, based on Census (1901), and Mudie-Smith, op. cit.

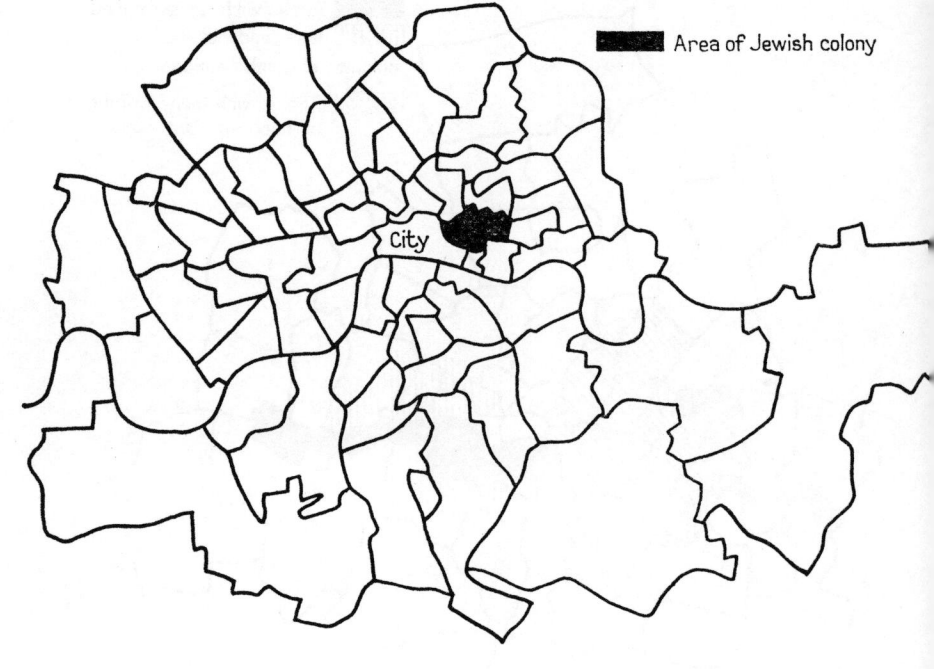

21. JEWISH COLONY. *c* 1900.

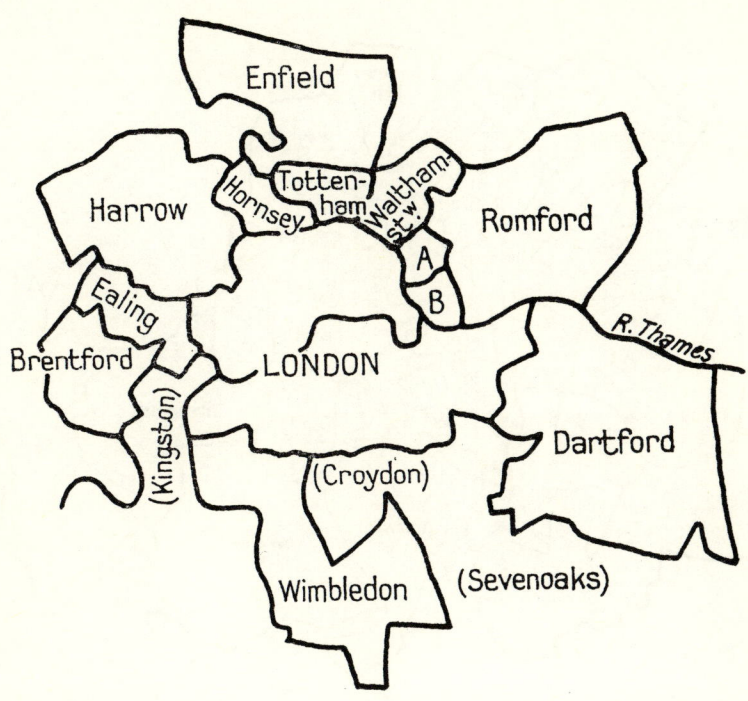

22 (a). CONSTITUENCIES. London, and adjoining country divisions and boroughs. Those in brackets are not included in the statistical tables. A, West Ham: B, West Ham South.

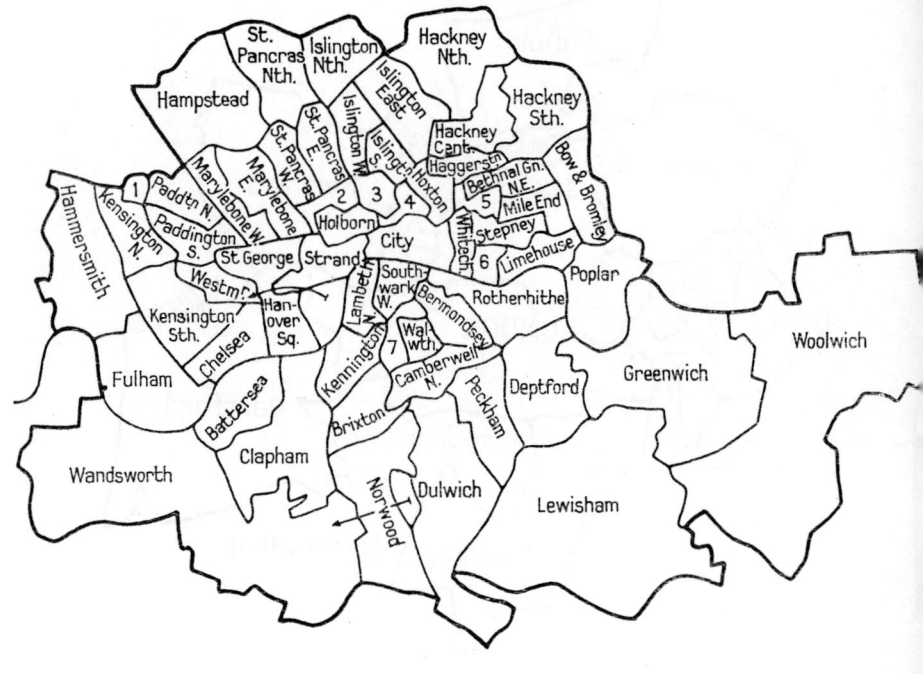

22 (b). CONSTITUENCIES. Metropolitan borough divisions.
1, Part of Chelsea; 2, St. Pancras South; 3, Finsbury Central;
4, Finsbury East; 5, Bethnal Green South West; 6, St George's in the East; 7, Newington West.

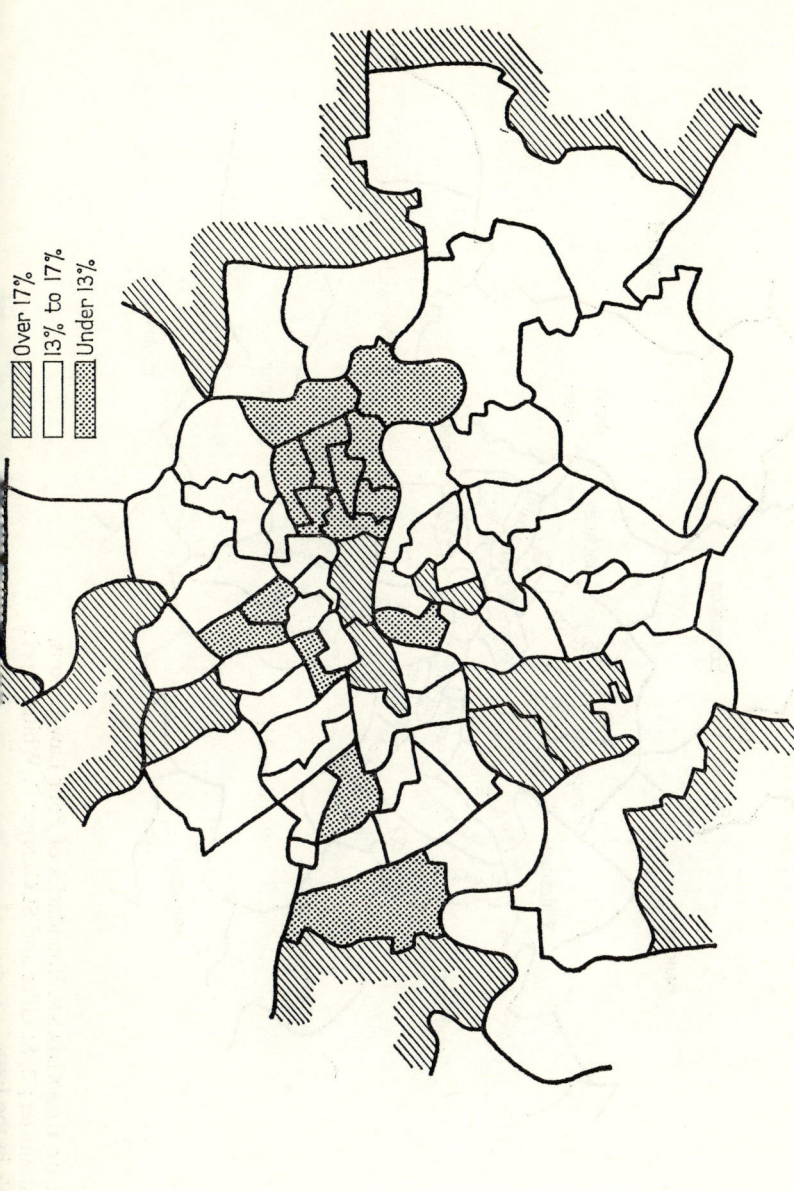

23. 1911: ELECTORATES OVER 17 PER CENT AND UNDER 13 PER CENT OF RESIDENT POPULATION. *London Statistics*, 1910–11, pp 19–20 and PP 1912–13 LXVII.

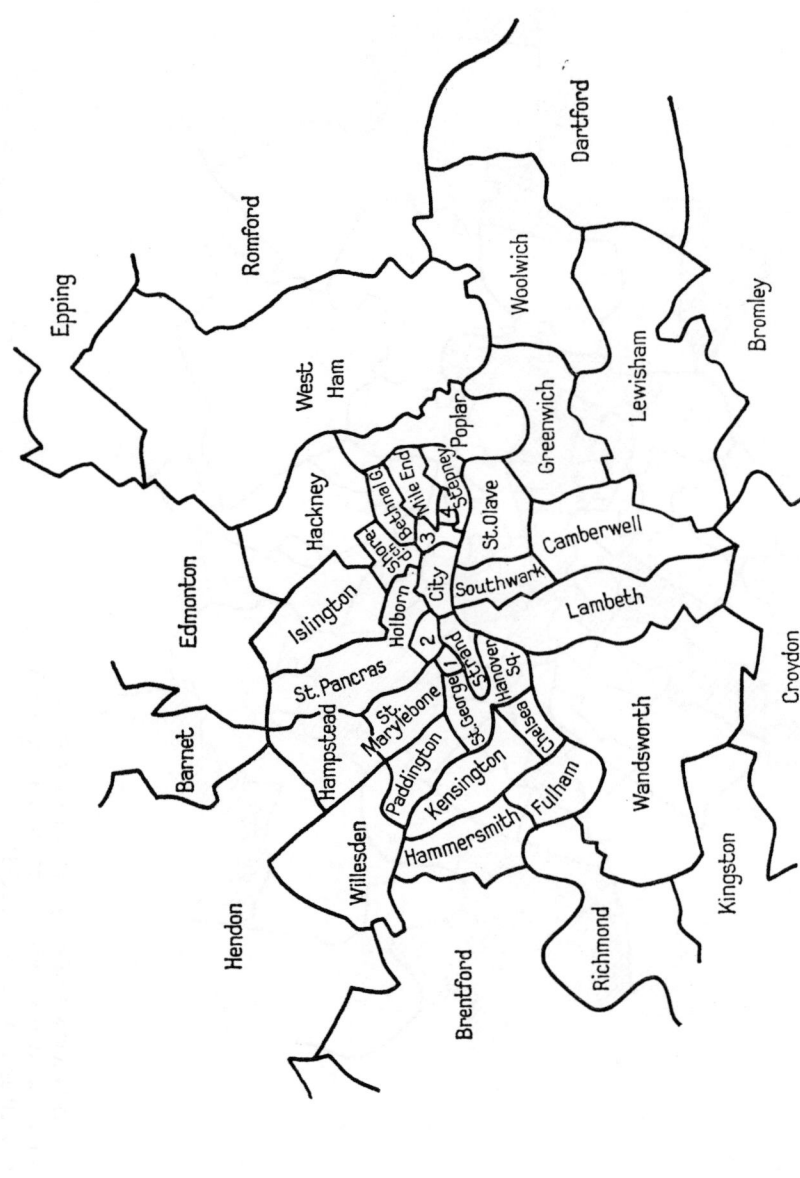

24. BOARDS OF GUARDIANS. Boundaries of Poor Law Unions, 1913. 1, Westminster; 2, St Giles and St George; 3, Whitechapel; 4, St George's in the East.

25. VESTRIES AND DISTRICT BOARDS: Boundaries in 1894.
1, Chelsea detached; 2, Westminster; 3, St George Hanover Square; 4, St Martin in the Fields; 5, St James Westminster; 6, Strand Board (six districts); 7, St Giles' Board (two districts); 8, Holborn Board (five districts); 9, Clerkenwell; 10, Stoke Newington; 11, St Luke; 12, Whitechapel Board (nine districts); 13, St George's in the East; 14, Limehouse Board (Limehouse, Ratcliffe, Wapping and Shadwell); 15, Bow; 16, Bromley; 17, Poplar; 18, Wandsworth detached; 19, Putney; 20, Wandsworth; 21, Tooting; 22, Streatham; 23, Clapham; 24, Lewisham; 25, Penge (Lewisham Board); 26, Southwark St George; 27, St Saviours Board (two districts); 28, St Olave's Board (three districts); 29, Deptford St Paul; 30, Deptford St Nicholas; 31, Greenwich; 32, Charlton; 33, Kidbrooke; 34, Lee; 35, Eltham.

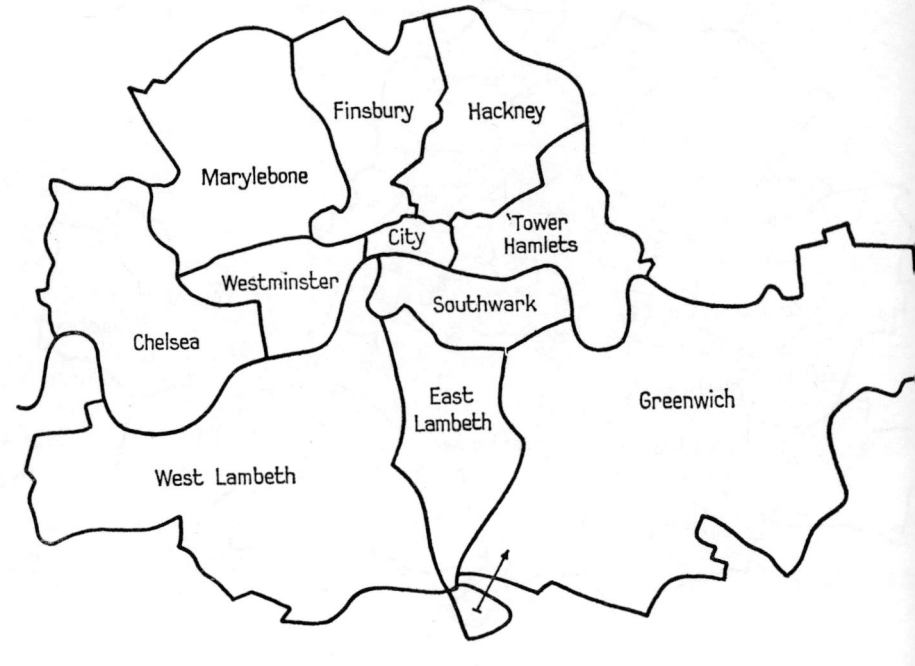

26. LONDON SCHOOL BOARD. Electoral divisions of the London School Board.

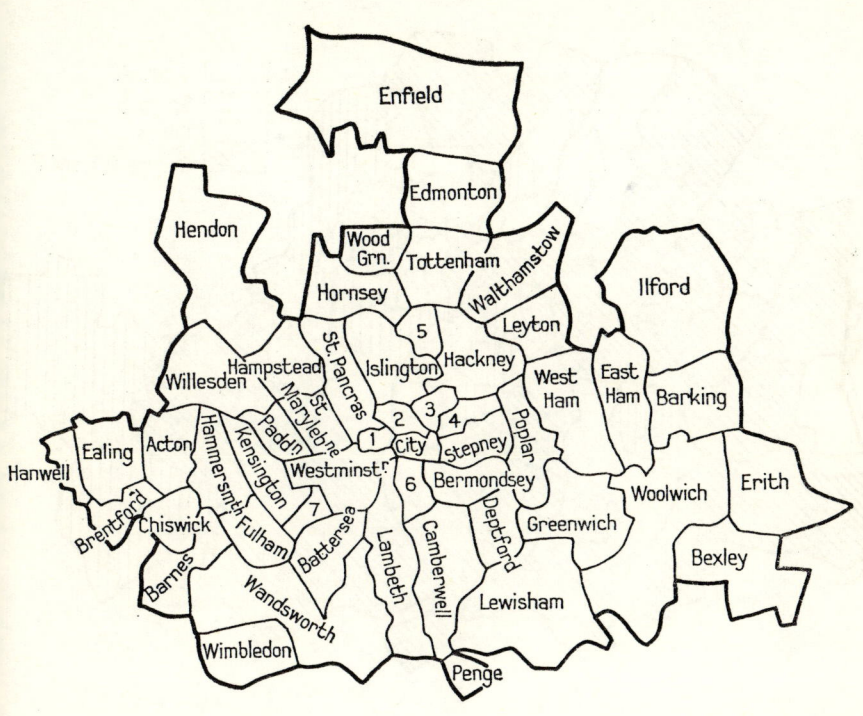

27. BOROUGHS AND URBAN DISTRICTS. Boundaries of County Boroughs, Metropolitan Boroughs and Urban Districts 1900–14. 1, Holborn; 2, Finsbury; 3, Shoreditch; 4, Bethnal Green; 5, Stoke Newington; 6, Southwark; 7, Chelsea.

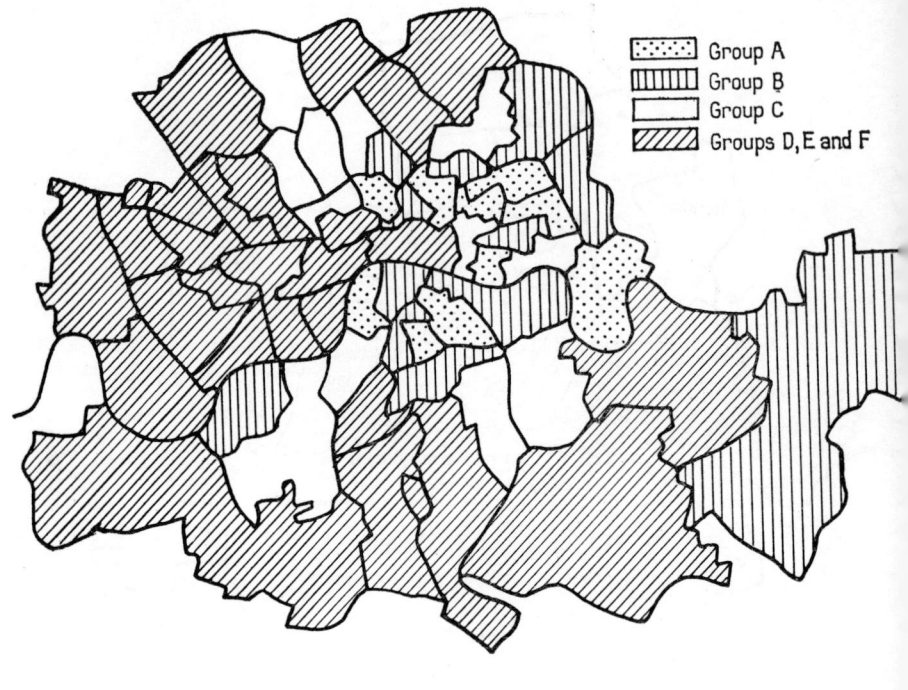

28. CONSTITUENCIES: SOCIAL COMPOSITION 1885–1900, *see* Appendix A.

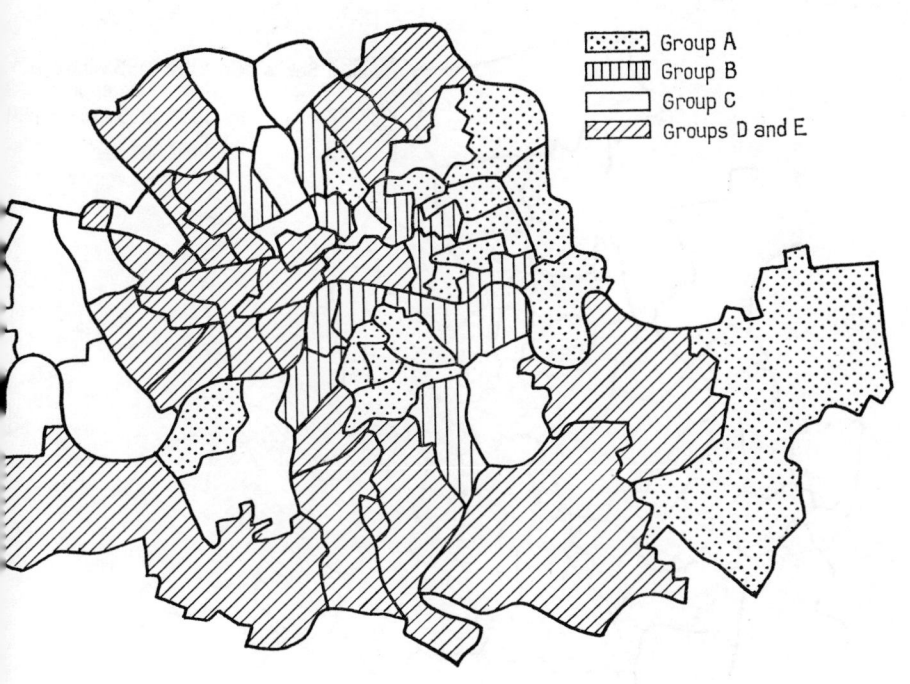

29. CONSTITUENCIES: SOCIAL COMPOSITION 1900–1914, *see* Appendix A.

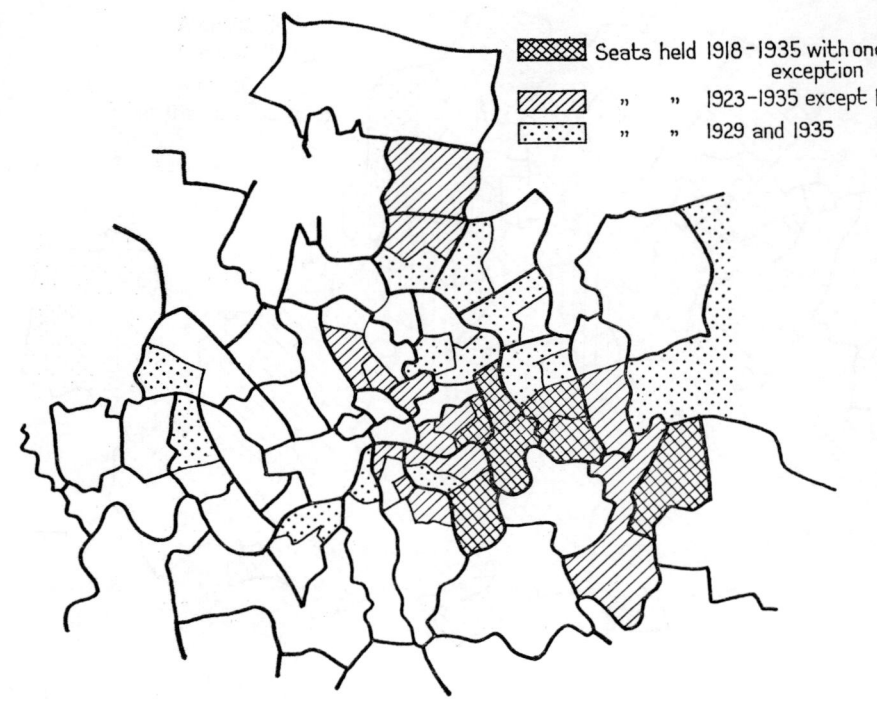

30. GROWTH OF LABOUR SEATS. (In order to facilitate comparison, divisional outlines are only indicated where essential.)

INDEX

Note: substantive footnotes are indexed, but not sources.

Acton, 136, 197, 319
Adams, Maurice, 33
Adler, Felix, 34
Advertising, 77, 182, 262
Alden, Percy, 132–3, 148, 175 215, 221
Aldred, Guy, 62
Aliens, Act, 29
Allen, Clifford, 220, 233, 292
Allen, E. J. B., 62
Alliance Cabinet Makers' Association, 54, 59
Amalgamated Farriers' Protection Society, 54, 59, 66
Amalgamated Omnibus and Tram Workers' Union, 56, 245, 316
Amalgamated Society of Carpenters and Joiners, 41–2, 54, 59, 66, 103, 231, 248, 268, 271
Amalgamated Society of Engineers, 41–2, 52, 54–7, 59–61, 65–7, 85, 132, 150, 170, 205, 212, 230–1, 236, 241, 248, 250, 252–3, 256, 271, 317
Amalgamated Society of Locomotive Engineers and Firemen, 59, 64, 66
Amalgamated Society of Railway Servants, 41–2, 54, 56, 59, 64, 170, 194, 241–2, 271–3, 320
Amalgamated Society of Tailors, 42, 53–4, 59, 66
Amalgamated Society of Watermen and Lightermen, 51, 54, 59, 63, 66, 87, 268–9
Amalgamated Stevedores Labour Protection League, 42, 48, 50–1, 54, 59, 63, 66, 169
Amalgamated Union of Operative Bakers, 54, 59, 66, 230–1
Amalgamated Union of Upholsterers, 59, 66, 103, 204
Ammon, Charles, 228, 231
Anderson, A., 192
Angell, Norman, 233
Arbeiter Freind, 30
Asquith, H. H., 85, 286, 295
Assistant Clerks' Association, 59, 66
Athey, W. R., 101, 133
Attlee, Clement, 232
Australia, 50, 53, 126, 150, 160, 249

Aveling, Edward, 33, 113–14, 118, 136–7, 150–3, 159–61

Ballard, Edward, 310
Banner, Robert, 136, 140, 149, 153, 158, 162, 251–2, 279
Bannochie, J. M., 224
Barefoot, William, 252, 257, 261–2
Bargebuilder's Union, 40, 53, 103, 270
Barking, 6, 101–2, 109, 115, 199, 311, 319
Barnes, George, 60–1, 212, 224, 231
Barnett, Canon Samuel, 22
Bateman, George, 104, 106
Battersea, 6, 16, 18, 38, 46–7, 56–7, 71–2, 87, 100, 102–3, 105–6, 109, 115–16, 118–22, 150–1, 155–6, 183–6, 198, 222, 227, 231, 243, 274, 287, 291, 299, 301, 308, 313
Baum, F. C., 103–4, 120, 146, 309
Bayswater, 37
Bax, Belfort, 203
Beal, James, 92
Beckton, 16, 42, 45–6
Beer, Max, 203
Belcher, Rev. J. H., 24, 36
Bellamy, Edward, 237
Belt, George, 172, 196–7
Benn, Sir John, 96, 105, 146, 175
Bennett, Arnold, 214
Bentham, Dr Ethel, 220, 227–8, 232
Beresford, Lord Charles, 254
Bermondsey, 6, 23–6, 63, 72, 115, 118, 168, 173, 176, 186, 197, 215, 227–8, 231–2, 234, 236, 242, 292, 299, 301, 308, 313
Berners Street Club, 30
Besant, Annie, 33, 45, 97–9, 118, 125, 137, 139–40, 148
Beth Din, 28
Bethnal Green, 9, 13, 19, 22, 94–5, 103, 120, 176, 183–4, 191, 198–9, 227, 231–2, 239, 242, 288, 291, 299, 301, 308, 313
Bingley, H. W., 224
Binning, Thomas, 55, 137, 153, 159
Birmingham, 2, 90, 92, 101, 188, 294
Blaiklock, George, 172, 178

INDEX

Bland, Hubert, 137, 214–15, 237–8
Blatchford, Robert, 77, 141, 200
Bloomsbury, 7, 136–7, 152–3, 158
Bondfield, Margaret, 65, 227–8
Booth, Charles, 8, 25, 53, 88, 96, 116, 287
Booth, General William, 18, 158
Boot trade, 12, 14, 28, 58, 183
Bottomley, Horatio, 74, 316
Bow and Bromley, 26, 74, 79, 85, 88, 103, 106, 110, 118, 126–30, 174, 176, 178, 193, 196–7, 200, 202, 205, 227–30, 232, 241, 281, 291, 299, 302–3, 310, 317
Bow and Bromley Socialist, 241
Bowerman, Charles, 55, 171, 205, 244–7 275, 278, 282, 287
Bowie, Rev. C., 96
Bowman, Guy, 62
Bradford, 53, 128, 160
Bradlaugh, Charles, 31–3, 35, 91–2, 139
Bramley, Fred, 197, 289
Bray, Reginald, 215
Brentford, 46, 51, 300, 302, 319
Brighton, 6
Brill, Harry, 270
Bristol, 50–1
British Brothers' League, 29
British Socialist Party (B.S.P.), 195, 200–11, 228, 235, 249, 261, 265, 272–3 282, 284–5, 289, 291, 307, 312–321
British Weekly, 17, 180
Brixton, 167–8, 277, 300, 302
Broad, F. A., 204, 291
Broadbank, R. W., 224
Brooke, Rev. Stopford, 174
Browning Hall, 24, 109
Brownlie, J. T., 65
Building industry, 8, 12, 15–16, 40–1, 55, 58, 64–5, 270–2, 289
Built-up area, 6–7, 337
Burgess, Joseph, 157–61
Burnley, 126
Burns, John, 46–7, 50, 52–3, 56, 96, 98, 100–1, 103–7, 113–14, 116–20, 146, 150–3, 155, 157, 170, 174, 185–6, 194, 216, 222, 229, 268, 273, 275–6, 278, 287, 308, 313
Burrows, Herbert, 33, 45, 114–15, 118, 125, 199, 202
Butler, J. G., 196, 204, 207, 291
Button, F. S., 65, 205
Buxton, Sydney, 29, 152, 174, 256

Camberwell, 20, 25, 71, 108, 120–1, 159, 195, 198, 210, 231, 239–40, 268, 288, 299, 302, 308, 314
Cambridge, 112, 232
Camden Town, 6
Cameron, A. G., 231
Campbell, Paul, 36, 157
Campbell, Rev. R. J., 24, 220, 234
Canning Town, 45, 101, 118, 130, 162
Cant, E. W., 292
Carlile, Rev. J. C., 96
Carlyle, Thomas, 135
Carpenter, Edward, 210, 233
Carr-Gomm, H. W., 74

Carson, Sir Edward, 113
Central Federation of Ratepayers' Associations of London, 181
Central Labour College, 65
Chamberlain, Joseph, 81
Chambers, Tom, 103
Champion, H. H., 98, 105, 113–14, 116–18, 140, 149–51, 160, 194
Chancellor, H. G., 215
Chandler, Dr., 22
Charity Organisation Society, 21–3, 122
Charrington, Spencer, 74
Chartism, 32, 40, 93
Chatham, 7
Cheesman, W. C., 55, 270
Chelsea, 6, 8, 75, 92–3, 103, 119, 155, 157–8, 163–4, 167, 178, 197, 239, 300, 302
Chesterton, Cecil, 218
Chiswick, 65, 158, 197, 319
Christian Social Union, 23
Christian socialism, 22–5, 38, 40, 131, 135, 229, 234, 252
Chubb, Percival, 33
Church of England, 18–20, 98, 350–1, 354–5
Churchill, Sir Winston, 216
Cigar Makers' Mutual Association, 40, 54, 59, 66, 103, 268
City of London, 7, 17, 40, 50, 68–70, 77, 79, 92–3, 231, 233–4, 239, 292, 300, 302, 304
Civil Service, 14–15, 42, 59, 66, 138
Clapham, 25, 103, 105, 128, 153, 157, 159, 223, 225–6, 231, 234–5, 300, 302, 311, 318
Clapton, 19
Clarion, 108, 125, 141, 157, 164, 200
Clarion movement, 128, 164, 197–8, 200, 206–7, 256
Clarke, Joseph, 224
Clerkenwell, 78, 82, 115, 128, 253, 308
Clerks, 14–15, 42, 343
Clery, W. E., 55, 244, 270
Clifford, Rev. John, 23, 96, 180
Clubs, 1, 19, 27–8, 30, 32, 91–5, 100, 114, 128, 131, 140, 152–3, 157, 177–8, 187, 194, 235, 242, 244–5, 251–4, 256
Cluse, W. S., 291
Coachbuilders' Union, 56
Cobbett, William, 5
Cobden, Richard, 222
Cobden-Sanderson, Annie, 222
Coit, Dr. Stanton, 34–5, 37, 222
Cole, G. D. H., 219
Cole, George, 315–16
Cole, J., 102
Collison, William, 60
Colne Valley, 197
Commonweal, 137
Communist Party of Great Britain, 183, 290–2
Commuting, 6, 13, 39, 251, 294, 296
Connell, Jim, 27, 108, 195
Connolly, F. V., 160
Congreve, Dr. Richard, 33
Conservative Party, 3, 19–20, 71, 73–6, 81, 86–90, 98, 109–10, 166–9, 171,

368

INDEX

173–4, 176, 179–82, 185–9, 208, 251, 253–5, 286–8, 295, 300–3, 310, 313–21, 349
Conurbation, 5, 294, 337
Cook, A. G., 99, 101
Cooper, Ben, 40, 103–4, 120, 148, 156, 227, 268, 276, 279, 287, 310, 317
Co-operative movement, 39–40, 206, 250–2, 284
Copeland, C., 316
Cornwall, Sir Edwin, 182
Corruption, electoral, 73–4, 181, 294
Costelloe, B. F. C., 27
Costermongers' Union, 87, 170
Cowen, Joseph, 112
Cox, E. W., 267
Crane, Walter, 203, 234
Cray, Edward, 103, 119
Cremer, W. R., 43, 94, 199, 268, 311
Crooks, Will, 40, 103–4, 122, 129, 140, 146, 148, 155, 178, 212, 215, 220, 223, 227, 246, 254–7, 268, 275, 278, 310, 317, 319
Croydon, 6–7, 36, 68, 277
Crusade, 216
Curran, Pete, 27, 164
Curwen, Spencer, 130–1

Daily Chronicle, 1, 89, 171, 173
Daily Citizen, 63, 207, 220, 229, 232, 272, 282
Daily Herald, 63–4, 170, 201–2, 207, 226, 229–30, 268, 270, 272
Daily Mail, 1
Daily News, 1, 173, 256
Dale, Gilbert, 227–8
Dartford, 6, 168, 172–3, 300, 302
Davidson, Thomas, 33
Davidson, Dr. W. T., 227, 232
Davies, Emil, 220, 233
Davis, C. F., 205
De Leon, Daniel, 62
De Mattos, W. S., 47, 140, 160
Dean, George, 320
Dear, C., 272
Deller, Michael, 27, 317
Democracy, 34
Deptford, 6, 16, 18, 27, 74, 103, 106, 108, 115, 120, 145, 149, 158–9, 163–4, 171–2, 175–6, 178, 187, 195, 197, 214, 216, 227–8, 231–2, 243–7, 263, 277–8, 285, 287, 291, 300, 302–3, 309, 314
Despard, Charlotte, 85, 122
Devenay, William, 231
Devonport, Lord, 63
Dew, George, 268, 315–16
Dewsbury, 275
Dickinson, W. H., 146
Dilke, Sir Charles, 92, 100
Disraeli, Benjamin, 112
Dobson, James, 157, 195
Dobson, John, 320
Dock, Wharf and Riverside Labourers' Union, 39, 51–5, 57–9, 63, 66, 101–3, 107, 118–19, 150–1, 169, 231, 241, 272, 289
Dockers' Record, 102

Docks, 12, 15–16, 40, 42, 45, 48–53, 58, 63, 109, 181, 226, 289, 346
Domestic service, 14–15, 42, 70, 87, 340, 356
Donald, A. K., 55, 159, 161
Drummond, Charles, 55
Dubery, Harry, 282
Dublin, 27, 65
Dulwich, 6, 20, 72, 103, 119, 300, 302
Duncan, Charles, 223

Ealing, 6, 162, 164, 300, 302, 319
East End, 17–18, 27–30, 54, 61, 63, 80, 84–6, 88–9, 94, 136
East Ham, 6, 16, 35, 57, 83, 102, 178, 225, 231, 235, 311–12, 319–20
Edmonton, 102, 172, 196–7, 202, 204, 210, 267, 274, 291, 312, 320
Edwards, Clem, 45, 53
Edwards, Passmore, 96
Education, 79, 82, 91, 96, 117, 197, 208–9, 213, 216, 237, 288, 297, 363
Electrical industry, 14–15, 55, 82, 109, 117, 181, 183–4, 226, 259, 288
Electrical Trades Union, 55, 66
Elliott, Jack, 164
Ellis, Ben, 120, 157, 159
Eltham, 257, 259
Employers' Federation of Engineering Associations, 60
Enfield, 6, 16, 300, 302
Engels, F., 97, 113–14, 118, 137, 139, 152–3, 252
Engineering and Shipbuilding Trades' Federation, 227
Engineering industry, 16, 40–1, 55–6, 58, 60–1, 65, 103, 108, 272, 345
Ensor, R. C. K., 124–6, 215, 219–20, 227–8, 230–2, 234, 280–1, 317
Erith, 6, 16, 56, 65, 168, 173, 197–9, 205, 247–50, 312, 320
Ervine, St. John, 218, 220
Escreet, Canon C. E., 23
Ethical movement, 33–7, 210, 222, 232–3
Ethical World, 34
Ethics, 34
Evelyn, W. J., 73

Fabian Society, 2–3, 24, 33–4, 47, 93, 95–100, 104–6, 108, 114, 121–2, 124, 133, 137–49, 154–5, 157–65, 199, 208–9, 212–23, 230–1, 233, 235–8, 243, 246, 255, 263, 269, 275, 279, 281, 284, 292–3, 296–7, 307
Fabian News, 104, 141
Fawcett Association, 54–5, 59, 231, 244, 270
Fawcett, Henry, 74
Fairchild, E. C., 206, 208
Federation of Metropolitan Trades and Labour Councils, 277
Federation of Trades and Labour Councils of the South and East of England, 277
Fellowship of the New Life, 33, 36
Fels, Joseph, 262
Fennell, E. T., 254, 259
Field, Arthur, 277

369

INDEX

Fineberg, J., 202–3
Finn, Joseph, 31
Finsbury, 11, 31, 82, 91, 93–4, 171, 176, 223–4, 231, 234, 242–3, 299, 302, 309, 314
Finsbury Park, 128, 191
Firth, James, 81, 99, 117, 145
Fitzgerald, Jack, 191–2
Food, 10–1, 15, 118, 184, 226
Foote, G. W., 32–3, 35, 92
Ford, W. C., 320
Forest Gate, 35
Freak, Charles, 103, 308
Freethinker, 32, 35, 92
Friendly Society of Ironfounders, 41, 59, 66
Fulham, 18, 35, 38, 75, 136, 168, 186, 196, 199–200, 222–4, 227, 242, 288, 300, 302, 309, 314
Furniture trade, 14–15, 40, 183

Galton, F. W., 176, 281, 292
Gardiner, Ben, 162
Garrity, Edward, 242–3, 314
Gas industry, 15, 42, 45–8, 58, 82, 99, 109, 117, 133, 163, 181
Gas, Light and Coke Company, 46
Gast, John, 40
Geddes, Patrick, 218, 233, 262
General Amalgamated Union of Labourers, 54, 59, 66, 270–1
General Railway Workers' Union, 54, 56, 59, 64, 101–2
General Union of Carpenters and Joiners, 54, 59, 66, 271
Gentry, R. M., 231
George, Henry, 93, 113
Germinal, 30
Gibson, J. V., 321
Gilbert, E., 227, 314
Gilbert, W. G., 235
Gladstone, Herbert, 1, 30, 171, 175
Gladstone, W. E., 152
Glasgow, 189
Glasier, Bruce, 124, 221
Glasier, Katherine, 233
Godbold, Walter, 133
Goddard, Dora, 232
Godfrey, Will, 155
Golders Green, 214
Goldsworthy, General, 76
Gooday, W. T., 204
Gordon, J. G., 204
Gosling, Harry, 63, 240, 268, 279, 287, 317–18
Gossip, Alex, 38, 231
Gould, A. T., 277, 316
Grant, Corrie, 96
Gravesend, 51
Gray, Mary, 122
Grays, 7
Grayson, Victor, 174, 197, 199–201, 205, 226, 234–5, 261
Great Eastern Railway, 39, 64
Green, J. F., 203
Greenwich, 6, 86, 119, 167, 183, 198, 227, 240, 243, 277–8, 287, 300, 302, 309, 314

Grimwood, H. H., 321
Grinling, C. H., 23, 257, 259, 262
Guest, Haden, 215, 219–20, 233
Guild of St. Matthew, 22–3
Guild socialism, 219

Hackney, 24, 28, 35, 71, 74, 93, 99, 154–5, 158, 162, 164, 167–8, 177, 196, 199, 202, 207, 224, 242, 277, 290, 299, 300, 302, 309, 314–15
Hagger, Fred, 197–8
Haggerston, 72, 94, 172, 215, 299, 302, 311
Haggerty, Dan, 58, 64, 274, 310, 318
Haldane, R., 152
Hales, John, 125
Hall, B. T., 159, 244–6, 309
Hammersmith, 6, 18, 35, 73, 75–6, 82, 84, 87–8, 92, 115, 136–7, 153–5, 157–8, 162, 171–2, 174, 178, 187–8, 196–7, 199, 222, 227, 232, 242, 278, 288, 300, 302, 309, 315
Hammill, Fred, 56–7, 104, 147–8, 156, 159–60, 164
Hampstead, 6, 11, 34, 36, 72, 75, 83, 115, 154, 162, 183, 214, 240, 300, 302, 309, 315
Hampton, Will, 248–50
Hannington, Wal, 291
Hardie, J. K., 36, 45, 106–8, 125, 130–1, 140, 144, 148, 150, 152, 157–8, 161–4, 174, 221, 234, 252
Harley, Rev. J. H., 224, 227
Harringay, 35
Harris, Sir Percy, 176
Harrow, 160, 300, 302
Hay, Claude, 89
Hayday, Arthur, 133
Haynes, Thomas, 311
Headlam, Rev. Stewart, 22, 96, 99, 137, 139, 148, 199, 213, 215
Headingley, A. S., 203
Health, 8–13, 28, 77–9, 81–3, 109, 181, 183–4, 226, 232, 237, 258–9
Henderson, Arthur, 278, 282
Henderson, Fred, 103–4, 146, 153–4, 157, 159, 311
Hennessey, D., 318
Hewitt, George, 206
Hicks, Amie, 118
Hicks, George, 64
Highbury, 128
Hill, C., 235
Hobart, H. W., 45, 118–19
Hobson, J. A., 34, 148, 209, 218
Hobson, S. G., 212–13, 215, 219
Holloway, 35
Holborn, 300, 302
Holmes, A. E., 172, 204, 274–5
Horne, George, 224, 227
Horniman, E. J., 178
Hornsey, 300, 302
Horsley, Rev. J. W., 23
Housing, 8–12, 78–9, 81–2, 98–100, 109, 117, 123–4, 133–4, 179, 184, 208, 226, 258–9, 297, 341
How, Bishop Walsham, 17
Howard, Ebenezer, 34

INDEX

Howell, George, 41, 43, 94, 120, 157, 308
Howlett, 320
Hoxton, 36, 89, 128, 153, 161, 299, 302
Hughes, Colonel, 251, 254
Hughes, Spencer, 173
Humphrey, A., 309
Humphreys, W. H., 227
Hutchins, Mark, 320
Hyndman, H. M., 30–1, 100, 104, 112–14, 134, 140, 142, 149, 151–2, 160, 190–1, 193–4, 202–3, 234, 237

Ilford, 6, 198
Independent Labour Party (I.L.P.), 3, 22, 24, 34, 38, 52–3, 104, 107–8, 113, 120, 122, 124–6, 128, 131, 133, 147–8, 153–5, 157–65, 168, 173–4, 184–5, 191–201, 203, 208, 220–38, 240–3, 246, 248–9, 252–4, 256, 261, 265–8, 275, 277–82, 284–5, 289, 292, 297, 307–21
Industrial Democracy League, 63
Industrial Freedom League, 181
Industrial Syndicalist, 62
Industrial Syndicalist League, 62
Industrial unionism, 62–5, 261
Industry, 13–16, 39, 41, 87, 288, 294, 296, 343–6
Inkpin, Albert, 202
International Federation of Ship, Dock and River Workers, 53
Irish, 8, 25–9, 49, 70, 96, 113, 167–9, 173, 180, 186, 191, 193, 204, 209, 212, 237, 240, 257, 270, 313, 319, 356
Irish National Society, 26
Isle of Dogs, 49
Islington, 36, 71–2, 156–7, 168, 197, 210, 228, 231–2, 235, 247, 268, 277, 287, 299–300, 302, 309, 315–6

Jackson, T. A., 127–8, 192, 235
Jacobs, Saunders, 132–3
James, Henry, 224
Jarrett, W. J., 228
Jeffreys, James, 178
Jephson, Rev. A. W., 26, 96, 140
Jessell, Captain, 77
Jesson, Charles, 186, 268, 275, 318
Jevons, Stanley, 138, 236
Jewish Chronicle, 28
Jews, 8, 20, 25, 27–31, 237, 357
John Bull, 74
Johnson, Hope, 234
Johnson, William, 279
Jones, Ben, 157, 163, 243, 251–2
Jones, F. G., 205
Jones, Jack, 162, 193–4, 205–6, 208–9, 272, 291
Jones, Rev. Jenkins, 223, 227, 236, 254
Journey to work, 6, 13, 39, 251, 288
Justice, 104, 114, 118–19, 125, 128, 134–5, 190–1, 202–3, 206, 243, 252

Kahan, Zelda, 203
Kautsky, Karl, 192
Kay, Harry, 53
Keddell, Frederick, 137
Keeling, Ben, 232

Kelly, 87–8
Kelly, W. T., 227
Kendall, Richard, 204
Kennedy, Rev. H. A., 22
Kennedy, Thomas, 206
Kennington, 115, 128, 174, 227–8, 300, 302
Kensington, 13, 35, 71, 73, 75, 81–2, 88, 102–3, 136, 163, 172–3, 227–8, 231–3, 242, 300, 302, 309, 316
Kentish Town, 35, 134, 202
Kerrison, Edith, 24, 162
Keylock, H., 103
Kilburn, 154, 158, 160, 162
King, James, 119
Kingsley, Charles, 135
Kitching, Charles, 154
Knee, Fred, 123, 140, 194, 202, 204, 208, 276, 279, 283, 285, 289
Krailing, F. C., 224
Kyd, David Hope, 29

Labour Church Record, 37
Labour churches, 34–7, 158, 164, 210
Labour Elector, 46, 149–50
Labour Electoral Association, 149–50
Labour Leader, 153–4, 162–4, 223, 227, 234, 252, 266, 275
Labour Protection League, 42, 48, 51–2, 54, 59, 63, 66, 256, 270, 276
Labour Representation Committee and national Labour Party, 1, 3, 24, 61, 67, 84–6, 110–11, 130, 166, 169–75, 178, 184–5, 190–8, 201–3, 205, 208, 213–21, 223, 225–6, 229–30, 235, 239–47, 253, 261, 264–87, 290–3, 295–6, 313–21, 353, 367
Labour Representation League, 86
Labour Union, 55–6, 153, 157, 159, 161
Lambert, George, 101
Lambeth, 20, 22, 71, 103, 119–22, 151, 168, 172, 174, 186, 197, 223, 227–8, 231, 247, 252, 277, 299, 302, 309, 317
Lancashire, 39, 41, 84, 87, 89, 114, 140, 190
Land League, 26
Land Restoration League, 121
Lane, Joseph, 136–7
Lansbury, George, 22, 35, 85, 106, 122–3, 125–7, 129–30, 134, 170, 174, 192–3, 199, 201, 205, 208, 215, 226–30, 233, 239, 241, 272–3, 278, 280–1, 291, 317–18
Lassalle, F., 262
Lawrence, Susan, 215, 220, 228, 282, 318
Lax, Rev. William, 23
Lea, river, 6, 16
Lee, H. W., 202
Leeds, 189
Leicester, 235
Leicester, Joseph, 94
Letchworth, 289
Lewis, Wyndham, 218
Lewisham, 88, 210, 224–5, 231, 240, 271, 300, 302, 317
Leyton, 199
Leytonstone, 155, 199

371

INDEX

Liberal Party, 1–2, 4, 19–20, 22, 24, 26–7, 30, 55, 71, 73–6, 81, 85–6, 89–112, 126, 128–34, 140–2, 147, 154–5, 166–89, 194, 197, 204, 208–9, 214–16, 220, 232, 242–7, 251–2, 255–7, 267–70, 272, 274, 276, 286–7, 293, 349, 352–3
Liberal Social Union, 33
Licensed Victuallers' Protection Societies, 79
Lidgett, Rev. Scott, 23, 26, 96
Limehouse, 4, 6, 16, 26, 36, 72, 157, 232, 300, 302, 310–11
Ling, W., 248–9, 312
Liverpool, 2, 89, 102, 188
Livesey, George, 46, 60
Lloyd, C. M., 220, 228, 232, 246
Lloyd-George, David, 4, 216–17, 286, 295
Local government organisation, 77–84, 361–4
London, 147
London Alliance of Industrial Unionists, 62
London Amalgamated Society of Boot and Shoemakers, 54, 59, 66
London Amalgamated Society of House Decorators and Painters, 41, 54, 59
London and Counties Labour League, 42, 54
London and Counties Liberal Union, 93
London and South Western Railway, 47
London Building Trades Federation, 55, 64
London Cabdrivers' Trade Union, 59, 276
London Carmen's Trade Union, 54, 56, 59, 155, 170, 270–1, 310
London Catholic Herald, 26, 180
London Consolidated Society of Bookbinders, 40, 54, 59, 63
London County Council (L.C.C.), 5, 11, 38, 52–3, 80–3, 96, 99–106, 109, 118–21, 142–8, 150–2, 155–61, 163–4, 173, 179–83, 197, 200, 208, 210, 212–5, 222–9, 233, 240, 244–6, 252–3, 256, 263, 268–9, 276, 278, 280–7, 289–91 296–7, 304–6, 308–21
London Glassblowers' Trade Society, 202, 204, 283
London Labour Party, 123, 202–3, 210, 216, 239, 247, 263, 265, 273–4, 278, 282–293
London Liberal and Radical Union, 94, 106, 143, 175
London Liberal Federation, 175, 265
London Master Printers' Association, 61
London Municipal Society, 76–7, 81, 109, 181, 265, 289
London Nonconformist Council, 96
London Owners' Committee, 86
London Printing Machine Managers' Trade Society, 54, 59, 66, 274
London Reform Union, 76, 81, 144, 147, 265, 281
London School Board, 32, 79–82, 86, 91, 96, 98–101, 103, 105, 115, 118–19, 121, 139, 152, 156, 180–1, 197, 363
London School of Ethics and Philosophy, 34
London Shipwrights' Union, 40–1, 48, 54
London Society of Compositors, 40–2, 50, 53–5, 57, 59–61, 66–7, 99, 101, 103, 108, 119, 169–70, 204–5, 230–1, 245, 247, 270–2, 274, 315–16
London Society of French Polishers, 59, 66, 170
London Society of Machine Rulers, 41
London Society of Tailors and Tailoresses, 61
London Trades and Labour Gazette, 276
London Trades Council, 41–3, 50, 52, 56–8, 61, 101–5, 119, 147, 150, 153, 155–8, 194, 202, 204, 208, 231, 266–8, 273–9, 282–4, 291
Lowe, Dr. G. C., 232
Lucraft, Benjamin, 86
Lyons, Lewis, 30, 53, 104, 118

Macdonald, James, 53–4, 61, 104, 113, 118, 194, 204, 273, 283
MacDonald, Margaret, 65, 232
Macdonald, Murray, 126
MacDonald, Ramsay, 33–4, 148, 172, 212–13, 221–4, 229, 234, 253, 256–7, 266–9, 275, 277, 279, 282
Mackail, J. W., 233
Macpherson, James, 55, 127, 205
Mahon, John Lincoln, 55, 137, 153, 159, 161
Maidstone, 277
Manchester, 2, 84, 102, 141, 157, 189
Mann, Tom, 50–3, 56–8, 60, 62, 101–4, 113–14, 116–18, 147–8, 150, 152, 156, 159, 161–2, 261
Mansfield House, 24, 132
March, Sam, 270
Marx, Eleanor, 136–7, 150, 152–3, 159
Marx, Karl, 113, 235–7, 262
Marxism, 3, 19, 31, 65, 105, 110–14, 135–8, 143, 191, 210, 235–7, 262, 297
Marylebone, 99, 158, 161, 240, 300, 302
Massingham, H. M., 34, 97, 147
Masterman, Charles, 175–7, 200, 221
Matchgirls, 45, 57, 118, 139
Maude, Aylmer, 215
Maurice, F. D., 22
McArthur, Mary, 65
McCabe, Joseph, 35
McCarthy, Tom, 27, 51
McDougall, Sir John, 227
McEntee, V., 291
McKinley, R., 224
McMillan, Margaret, 34, 36, 140, 157, 232–3
Mellor, William, 219
Mercer, A., 103, 310
Metivier, E. E., 126–7
Metropolitan Asylums Board, 79
Metropolitan Board of Works, 9, 79–80, 82–3, 100
Metropolitan Board Teachers' Association, 42
Metropolitan Cabdrivers' Trade Union, 54, 56
Metropolitan Radical Federation, 32, 91, 93–4, 103, 108, 177–8, 194, 265

372

INDEX

Metropolitan Trades Committee, 40
Metropolitan Water Board, 7
Middle Class Defence League, 83
Middlesbrough, 106, 174
Migration, 13, 25, 27–9, 39, 69–72, 87, 288
Mile End, 28, 35, 74, 102, 299, 302, 310–11
Millwall, 49, 52
Miners' Federation, 45
Mitchell, Isaac, 223, 231
Moderate Party, 81
Moir, Dr. John, 131
Money, Chiozza, 182, 215
Montagu, Samuel, 28–9, 126
Montefiore, Dora, 84, 203
Morgan, W., 130
Morning Leader, 173
Morning Post, 290
Morris, William, 23, 113–14, 124–5, 127, 135–7, 140, 151, 154, 207, 210, 233–4, 236–7, 262
Morris, Rev. W. A., 22
Morrison, Herbert, 192, 283, 289–92
Muirhead, J. H., 34
Municipal Employees' Association, 59–60, 66
Municipal Reform League, 93
Municipal Reform Party, 180–2
Musicians' Union, 186, 268

National Amalgamated Coal Porters' Union, 54, 56, 59, 66, 270, 310
National Amalgamated Furnishing Trades' Association, 38, 58–9, 66, 230–1
National Amalgamated Sailors and Firemen's Union, 45, 50, 63, 101, 103, 106, 131
National Amalgamated Sheet Metal Worker's Society, 66, 204
National Amalgamated Society of Printers' Warehousemen, 59, 66
National Amalgamated Tin and Iron Plate Workers' Society, 59, 204
National Association of Operative Plasterers, 54, 59, 66, 271, 315, 317–18
National Association of Operative Printers' Assistants, 54, 59, 61, 66
National Association of Theatrical Employees, 279
National Committee of Organised Labour, 24
National Democratic League, 53, 108, 194–5, 212, 253–4, 270
National Federation of Labour Union, 55, 58, 118
National Federation of Women Workers, 65
National Free Labour Association, 60–1
National Insurance Act, 66
National Movement of Conservative Working Men, 88
National Municipal and Incorporated Vestry Employees' Association, 54, 102
National Reformer, 31
National Secular Society, 32
National Transport Workers' Federation, 63, 268

National Union of Bookbinders and Machine Rulers, 66, 170
National Union of Boot and Shoe Operatives, 42, 53–4, 59, 66, 103, 170
National Union of Clerks, 55, 59, 63, 66, 269–70
National Union of Gas Workers and General Labourers, 22, 45–8, 50–2, 54–5, 57–60, 63, 66–7, 101–3, 106–8, 118–19, 127–31, 150, 152–3, 158, 164, 193, 205, 209, 230, 240–1, 252, 272, 311–12, 319, 320
National Union of Railwaymen, 64, 66–7, 289
National Union of Ships' Stewards, Cooks, Butchers and Bakers, 66
National Union of Shop Assistants, 55, 59, 63, 66–7, 127, 205, 271–2
National Union of Teachers, 42, 269
National United Society of Smiths and Hammermen, 66, 314
Navvies, Bricklayers' Labourers and General Labourers' Union, 54–5, 59, 270
Naylor, Tom, 230, 315–16
Neighbourliness, 13, 19, 39, 288, 296
Neumann, Hans, 192
New Age, 218–19
New Leader, 292
New World, 207
Newcastle-upon-Tyne, 11, 106, 112, 140, 142
Newington, 23, 299, 302, 310–11
Newspapers, 1, 77, 197, 207, 262
Newton, William, 41, 85
Nonconformity, 1, 18–21, 24, 90–2, 95–6, 98–9, 110, 125, 131, 168–9, 171, 179–80, 185–8, 193, 209–10, 213, 234, 237, 251, 269, 293, 295, 297–8, 315–16, 350–1, 354–5
Norfolk, Duke of, 181
Northfleet, 7
Norwood, 20, 72, 300, 302
Nottingham, 23

Oakeshott, J. F., 33
O'Connor, James, 310
O'Connot, T. P., 27, 97–8
O'Dell, G. E., 232
O'Donnell, F. H., 253
Olivier, Sydney, 33, 137, 148, 219
Operative Bricklayers' Society, 41–2, 54, 59, 64, 66, 103, 268, 270–1
Operative Stonemasons' Society, 41–2, 54, 59, 66, 270–1
Orage, A. B., 218
Osborne, W. V., 64, 169–70, 192, 231, 270–1, 273, 316
Otley, T., 271, 318
Oxford, 219, 232
Oxford, Rev. A. W., 96

Paddington, 8, 23, 36, 158, 172–3, 182, 300, 302, 310, 317
Paine, Tom, 31–2, 93
Pall Mall Gazette, 94, 100
Palmer, Nelson, 121, 157
Pamphilon, 104

373

INDEX

Pankhurst, Emmeline, 84–5
Pankhurst, Christabel, 84–5
Pankhurst, Sylvia, 84–5
Paris, 62, 117, 124
Parker, W. B., 315–16
Parliamentary constituencies, 68, 299–300, 358–9
Parlimentary election costs, 72–3
Parliamentary electoral franchise and registration, 68–72, 84–5, 110, 176, 206, 240–1, 244–5, 260, 288, 295, 299, 305, 360
Patterson, G., 205
Pearce, W., 74
Pearson, Will, 119, 121, 125
Pease, Edward, 140, 143, 213, 215, 217, 269
Peckham, 35, 115, 120, 163, 191, 227, 300, 302
Penfold, F. W., 224
Penge, 155
Pentonville, 33
People, 128, 191
Peters, 87–8
Peters, Arthur, 235
Pethick-Lawrence, Emmeline, 84–5
Pethick-Lawrence, Frederick, 84–5, 215
Pethybridge, 245
Phillimore, R. C., 215, 243, 246
Phillips, Harry, 131
Phillips, Marion, 220, 232
Pickersgill, E. H., 176
Pincombe, W. J., 224
Plumstead, 35, 252, 256, 259, 310–11
Plumstead News, 262
Police, 7, 226
Political theory, 3, 19, 30–1, 43–5, 62–3, 93, 105, 110–11, 114–15, 128, 137–8, 142–8, 191–2, 208–10, 234–8, 252, 295–7
Pope, J. J., 320
Poplar, 6, 16, 22–6, 60, 80, 82–3, 102–5, 120–3, 128–9, 154–5, 162, 174, 181, 183, 187, 196–7, 199, 201, 204–5, 227–33, 240–2, 255–6, 267, 272, 278, 285, 299, 302, 310, 317
Population, 5, 7
Port of London Authority, 49, 63, 268
Porters, 40–1
Postal Telegraph Clerk's Association, 54, 59, 66
Postmen's Federation, 54–5, 59, 66, 271
Postmen's Union, 55
Poverty, 12–13, 90, 251, 256, 288, 339
Preston, 17
Primrose League, 73–5
Prinsep, Val, 253
Printing industry, 14, 28, 40–1, 54, 58–9, 63
Progressive Party, 1, 33, 53–4, 76, 80–1, 96–109, 118–124, 129, 132–4, 139, 154–6, 163–4, 168, 173, 177–88, 197, 213–16, 223–4, 226–8, 233, 239–40, 243, 252–9, 263, 268–9, 271, 275, 278, 281–2, 285–6, 289, 293, 296, 304–6, 308–21
Propaganda, 1, 76–7, 115, 127–8, 182, 206–7, 234, 289

Quelch, Harry, 51–2, 113, 116, 118–19, 123, 125, 156, 190–1, 196, 202, 204, 275–6, 283

Radical, 33, 93, 112
Radicalism, 27, 32–3, 42, 53, 90–101, 107–12, 114, 116, 126, 177–9, 194–5, 217, 242–3, 251, 253–6, 269
Railways, 6, 39, 41–2, 47, 56, 59, 64, 181, 237, 268, 272, 289, 346
Railway Clerks' Association, 59, 64, 66, 269
Rees, Tom, 65
Religion, 1, 17–38, 89–92, 95, 98–9, 125, 167–8, 180, 186–7, 209–10, 234, 237, 251, 293, 297–8, 347–8, 350–1, 354–7
Reynold's Newspaper, 171, 179, 194
Riley, Rev. William, 74
Roberts, R. H., 74
Robertson, J. M., 35
Rogers, H. B., 119
Rogers, Thorold, 237
Roman Catholicism, 18, 25–7, 31, 89, 114, 167–8, 180, 186, 313
Romford, 300, 302
Rosebery, Lord, 5
Rotherhithe, 26, 299, 302, 308, 310
Rothschild, Lord, 30
Rothstein, Theodore, 190, 203
Rowlands, James, 92, 94, 168, 310
Roy, J., 119
Royal Army Clothing Employees' Union, 204
Ruskin, John, 135, 236–7, 252, 262

St. George's Hanover Square, 70, 300, 302
St. George's in the East, 21, 25–6, 28, 70, 80, 103, 167, 172–3, 177, 180, 268, 299, 302, 310–11
St. Giles, 25
St. Luke, 310
St. Pancras, 18, 142, 158, 161, 163, 178, 187, 197, 201, 224, 227, 247, 300, 302, 311, 318
Salisbury, Lord, 81
Salter, Dr. Alfred, 173, 227–8, 232, 292
Salvation Army, 18, 21–2, 158, 223
Samuel, Herbert, 148
Samuel, Montagu, 29
Samuels, H. V., 160–1
Sanders, William, 34, 120, 185, 222–3, 278, 281
Schloesser, H. H., 220, 233
Scientific Instrument Makers' Society, 66, 204
Scotland, 2, 31, 251
Scurr, John, 27, 199
Seager, Renwick, 94–5, 97, 129, 175
Secularism, 19, 31–3, 91–3, 97, 100, 110, 209, 237, 242, 293, 297–8
Seedtime, 33
Shallard, S. D., 119
Sharp, Cecil, 216–17
Shaw, C. N. L., 215
Shaw, Charlotte, 148
Shaw, G. B., 33, 97–8, 114, 137–8, 141–4, 146, 160, 212–15, 218–19, 237, 318
Shearman, Montagu, 215
Sheffield, 101, 188

INDEX

Shipbuilding industry, 16, 40–1
Shipton, George, 42, 50, 57, 61
Shoreditch, 120, 170, 197, 199, 201, 228, 242, 311, 318
Sickert, Walter, 218
Silvertown, 46–7, 134
Slums, 8, 13, 341
Smith, Aeneas, 103
Smith, Frank, 103–4, 140, 146, 148, 157–9, 162–4, 223–4, 227–8, 278, 280–1, 309, 314, 317
Smith, Harry, 88
Snell, Harry, 34, 220
Snow, William, 119
Snowden, Philip, 221
Social class:
  conflict, 8–9, 13, 209–10, 217, 271, 275
  ecology, 7–8, 13, 240, 287–8, 295–6, 339, 365–6
  and electoral system, 69–74, 85
  and religion, 17–21, 25, 32, 187
  and Conservative Party, 19–20, 48, 73–4, 86–90, 94, 166–7, 181, 251, 288, 295
  and Fabian Society, 104, 138, 140, 214, 217
  and I.L.P., 125, 230–4
  and Liberal Party, 20, 73–4, 86, 89, 91–6, 105–10, 166–7, 179, 183–4, 295–6, 299–303
  and London Labour Party, 290–1
  and S.D.F., 108, 115–16, 203–4
  and Woolwich Labour Party, 256
Social Democratic Federation (S.D.F.), 3, 30–1, 38, 47, 51, 61, 89, 93, 100, 103–5, 108–40, 149, 151, 153, 156–60, 162–5, 190–211, 221–2, 225, 228–31, 233–8, 240–3, 246, 248–9, 251, 256, 263, 265–70, 272, 275–9, 281–2, 285, 287–93, 296–7, 307–21
Social Democratic Party (S.D.P.), 200, 307, 312–21
S.D.P. News, 206–7
Socialist International, 48, 125, 252, 210
Socialist Labour Party, 62, 191, 198
Socialist League, 114, 120, 136–9, 149, 152–3, 157, 160, 251, 307–312
Socialist Party of Great Britain, 191–2 194, 198, 235
Socialist Sunday Schools, 35, 38, 207, 210, 231–2, 250
Socialist Workers' Circular, 207
Solidarity, 63
South Africa, 53
South Metropolitan Gas Company, 46
Southgate, 198
Southwark, 11, 25, 71, 102, 109, 119, 183–4, 231, 243, 277–8, 285, 299, 302, 311, 318
Soutter, F. W., 118
Sparling, Halliday, 122
Speaker, 105, 107–8, 145
Spender, Harold, 129, 224
Standring, George, 33
Star, 1, 27, 46, 50, 57, 80, 95, 97–101, 105–7, 116, 119, 122, 141–5, 152, 173
Stead, Herbert, 24
Stead, W. T., 33

Steadman, Will, 40, 53, 76, 102–4, 119, 146, 155–6, 171, 212, 223–4, 240, 242, 268, 270, 273, 275–6, 278, 310, 314, 318
Stephenson, J. J., 227, 231, 317
Stepney, 21, 25, 27, 79, 103, 109, 120, 155, 159, 172–3, 176, 186–7, 202, 204, 231, 239–40, 242, 274, 287, 299, 302, 310–11, 318
Stevenson, W., 58, 315
Stick Umbrella Makers and Mounters' Trade Union, 204
Stoke Newington, 83, 235, 239
Stokes, John, 202, 204, 283, 289
Strand, 69–70, 300, 302
Stratford, 39, 102, 172, 194, 272–3
Stratton, Dr., 232
Streatham, 159, 198
Stuart, Professor, 99, 145
Suburbs, 6–8, 13–14, 83
Sumner, Charles, 127
Sun, 53, 74
Sutherst, T., 56
Sydenham, 6
Syndicalism, 62–5, 170, 201, 205, 219, 226, 272–3
Syndicalist Railwayman, 64

Tailoring trades, 12, 14, 28, 40, 53, 61, 63, 288, 344
Taine, H., 5
Tariff Reform League, 88
Tawney, R. H., 262
Taylor, H. R., of Camberwell, 103–4, 240, 268, 308
Taylor, H. R., of S.D.F., 119–20, 156–7
Tea Operatives and Dock Workers' Union, 45, 50
Temperance, 45, 89, 116, 125, 133, 162, 179, 188, 209–10, 249, 253, 269
Terrett, J. J., 132, 135, 205
Thames, river, 5–6, 16, 60, 181, 250
Theosophy, 33, 139
Thompson, W. M., 194
Thorne, Will, 45–8, 51, 61, 101–3, 117–18, 129–34, 152, 162, 192–4, 205, 273, 291
Thornycroft, Hamo, 253
Thorogood, A. J., 224
Tilbury, 7, 45
Tillett, Ben, 39, 45, 50–3, 57, 61, 63, 101–5, 108, 117–18, 146, 150, 155, 159, 205, 272
Times, 203
Tims, James, 103
Tooting, 118, 318
Tottenham, 6, 18, 36, 47, 53, 57, 115, 119, 128, 172, 224, 234, 267, 291, 300, 302, 312, 320
Tower Hamlets, 41, 86, 99, 121, 197
Toynbee Hall, 22–4, 34, 232, 246
Trade cycles, 12, 16, 42–5, 58, 60, 100–1, 104, 107, 116, 164, 169, 298
Trade Union Congress, 41, 45, 147, 149, 190, 208, 268
Trade unionism, 39–67, 101–4, 107–9, 169–70, 188, 204–5, 230–1, 241, 247, 256, 258, 261, 263–4, 266, 269–73, 284–5, 288–9, 293, 295–6

375

INDEX

Tramways, 6, 82, 109, 117, 163, 179, 181, 250, 259
Transport, 6, 15–16, 42, 56, 63, 82, 109, 117, 250, 288
Trevelyan, C. P., 148
Trevor, Rev. John, 36
Tufton, A. G., 62
Turner, John, 55

Unemployment, Boards of Guardians and Poor Law, 12, 21–2, 28, 44, 49–50, 78, 80–4, 96, 98–9, 107, 109, 114, 117, 120, 122–3, 129, 133, 164, 174, 181, 183, 197, 208, 216–17, 229, 258–9, 291, 297, 341, 361
Unionist Labour League, 88
United Builders' Labourers' Union, 54, 58–9, 64, 66, 271, 274, 310, 315, 318
United Clothing Workers' Union, 30
United General Order of London Labourers, 59, 66
United Irish League, 26, 257
United Ladies' Tailors and Mantle Makers' Union, 31
United Operative Plumbers' Association, 54, 59, 66, 271
United Society of Boilermakers, 42, 54, 59, 66
United Society of Brushmakers, 40, 157
United Society of Coopers, 40, 66, 103
University of London, 68, 300, 302, 304

Vaughan, Joe, 183
Vauxhall, 46
Vellum Binders' Trade Union, 40
Vivian, Herbert, 171
Voice of Labour, 62
Votes for Women, 84

Wages, 10, 12, 42, 163, 288
Wales, 1, 39, 51, 65
Wall, Tom, 196
Wallace, Rev. Bruce, 36
Wallas, Graham, 96, 137, 139–40, 148, 213
Walsh, T. M., 101, 131
Walthamstow, 36, 38, 62, 102, 109, 172, 199, 207, 224, 242, 271, 274–5, 291, 300, 302, 312, 321
Walthamstow Reformer, 207
Walworth, 18–19, 23–4, 72, 92, 120–1, 126, 176, 232, 268, 299, 302
Wandsworth, 72, 103, 115, 118–19, 162, 164, 240, 300, 302, 311, 318
Ward, William, 133
Ward, John, 47, 55, 103, 118–20, 270
Warren, Rev. Tom, 162
Warwick, Lady, 206
Water, 7, 9, 109, 117, 133, 163, 181
Watford, 6–7, 36–7, 198
Watkins, Charles, 64
Watson, Campion, 102, 245, 314, 316
Watson, W. F., 65
Watts, A. A., 127, 206, 291
Watts, Charles, 33, 35
Watts, Hunter, 128, 202
Webb, Beatrice, 33, 97, 104, 144, 148, 163–4, 212, 215–17, 219–23, 229, 233, 292, 297

Webb, Sidney, 97–9, 103–4, 106, 137, 139, 142–8, 159–60, 164, 212–17, 219–21, 243–4, 292, 297
Webster, Hume, 73, 130–1, 134
Wedgewood, Josiah, 233
Wells, H. G., 212, 215, 218–20
West End, 8, 16–18, 28, 54, 61, 70, 288
West Ham, 6, 8, 16, 24–5, 28, 35, 38–9, 46, 49, 57, 64, 68, 72–3, 83, 94–5, 101–3, 105–6, 110, 120–1, 123–5, 129–35, 150, 155, 162–4, 171–2, 174, 185, 187, 193–4, 196–7, 199, 201–2, 204–6, 220, 224, 230, 240–1, 252, 267, 272–3, 291, 300, 302, 312, 320–1
Westbourne Park, 8, 96
Westcott, J. T., 227
Westminster, 70, 77, 79, 197, 199, 223–4, 240, 274, 300, 302
Whitechapel, 8, 18–22, 27–9, 87, 126, 300, 302, 311
Whitman, Walt, 210
Wicksteed, Philip, 36
Widger, J. O., 259
Willesden, 18, 154, 168, 224, 242, 312, 321
Williams, Jack, 114, 118, 122, 208
Williams, Robert, 223
Wills, Jack, 63–4
Wilson, Charlotte, 137
Wilson, Havelock, 45, 106, 174
Wimbledon, 6, 191, 300, 302
Women: and franchise, 69, 84–5, 113, 201, 222, 226, 229–30
  and political parties, 75, 182, 203–4, 247, 260, 284–5
  and trade unionism, 47, 65–6, 230
Women's Freedom League, 85
Women's Labour League, 285
Women's Social and Political Union, 84–5
Wood, McKinnon, 182
Wood Green, 6, 35, 38, 115, 128, 172, 191, 242, 267, 312, 321
Woods, Sam, 312
Woolwich, 6, 16, 23–5, 39, 47, 52, 57, 65, 72, 75, 78, 87, 89, 103, 105, 110, 115, 136–7, 149, 155, 157–8, 162, 171, 176–8, 183, 187, 197–8, 200–1, 223–8, 231, 235–6, 240–1, 248, 250–63, 277–9, 285, 287–8, 291, 299, 302–3, 310, 319
Woolwich Labour Journal, 253, 257, 262
Woolwich Labour Notes, 252–3
Woolwich Pioneer, 262–3
Worker's Circle, 30
Worker's Cry, 158
Worker's Union, 58, 66
Workmen's Cheap Trains Association, 268
Workmen's National Housing Council, 108–9, 123, 194, 208
Workmen's Times, 157, 160–1
World's End, 119

Yarrow, Alfred, 60
Yorkshire, 39
Young, Robert, 65
Young Socialist, 38